Evidence Based Design
A Process for Research and Writing

DAK Kopec
Newschool of Architecture and Design

E. L. A. Sinclair
Naval Facilities Engineering Command

Bruce Matthes
Newschool of Architecture and Design

Art Institute of San Diego

Prentice Hall

Boston Columbus Indianapolis New York San Francisco Upper Saddle River
Amsterdam Cape Town Dubai London Madrid Milan Munich Paris Montreal Toronto
Delhi Mexico City Sao Paulo Sydney Hong Kong Seoul Singapore Taipei Tokyo

Editorial Director: Vernon Anthony
Acquisitions Editor: Sara Eilert
Editorial Assistant: Doug Greive
Director of Marketing: David Gesell
Marketing Manager: Harper Coles
Senior Marketing Coordinator: Alicia Wozniak
Senior Marketing Assistant: Les Roberts
Project Manager: Holly Shufeldt
Senior Art Director: Jayne Conte
Cover Designer: Suzanne Behnke
Manager, Rights and Permissions: Karen Sanatar
Cover Art: Fotolia
Full-Service Project Management/Composition: Aptara®, Inc.
Printer/Binder: Courier
Cover Printer: Lehigh-Phoenix Color

Photo Credits: Giordano Aita, p. 1; Andrejs Pidjass, p. 17; ArchMen, p. 30; victor zastol'skiy, p. 44; Subbotina Anna, p. 65; Roman Sakhno, p. 79; arquiplay77, p. 96; George Mayer, p. 110; George Mayer, p. 129; archideaphoto, p. 144; Albo, p. 160; Gautier Willaume, p. 174

Copyright © 2012 Pearson Education, Inc., publishing as Pearson Prentice Hall, One Lake Street, Upper Saddle River, NJ 07458. All rights reserved. Manufactured in the United States of America. This publication is protected by Copyright, and permission should be obtained from the publisher prior to any prohibited reproduction, storage in a retrieval system, or transmission in any form or by any means, electronic, mechanical, photocopying, recording, or likewise. To obtain permission(s) to use material from this work, please submit a written request to Pearson Education, Inc., Permissions Department, Pearson Prentice Hall, One Lake Street, Upper Saddle River, NJ 07458.

Many of the designations by manufacturers and seller to distinguish their products are claimed as trademarks. Where those designations appear in this book, and the publisher was aware of a trademark claim, the designations have been printed in initial caps or all caps.

Library of Congress Cataloging-in-Publication Data
Kopec, David Alan.
  Evidence based design : a process for research and writing / David Kopec, Edith L.A. Sinclair, Bruce Matthes. — 1st ed.
     p. cm.
  Includes bibliographical references.
  ISBN-13: 978-0-13-217406-0
  ISBN-10: 0-13-217406-5
  1. Evidence-based design--Research.   2. Architectural writing.   I. Sinclair, Edith L. A.
II. Matthes, Bruce.   III. Title.
  NA2570.K67 2010
  720.72'1—dc22
                                                   2010049485

10 9 8 7 6 5 4 3 2 1

Prentice Hall
is an imprint of

www.pearsonhighered.com

ISBN 10:   0-13-217406-5
ISBN 13: 978-0-13-217406-0

Dedication

This book is dedicated to all of those designers who engage in evidence-based design research as a means to make the world a better and safer place. THANK YOU!

BRIEF CONTENTS

CHAPTER 1   Call for Methods-Based Research   1
CHAPTER 2   Importance of Citations   17
CHAPTER 3   Developing a Line of Logic   30
CHAPTER 4   Formation of a Topic and Argument   44
CHAPTER 5   Review of Literature   65
CHAPTER 6   Issues in Research   79
CHAPTER 7   Methods   96
CHAPTER 8   Site Analysis and Case Studies   110
CHAPTER 9   Surveys, Interviews, and Observations   129
CHAPTER 10   Historical Analysis Method and Photo Analysis Method   144
CHAPTER 11   Experimentation and Computer Modeling   160
CHAPTER 12   The Final Phase   174
REFERENCES   **195**
INDEX   **197**

CONTENTS

CHAPTER 1   **Call for Methods-Based Research**   1

Introduction   1

Research and Design   4
- Design Education   4
- Trends in Design Education   5

The Role of a Thesis or Dissertation   6

The Research Process   7
- Developing a Chain of Logic   9
- Developing a Position   9

Pursuit of Research   10

Types of Studies   13

Summary   15

Glossary   16

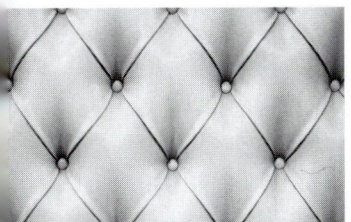

CHAPTER 2   **Importance of Citations**   17

Introduction   18
- APA & MLA   18
- Purpose   18

Terminology and Fundamental Differences   19

Plagiarism   20
- Forms of Plagiarism   20

In-text Sources   21
- Summarizing   21
- Paraphrasing   22
- Quotations   23
  - *Direct Quote*   23
  - *Quote with Signal Phrase*   23
  - *Long Quotes*   24

Tools of Organization and Documentation   25
- Citation Management   25
- Formatting Final Lists   25
- Abbreviations   26

Summary   29

Glossary   29

CHAPTER 3   **Developing a Line of Logic   30**
   Introduction   30
   Stages of Research   32
      The Formation Stage   32
         Quantitative and Qualitative Approaches   33
      The Development Stage   34
         Information Gathering   34
         Inductive versus Deductive Reasoning   36
      The Outcome Stage   39
         Illogical Argumentation and Conclusions   39
         Leaps of Faith   40
         Overstating the Research   41
   Summary   42
   Glossary   43

CHAPTER 4   **Formation of a Topic and Argument   44**
   Introduction   45
   Identifying a Topic   45
   Preparing a Thesis Statement   48
   Forming a Research Question   49
      Concept Mapping   49
      Developing a Research Question   49
   Beginning the Process   53
      The Abstract   53
      The Introduction   54
   Dissecting an Argument   57
      Logic Mapping   59
   Selecting Research Objectives   60
      Recognizing Objectives   60
      Specify Objectives   61
      Organize Objectives   61
      Define Objectives   62
   Summary   63
   Glossary   64

CHAPTER 5 **Review of Literature** 65

Introduction 66

Assessing the Literature 67

    What's in a Credential? 68

    What's in a Title? 68

    What's in a Publication? 69

    Assessing Bias 69

Preparing a ROL 69

    Stage 1: Define the Topic 70

    Stage 2: Search and Organize 70

    Stage 3: Evaluate and Assess 73

    Stage 4: Analyze and Interpret 73

Assembling an ROL 74

    The Introduction 75

    The Body 75

Concerns and Considerations 77

    An Invalid ROL 77

    Plagiarism 77

Summary 77

Glossary 78

CHAPTER 6 **Issues in Research** 79

Introduction 80

Ethics 80

    Institutional Review Board 81

Variables 82

Biases 85

Sampling 88

    Probability Sampling 88

        Simple Random Sampling 88

        Stratified Random Sampling 88

        Systematic Sampling 89

        Cluster Sampling 90

    Non-Probability Sampling 91

        Availability Sampling 91

        Quota Sampling 91

        Purposive Sampling 91

        Snowball Sampling 91

Choosing a Sampling Method 92

Summary 94

Glossary 94

CHAPTER 7 **Methods 96**
- *Introduction 97*
- *Formatting the Methods Section 98*
- *Data Gathering and Analysis 99*
  - Quantitative and Qualitative Approaches 99
- *Phenomenology and Design 101*
- *Ethnography 102*
- *Other Research Approaches 105*
  - Mixed Methods 107
- *Summary 108*
- *Glossary 108*

CHAPTER 8 **Site Analysis and Case Studies 110**
- *Introduction 110*
- *Site Analysis 111*
  - Implications and Purpose 113
  - Tools and Diagramming 114
  - Process and Procedure 117
  - Analysis and Interpretation 118
  - Presentation of Findings 119
- *Case Study 121*
  - Technique and Process 123
  - Resources 125
  - Building Typology Study 125
- *Summary 128*
- *Glossary 128*

CHAPTER 9 **Surveys, Interviews, and Observations 129**
- *Introduction 130*
- *Developing Questions 130*
- *Surveys 131*
  - Survey Construction 132
  - Survey Dissemination 133
  - Electronic Surveys 135
- *Interviews 135*
  - Initiating Interviews 137
  - Face-to-Face Interviews 138
  - Community Forums and Focus Groups 139
  - Electronic Media 141
- *Observations 141*
- *Summary 143*
- *Glossary 143*

CHAPTER 10   **Historical Analysis Method and Photo Analysis Method**   144

Introduction   145

Historical Analysis Method   145

   Areas of Research   146

   Historic Documents   148

      Popular Media   148

      History Books   149

      Census Data   149

      Public Records   150

   Data Analysis   150

Photo Analysis Method   152

   Process   153

   Approaches   153

   Analysis Criteria   154

   Photo Modification   155

Summary   159

Glossary   159

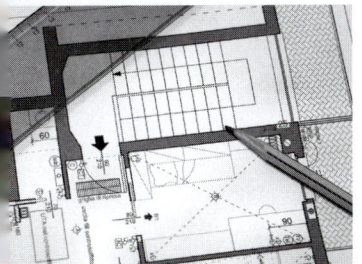

CHAPTER 11   **Experimentation and Computer Modeling**   160

Introduction   161

Experimental Methods   162

   Types of Experiments   162

   Control and Experimental Groups   163

   Variables   163

   Analysis   165

Computer-Related Methods   166

   BIM   167

   Analysis   169

   GIS   170

   Analysis   171

Summary   172

Glossary   173

CHAPTER 12   **The Final Phase**   174

Introduction   175

General Guidelines   175

   Resources   175

      Time-Management   176

   Formatting   177

Citations   177
Embellishments   178
   Fold-out Pages   178
   Pocket Material   179
   Miscellaneous   179
Final Assembly   179
The Title and Cover Page   179
Front Matter   180
   Copyright Page   181
   Signature Page   182
   Dedication Page   183
   Table of Contents Page   183
   Tables, Figures, Illustrations, Charts, and Graphs   183
   Nomenclature List   185
   Abstract Page   185
Main Text   186
   Chapter Headings   187
   Review of the Literature   187
   Methods   187
   Results   188
   Discussion and Design Application   189
Back Matter   190
   Reference (APA) or Works Cited (MLA)   190
   Appendices   190
   Glossary of Terms   191
   Curriculum Vitae or Author's Biography   191
Electronic Submission   191
Electronic Thesis or Dissertation   191
   Security concerns   192
Summary   192
Glossary   193

REFERENCES   **195**

INDEX   **197**

PREFACE

The U.S. culture continues to demand greater justification and verification for actions taken by professionals. Just as many people now question their physicians and pursue their own knowledge regarding a certain health condition or prescribed medication, many are starting to question the logic behind design. Like medicine, design education has a long tradition of apprenticeships and studio-based learning. Through these media, the student is able to question and explore ideas and concepts in relation to the manifestation of the physical form. Unlike medicine, which has evolved from the "healing arts" into a research-based profession, design remains the domain of ethereal thought guided by subjectivity and then applied to the built environment. Recent trends seem to indicate that a paradigm shift is occurring and a greater demand is being placed upon design education to produce evidence-based design. As the demands that society places on designers increase, so too must the educational curriculum. This places design schools in the position of either elevating their curriculums to include quantitative and qualitative research methods, or running the risk of having their program devalued. This idea can be threatening for those who view evidence-based design as a future trend toward prescriptive design.

There have been many books written on the topic of research methods, but few on the process and procedures of writing a thesis or dissertation for the design curriculum. This book attempts to fill that gap by providing an overview of the contents found within a traditional academic thesis or dissertation and relating that information back to the design process. Although this book is not intended to be a standalone research writing guide or a research methods text, it does contain an overview of each subject along with activities for practical application. The primary purpose of this book is to serve as a guide to help students conceptualize and formulate their design ideas and then to evaluate and test those ideas through an organized and structured process. The result of this process will be the culmination of a comprehensive document that articulates a design concept and justifies key design attributes.

Overarching themes in this book include the development of a critical position, the process and importance of performing a thorough review of the literature, and an overview of common research methods. This book thus serves as a guide for the student as he or she embarks upon the process of producing an evidence-based thesis or dissertation.

ACKNOWLEDGMENTS

The authors acknowledge the following individuals for their review of the manuscript: Zane Curry, Texas Tech University; Carol Caughey, Oregon State University; Maruja Torres-Antonini, University of Florida; Phillip Tebbutt, Louisiana State University; and JoAnn Wilson, Utah State University.

ABOUT THE AUTHORS

DAK Kopec is Associate Professor at Newschool of Architecture and Design. He is an ASID distinguished speaker, recipient of the Joel Polsky Prize, and listed as a Fullbright Specialist. In addition to serving as a visiting professor at the University of Hawaii at Manoa, and visiting lecturer for Virginia Commonwealth University in Doha Qatar, Dr. Kopec is active in the promotion of interdisciplinary approaches to design and design research.

E.L.A. Sinclair has an interdisciplinary background in architecture, business, and research methods. She draws upon this background to promote her passion for more Evidence-based designs. Among Ms. Sinclair's academic and professional service, include: participation on an international panel for the discussion of Evidence-based design and acting as an expert reviewer for facilities based journal articles. On a local level she has acted as facilitator for community-design charettes. Currently Ms. Sinclair works for the Department of Defense in the Architectural division of Naval Facilities Engineering Command (NAVFAC).

Bruce Matthes is Assistant Professor at the Newschool of Architecture and Design and adjunct faculty member of the Art Institute of San Diego. Mr. Matthes teaches an array of courses in English and has developed a specialization in the linkages between visual and written arts as a pedagogical practice for teaching design students.

Call for Methods-Based Research

CHAPTER 1

> " A love affair with knowledge will never end in heartbreak."
> —Michael Garrett Marino

chapter objectives

By the end of this chapter, students should be able to:

- Analyze the role of research in the design process.
- Discuss the value that research can contribute to the design process.
- Identify the trends related to design research.
- Make a case for greater research in design education.

Introduction

Design professionals are responsible for making some of the most important decisions regarding our built environment. The built environment, however, has no meaning without human interaction. Because of concerns pertaining to the human–environment relationship, architects must be licensed, or work under another architect's license. Likewise,

chapter outline

Introduction

Research and Design
Design Education
Trends in Design Education

The Role of a Thesis or Dissertation

The Research Process
Developing a Chain of Logic
Developing a Position

Pursuit of Research

Types of Studies

Summary

many states require licensure for interior designers. A fundamental premise for licensure in any state is the establishment of a direct threat to human health, safety, and welfare. There must be proof that a building or design is to be developed by a person who has a verifiable credential attesting to a higher-than-average expertise in a given area and who is therefore uniquely qualified to ensure the health, safety, and welfare of human occupants. Because this is a common denominator within licensure and therefore within architecture and interior design, this book will focus on research and research methods as they pertain to health, safety, and welfare. It should be noted that research can, and should, be conducted on other aspects of design and the design process and that there are other methods to conduct research.

Many studies have shown that the built environment has an impact on human health and behavior. Therefore, the level of and responsibility for acquiring the expertise, knowledge, and practical experience that are required to protect the life, safety, and well being of end-users is extraordinary. Architects, landscape architects, interior designers, and other design professionals have a long and respected history of creating environments, although the climate they work in has changed. In an effort to remain competitive in a world that is becoming increasingly specialized, the design profession has risen to meet yet another challenge. Architects in particular are accustomed to public and judiciary bodies holding them accountable—long after they have finished a project. However, the most recent change voiced by the architectural community is that clients are beginning to demand credible data and assurances of building performance to validate the rising costs of design and construction. Therefore, in response to "value engineering," some of the larger firms have made the strategic decision to incorporate rigorous research into the design process to satisfy public demands; this research is called *evidence-based design*. Hamilton and Watkins (2009) sum up the situation:

> If a modest change in practice can lead to better decisions, increased rigor, and the capture of relevant data that offer the potential for a competitive advantage, design practitioners would be well advised to adopt an evidence-based model. If widespread use of such a model improves the credibility and prestige of the profession, the leadership of the field should encourage its adoption. If such a model improves the standing and performance of the profession, the structure of professional education must adapt. (p. 6)

This call-to-arms of the next generation of design professional to learn *how to research* is the predominate reason for writing this book. *Evidence Based Design: A Process for Research and Writing* addresses the process of the first true research a person might be exposed to—the thesis or dissertation. The scientific-based process used for developing a thesis or dissertation is the best way for a young designer to delve into the world of research procedures. As this is only one way to approach design research, it behooves the student to explore other perspectives as well, in order to understand the full breadth of the research options available.

Research does not begin with a survey, focus group, or even a design charrette. Research begins with the researcher. The researcher must be fully aware of his or her position and its relationship to the overarching theme of that research and how this position conforms or conflicts with society. As researchers explore a given topic, they must ensure personal and professional adherence to ethics. They must be mindful that their beliefs and values can often influence the interpretations of the subject matter being investigated, as well as the method used to gather additional information. In short, we can say that research for the purpose of designing is an organized formal inquiry for the purpose of obtaining information that can be used for making design decisions.

"Design research" refers to the procedures and techniques involved in a method of inquiry, data collection, analysis, and the presentation of the information that leads to design-related decisions. An area where *design research* differs from *academic research* is in the "application." Design research produces information that designers need to make decisions. In some cases, this information will generate a verifiable outcome (a specific design feature), and in other cases, it may be inconclusive. It is common knowledge among designers that generating a project from a baseline of knowledge (e.g., codes, zoning) and doing "one's due diligence" (e.g., checking safety ratings) is an ethical obligation. However, design research is different in this way: it focuses on answering important questions that arise from the design *process*, not the *product*, and the answers are then applied to the design. Designers who lose sight of this difference are likely to encounter one of two outcomes:

1. Failing to collect information that is required
2. Collecting information that may be of interest, but that is unimportant to the application of design

Table 1.1 — Examples of Early Research

Study Method	Area of Study	Application
Observation	Solar cycles	Building site and configuration
Assessment (trial and error)	Built forms and materials	Indigenous methods and materials
Monitor and record	Weather patterns	Crops and travel

Therefore, the basic purpose for design research is to reduce uncertainty or error when designing environments for human occupation and aid in making crucial design decisions. Although certainty cannot be guaranteed, research allows for the reduction of uncertainty.

Early philosophers conducted much of the first documented design research. The premise of this research was derived from logical reasoning and observations. One could argue that in many respects, the design fields evolved from this basic premise and that designers have therefore conducted preliminary forms of research such as observation and assessment for many years. For example, early people would monitor and record weather patterns and then draw conclusions as to when a crop should be planted, where a home might be best situated, or how much food should be stored. Other forms of early research occurred through trial and error. Early builders learned from their mistakes as they built various structures and experimented with form. This knowledge was then passed down through the generations via the oral tradition. Later, the data obtained from these early studies was published in written documents such as the *Farmers Almanac* or the *Architectural Graphic Standards* or within cultural and religious traditions such as feng shui. See Table 1.1.

The design research process starts by identifying and defining an issue or an opportunity. When design decisions arise, they can be addressed through a four-step process:

1. Identification of an issue or opportunity
2. Definition of the issue or opportunity
3. Identification of alternative courses of action
4. Selection of a specific course of action

An *issue* is something that affects the design process, such as local building codes or a specific need of a given user group. An *opportunity* allows a designer to contribute something of interest to the design community by adding to the body of knowledge. For example, the recent "green" movement and the "sustainability" movement have afforded the design community with many opportunities to break from the traditional design methods and explore new ways of designing buildings. This too must be learned. Quite a few groups and organizations have been formed to educate, monitor, and certify design professionals in their ability to "design sustainably" (e.g., the U.S. Green Building Council and Leadership in Energy and Environmental Design or LEED certification).

Once a larger concept has been identified, the next step is to assign definitions to various attributes. In some situations, an entire research project may be devoted to the definition of an issue or an opportunity. The term "sustainability," for example, has grown to encompass environmental conservation, energy efficiency, preservation of human health, and a host of other conditions that have been traditionally unrelated. Distinctions in definitions are important because they are the crux of research expectations. Put another way, if a client regards sustainability as recycled materials and the design firm approaches sustainability in terms of energy conservation, the client may then be disappointed with the outcome. See Activity 1.1.

When the purpose of research is to identify a phenomenon or causal factor and there is little or no previous research, it is called an **exploratory study**. This type of study is undertaken to better comprehend the nature of a given problem. The ability to estimate the relative importance and overall impacts of a design choice is the cornerstone of design intelligence. The process of research conveys this intelligence and allows the designer to estimate the cause-and-effect relationship of multiple design interventions, which allows the designer to make informed choices. Once architects and designers are capable of providing these credible and scientific facts to their clients, they not only justify their designs but also add to the knowledge of the entire design community.

ACTIVITY 1.1 — Exploration of Issues and Opportunities

Explore preliminary research ideas. First, identify your issue or opportunity to research. Second, define the core of the issue or opportunity. The key here is to reduce your theory to the smallest possible component from which to research. Second, to do this, continue to ask the question "Why or what is the principle element of this issue?" Third, pose possible alternative ways to view the same issue or ask a friend. Finally, plan a course of action that would warrant the most information to apply to your design.

Issue/ Opportunity	Define	Alternatives	Action
Example			
Issue: Needs of the blind	Existing wayfinding methods	Audio cues	Interview blind people
Opportunity: Design for touch, sound, and smell	User wayfinding language Wayfinding clues	Thermal cues Textural cues	Test materials Demonstrate use
Issue: Opportunity:			
Issue: Opportunity:			

Research and Design

DESIGN EDUCATION

Design education presents an interesting conflict between theory and practice, and between science and philosophy. Likewise, much of today's design professions are conflicted between the practical aspects of project budget and time expenditures and the philosophical and scientific approaches to design. The philosophical approaches are often based on critiquing existing designs and developing metaphorical symbolism. A scientific approach generally takes a more defined and functional perspective. Designers who embrace the scientific approach gain knowledge through a variety of methods related to experimentation and observation. Once again, Hamilton and Watkins (2009) explain the circumstances succinctly:

> The issue, however, is this: the education most architects receive is ill suited to providing the kind of knowledge that can consistently assist clients in achieving goals that go beyond (1) aesthetics, (2) efficiency, (3) schedule and budget compliance, (4) technical accuracy, and (5) functionality. (p. 251)

The concern here is that the current disconnect between philosophical and scientific approaches could possibly lead to a future fracturing within the design community rather than the integration of a diversity of design approaches for the next generation of designers.

Architectural and design education has roots firmly tied to art. Efforts to reform architectural education have emerged throughout history; from the Beaux-Arts to Bauhaus training, to John Dewey and Alfred Whitehead in the early twentieth century, to the experimental colleges of the 1960s. These movements all helped promote philosophical approaches to exploration and inquiry. It wasn't until recently that ideas of evidence-based design permeated the design curriculum. Notwithstanding the valid concerns of the faculty of many design schools, this book will endeavor to fill the void for the evidence-based design curricula that will support offering students a well-rounded design education. For some students who have been educated from an art-based pedagogy, the risk is that recent scientific advancements will overwhelm them and put them at a distinct disadvantage for employment. For the purposes of this book we will use the operational definition of all careers, business, academia, and design as a "profession." With architecture and interior design, the number of required years for an apprenticeship can be reduced by first obtaining a professional degree (a highly specialized degree that prepares a student to perform certain tasks) at either the bachelors, masters, or doctorate level (B.Arch, M.Arch, and D.Arch, respectively). Although most design fields offer the option to pursue an academic degree (a broad-based education with an interdisciplinary foundation) such as a Bachelor of Arts (BA) at the undergraduate level, a Master of Arts (MA) or Master of Science (MS) at the graduate level, and a PhD at the doctorate level; in order to be a practicing architect or interior design (in some states), a person must complete an apprenticeship, now called an *internship*. The goal of the internship is to provide the student with technical hands-on experience so the intern can learn about the practice under the guidance of someone with greater experience. In this way, design education can be likened to other occupations that require a similar apprenticeship-type education, such as medicine, which requires that interns know how to research.

What separates a professional degree from an academic degree is *scientific inquiry*, otherwise known as research. The final project required for some professional degrees is often a capstone or other comprehensive project demonstrating that one can perform the typical duties of a given occupation. The award of an academic degree requires the completion of a heavily researched and documented study. In many respects, architects are great at searching but not at the process of research. This distinction has many implications. A professional education presupposes some form of apprenticeship, whereas an academic degree presupposes rigorous research. From this dichotomy, design is in a position to do as other professions such as medicine and law have done: merge a professional education with an academic discipline to develop a student who knows how to do something and has cultivated the higher-cognitive thought process to support their actions with logical and well-thought-out justifications. In this format, the *design thesis or dissertation* satisfies the need for the student who on entering the work environment is an experienced designer and researcher.

In 1996, the Carnegie Foundation published the report *Building Community: A New Future for Architecture Education and Practice*, which—when coupled with the American Institute of Architecture Students (AIAS) report, *The Redesign of Studio Culture*—indicates numerous missed opportunities at the undergraduate level to take full advantage of interdisciplinary collaboration and exposure to the research process typically associated with an academic degree. One might therefore argue that a professional degree at the undergraduate level may be too narrow and lack an interdisciplinary foundation. An education in evidence-based design and a design thesis or dissertation resolves this issue.

There has been a long-standing debate among design educators about the role of research-based knowledge in design. Some have posed the argument that formal academic research is not a necessity for design and some even suggest that research compromises the artistic integrity of design. Their opposition is based on the thinking that the research results will drive form without consideration for the artistic aspects of design. Still others have argued that traditional teaching practices rely too much on the encouragement of students to develop form-generation skills obtained through intuition, reflective observation, and concept formation. This sentiment is echoed by Hamilton and Watkins (2009): "The days of architects relying largely on intuition, personal experience, or even examples of comparable projects as models for design are over". Whereas, socializing students into a solely artistic paradigm is a condition that, as Salama (2005) warns, "emphasizes personal feelings, subjective judgments, intuition and imagination at the expense of social and professional responsibilities" (p. 8).

TRENDS IN DESIGN EDUCATION

Recognizing architecture's precarious position in society, several deans from the schools of architecture, along with practitioners from some of the larger firms, convened in the 1990s to discuss possible reasons for the neglect of research within the field. The general consensus appeared to be a lack of easily accessed information and previous research. In 2002, the American Society of Interior Design (ASID), recognizing this need for its profession to gain access to design research databases, teamed up with the University of Minnesota to create InformeDesign, an easy-to-use database that provides succinct environment and design information obtained from peer-reviewed scientific journals. *Harvard Design Magazine* author Fisher (2004/2005) expects that as similar types of databases become more common, clients will have greater expectations of designers and expect them to know the research. Increased client expectations would mean that if a designer failed to consider a human condition known to derive from the built environment, the designer could be found legally negligent. If greater client expectations drive the future of design, then it is necessary to incorporate evidence-based design into the curriculum of design schools immediately. To further meet the challenge of increasing the academic rigors of design education, the scholarly journal of the interior design profession, the *Journal of Interior Design*, has been altered to reflect greater involvement in social science research, and many departments of interior design are increasingly recruiting new faculty with research training backgrounds. Hence, if the design profession as a whole is to keep pace with this trend, educators will need to change the existing paradigm, particularly within the studio culture. Studio instructors themselves will need to evaluate students based on scientific measurement to support the propositions of human activity in combination with aesthetics and require students to demonstrate their designs with verifiable facts. Fisher (2004/2005) suggests that most studio reviews, concentrate on what a student intended to do and how the results did or did not achieve those intentions. The research expected from the student is limited to site-, program-, or precedent-specific inquiries. In many respects, one might conclude that this is inevitable; disregarding perspective, site, program, or precedent is only one way to look at things.

Amos Rapoport (1994) states that the discipline of architecture needs to develop a quantifiable body of knowledge. He believes that it is time for the discipline to depart from the current art paradigm that the profession and its education are based on and to develop a new professional paradigm based on science and research. Others believe that as early as the undergraduate level, the architectural student should be involved in research and that evaluation research needs to be included into architectural pedagogy. For example, students could engage in ethnographic studies, spending several hours engaged in structured observation and recording of data as part of their existing site visits and walkthroughs of the built environment. Through the use of this method, students will gain more than a cursory overview of how people use the space; they will develop instead a deeper understanding of the various nuances or phenomena that occur together with other environmental forces (e.g., noise, light, weather), people, and buildings. Hence graduating students will be better able to understand what they see and better trained to know what to look for in the built environment.

The Role of a Thesis or Dissertation

The fields of design (e.g., architecture, industrial design, interior design, landscaping) are all fortunate because research can be approached from many varied perspectives. To illustrate this point, consider the research perspectives associated with the fields of medicine, which are often limited to biology and behavior. Design, on the other hand, can pursue research from the diverse perspectives (see Figure 1.1) of art and philosophy (symbolic meaning and metaphor), science and technology (structural or automation), urban and community planning (navigability and public safety), or psychology (behaviors and attitudes). These research perspectives are often bundled into the term "human factors."

Although these diverse perspectives offer a wide breadth of subject matter within the academic curriculum, the ability to acquire depth of knowledge can be compromised simply because of time constraints; it would likely take a

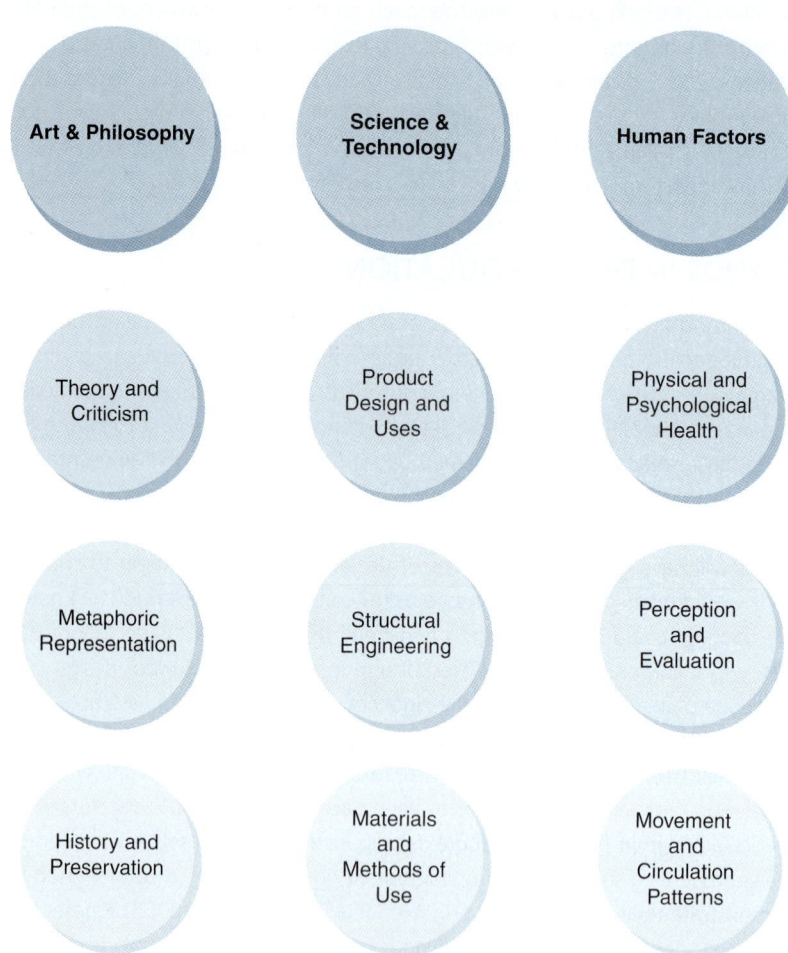

FIGURE 1.1 Design Research Perspectives.
From a design standpoint, research can pursue theories from many diverse perspectives.
Source: Kopec, D. (2009).

student ten or more years to complete a program that provides a sufficient depth in art, science, technology, and human health and behaviors. However, the thesis or dissertation offers a solution to this conundrum because the student can self-select a single perspective of interest to focus on.

The completion of a thesis or dissertation requires the pursuit and acquiring of in-depth knowledge that goes beyond the academic curriculum. In this situation, the design student must be willing to accept the challenge of taking responsibility for a portion of his or her own education by specifying and defining his or her project and then developing individual learning outcomes to achieve throughout the process. The thesis includes but is not limited to the following:

1. Undertaking an independent project of a demanding nature
2. Pursuing an in-depth investigation into a subject of interest
3. Developing and documenting research methodologies
4. Analyzing data sets for recurring themes or emerging ideas
5. Logically ordering and reporting information in a written format

It is important to understand that a thesis or dissertation goes beyond knowing how to perform a skill or function. It requires the aggregation and analysis of multiple perspectives that are then synthesized into a critical and thoughtful discussion. Learning and embracing the research process gives the design student fortitude and discipline that can be applied to life, a career, or both. In order for this critical thought process to occur, conceptual, temporal, and other boundaries must be defined so that the subject can be researched without contamination or bias.

The Research Process

Research is a process that many students find abstract, complicated, and perhaps even frightening (Figure 1.2). Fortunately, it is much like the process of design; research has a beginning, a middle, and an end. The beginning portions are about the researcher's assumptions and how the researcher comes to understand those assumptions in the greater context of the world. In order to gain this understanding, there are a multitude of perspectives from which

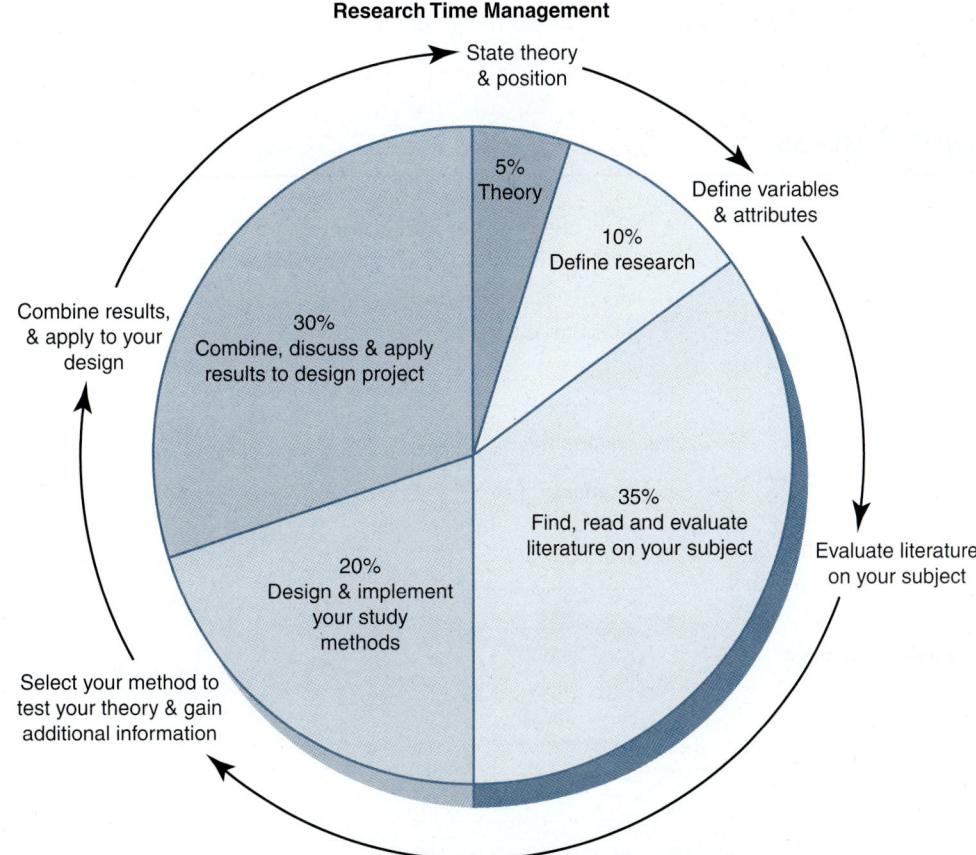

FIGURE 1.2 The Research Process. The research process can be easily managed when thoughtful planning and time management procedures are implemented in the early stage. The management of time during the research process is crucial. This graph reflects how much time should be allotted for each phase.
Source: Sinclair, E. (2009).

BOX 1.1 — Reasons for Research

There are four reasons to perform research:

1. Explore an idea or concept
2. Describe or better understand new information or relationships
3. Provide an explanation for a given phenomenon
4. Evaluate the efficacy or viability of a process, procedure, or practice

---

researchers can frame their thoughts (e.g., constructivism, deconstructivism, relativism, feminism). There are two overarching approaches that are important to understand: **positivism** and **postpositivism**.

Positivism is a theoretical position that demands scientific explanations and rejects intuition and perception. For example, a straightforward experiment, such as one that seeks to understand water flow capacity for drainage purpose, would follow a positivism line of inquiry. Postpositivism, also known as postempiricism, contends that human knowledge is not based on absolute ideas, but has speculative elements. According to postpositivism, the knower and known cannot be separated, and therefore they influence each other. By and large, design research follows the theoretical position of postpositivism because much of the research related to human perceptions and behaviors are interpretive. Student researchers opting for the postpositivist position need to understand the importance of multiple sources of data and the triangulation of all the information to come to any thoughtful conclusions. Once the researcher has established the position best suited to view the subject matter, he or she must then identify the *reason* for the study.

There are generally four reasons to perform research: (1) to explore an idea or concept, (2) to describe or better understand human–environment relationships, (3) to provide an explanation for a given phenomenon, and (4) to evaluate the efficacy or viability of a process, procedure, or practice. (See Box 1.1 and Activity 1.2.)

When selecting a topic or subject area for a thesis or dissertation, students must first understand their area of interest. This is important because a given subject area can be approached from many perspectives. Sensation, for example, can be explored from the perspective of sensory development or rehabilitation: neurobiological interpretations of sensation, sensory association, or philosophical interpretations. Consequently, student researchers must identify their interest and define those parameters for the reader. During this process, the boundaries of the topic are accessed. Therefore, the goal of research is to obtain detailed and in-depth information within a specific area.

ACTIVITY 1.2 — Thought Process

Example

Idea: Pets have taken the place of children for many young couples.

New Information: During the past few decades, pets have evolved from personal property to valued members of a family in the minds of many people.

Explanation:
- In a highly competitive and stressful world, pets provide unconditional love.
- People have an innate desire to love and care for another, but because children require much attention, a pet can be a viable second option.
- It is easier to work a pet into a busy lifestyle than it is a child.

Effects:
- Pets need access to outdoor facilities for urination, defecation, and exercise.
- Many people suffer from allergies or asthma-related symptoms in direct response to the presence of animal dander.
- Pets require specialized health care services provided by a veterinarian.

Idea: _____

New Information: _____

Explanation:
- _____
- _____
- _____

Effects:
- _____
- _____
- _____

Because of this depth, the researcher must dedicate numerous hours to the understanding of the subject matter. This is why it is vital that the topic or subject area be an area of interest to the researcher. If the subject has little appeal to the researcher, concentration will not be sustained throughout the duration of the research process, and any lackluster enthusiasm will come across in the written document. Likewise, as the research goes deeper and deeper into the subject area, the researcher must attempt to solve only one piece of the problem at a time. Like a chain being submerged into water, it goes one link at a time. Each link can be likened to a piece of the greater problem.

DEVELOPING A CHAIN OF LOGIC

One issue of concern for beginning researchers and even for seasoned researchers is tangents. Because many diverse factors are linked, many beginning researchers either stop delving into the depths of their subject matter or overcomplicate the research process by digging too deep. This can cause a host of problems for the researcher, including losing a great deal of time or overstating a conclusion. Considering that many career researchers have often dedicated their lives to a single topic or subject area, it is not realistic for beginning researchers to attempt to understand the depth and breadth of their subject in only one or two years. Therefore, the researcher must keep his or her research expectations focused and realistic.

DEVELOPING A POSITION

The process of research entails the development of a theory or theoretical proposition. Next, the theoretical constructs must be established, along with the relationship between variables. A *theoretical construct* is a specific instance that may have a connection to another instance. *Theories* are composed of statements that indicate a relationship between constructs; that is, particular conceptions that are labeled by a term. These constructs should be conceptualized and the concept clearly defined. Then, those concepts can be operationalized or tested, as specific indicators to measure in terms of their different constructs. See Box 1.2.

Concepts can be defined in two steps. The first step is a **nominal definition**, which provides a precise meaning to a term that cannot be observed. The second is the **operational definition** of the concept, which defines in detail how it is to be measured or observed. For example, *beauty* is a concept, but it cannot be precisely defined or measured because it has different meanings to different people; therefore, we can apply only an operational definition. We could develop a set of criterion such as shape, dimension, color, and so on that can be used as our operational

---

BOX 1.2   Theory and Constructs

Theory:

"Cork flooring is the best all-around type of flooring for people who live in condominiums and suffer from allergies."

Theoretical construct 1:

"Because cork resists the growth of mold and because mold is an allergen, it stands to reason that cork is a good flooring option for those who suffer from mold allergies."

Theoretical construct 2:

"Because cork is a porous material, it is a good sound dampener, ideal for condominiums located on the second and higher level floors."

The *person* is the relationship between the two theoretical statements:

"A person living in a second-floor condominium who also suffers from mold allergies would be well served by cork flooring."

Concepts are operationalized or tested:

Experimentation and testing for mold threshold, as well as acoustic levels, must be undertaken.

The experimental objectives:

Objective 1: "Identify the type and level of fungal growth to occur on a water-saturated sample of cork flooring that is placed in a dark closet with an ambient temperature of 72 degrees."

Objective 2: "Analyze the different decibel readings obtained from various objects dropped onto a cork floor from the unit directly below the sample flooring system."

definition of beauty. Without operational definitions, it is difficult to say what is beautiful versus what is ugly, what is painful versus what is pleasurable, what is noise versus what is music, and so on. What can cause confusion in nominal and operational definitions is the imprecise nature of the English language. For example, the English language has *homonyms*: words with multiple meanings and spellings that sound the same but have completely different definitions. These include, but are not limited to, past and passed, duel and dual, and write and right. In this computer age, spell-checking will not catch these words, and if spelled incorrectly, they can change the meaning of a sentence. A third concern is the lack of clarity associated with a word. The word "see" can be used to describe an action such as watching the sunset on the horizon (*I can see the sun setting on the horizon*) or as a description to convey understanding (*I see what you mean*). Within the fields of design, the use of the word "feeling" is often used to describe experiential qualities. This common catch-all word can be used to formulate a question such as, "How does the room feel?" However, without clarification of the researcher's intended use of the word, one response might be "hot," indicating a response to the temperature. Another response might be "hot," a slang word that indicates something beautiful and trendy. Therefore, it is important to understand and clarify nominal and operational definitions within the research document in order to avoid confusion and misunderstanding.

Once a topic or subject matter has been selected and defined, it is important that the researcher gain a thorough understanding of its complexities and intricacies. This can be accomplished by reading broad-based documents and by reading what others have said about the subject. It is essential that the researcher does not accept everything read as an absolute truth. Instead, the researcher should critically analyze what is being stated and compare it with information from other authors. The culmination of this information will be used for a comprehensive discussion that will appear in the final thesis or dissertation as the review of literature (more on the review of literature can be found in Chapter 5).

Pursuit of Research

Design research as compared with scientific research is the quest to examine and understand the realities of the physical environment in a systematic way. It is a step-by-step process, which allows those who are methodical and creative in their thinking to explore how ideas and concepts come together. However, this same opportunity can result in much difficulty for researchers who have not properly prepared themselves for the endeavors associated with research. To illustrate, here are just a few of the most common research problems stemming from unprepared researchers:

- Incomplete conclusion due to complicated subject or scope that is too broad
- Lack of sufficient understanding of the subject matter due to a weak research question
- Disorganization due to continually changing the research topic
- Lack of development due to "putting off" the research until too late

There are different reasons to pursue design research: to test, to explore, or to establish probable cause. When testing a hypothesis or theory, one might state that "the use of rounded edges, curved walls, and hallways facilitate better wayfinding." This is an idea that would need to be tested and found to be either supported or unsupported. The second reason might be to explore a phenomenon associated with an object or event. For example, "At what point in the design process does design become more about art and less about function?" Research in this area would undoubtedly require the researcher to shift from an inductive thought process to a deductive one. A **deductive process** begins with a guiding theoretical logic; an **inductive process** begins with a blank slate and explores a subject area in order to identify theoretical logic.

As previously mentioned, research is a systematic, logical, and empirical process. It requires the understanding of past and present knowledge related to the subject, as well as the development of a method best suited for gathering additional knowledge on that specific subject. The additional knowledge gathered from a research method is then integrated with the knowledge obtained via the review of literature to form inferences that bring clarity to a problem. These inferences can be causal or probabilistic. **Causal inferences** are a set of circumstances based on causality (causing something), whereas **probabilistic inferences** have a probability of being accurate. However, the cultural orientation and personal beliefs of researchers have the potential to influence the conclusions and may lead to overgeneralizations of the data. An example of an overstatement or overgeneralization is when a research study states that "natural views assist in the healing process" and the researcher then makes the claim that "a landscape painting will assist in the healing process." In this case, a living three-dimensional landscape is very different from a two-dimensional representation of a

ACTIVITY 1.3 — Exploration of Variables and Attributes

Use the following example as a guide to explore your subject in terms of variables and their attributes.

Variable (characteristic or unit of analysis)	Attributes (features or traits)
Example	
Hallways	Move people
	Move materials
	Narrow hallway
	Curved hallway
Variable	**Attributes**

---

landscape. Hence, it should be the personal goal of each student researcher to conduct research thoroughly and without personal judgment or bias. Some of the more common mistakes made during the research process include:

1. *Ex post facto (after the fact) reasoning:* Working backward to deny a theory or entirely restating the theory after the facts are observed but not tested (study appears irrational).
2. *Researcher over-involvement:* Researchers become too close to the subject matter, which interferes with their objectivity.
3. *Mystification:* Findings attributed to supernatural causes.

There are two mainstays of design research that are based on logic and patterns. Many contend that it is neither buildings nor designs that are directly researched, but rather the individual variables or attributes that compose them. A **variable** is a characteristic of the building or design, and the **attributes** are the different ways in which the variable can occur. For example, hallways within a building can be a variable and the ways in which those hallways are used (e.g., to move guests, to transport materials) are the attributes. All the relevant attributes of the subject (different uses and sizes of the hallway) are variables, which should be mutually exclusive. This means that two events should not occur without a common outcome. Examples of multiple variables without a common outcome are the uses of a hallway. It can be used as a place to sit and rest or as a place to move people and objects from one point to another. However, in ordinary situations, a single person cannot sit *and* move through the hallway simultaneously.

There are four common types of variables: **nominal**, **ordinal**, **interval**, and **ratio**. A **nominal variable** is one for which the attributes are irrefutably different, such as the case of the permeability of materials—materials are either permeable or not. Even semipermeability is permeable. In this case, permeability would be the nominal variable. A second type of variable is ordinal. This occurs when a variable can be ranked. Using the same example, an **ordinal variable** is the degree of permeability. Therefore, information would be gathered that would prove, for example, that "Unsealed concrete is generally more permeable than wood and quarried rock is less permeable than wood." Interval is a third type of variable. An **interval variable** is the distance between attributes in an order that is precise and meaningful, as in "Unsealed concrete is three times more permeable than wood, but wood is only two times more permeable than quarried rock." The last type of variable is called ratio. A **ratio variable** has an absolute zero point, such as the date construction began. This might be used to calculate the life span of certain materials within a given climate. It is also important to understand that variables can be linked. For example, a researcher might want to measure the lifespan of a 4 × 4 redwood beam with respect to ratio, interval, ordinal, and nominal variables. The variable can be portrayed as a ratio because the absolute zero point of when the beam was formed can be determined. It could be defined as an interval variable if the researcher were to measure the degree of decay from season to season. It could also be defined as an ordinal variable if the decay were being tracked and correlated from week to week or month to month. Finally, it

ACTIVITY 1.4 — Exploration of Different Variables

Follow the example in this table as a guide to input the variables of your chosen research subject.

Variable	Type of Variable			
	Nominal (features are definitely different)	**Ordinal** (features can be classified or ranked)	**Interval** (measurable difference between features)	**Ratio** (feature has an absolute point of zero)
Example				
Materials	Permeability	Degree of permeability	Temperature	Date of construction

could be defined as a nominal variable because there is an absolute point at which the redwood beam could no longer provide support. The key in this discussion is the understanding and articulation of what the researcher wants to measure.

From this point, researchers can develop theories to help explain relationships between variables, termed the independent and dependent variables of a situation. (Variables are discussed further in Chapters 5 and 6, but as an introduction, **independent variables** are factors of measurement that the researcher does not have control over, such as age, race, and the like. **Dependent variables** are factors of measurement that change and the researcher can experimentally manipulate and document those changes.) Variables are units of analysis that have different attributes or events that have an immediate or potential relationship to a subject under investigation. Units of analysis in design research typically include unique environmental conditions. An environmental condition can be any number of situations within a space. An example of a condition within an environment that can be analyzed is the change in spatial density or, in other words, the concentration of people in an area. A researcher could measure the spatial density in a shopping center during a holiday season compared with nonholiday times. Another unit of analysis could be the airflow patterns of a mechanical HVAC system versus the passive ventilation of operable windows in an office. By testing and measuring the conditions, documenting the results, and analyzing the data, one could begin to predict relationships. For instance, relationships about the spatial density of crowds during the winter holiday season may have a relationship to the configuration of benches and planters in the shopping center walkways. HVAC airflow patterns or occupant window use may have a relationship to office employee sick leave statistics. However, when developing these predictions and relationships, it is important the researcher not fall victim to one of these two traps. The first is **ecological fallacy**, which means that the researcher has arrived at an erroneous conclusion based on findings about groups or aggregations. Essentially, an ecological fallacy is a *stereotype* or the profiling of a group of people. The other trap is the idea of **reductionism**, which occurs when the researcher ascribes a cause from a limited and narrow perspective. For example, a researcher should not ascribe attributes such as a preference to individuals, but rather develop clusters of traits that have a likelihood of leading to a preference.

BOX 1.3 — Conclusions to Avoid

Ecological fallacy

- Erroneous conclusion based on findings more closely aligned with group stereotypes than with factual data.

  Example: "More women go to malls than do men."

Reductionism

- Assigning cause and effect of a broad subject from a limited and narrow perspective or a small group of people to sample-test.

  Example: "Preference for the configuration of sidewalks is a factor of marital status."

> **BOX 1.4 Reliability and Validity**
>
> **Assessing results**
>
> **Reliability**
>
> - The same results are achieved by several studies or experiments, testing the same thing in the same way.
>
>   *Example: "This study has produced the same results with the same conditions, reproduced several times over the last ten years by different researchers."*
>
> **Validity**
>
> - The conclusion is the result of the culmination of universal proof.
>
>   *Example: "This study has proven the concept of $1 + 1 = 2$ as a mathematical truth."*

The next step in the research process requires the measurement of indicators followed by an analysis of the results. Design research has the added step of applying that information to a design project. Hence, the researcher must approach the subject matter through a deductive or inductive process of reasoning. In its simplest form, to *deduct* is to reduce or bring down to a conclusion (the general to the specific). To *induct* is to lead into a conclusion (the specific to the general). As these are abstract concepts, these examples should provide clarity. Sherlock Holmes, the private detective in the stories by A. C. Doyle, often uses *deductive reasoning*. Holmes has a general theory about a criminal event; he looks in the areas that have a likelihood of providing evidence, makes an observation of something, deduces what has happened, then confronts the alleged villain (who willingly confirms Holmes's theory). Whereas in the popular television series *House, M.D.*, Dr. Gregory House can generally be seen using *inductive reasoning*. Dr. House documents all the patients' specific symptoms and odd personality traits and works with his team to find connections among all the characteristics that lead them to one general conclusion or diagnosis—usually just in the nick of time. (Inductive and deductive processes are discussed in Chapter 3.) Whether it is an inductive or deductive approach, the measurements must be precise, reliable, and valid. **Reliability** and **validity** refer to the relationship between the measurement and the concept. Consider if a friend called you "unreliable"—they would be saying that you are not to be trusted. Reliability describes a concept in which the results are *consistent* over time within identical parameters as in the original study (i.e., the same methodology and target population). When assessing a study for its reliability, it can be viewed in terms of producing the same results within a specified time period. Now consider if a friend called you "invalid"—he or she would be insinuating you are either unhealthy or unfit. The same is true with research validity; the underlying premise of validity refers to the *quality* and *truth* of various conclusions that have been reached. The traditional criterion for validity has its roots in positivism, which was discussed earlier, and derives from the culmination of other empirical conceptions: universal laws, evidence, objectivity, truth, actuality, deduction, reason, and mathematical results. Though both reliability and validity are research goals, there often must be a trade-off. In order to achieve reliability, sometimes the validity of the study results may have to be compromised, or vice versa. Notwithstanding, reliability is a much easier criterion to meet because the researcher can control the experimental variables.

Types of Studies

Within research, there are several different types of studies that range from a relationship between two events (such as natural light and level of learning) to the prediction of performance or behaviors within a given scenario (such as that natural light produces higher test scores in children). The identification and understanding of how a study will be carried out and the type of data it will generate is an important step in the overall framework of the research. Within the different studies are a variety of methods that can be used to gather data (more on research methods in Chapter 7). Some of the studies that researchers are likely to engage include the following:

- Causal-comparative research
- Correlational research
- Descriptive research
- Experimental research
- Historical research
- Qualitative research

Table 1.2 Types of Research

Study	Description	Example
Causal-comparative	A type of research used to determine the cause of existing differences in outcomes	Why do similar building layouts cause wayfinding confusion for some people but not others?
Correlational	An examination that uses statistics to identify the relationship between two or more variables. This type of research doesn't seek to answer questions	Identify the frequency of disorientation between building plans A, B, and C.
Descriptive	A statistical representation of data and characteristics about the subject or phenomenon under investigation	What are the cost/benefit savings over a ten-year period for different ventilation devices deemed as sustainable?
Experimental	When the investigator manipulates and controls one or more independent variables to determine their effects on the subject or phenomena	What are the thermal differences in a 10 × 10 room with the use of three different types of window treatments?
Historical	A process of analyzing past events in an effort to reconstruct and understand past events	Identify the sociopolitical conditions that were reflected in the design of Europe's grand cathedrals.
Qualitative	The formulation of detailed descriptions of characteristics, cases, and settings	How did a series of designers address the issues of ergonomics in the past?

See Table 1.2 for a brief description of each.

Within each of these studies, observations can be conducted in one of two different ways. The first way is a **longitudinal study**, which occurs over the course of multiple years or decades. Longitudinal studies are expensive and time-consuming, but the results obtained from them tend to have greater validity and truth. To illustrate, consider the human life span. Humans live on average more than 70 years. However, we have no way of absolutely knowing the effects of some of our newer products (such as microwave ovens) on human health because many of these products were released within the last 30 or 40 years. Hence, it would not be until a **cohort** (specific group) of children who were born when these products were already in use reaches the age of 70 that we would know for certain whether these products have any long-term effects on human health. In this situation, a longitudinal study would be needed to track diseases and illness throughout the life of a person born into a world where a given item is in use before the health implications could be answered with certainty and truth (see Box 1.5 and Figure 1.3).

The **cross-sectional study** is what most thesis or dissertation researchers are likely to pursue. This is a study that examines a subject or phenomenon at a given point in time. The benefit of this type of study is that it can be conducted in a relatively short period of time. However, the results are only a snapshot in time with a small sampling of test participants. The overall findings are based on the behaviors of those targeted and the assumption that the sample behaviors

BOX 1.5 Longitudinal Study

To get an idea of a longitudinal study, let's analyze the effects of synthetic carpeting on human health. The first variable of consideration is the advent of carpeting into mainstream homes. The literature is likely to show that it was during the 1960s that small areas of carpeting became cost-effective for the mainstream population. The next variable would be the quantity of carpeting. Again, the literature will probably reveal that deep-pile, wall-to-wall carpeting became popular in mainstream America during the 1970s. A third variable would be length of exposure. For a true longitudinal study, we have to look at someone who was born into a home with wall-to-wall carpeting and has therefore lived in a home that has always had such carpeting. This is where a longitudinal study becomes compromised. A person born in 1960 would be only fifty years old in 2010. So the first flaw in the argument that synthetic carpeting is absolutely safe is that we cannot know this for sure because humans live into their seventies and the generation that grew up with carpeting is only in their fifties. A confounding variable in such a study as this would be a person's duration and exposure to carpeting throughout their lives. This is a confounding variable because we cannot be certain how long a person is exposed to carpeting throughout the course of a 24-hour day, nor can we know if the person has had carpeting in their home throughout his or her lifetime. Therefore, at this point in history, we cannot say for certain whether synthetic carpeting is safe for human health.

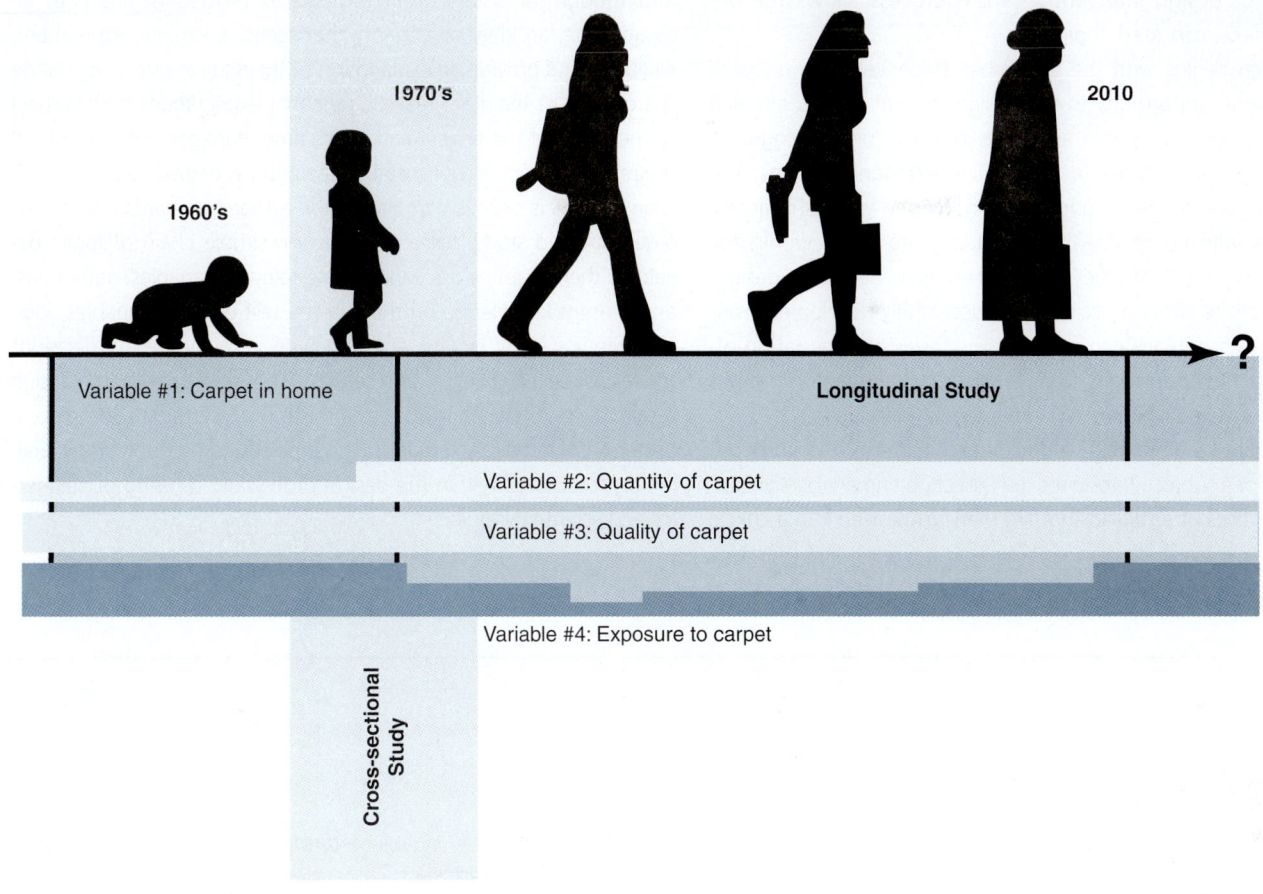

FIGURE 1.3 Longitudinal Study vs. Cross-Sectional Study. This graphic illustrates the difference between the longitudinal studies and cross-sectional studies. The variables represented by colored bars shows an approximation of the time each of the study participants might have been exposed to each variable throughout the course of their lives. Only the longitudinal study can account for all the variables in different amounts, whereas the cross-sectional study remains a "snapshot in time."
Source: Sinclair, E. (2009)

are typical of all people. Because humans and their environment are continually evolving, the number and degree of variables that may affect the outcome are in a constant state of flux. This means that the results from a cross-sectional study are only *estimates* and carry only the *probability* of being accurate. With some exceptions, the passing of time will render many cross-sectional studies less relevant. To illustrate, consider the role of carpeting within the built environment. In the 1950s and early 1960s, most carpeting was not wall to wall. In the 1970s, the carpeting not only extended from wall to wall, but also had deeper pile, thereby bringing greater quantities of the synthetic material into the environment. Later, in the 1980s, there was a resurgence of tile and other types of flooring. Therefore, it is nearly impossible to obtain a true longitudinal study of the effects of carpeting on human health because the variable (carpeting) and its attributes (size and quantity) has changed throughout time. Instead we use cross-sectional studies that give us data from points in time and then we correlate that data with other data, which leads to suppositions. Along with most research, we must be cautioned that these correlations do not always equate to cause; sometimes the correlations lead instead to educated speculation—which is always respected more than mere intuition.

Summary

The call has come for the design community and design schools to embrace evidence-based design. Both large design firms and design schools have begun to incorporate research into the design process because they realize that empirically derived research provides designers with the information needed to make design decisions. The basic purpose of research is to mitigate uncertainty. Early research methods were composed of predominately rudimentary observation and assessment, with the information being passed down through the generations. The modern design research process is a step-by-step process to estimate the cause and effect of design interventions. This process allows the designer to make informed choices.

Research begins with the researcher. Evidence-based research offers a unique opportunity to the design student via the research process; the individual is trained to develop higher cognitive thought processes in order to support their design decisions. The student develops a deeper understanding of the various nuances, phenomena, and environmental forces that are active within the built environment that they themselves will one day design. Students learn to draw on science to successfully develop environments in which humans can flourish. The thesis or dissertation offers students the opportunity to be exposed to the scientific process from which an area of interest can be deeply examined.

The goal of a thesis is the pursuit and acquisition of in-depth knowledge of a subject. It requires the collection and analysis of multiple perspectives of a subject that are then synthesized into a critical and thoughtful discussion. The research process begins with an assumption, an idea, or a theory that seeks to explore, experiment, evaluate, and provide an explanation of the issue in question. The researcher must maintain realistic personal expectations with respect to the scope of the project and utilize time management throughout the research process. The step-by-step process of writing a design research thesis is only as complex as the researcher wants it to be. As a self-directed study, research follows a simple chain of logic: develop a theory, define the concept and relevant variables, gather past and present knowledge on the subject, test or study variables, logically discuss study results, and conclude with the design decisions made as a result of the research. The evidence-based design research—or, more simply put, the thesis or dissertation—develops a better-prepared design student who is poised to tackle the new challenges forecasted within the design profession: a fusing of aesthetics and scientific inquiry.

Glossary

Attributes—Descriptive information about features or elements.

Causal inferences—Describes ideas about the nature of the relations of cause and effect.

Cohort—Group of subjects who have shared a particular experience during a particular period of time.

Cross-sectional study—A study conducted at one point in time.

Deductive process—A form of reasoning in which conclusions are formulated about particulars from general or universal premises.

Dependent variable—A variable in an experiment that is altered by a change in the independent variable.

Ecological fallacy—A false conclusion that research obtained on groups hold true for individuals.

Exploratory study—A preliminary study to provide information on the topic in effort to understand the problem better.

Independent variable—A variable whose values are independent of changes in the values of other variables.

Inductive process—Specific observations that lead to broad generalizations and theories.

Interval variable—A variable in which both order of data points and distance between data points can be determined.

Longitudinal study—A study conducted over a long period.

Nominal definition—Defining a complex or vague concept by using other ideas which people may understand better. (i.e., "Art is a thing people either love or hate, but never ignore")

Nominal variable—A variable determined by categories which cannot be ordered, such as gender.

Operational definition—A clear and precise description of a particular term or item used in the process.

Ordinal variable—A variable in which the order of data points can be determined, but not the distance between data points.

Positivism—Holds science to be the only valid source of knowledge.

Postpositivism—Values qualitative over quantitative research; questions the possibility of objectivity.

Probabilistic inferences—Assumptions based on uncertain reasoning derived from empirical learning.

Ratio variable—Similar to an interval variable, but has a clear zero point.

Reductionism—A theory that all complex systems can be completely understood in terms of their components.

Reliability—Consistency in measurements, or the degree to which an instrument measures the same way each time.

Validity—Strength of conclusions, inferences, or propositions.

Variable—An identified piece of data.

Importance of Citations

CHAPTER 2

 Style helps us express the key elements of quantitative results, choose the graphic form that will best suit our analyses, report critical details of our research protocol, and describe individuals with accuracy and respect."

—Gary R. VandenBos

chapter objectives

By the end of this chapter, students should be able to:
- Understand both APA and MLA publication styles.
- Summarize and paraphrase in order to avoid plagiarism.
- Use in-text references or in-text citations.
- Generate tools for organization and documentation.
- Formulate an accurate list of references or works cited.
- Identify and use common abbreviations.

chapter outline

Introduction
APA & MLA
Purpose

Terminology and Fundamental Differences

Plagiarism
Forms of Plagiarism

In-text Sources
Summarizing
Paraphrasing
Quotations
  Direct Quote
  Quote with Signal Phrase
  Long Quotes

Tools of Organization and Documentation
Citation Management
Formatting Final Lists
Abbreviations

Summary

Introduction

In order to answer the call of evidence-based design and participate in the research process, it is critical that design students become experts in using citations within their theses and dissertations. Aside from the legal and ethical reasons, citations demonstrate to the reader that an author has gained a diverse and thorough understanding of the topic. The **American Psychological Association (APA)** and the **Modern Language Association (MLA)** rigorously established writing styles in order to meet the needs of academic and scientific research. These styles consistently evolve in order to adapt to the ever-changing mediums of data collection and publication that result from a steady progression of technological mediums such as the Internet. To address the evolving nature of these styles, the most recent publication manuals are referenced in this chapter. Although a good overview of both styles will be discussed here, it is highly advised that all writers use the resources provided in Table 2.1 because both styles continue to evolve; therefore, updated publications must be referenced.

For some students, the acronyms of APA and MLA generate a form of anxiety that has come to be synonymous with other acronyms in education such as SAT or GRE. This anxiety is understandable because of the broad range of guidelines and rules that APA and MLA styles prescribe. This chapter seeks to demystify the usage of both styles by discussing them simultaneously. It is important to remind the student-researcher that these styles are not arbitrary rules of constraint, but rather formulas that help guide the researcher in his or her scholarship. Furthermore, these writing styles promote organized scholarship across all disciplines by giving earned credit to academics, architects, artists, authors, designers, and scientists by providing clear parameters for the production of original and organized research. This organized research, in turn, allows the writer to avoid the pitfalls of **plagiarism**, which is the literary term for stealing someone else's work.

APA AND MLA

Both APA and MLA styles are very difficult to memorize in their entirety, if not impossible; however, with frequent usage the student will become familiar with them by identifying the similarities and differences between the two styles. A clear understanding of each style enables the student-researcher to communicate his or her ideas and findings more effectively. Peer-reviewed journal articles and other student theses and dissertations can be used as examples and valuable resources of either style in professional practice. However, the researcher must remain mindful and cautious that models may include errors. Therefore, when searching for sample theses or dissertations, it is best to inquire (with instructors, department chairs, librarians, and thesis committee members) as to which former student works would be appropriate models to investigate. Many colleges and universities have a style guide that details how a student should prepare his or her document. This style guide will be an invaluable tool when answering an assortment of questions that may arise.

PURPOSE

Citations in scholarship—specifically, when used in academic and scientific research—are vital tools for the writer because they give an authority to the writer's claims and thesis. Furthermore, they are crucial tools for the reader as they become a compass that guides them through the research. Proper citations allow the reader to identify the who, what, when, where, how, and why of explaining research studies. For example: Who conducted the study, and (in the case of research involving humans) who was being studied, and how old is the information? What exactly did the researchers measure and under what conditions? Where did the author(s) obtain the infor-

Table 2.1 Citation Styles Resources

Style	Resource
APA American Psychological Association http://www.apa.org	*Publication Manual of the American Psychological Association*, 6th ed. (Washington, DC: APA, 2010)
MLA Modern Language Association http://www.mla.org	*MLA Handbook for Writers of Research Papers*, 7th ed. (New York: MLA, 2009)

mation or where was the research conducted? How exactly was the study conducted? Why or for what purpose was the study conducted and why is it important to this particular thesis or dissertation? Citations also help the reader determine whether the research is current, valid, bias, or useful to his or her own scholarship. Because the reader can generate a seemingly infinite number of questions and/or concerns when reading a research paper, it is imperative that the writer use APA or MLA citation correctly to successfully guide the reader and to effectively avoid plagiarism.

Terminology and Fundamental Differences

Perhaps the greatest difference between these two styles is that they tend to be used exclusively by different fields. APA style is commonly associated with:

- Behavioral and social sciences
- Education
- Business
- Engineering

MLA is commonly associated with:

- Humanities
- Languages
- Literature

Notice that design and architectural studies have not been included in this list. This is because the call for research studies in these fields is evolving. The current trend of evidence-based design is making it acutely necessary for design students to learn how to navigate and write in both styles because their research model may be addressing issues from a multimodal perspective that reaches across disciplines. For example, a student may seek to combine ideas from the humanities such as an analysis of mysticism through the lens of Carl Jung and combine his or her theories with data derived from the behavioral sciences in order to guide his or her research on spiritual centers. It is likely that in this example some of the literature concerning Jung might be published in MLA style, with other research data style published in APA style. This multimodal approach assists design students by preparing them to connect the academic, artistic, and scientific perspectives into one cohesive research document. It is always important to consult with the thesis committee or individual instructors regarding which style to use because the requirements for research papers tend to vary—whatever the requirement. Use only one style when writing a thesis or dissertation.

There are also a few terminology differences between APA and MLA styles that can lead to confusion. The final listing of all sources used at the end of a research paper is referred to as **References** by APA, whereas MLA refers to this as **Works Cited**. Similarly, the words "reference" and "citation" are often used interchangeably. The word *reference* means to recommend or make mention of; the word *cite* means to quote directly or to summon forth. **In-text citations** and **In-text references** are ways to give formal credit to the source author for the information used within the text. This brief bit of information includes the last name of the author and the date of publication and/or page number; this information is placed at the end of a summary, paraphrase, or quotation as a **parenthetical reference**, called thus because it is positioned *inside* parentheses. In addition, both types give credit to the works of others within the text—which is why they are called "in-text" referencers. (See Figure 2.1 for a graphic representation of the differences.)

One clear distinction between the two styles of crediting sources within the text is that APA style emphasizes the author and the date of publication; for example (Sallis, 2009). MLA style emphasizes the author and the page number where the information or quote can be found in the publication; for example (Campbell 71). This emphasis may be attributed to the tendency of behavioral and social sciences to focus on who (researcher) was conducting the research and when (year) the study was conducted or published, whereas in the humanities much of the focus is on where (page number) and how the language (direct quote) is being used by whom (author). However, both styles may or may not include page numbers in the in-text citations. Examples of specific in-text citations and parenthetical references for both styles are included within this chapter in the next two sections, and in Table 2.3.

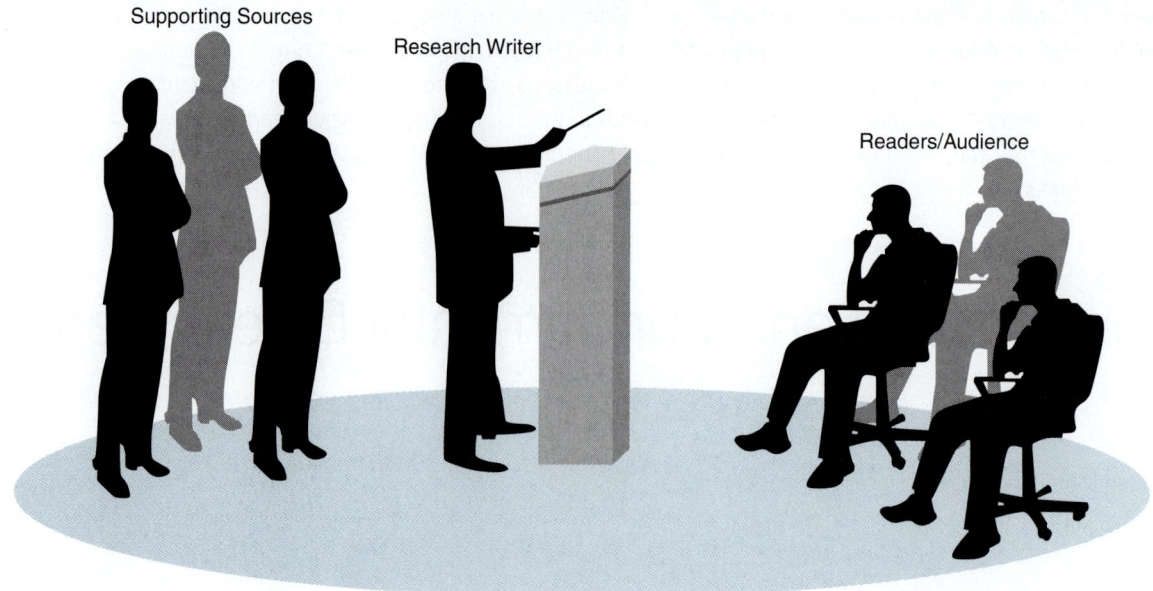

FIGURE 2.1 References and Citations. Design students can think of the difference between an in-text reference and an in-text citation in terms of their literary position while delivering the message of their thesis. It is more easily grasped if a *reference* is thought of as a "recommendation" and a *citation* as the "summoning of another."
Source: Sinclair, E. (2009).

Plagiarism

As previously stated, citing sources gives credit to previous authors and helps avoid the pitfalls of plagiarism. All individuals whose work, ideas, theories, or previous studies have influenced the research of the student must be properly cited. Respecting the work of others means giving credit whenever a reference is made to any work in any form or medium. However, students should not cite sources unless the complete work was read and studied. **Padding** the references or works cited list is highly frowned upon. Plagiarism must be taken seriously because it is a legal concern with regard to copyright, and within education it is reason from expulsion for an educational institution.

What is considered plagiarism? Most students are surprised to find out that when paraphrasing another's words (by adhering to the common phrase of "putting it in [their] own words") without acknowledging the original author, that they have committed plagiarism. To plagiarize means to represent ideas and concepts whether verbatim or paraphrased as one's own and without giving credit. Simply put, it is stealing someone's intellectual work. Plagiarism occurs commonly in two forms (copying text or copying ideas) and occasionally in a third form called self-plagiarism.

FORMS OF PLAGIARISM

The first form of plagiarism occurs when a person copies a group of words (phrase or sentence) of an author word for word, fails to place the words in quotation marks, and then references the author. In this instance, the researcher can avoid plagiarizing by placing the words or phrase in quotation marks and citing the author (source). A second common form of plagiarism may occur when an idea or concept is represented as one's own. These two forms of plagiarism have been further complicated by the use of technology and the Internet for research writing. When writers simply copy and paste text from one document to another, the likelihood of plagiarism increases exponentially. Therefore, this process should always be avoided.

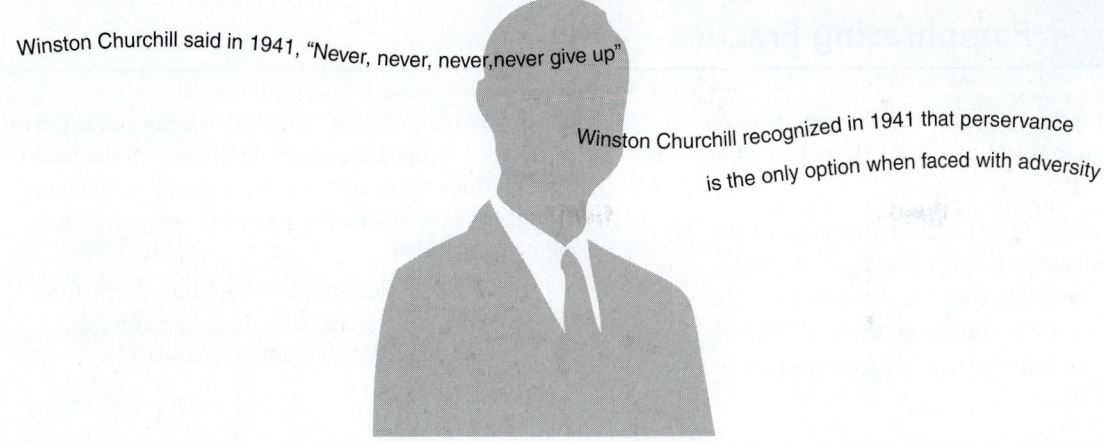

FIGURE 2.2 The Process of Paraphrasing. As writers read the words of previous authors, they take in the information as direct quotation, process the information, translate the words, filter the meaning, and, in the end, recreate a statement that explains the idea without using the same words: all while giving credit where credit is due.
Source: Sinclair, E. (2009).

A less common form of plagiarism is **self-plagiarism**. This form results when the writer presents his or her own words in a new document that has been previously published without referencing the previous document. It may seem odd to be capable of plagiarizing oneself, but when a writer presents past ideas or data as being new and never before published, this misrepresentation can potentially misguide the reader and interfere with his or her own research process. Once again, participation in academic writing highlights the imperative that the student-researcher must always be aware of how proper citation affects other researchers, and therefore must never mislead readers.

When conducted with diligence, the thesis or dissertation is not just a "rite of passage" for the design student, but is rather a piece of the proverbial design puzzle that contributes to the advancement and progression of the entire design profession. In order to avoid any form of miscommunication between writer and reader, the student must learn how to:

- Properly summarize, paraphrase, and quote sources.
- Properly cite or reference sources within the text.

Both are important processes at the foundation of all good writing. The goal of all writing—whether personal, creative, academic, or scientific—is to "show, don't tell" the reader why something is or should be a certain way. Citations are a scholar's way to "show" the reader where the evidence is for each claim; whether the research is accurate or controversial; and, specifically, how the thesis or dissertation is supported. In scientific writing (and, more specifically, in APA style), the desire is for clear linear writing devoid of redundancy and literary tangents. Although the mantra of "put it in your own words" is appropriate for staying on task while writing, from a research-writer perspective, it fails to outline the complex steps of summarizing, paraphrasing, and quoting in order to properly use in-text citations and parenthetical references (see Figure 2.2).

In-text Sources

In-text information sources are called in-text *references* by the APA, in-text *citations* by the APA and the MLA, and are also referred to as *parenthetical references* by both APA and MLA. Although these terms all refer to the same procedure, the formatting is slightly different. Specifically, they are references that the writer places within the written thesis or dissertation in order to direct the reader to the references (APA) or works cited (MLA) document at the end of the research paper. They also serve to point the reader to the original source for further investigation. Student-writers should begin using in-text references and/or citations as soon as the writing process begins.

SUMMARIZING

Summarizing allows the researcher-writer to sum up or condense a large amount of information with limited words. It is a long paraphrasing, with the key points and the essential thesis argument included. However, when summarizing

ACTIVITY 2.1 Paraphrasing Practice

The following activity will prepare you to write longer, more in-depth summaries and paraphrases that will be required for a thesis or dissertation.

Step 1: Gather three pieces of information that support a central thesis. (This is *practice* for your thesis, so start on a small scale—gather newspaper clippings or magazine articles about your favorite sport or music genre, for example.)

Step 2: Read the articles and highlight key facts that will support your practice thesis.

Step 3: Put all the gathered information away and begin to write a *quickly* composed passage that sums up the facts or ideas of all three of the authors and attempt to "build up" or organize the facts in such a way as to support each following fact or idea.

Step 4: Bring the articles and facts back into the picture and use them to double-check the facts and add the author's in-text credits (APA or MLA) if applicable.

---

other's ideas, it is critical to maintain an objective voice. An objective voice is sometimes called a *third-person objective* narrative. The author takes the stance of reporting facts without a personal or emotional interpretation of the information. This is accomplished by writing in one's own voice, yet avoiding any deviation from the ideas, facts, or figures written by the original author(s). One way to practice paraphrasing skills is to avoid writing your summaries or paraphrases while in clear sight of the original document. To accomplish this, the student should close the book, close the laptop, move away from the computer, put away notes, and refer to these resources only when gathering specific quotations, technical terms, or numerical data. See Activity 2.1.

The best paraphrases come when the writer simply *writes*. The design student should allow his or her internal processor to form ideas that have been synthesized into new and articulate ways of stating the information. This technique not only helps to limit the likelihood of plagiarism, but also assists in providing the writer with a deeper understanding of the research. Of course, it is always essential to cite the original source of the words or ideas after the summary. For example: (Kopec p. 8), APA; (Sinclair pp. 7–15), APA; (Matthes 7–15), MLA. Note: APA abbreviates *p.* for page and *pp.* for pages, whereas MLA cites only page numbers without any abbreviation.

PARAPHRASING

Paraphrasing is synonymous with summarizing. In fact, the two words are often used interchangeably. However, paraphrasing is not condensing the information; it is saying the same thing in about the same amount of words, but in a recognizably different manner or "putting it in your own words." *Warning:* merely changing a few words or reversing the word or sentence order is not proper paraphrasing—it is plagiarism. At first glance, the following three sentences appear to be very similar, but by examining them individually, the reader can witness the transformation. Read the following three sentences and analyses:

    1. Although walking to school provides an excellent opportunity for children and adolescents to take advantage of the health benefits of physical activity, the fact remains that most children and adolescents simply do not walk to school. It is estimated that only about one out of every nine children in the United States walks to school.

    Sentence #1: Direct quote from secondary author: Not in quotations, no paraphrasing of ideas, no citation of original or secondary source = plagiarism

    2. It is estimated that only about 11% of children in the United States walk to school. The fact that most children do not walk to school shows that they are not taking advantage of their excellent opportunity for the health benefits of physical activity (Eggerman, 2007).

    Sentence #2: Failed paraphrase: Attempted paraphrase but only rearranged sentence sequencing and a few words, and citation of secondary source only = plagiarism.

    3. One possibility for American children and adolescents to benefit from physical exercise is to walk to school. Unfortunately, estimates suggest that for every nine children attending school, only one gets there by way of walking (Staunton, Hubsmith, & Kallins, as cited in Eggerman, 2007; APA quoted in Eggerman 10).

    Sentence #3: Successful paraphrase: Has a distinctly different voice, maintains objectivity of authors original statement, and includes citation of both original and primary source = correct paraphrase and in-text citation, therefore, not plagiarism.

These examples highlight the complexity of citations. It is always best to use the original source, but occasionally the original source is not available. In the previous examples, which were taken from the thesis of Eggerman, the *original source* must be cited because the ideas belonged to other researchers and not to Eggerman.

When paraphrasing, it is important to cite only the portion of a sentence, idea, or concept that belongs to the original author; this means that if the author has a concept but only a portion of that concept is citable, then the student should cite that portion and maintain an objective voice by not suggesting or inferring that the author stated something that he/she did not. For example, consider the following two sentences. Sentence 1 is a paraphrase of the author's literal words and ideas:

1. Graduate school requires, on average: one pizza, eight double espressos, two to four hours of sleep, and a whole lot of humility (Kopec, 2008).

Sentence 2 is an attempt to paraphrase, with two potential problems:

2. Researchers in graduate school require, on the average, one pizza, eight double espressos, two to four hours of sleep, and a whole lot of humility, which suggests that graduate school promotes an unhealthy lifestyle (Kopec, 2008).

Kopec did not suggest, or state, that graduate school is unhealthy; rather, the student-writer *inferred* that by suggesting it to the reader by writing "promotes an unhealthy lifestyle" and by moving the in-text reference to incorporate the entire idea. The first problem is that this inference fails to maintain the *objective voice* by misrepresenting the original author's words or ideas. The second problem is that the sentence is nearly identical to the original author's voice and writing style, so it should have been either rewritten or put in quotation marks as a direct quote—as it is written, it is plagiarism.

QUOTATIONS

When direct quotes are used, both quotation marks and citations are required. The citation requires the author (APA and MLA); year of publication (APA), and the page number or range (APA and MLA). It is more common to see direct quotations used in MLA style because of the nature of the research; however, both styles use direct quotes to help the writers emphasize and support their thesis.

Direct Quote

In the first sentence in Box 2.1, the APA parenthetical includes a comma after the name, and the year. In the second sentence in Box 2.1, the MLA parenthetical includes only the author's last name and the page number. In both parenthetical references, the period is *after* the parentheses. The quote can also be reproduced by first mentioning the author's name.

Quote with Signal Phrase

In Box 2.2, the first sentence shows the in-text citation in APA style: the **signal phrase,** "According to . . . ", is followed by the author's last name, then the year of publication within parentheses, and then the subsequent quote

---

BOX 2.1   Direct Quote Examples

APA Style:

1. "Graduate school was the toughest and most rewarding time of my life" (Kopec, 2008, p. 88).

MLA Style:

1. "Graduate school was the toughest and most rewarding time of my life" (Kopec 88).

BOX 2.2   Direct Quote with Signal Phrase Examples

APA Style:

1. According to Kopec (2008), "Graduate school was the toughest and most rewarding time of my life" (p. 88).

MLA Style:

1. According to Kopec, "Graduate school was the toughest and most rewarding time of my life" (88).

> **BOX 2.3 Typical Signal Words**
>
> A signal word or phrase is a word(s) that readers come to anticipate as being followed by a quote or paraphrase. Student researchers should vary the use of signal words in order to *activate* their work. In other words, do not use the same signal word over and over.
>
> | | | | | | |
> |---|---|---|---|---|---|
> | Acknowledges | Argues | Comments | Declares | Implies | Rejects |
> | Adds | Asserts | Compares | Denies | Insists | Reports |
> | Admits | Believes | Competes | Disputes | Notes | Responds |
> | Addresses | Challenges | Confirms | Emphasizes | Observes | Suggests |
> | Agrees | Claims | Contends | Endorses | Points out | Thinks |
> | | | | Found | Reasons | Writes |
> | | | | Grants | Recognizes | |
> | | | | Illustrates | Refutes | |

follows. The specific page is cited at the end of the sentence, within parentheses. In the second sentence, the in-text citation is in MLA style; the sentence opens with the signal phrase, followed by the author's last name, the quote, and then the specific page number is included at end of the sentence within parentheses (without any abbreviation for "page"). Again, the period is placed after the parentheses. A signal word or phrase is one that readers come to anticipate as followed by a quote or paraphrase. When using signal words and phrases to introduce or describe earlier research, both APA and MLA styles generally expect the word tense to be in past or present perfect tense (see Box 2.3).

Long Quotes

In some research documents, it is necessary to use a long quotation (40 or more words) to get a point across; however, the researcher should be cautious and rarely use long quotations. The overuse of long quotations lessens the quality of the work and places the researcher's due diligence into question. When using long quotations in APA, start the quotation on a new line that is indented five spaces from the left margin; there is no need to use quotation marks. Keep the entire quotation within this indentation. For example, Kopec's (2008) study revealed that:

> Researchers pursuing a design education have the added burden of applying their research results to a prototype in order to assess feasibility. This added responsibility forces the researcher to bring research results directly into practice. This differs from researchers who conduct research in other fields where the results may or may not get published or tested within a practice setting (p. 19).

In MLA, for four or more lines of prose or three or more lines of poetry, double-space the quotation and indent it one inch from the left margin. Again, there is no need for quotation marks. For example, Stephen Spender directly relates painting to writing:

> When they paint, painters are exercising some of the qualities essential to good writing. Apart from the most obvious of these—the organizing power of visual imagination—they observe what Blake called "minute particulars." They create images and store memories. (140)

Note that in a long quotation in MLA style, the parenthetical reference places the period at the end of the sentence instead of at the end of parentheses, as is the case with regular parenthetical references. Again, the APA reference includes the abbreviation *p.* for "page number" and the MLA citation includes just the number. Some final notes of caution regarding the long quotation: using more than one long quotation per chapter is seen as a sign of lazy writing and weak analytic skills. In addition, researchers wishing to quote more than 500 words from a single published source must secure legal permission from the author(s) or publisher (whichever holds the copyright). Long quotations are more common in MLA style, as the nature of literary criticism and critical analysis of theory requires detailed explications of entire written passages.

Tools of Organization and Documentation

As soon as the research process begins, it is crucial for student-researchers to generate a system for organizing and documenting all of their information related to their thesis. Data, charts, quotes, figures, concepts, illustrations—quite literally *everything* that may end up in the writing—must be kept and organized in a manner that allows the writer to quickly access these sources.

CITATION MANAGEMENT

The organization of sources helps facilitate the research process and is vital to the management of information to avoid plagiarism. If file folders are organized on the computer, they should be backed up in at least three locations. Some theses and dissertations have organizational tools such as outlines that are required during the research process. It is best to always check with the instructor and/or thesis committee for specific instructions. Writing from an outline promotes linear logic. If an organizational tool is not readily available, the student can generate his or her own tool. The References (APA) or Works Cited (MLA) page should be the first document generated in order to ensure that every original source is properly documented and cited throughout the writing process. See Table 2.2 for a brief listing of several citation management systems.

FORMATTING FINAL LISTS

Both APA and MLA styles utilize similar formats for creating the final list of sources (References or Works Cited) by using hanging indents: the first line has the standard one-inch margin and subsequent lines are indented so that the author's information is easily visible or "hanging" on the left margin (equivalent to a half-inch indent). As every computer

Table 2.2 Citation Management Tools

One of the most important things that can be done to maximize the success of a research project is to implement a citation management tool. Gathering, organizing, and managing citations and references is easily done when a system is put into place *immediately* upon embarking on a research project. Here is a small listing of the many citation management tools available. When in doubt, ask a librarian or professor, or search for "citation management" on the Web.

System	Format	Process	Cost
NOTE CARDS			
Hard copy	Paper	Write each citation on an index card and file in desired order (alphabetical or by topic).	Cost of index cards (colored, lined, or blank)
Digital	Computerized	Microsoft Word > Tools > Envelopes and Labels > Avery 5315 (Note cards) > type in each citation and save.	Free with program
Notebook	Paper	Write each citation on a page of the notebook in chronological order.	Cost of notebooks
Slideshow	Computerized	Microsoft Word/PowerPoint: Type each citation onto a new slide; color-code slides by changing the background color to indicate general topic.	Free with program
Digital File	Computerized	Select any document, spreadsheet, or publishing software and create a standalone file. Enter all citations throughout the research process and in the end bring (or copy and paste) the list into the final research paper. FYI: Change the font color of all citations in the main text until confirmed prior to final printing.	Cost of program
Software (visit websites for most current information)			
RefWorks	Web-based	http://www.refworks.com	Free at some school libraries
Zotero	Web-based	http://www.zotero.org	Up to 100 MB file storage: free
CiteULike	Web-based	http://www.citeulike.org	Free
Connotea	Web-based	http://www.connotea.org	Free

platform and word-processing software application handles document formatting differently, students should familiarize themselves with their software as soon as possible. Once the citation is placed in the references document, it will be listed alphabetically by author and titles; refer to the following formatting examples. This is a sample of an APA-style journal article entry with three to six authors:

References

Kligerman, M., Sallis, J. F., Ryan, S., Frank, L. D., & Nader, P. R. (2006). Association of neighborhood design and recreational environment variables with physical activity and body mass index in adolescents. *American Journal of Health Promotion, 21,* 274–277.

This is the same entry in MLA style:

Works Cited

Kligerman, M., et al. "Association of neighborhood design and recreational environment variables with physical activity and body mass index in adolescents." *American Journal of Health Promotion*, 21.2 (2006): 274–277.

Notice the many differences:

1. APA includes all authors, whereas MLA uses "et al." for four or more authors.
2. MLA puts title in quotes and underlines publication.
3. APA italicizes publication.
4. MLA moves publication date after volume number and places a colon before page number.
5. In APA, the volume number is italicized; in MLA, it is not.

As stated previously, APA research often focuses on *who* conducted the research study and *when* the research was conducted, so it makes sense to have authors listed first and then the publication date. In MLA, the emphasis is the author of the journal, then the "title," which is put in quotations. Samples of several common source citations for a Reference List (APA) or Works Cited (MLA) are in Table 2.2

The examples in Table 2.3 are only some of the possible common citation formats for References and Works Cited documents. Due to the numerous possibilities of sources used in research for a thesis or dissertation, it is always necessary to consult a current APA or MLA manual.

ABBREVIATIONS

There are hundreds of abbreviations used in research writing, especially in scientific writing. Box 2.4 is a short list of common abbreviations that the student is likely to encounter during research and may decide to use while writing a thesis or dissertation.

MLA style uses only lowercase abbreviations; APA style uses both lower- and uppercase. It is always best to check

Table 2.3 Format Examples

The reference format for APA style as described in the sixth edition of the *Publication Manual of the American Psychological Association* (2010) and the seventh edition of the *MLA Handbook for Writers of Research Papers* (2009).

	APA Styles	MLA Styles
Journal Article, One Author	Bearer, C. (1995). Environmental health hazards: How children are different from adults. *Future of Children, 5*(2), 11–26. **In-text:** Bearer (1995) **Parenthetical:** (Bearer, 1995)	Bearer, C. "Environmental Health Hazards: How Children Are Different from Adults." *Future of Children* 5.2 (1995): 11–26. **Parenthetical:** (Bearer, 11–26) or (11–26)
Journal Article, Two Authors	Kopec, D., & LaCapra, D. (2008). Design cognitive stimulating environments for infants and toddlers. *Journal of Interior Design, 33*(3), 10–36. **In-text:** Kopec and LaCapara (2008) **Parenthetical:** (Kopec & La Capara, 2008)	Kopec, D., & LaCapra, D. "Design Cognitive Stimulating Environments for Infants and Toddlers." *Journal of Interior Design* 33.3 (2008): 10–36. **Parenthetical:** (Kopek and LaCapara, 10–36). or (10–36)

	APA Styles	**MLA Styles**
Journal Article, Three to Six Authors	Hubble, J. P., Cao, T., Hassanein, R. E., Neuberger, J. S., & Koller, W. C. (1993). Risk factors for Parkinson's disease. *Neurology, 43*(9), 1693–1697. **In-text:** Hubble, Cao, Hassanein, Neuberger, and Koller (1993) or Hubble et al. (2008) **Parenthetical:** (Hubble, Cao, Hassanein, Neuberger, & Koller, 1993) or (Hubble et al., 1993)	Hubble, J. P. et al., "Risk Factors for Parkinson's Disease." *Neurology,* 43.9 (1993): 1693–1697. **Parenthetical:** (Hubble and Cao, et al. 1693–1697).
Journal Article, Six or More Authors	Verghese, J., Lipton, R. B., Katz, M. J., Hall, C. B, Derby, C. A., Kuslansky, G., et al. (2003). Leisure activities and the risk of dementia in the elderly. *New England Journal of Medicine, 348*(24), 2508–2516. **In-text:** Verghese et al. (2003) **Parenthetical:** (Verghese et al., 2003)	Verghese, J., et al. "Leisure Activities and the Risk of Dementia in the Elderly." *New England Journal of Medicine,* 348.24 (2003): 2508–2516. **Parenthetical:** (Verghese, Lipton, et al. 2508–2516)
Book, One Author	Kopec, D. (2006). *Environmental psychology for design.* New York: Fairchild Books. **In-text:** Kopec (2006) **Parenthetical:** (Kopec, 2006)	Kopec, D. *Environmental Psychology for Design.* New York: Fairchild Books, 2006. Print. **Parenthetical:** (Kopec 10–27)
Edited Book, Two Authors	Stokols, D. & I. Altman (Eds.). (1987). *Handbook of environmental psychology.* Hoboken, NJ: Wiley. **In-text:** Stokols and Altman (1987) **Parenthetical:** (Stokols & Altman, 1987)	Stokols, D. and I. Altman, eds. *Handbook of Environmental Psychology.* Hoboken, NJ: Wiley, 1987. Print. **Parenthetical:** (Stokols and Altman, *Handbook* 12–99)
Book, No Author or Editor	*Merriam-Webster's Collegiate Dictionary* (10th ed.). (1993). Springfield, MA: Merriam-Webster. **Parenthetical:** (*Merriam-Webster's*, 1993).	*Merriam-Webster's Collegiate Dictionary.* 10th ed. Springfield, MA: Merriam-Webster, 1993. Print. **Parenthetical:** (*Merriam Webster's Collegiate Dictionary*)
Book, Revised or Specific Edition	Gifford, R. (2002). *Environmental psychology: Practice and principles* (3rd ed.). Victoria, Canada: Optimal Books. **In-text:** Gifford (2002) **Parenthetical:** (Gifford, 2002) U.S. Environmental Protection Agency. (April 1991). *Indoor Air Facts No. 4 (revised): Sick Building Syndrome (SBS).* http://www.epa.gov/iaq/pubs/sbs.html. **In-text:** *Indoor Air Facts* (1991) **Parenthetical:** (*Indoor Air Facts*, 1991)	Gifford, R. *Environmental Psychology: Practice and Principles.* 3rd ed. Victoria, Canada: Optimal Books, 2002. Print. **Parenthetical:** (Gifford, *Environmental*) U.S. Environmental Protection Agency. *Indoor Air Facts No. 4 (revised): Sick Building Syndrome (SBS).* April, 1991. <http://www.epa.gov/iaq/pubs/sbs.html>. **Parenthetical:** (*Indoor Air Facts*)
Translated Book	Laplace, P. S. (1951). *A philosophical essay on probabilities.* (F. W. Truscott & F. L. Emory, Trans.). New York: Dover. (Original work published 1814). **In-text:** Laplace (1814/1951) **Parenthetical:** (Laplace, trans. 1814)	Laplace, P. S. *A Philosophical Essay on Probabilities.* Trans. F. W. Truscott & F. L. Emory (1814). New York: Dover, 1951. Print. **In-text citation:** (*A Philosophical*).
Magazine Article	Kandel, E. R. & Squire, L. (2000, November 10). Neuroscience: Breaking down scientific barriers. *Science, 290,* 1113–1120. **In-text:** Kandel (2000) **Parenthetical:** (Kandel, 2000)	Kandel, E. R. & Squire, L. "Neuroscience: Breaking Down Scientific Barriers." *Science* 10 Nov. 2000: 1113–1120. Print. **Parenthetical:** (Kandel 1113–1120).

(Continued)

	APA Styles	MLA Styles
Daily Newspaper Article, No Author	New drug appears to sharply cut risk of death of heart failure. (1993, July 15). *Washington Post*, p. A12. **Parenthetical:** (New Drug Appears, 1993).	"New drug appears to sharply cut risk of death of heart failure." *Washington Post* 15 July 1993: A12. Print. **Parenthetical:** ("New Drug Appears")
Article, Internet-only journal	Fredrickson, B. L. (2000, March 7). Cultivating positive emotions to optimize health and well-being. *Prevention & Treatment, 3,* Article 0001a. Retrieved November 20, 2000, from http://journals.apa.org/prevention/volume3/pre0030001a.html **In text:** Fredrickson (2000) **Parenthetical:** (Fredrickson, 2000)	Fredrickson, B. L. "Cultivating Positive Emotions to Optimize Health and Well-Being." *Prevention & Treatment*, 3, Mar. 7 (2007): Article 0001a. org. Web. 20 Nov. 2000. <http://journals.apa.org/prevention/volume3/pre0030001a.html>. **Parenthetical:** (Fredrickson, "Cultivating")
Message posted to a newsgroup	Chalmers, D. (2000, November 17). Seeing with sound [Msg 1]. Message posted to news://sci.psychology.consciousness **In-text:** Chalmers (2000) **Parenthetical:** (Chalmers, 2000)	Chalmers, D. "Seeing with Sound." [Msg 1]. Online posting. 17 Nov. 2000 Web. 17 Nov. 2000. <news://sci.psychology.consciousness>. **Parenthetical:** (Chalmers, Seeing)
Website	American Lung Association (n.d.). It has a name: COPD Chronic Obstructive Pulmonary Disease. Retrieved April 30, 2008 from http://www.lungusa.org/site/pp.asp?c=dvLUK9O0E&b=38502 **Parenthetical:** (American Lung Association, 2008)	"*It has a name: COPD Chronic Obstructive Pulmonary Disease.*" n.d. American Lung Association. Web. 30 Apr. 2008. <http://www.lungusa.org/site/pp.asp?c=dvLUK9O0E&b=38502>. **Parenthetical**: ("It has a name")

BOX 2.4 Common Abbreviations

Abbreviations that APA & MLA share:

chap.	chapter
ed.	edition
et. al	and others
p.	page
pp.	pages
pt.	part

Common APA abbreviations:

No.	number
Ed.	editor
Rev. ed.	revised edition
2nd Ed.	second edition
Suppl.	supplement
Trans.	translated by
Vol.	volume
Vols.	volumes

Common MLA abbreviations:

bk.	book
ed.	editor
doc.	document
fig.	figure
no.	number
n.	note
nn.	notes
par	paragraph
pseud.	pseudonym
trans.	translator
vol.	volume
vv.	verses

Abbreviation to avoid when using APA:

cf.	confer: (use instead: "compare")
e.g.	*exempli gratia*, Latin for "for example": (use instead: "for example")
etc.	et cetera: (use instead: "and so forth")
i.e.	*id est*, Latin for "that is": (use instead "that is")
viz.	*videlicet*, Latin for "permitted to see": (use instead: "namely")
vs.	versus: (use instead the full word "versus")

Summary

The American Psychological Association (APA) and the Modern Language Association (MLA) have rigorously established writing styles to standardize research writing. Formalized research writing allows writers freedom to study without fear of plagiarism. *Plagiarism* is the literary term for stealing someone else's work, which can be avoided by following the guidelines of the APA and/or MLA styles. Citing one's sources used in academic and scientific research provides authority to the writer's claims, thought process, and thesis. Design students must learn both main styles because their research is likely to address issues from several disciplines.

The word "reference" means to recommend or make mention of; the word "cite" means to directly quote or to mention someone else's work. Both in-text citation and in-text references are ways to give formal scredit to a source author within the text. While summarizing allows a large amount of information to be presented in a small amount of words; it is called a long paraphrase which does not seek to condense the information. Researchers should be extremely cautious and rarely use long quotations (40+ words) to get a point across, as it is seemingly lazy writing. Paraphrasing says the same thing in about the same amount of words but in a recognizably different manner. When direct quotes are used both quotation marks and citations are required.

Generating a system for organizing, documenting and managing all of the information related to a formal study is vital to a researcher. There are many ways to organize the information depending on the comfort level of the student. Such that if someone prefers to work with their hands, pen and paper; a note card system might be the best fit. Although, keeping in mind that the information must be put into a typed format conducive for printing for the final thesis or dissertation document. To sum up, due to the numerous possible sources used in researching, it is always necessary to consult a current APA or MLA manual and to manage the sources appropriately and efficiently.

Glossary

American Psychological Association (APA)—A scientific and professional organization that represents psychologists in the United States.

In-text citation—A reference to a source inside the body of a paper.

In-text reference—A reference cited in the text of a research paper and within the reference list.

Modern Language Association (MLA)—An organization dedicated to the promotion and study of language and literature.

Padding—Adding references that were not actually used in the document.

Parenthetical reference—A portion of the in-text citation.

Plagiarism—A piece of writing that has been copied from someone else and presented as one's own writing.

References—A list of works that have been addressed as part of the research process.

Self-plagiarism—Presenting established thoughts as new ideas within current research.

Signal phrase—An indication that something is a direct quote.

Works cited—A list of items that have been included in the bibliography of a research paper.

CHAPTER 3

Developing a Line of Logic

chapter outline

Introduction

Stages of Research
The Formation Stage
  Quantitative and Qualitative Approaches
The Development Stage
  Information Gathering
  Inductive versus Deductive Reasoning
The Outcome Stage
  Illogical Argumentation and Conclusions
  Leaps of Faith
  Overstating the Research

Summary

> "All science is concerned with the relationship of cause and effect. Each scientific discovery increases man's ability to predict the consequences of his actions and thus his ability to control future events."
>
> —Laurence J. Peter

chapter objectives

By the end of this chapter, students should be able to:

- Identify the merits of quantitative and qualitative approaches in design research.
- Describe the differences between an inductive versus a deductive line of reasoning.
- Analyze various approaches to the conceptualization of a research project.
- Identify potential flaws in a thesis statement that could affect the research process.

Introduction

The process and execution of a thesis differs between academic programs and design programs. The key difference between the two programs is the end product. The main similarity is that both—regardless of the degree or program—are research papers, albeit large research papers. All theses and dissertations:

- Propose an idea
- Select a method

- Implement a method
- Analyze results

Design students have the added challenge of incorporating those results into a design prototype. Hence, students must select not only a question of inquiry, but also a building type (typology) or environment from which the question can be answered with the physical prototype.

Evidence-based research (also known as *methods-based research*) teaches students how to obtain objective facts and add to the knowledge acquired from previous discoveries. Students also learn how to identify and accurately measure the variables under investigation. Design research specifically allows students to gain specialization in a particular area of interest and connects them to the occupant populations. The skills acquired from evidence-based research enables students to accurately and systematically collect data that will, in turn, answer questions; to address problems from a rational and lucid perspective; and to logically articulate and justify their design approaches.

In the professional world, this same process has been dubbed *evidence-based design*, a term borrowed from the medical community to signify that the final design was generated from extensive research. Along the lines of research terminology, "methods-based research" and "evidence-based research" are, as mentioned previously, the same thing. The authors of this book made every effort by way of many examples to make the thesis process as easy to understand as possible, though we fully understand that the terminology tied to research can be initially overwhelming. Be cautioned as well that some words found within research are used interchangeably, such as:

- Researcher, designer, and experimenter
- Thesis, research, and study
- Data, information, knowledge, and findings
- Cohort, participants, and study group

Therefore, the glossary was developed to help alleviate confusion brought on by terms used in this book. As a matter of course, a good dictionary should be purchased prior to beginning your research—it is an invaluable tool.

As design students embark on the path of research, they can conceptualize the stages of the research process as *formation*, *development*, and *outcome*, or, in a more universal language, beginning, middle, and end. The aim of this chapter is to highlight the thesis process in terms of the progression of logic required to successfully complete the research. During the *formation* stage, the researcher begins to understand and define the thesis direction. The next step is the *development* and acquisition of information. In this step, researchers gather previously researched information (primary data) and implement a method to gather new information (secondary data) related to their subject matter. The final part of the research process is the *outcome*, in which researchers combine, evaluate, and summarize all the information they have gathered and apply it to a studio-generated prototype.

BOX 3.1 Stages of Research

Stage	Paper Section	Objectives
Formation (Beginning)	Introduction	Develop and define theory and relevance State and define variables Decide position and approach
Development (Middle)	Review of Literature Methods Findings	Collect primary data on subject Collect information on methodologies Perform method and organize all data/findings
Outcome (End)	Analysis Discussion Conclusion	Analyze all information Delineate and discuss findings Apply solution or findings to design

Stages of Research

THE FORMATION STAGE

During the formation stage of research, students:

- Develop a theory.
- Clearly define all aspects of the theory.
- Learn about the environment type.

Good research comes from objective, unbiased assessments that can be repeated and are able to be built upon in the future by other researchers. Therefore, in the early stage of a thesis or dissertation, students must exercise care to remain focused and dedicated to their projects, because the approach, data, or analysis might pave the way for future research in that area. Hence, the first step of research actually starts with the *researcher*.

Know thyself. The first step of a research project is to determine what you want to study. Initially, this might cause a crisis situation for a student, but there are a few simple techniques to get over this first hurdle. Every person has a basic understanding of their own personal learning style or information preference. Therefore, the statements in Activity 3.1 offer some insight into the type of research best suited for each individual.

A student more inclined to gravitate toward facts and figures would find his or her skills applicable to experimentation and quantitative measures. A student who enjoys searching for humanistic meaning would more than likely enjoy more robust research methodologies and qualitative measures. Students who work diligently toward satisfying the requirements of their chosen degree program may thrive with a research project limited in scope but with a genuine and motivating topic of interest.

Developing and refining a research question involves some preliminary reading of literature available on the selected subject, finding an angle appropriate to the chosen degree program, and assuring that the subject is "researchable." A **hypothesis** is defined by the Merriam-Webster dictionary (2009) as "a tentative assumption made in order to draw out and test its logical or empirical consequences." Simply put, a hypothesis is a clear and concise statement of the researcher's hunch or "gut feeling" about a relationship between two things that the researcher plans to test. A **research question** cannot be tested so easily, as it is a question that guides the research, such as, "What is the experience of a newly immigrated Middle Easterner to a typical American classroom?" The decision whether to use a research question or hypothesis can be determined by referring to Activity 2.1. (Chapter 4 provides an in-depth focus on tips and techniques for developing a research topic.) If a student prefers to seek meaning and rich descriptions with their research project, he or she should use the research question to guide them; all others might consider using the hypothesis option to test their theories.

Once the research topic is absolutely clear, research is much easier. However, there are a few items of caution with regard to the motivations for selecting a research topic. First, the topic should have relevance to your chosen degree program. Next, the researcher should be without extreme prejudice toward the subject matter. The motivation should not be to "settle a score." Such research lessens a researchers credibility. And finally, the research subject should not be of such a personal nature that the student loses objectivity early on in the research process. Ultimately, a cognizant and firm understanding of the significance of the project is a healthy start toward pursuing research.

Developing a position from which to research, whether it is scientific or more closely aligned with intuition, is a case for positivism and postpositivism. As mentioned in Chapter 1, *positivism* is a theoretical position that demands scientific explanations and rejects intuition and perception. Postpositivism contends that human knowledge is not based on absolute ideas, but rather speculative elements that require the voices and the interpretations of many people. By and large, design research follows postpositivism because much of the research related to human perceptions and behaviors (with respect to the environment) are interpretive. On establishing the

ACTIVITY 3.1 Learning Style Evaluation

Select the statement that describes you best:
- I am interested in facts and figures.
- I enjoy searching for meaning.
- I just need to fulfill my scholarly obligations.

BOX 3.2   Hypothesize or Question?

The words displayed in bold letters denote the differences between framing a similar concept in hypothesis form and question form.

Hypothesis	"**If** low test scores **are related** to cultural education experiences, **in that case** students who have recently immigrated to the United States **may have** a higher frequency of academic failure."
Research Question	"**What is** the experience of a newly immigrated Middle Easterner **to a** typical American classroom?"

BOX 3.3   Motivations to Avoid

Relevant to degree	Architecture degree
Paper Title:	"The Behaviors of Ghosts and Mythical Creatures"
Result:	Research with regard to professional employment may be ill-fated
Prejudice	I hate apartments!
Paper Title:	"The Eradication of the Spirit-Sucking Apartment Dwelling"
Result:	Research lacks scientific emotional detachment and credibility
Too Personal	My car tire keeps going flat.
Paper Title:	"The Manufacturing Flaws in the Acme Tire #A2578DGH83R14"
Result:	Findings may lead to "closure" but not to objective advances in society

position, variables, and definitions of the research topic, students must decide on an approach from which to continue their investigation (see Table 3.1).

Quantitative and Qualitative Approaches

Once the researcher has a perspective from which to conceptualize the research project, the next step is to identify an approach that allows for the greatest acquisition of new information. In general, there are two approaches to gather and interpret data. These approaches are described as **qualitative** and **quantitative**. Each has its own advantages and disadvantages, and each can add value to the overall body of knowledge, albeit from different perspectives. Chapter 7 goes into detail regarding the implications of each of these approaches. Basically, quantitative results are in *quantities* and qualitative results are in the *quality* of the narrative and interpretations from study participants. See Table 3.2.

The primary differences between quantitative and qualitative research approaches are the scope and type of data obtained. Each approach also carries its own inherent ability or limitation to **generalize** that data to other similar situations or groups of people. For the design student, this might translate to the exploration of a design concept as it

Table 3.1   *Positions: Positivism vs. Postpositivism*

	Positivism	**Postpositivism**
Position to research with:	Scientific methods	Exploratory methods
Objective	Measure and test	Discover and describe
Scope	Factual knowledge	Human knowledge

Table 3.2 — Approaches: Quantitative vs. Qualitative

	Quantitative	Qualitative
Functions in	**Quan**tities	**Qual**ity
Utilizes	Numbers	Narratives
Findings in	Graphs and charts	Interviews and observations

pertains to different environments or geographic regions. For example, the design concept of an open-air restaurant with a Hawaiian theme might be exported to other Polynesian Islands, but it is unlikely to be exported to the Virgin Islands because Hawaiian cultural values and subsequent design traditions can be generalized only so far. However, the core design style might be generalized from place to place and then *adapted* to a new area. Therefore, for the most part, data obtained from quantitative methods tends to be more generalized and applicable to other regions or groups of people, and data collected through qualitative methods tends to be less generalized and more specific to an individual situation, location, and specific group of people.

One advantage of qualitative data is that it can be quantified through the assignment of a numeric value. In other words, people's opinions can be counted. For example, a researcher might be determining why a high rate of people are getting sick within a specific building. He or she hypothesizes that these rates are a result of the ventilation system, then decides to design a ventilation system that provides better filtration, thereby decreasing the rate at which people become sick. The researcher decides that in order for the ventilation system to have the desired effect, delving deep into the employee's perceptions of the building's existing ventilation is also appropriate. The researcher opts to pursue a qualitative approach in which responses to open-ended questions asked during interviews identify employee predisposition. In addition to video recording the participant's responses, the interviewer also observes the participant's body language and vocal tone. As a means of quantifying some of this qualitative data, the student measures vocal tone with a decibel meter, and numerically categorizes and compares the number of positive words to negative words used by the participant during the interview. Although the student is able to quantify some of the qualitative data, the reality is that the data is very specific to a particular group of people and thus lacks the ability to be generalized.

Recognizing the similarities between qualitative and quantitative data analysis provides multiple perspectives that might otherwise be neglected. Research obtained from quantitative and qualitative approaches have valuable contributions in and of themselves, but a combination of the two within a particular research project adds another dimension and degree of authenticity to the results. This is commonly referred to as a **mixed-methods** approach. The next important phase of a design research project involves the gathering of research data, which is likely to appear in both the methods and results sections of a thesis or dissertation.

THE DEVELOPMENT STAGE

Information Gathering

The first step in the developmental stage is to gather and analyze data from other literature sources for the **review of literature (ROL)** regarding the research topic, as well as information about the intended method of inquiry the researcher intends to use. (See Chapter 5 for instructions on review of literature and Chapter 7 for a list and discussion of different methods.) For example, if a research topic were an aquatic center, then knowledge would have to be acquired about the unique and special issues common to such a center, including (but not limited to):

- Health and safety issues as they pertain to filtration devices
- Ventilation and surface materials
- Growth of fungi and manifestation of slippery surfaces

Each of these unique factors when applied to an environmental type contributes to the student's review of the literature, which might include trade magazines, manufacturer's testing results, or health department safety reports.

Building on the example of the aquatic center, the researcher may have a desire to include a sustainable attribute into the project, such as a water-use reduction plan and a recycling plan. The research method might then be experimental because several models that demonstrate how water can be recycled and reused efficiently need to be constructed (quantitative data). Another option for the researcher might be to direct the method to the

Table 3.3 Evaluation Types

Time Period	Design Report Type	Description
Formative	Predesign Research Evaluation (PDR)	This evaluation requires that the student understand the environment type and accesses the needs of the users. (For example, if a student wishes to design a high school, then information on how a school operates and a "needs assessment" must be completed for all users: faculty, administrators, and students.) The knowledge acquired provides the basis for a review of the literature (ROL).
Process	Occupancy Evaluation	During this evaluation, students actually implement the method or their design changes into the environment and record the user's reactions. (For example, a student might build a model and perform tests on it or administer a survey.)
Summative	Post-Occupancy Evaluation (POE)	This evaluation is done after the experiment to assess the relationships and outcomes of the interventions applied.

discovery of how a more elaborate and sophisticated locker/shower room would be perceived by regular swimmers. In this situation, the student might draft a survey to disseminate among people who currently use an array of aquatic centers to gain the swimmers' insight or preferences (qualitative data). What is important to know about this process is that students have multiple methods to utilize when determining what type of information is needed, as well as when and how the information will be gathered.

There are three time periods that a design researcher might wish to acquire specific information from which to evaluate: **formative**, **process**, or **summative**. These time-specific evaluations (see Table 3.3) were developed to assess programs and projects *prior*, *during*, and *after* the design interventions. The final document is considered complete when all of the evaluations are included:

- Situation prior to implementation of the design (formative)
- Immediate effects and impact of the design (process)
- Long-term effects of the design (summative)

Formative research is essentially the procedure that establishes the needs or current conditions of the subject prior to being researched. This type of study seeks to identify areas of need, improvement, or further exploration. The process evaluation documents the immediate changes that an experiment causes. Summative evaluations examine the final outcomes. Once a good deal of information has been acquired, it is natural for a researcher to start to draw preliminary conclusions, though the very nature of research is to *discover*. Therefore, there is a formal method for applying assumptions to the scientific method.

In order to write a well-thought-out research paper, students must understand that they are embarking on a formal scientific investigation. There are key assumptions about all scientific endeavors; these assumptions are referred to as **operationalism**, **determinism**, and **invariance** (see Table 3.4). Operationalism is the ability to actively identify research variables and then objectively and accurately measure them. Determinism is the scientific premise that there is a reason or cause for everything. Deterministic logic follows this line of thought: "if this, then that" or "X causes Y." Researchers should be careful with this line of logic; see Box 3.4.

Invariance is the rule that "natural laws do not change." An example of a natural law is gravity. Hence we can say with absolute certainty that if a person were to drop a penny from the Seattle Space Needle, the penny (unimpeded) would eventually hit the ground. Together, operationalism, determinism, and invariance serve as the basic tenets of research as the topic is being developed. During the developmental stage, the research subject moves from its original form of a statement or question into a phase of reasoning and logic that will be tested and measured.

Table 3.4 Scientific Assumptions

	Operationalism	Determinism	Invariance
Research operation	Identify and measure	X causes Y	Natural laws

| BOX 3.4 | **Sample Deterministic Statement** |

"Increased natural light contributes to happiness. Therefore, natural light should be included in all environments to promote happiness."

Notice how this statement is flawed because it is nearly impossible to ascribe an absolute outcome such as "happiness" to a single cause. It is therefore crucial that students refrain from making assumptions about a phenomenon without legitimate proof.

Inductive versus Deductive Reasoning

Inductive and **deductive reasoning** are two techniques to formulate a logical thought process from which the student can seek further knowledge. Each method represents one way to explore a research topic. To help grasp these concepts, "induct" is *adding* to something to arrive at a conclusion, and "deduct" is *subtracting* from something to obtain results.

With inductive reasoning, one examines a situation from the inside and continues to move outwards with each additional piece of data towards the conclusion. The researcher starts with a specific subject from which patterns develop and add up to an outcome. Typical conclusions of inductive reasoning are that similar patterns always lead to similar outcomes. This leads to generalized conclusions, which are good, in a way, because the conclusions are then applicable to other common situations. An example of an inductive process is: "All carpeting contains allergens; therefore, all carpeting is bad for people who suffer from allergies." On the surface, inductive reasoning makes gross generalizations, but it is from those generalities that many scientific discoveries are made (e.g., additional research may prove that only some carpeting holds allergens). But a key word with inductive reasoning is "discovery." See Figure 3.1.

A deductive line of reasoning starts from the outside and looks inward, continually removing data and refining the statement. This line of reasoning starts with a general rule, a premise that we know to be true or accept to be true within

(a)

(b)

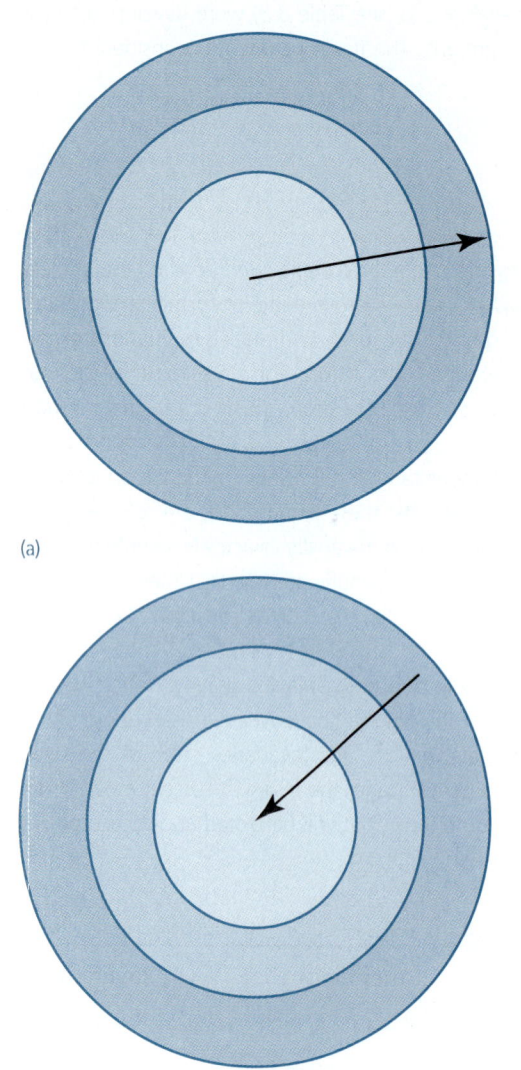

FIGURE 3.1 A&B—Inductive vs. Deductive Reasoning. (a) Inductive reasoning starts with a problem (specific) and works outward in attempt to solve the situation (general). National monuments are often symbolic representations, but one could ask, "What and where did the representation originally derive from?" (b) Deductive reasoning starts from the outside (general) and works inward toward specific details (specific). "Respiratory problems are common in building interior environments." The identification of causal agents for respiratory disorders is an example of deductive reasoning.
Source: Kopec, D. (2009).

a set of circumstances. In this situation, the student starts with a general theory related to his or her topic and then narrows the topic to one specific idea. As the student collects information, the ability to continually refocus in on the idea is intensified. At the onset, deductive reasoning is always general and moves the investigation forward by ruling out or subtracting probable contributing factors to reach a specific conclusion. An example of deductive reasoning follows this line of thinking: (1) All carpeting contains allergens; (2) there is carpeting in the bedroom; (3) I spend 60 percent of my day in the bedroom; (4) therefore, I conclude that it is the carpeting that is the source of my allergies. This conclusion is logical, given the assumption that the statement "all carpeting contains allergens" is true. The weakness with this example is that new information was not obtained during the reasoning process. That is, inductive reasoning points a person in the right direction; deductive reasoning provides the venue to prove an idea or hypothesis. Because any given situation has countless covariable influences, it behooves a student to avoid aimlessly using deductive reasoning. Inductive reasoning, on the other hand, allows students to discover information that they can prove or disprove later.

Research within design education follows both inductive and deductive reasoning, such that in the studio environment students are often asked to think inductively. They identify a concept, analyze case studies, and perform a site analysis. In contrast, the fundamental goal of research is for the student to develop an idea with the intent of seeing how that idea will affect a design. Deductive approaches are well suited for investigating environmental conditions because they allow the student to focus on the problem. For example, we know that many environmental contaminates are found within heating, ventilation, and air conditioning (HVAC) systems. Therefore, if an outbreak of some illness occurs within a building, the HVAC system is often the first place investigated. This building system is the one "common denominator" (the general theory) to all the occupants of the building; utilizing deductive reasoning requires all parts of the system to be tested individually for contamination, continually ruling out elements, "deducting" until the culprit is found—perhaps one lone filter inundated with mold spores.

To get a better sense of inductive and deductive reasoning, consider a case in which a researcher wants to decrease asthma symptoms in the workplace environment. The first step would be to identify the triggers of asthma symptoms within a workplace setting. As this is an exploratory process (discovery), it would follow an inductive line of reasoning. But in order to pinpoint the specific asthma triggers, it is likely that deductive research measures would be included. Although it may be impossible to address *all* of the factors known to cause asthma, the researcher can address the most influential factors. Hence, using deductive reasoning to rule out the factors that play only a small role in triggering asthma symptoms will result in an accurate assessment.

Although it might seem as if design research is predominantly about inductive reasoning (only exploring and rarely proving), a design researcher might analyze several buildings using deductive reasoning in order to identify common denominators (called a *comparative case study*) that will be addressed in the construction of a prototype. The following are excerpts from design theses. As you read the following overviews, notice the different approaches:

Overview 1

A society's culture and social depth are often evaluated through its art and science. Therefore, one could argue with some certainty that the world's architecture and design serve as a type of historical record. Buildings, with their stylistic attributes and interior design, express the sociopolitical climate of an era. Europe and the northeastern parts of the United States have long been heralded for their stunning and informative architecture and design. However, with the advent of uncontrolled capitalism and a media-crazed "pop culture," much design has become aesthetically sterile and a gross montage of fictional realities based on reproduced images. This has led to a fracturing within the design professions between those who can design inexpensively and those who design as if the world we live in is nothing more than a Hollywood set.

Via an exploratory process of identifying multiple design types throughout history, one can start to identify common attributes that are representative of a period in time. Through this identification, we can list important attributes of design and then infer their metaphoric representation to the sociopolitical climate of the era. This will provide us with a set of criteria enabling us to design in a way that represents the current sociopolitical climate without further fictional representations of a bygone era.

In this statement, the researcher seeks to understand how design mirrors the sociopolitical climate in the era in which it was conceived. For this exploration, the researcher will develop a method that modern-day designers can use to continue the evolution of social culture by using design as a means to document the sociopolitical climate of their era. Notice how the researcher started with very broad knowledge and then slowly moved toward the application of that knowledge to a design style. This is a classic deductive approach.

Overview 2

Each year, thousands of people have their lives changed forever as a result of a debilitating accident. This poses a unique situation within the health-care environment, because the patients who were likely fully functioning individuals in one moment had their lives changed forever in another. Therefore, social support is an important part of recovery. The primary support will likely come from friends and family, with secondary support from other patients. However, the health-care environment has a long tradition of being a tightly controlled environment with little regard for the unique situations of its patient population.

Studies have shown that the environment has a direct effect on patient recovery (e.g., Ulrich 1984) and motivation (Shaw 2004). This project seeks to design a rehabilitation center where the physical and psychological needs of the patient are addressed through environmental design. To support this effort, the design will seek out ways to create an environment, which will reintroduce the patient to events that occur daily. Such an environment will lead to better overall rehabilitation of individuals and their physical, emotional and mental readaptation to their everyday lives. For that reason, importance should be placed on the design and offerings of the environment to motivate recovery.

This statement has strong inductive and deductive components. The researcher begins with the assertion that rehabilitative patients have unique environmental "needs." The discovery of those "needs" will be an inductive process. Once the researcher identifies those "needs," the next step is to decide which "needs" will be addressed via the design. This will be a deductive process. Although a particular study may look deductive, most research that involves the human condition involves both inductive and deductive reasoning. As a result, it is not uncommon to observe data patterns that result in the formation of completely new ideas. See Activity 3.2.

ACTIVITY 3.2 Inductive versus Deductive Reasoning

Analyze the following statements and identify each as an inductive or deductive thought process. Then discuss why they are either inductive or deductive.

Identify environmental attributes that will support the unique needs of an aging adult.

Is it an inductive or deductive statement?	Why?
Deductive	The statement asks for the identification of environmental factors—we need to look at all of them and reduce the list to the factors supportive of only the specific older user.

Discover the ways in which autistic children interpret an environment.

Is it an inductive or deductive statement?   Why?

Identify attributes of a vacation resort that are most important to patrons.

Is it an inductive or deductive statement?   Why?

Identify the importance of public spaces to neighborhood residents.

Is it an inductive or deductive statement?   Why?

Classify the different family member perceptions as they relate to privacy within a residential environment.

Is it an inductive or deductive statement?   Why?

Analyze ways in which the workplace environment can support employee retention.

Is it an inductive or deductive statement?   Why?

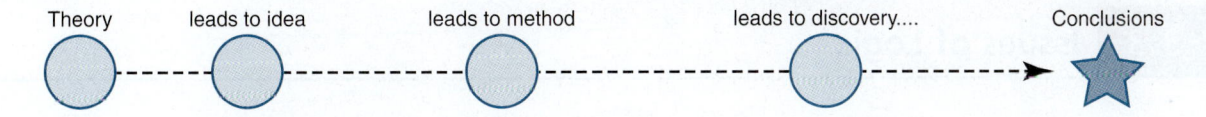

FIGURE 3.2 Logical Thought Process. Reflects a logical thought process of the streamlined flow of information that the reader understands and thereby trusts.
Source: Sinclair, E. (2009).

THE OUTCOME STAGE

Within the methods and results sections of a thesis or dissertation, it is important for the researcher to document and discuss the findings. A **logical thought process** (see Figure 3.2) begins with a concise statement of direction and follows a flow of information that comes across in the writing of the thesis or dissertation document. The cohesive nature of a well-thought-out and precisely executed research paper lends itself to the hallmarks of good research—reliability and validity. However, there are three fundamental flaws that plague many beginning researchers when they are writing their methods, results, and ultimate conclusions:

1. Illogical argumentation or conclusions
2. Leaps of faith
3. Overstating the results

Illogical Argumentation and Conclusions

An **illogical argument** or conclusion results from meanings derived from similar but different variables. To get a better idea of this situation, consider this sentence: "I was hungry, so I went to the coffee shop." The first issue with this sentence is the lack of agreement between *hungry* and *coffee shop*. As written, the sentence presupposes that coffee would satisfy hunger, but that is not true; therefore, it is illogical. A solution would be the addition of detail. For example, "I was hungry, so I went to the coffee shop to get a sandwich." Now the variables are *hungry* and *sandwich*—and a sandwich can satisfy hunger.

As the researcher assembles his or her thesis, logic must be maintained and documented throughout. In any given research, periodic assessments are made that inform the researcher regarding modifications that should be made prior to proceeding. Figure 3.3 depicts the points in a thought process that represent a decision or knowledge for the researcher. Each of these points and decision pathways must be explained so that the reader understands the researcher's thought process as well as the rationale. See Activity 3.3.

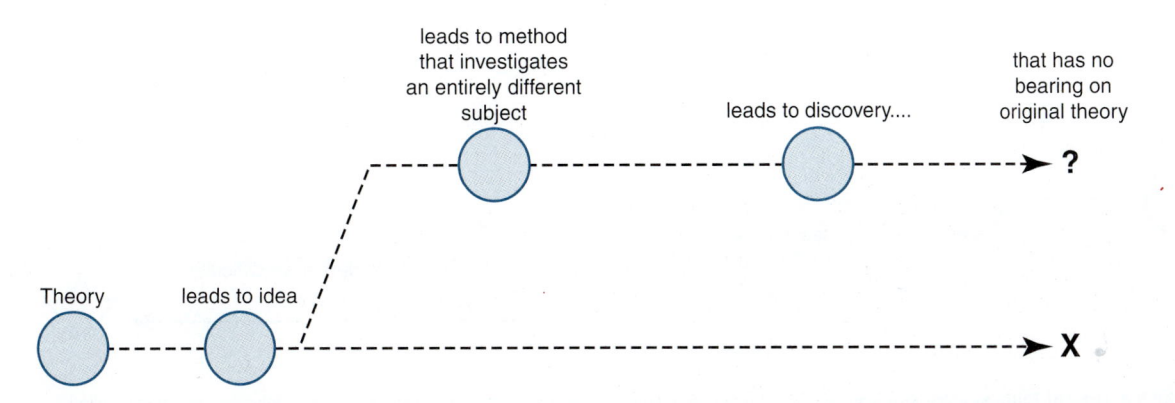

FIGURE 3.3 Illogical Thought Process. A departure from linear logic results in a conclusion that is unreasonable, or illogical.
Source: Sinclair, E. (2009).

ACTIVITY 3.3 Issues of Logic

Identify the issues of logic within each of the following sentences:

1. A center for autistic children will help educate the community about autism.
2. The deterioration of the family structure results in increased aggression.
3. In recent years, much research has concluded that green spaces are beneficial. Because of the increased level of green spaces within the city, there has been a significant decline in urban crime.

Discussion: Identification of flaws in the previous statements.

- In the first statement, a center is a thing and a thing cannot provide education. People can provide education and a design might even be able to educate, but a thing is just a thing. Therefore, this statement is illogical.
- The second statement lacks supporting data, and as currently stated requires a huge leap of faith, because not all deteriorations within a family lead to aggression. Some cause a person to thrive. Others lead to depression. Therefore, we can not ascribe an absolute outcome to a single event.
- The third statement is flawed because there is no relationship between green spaces and lower crime. Like the second statement, the latter may or may not have influenced the former. What separates this statement from the second is the use of research to support a statement. However, the use of the research has been overstated. There was nothing in the original research that suggests that green spaces lower crime; it claimed only that green spaces are *beneficial*.

Leaps of Faith

The second common flaw that plagues researchers when developing their thesis or dissertation is **leaps of faith**. These occur when the researcher fails to completely document each step of the process or fails to address all aspects within the discussion. The result is that the reader must make grand assumptions or *leaps of faith* to arrive at the same conclusion as the researcher. Figure 3.4 depicts an example of a leap of faith within a line of logic. The theory and research are disjointed, requiring the reader to leap over the gap in order to arrive at the same conclusion. Hence, readers have to rethink their own thoughts. This is akin to reading an exciting novel only to discover that a few of the last pages have been removed. Therefore, it is likely that such a flaw will result in a negative assessment of the researcher's work.

Another way that a leap of faith can occur is through inference. If we look at the sentence "I was hungry, so I went to the coffee shop," the word *went* infers a transition from one place to another. The question of how the individual transitioned from place to place then becomes germane or relevant. One reader might imagine a person walking from a home to the coffee shop; another reader might image the person riding a bike from school to the coffee shop; and still another might image the person leaving from work in a car and driving to the coffee shop. As one can see, three different sets of interpretations and subsequent conclusions were made in relation to one sentence. This is why it is very important for the researcher to be very clear in the documentation of research.

When documenting research, the researcher should always keep in mind a few essential components of good writing: who, what, when, where, how, and why. To get a better idea of these ideas, consider the following sentence:

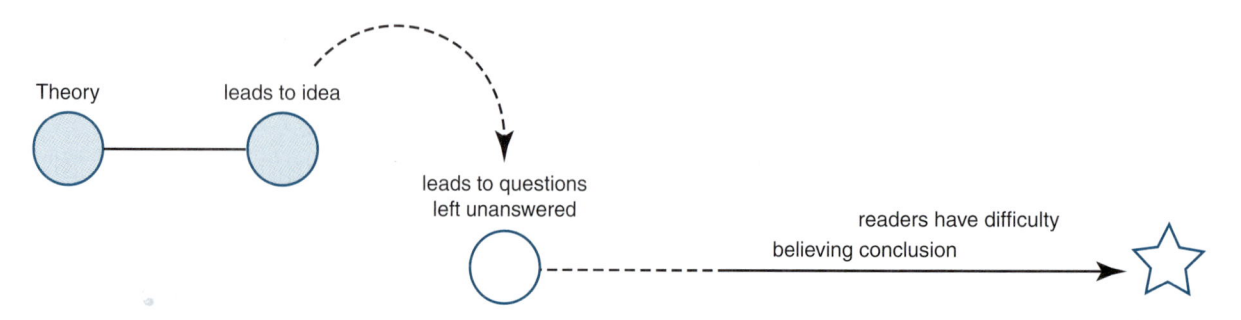

FIGURE 3.4 Leap of Faith. Readers must leap over the gap created by unanswered questions and believe the stated conlusions by acting on blind trust, rather than by considering the logical evidence presented by the researcher.
Source: Sinclair, E. (2009).

"I was hungry, so I rode my bike to the coffee shop to get a sandwich."

The *who* is:	"I"
The *what* is:	"Hunger"
The *where* is:	"Coffee shop"
The *why* is:	"To get a sandwich"
The *how* is:	"Bike"

In this example, the *when* is missing, so we must modify the sentence. The improved sentence reads: "At 3:00 p.m., I was hungry, so I rode my bike to the coffee shop to get a sandwich." The *when* is answered: 3:00 p.m. With this formula, all of the reader's questions are now answered and there is little room for leaps of faith to be necessary within the sentence. The subsequent sentences within the paragraph should answer any peripheral questions. To illustrate, consider our original sentence: "At 3:00, I was hungry, so I rode my bike to the coffee shop to get a sandwich." Some of the peripheral questions might be:

- Why bike? Why not walk? Why not drive?
- Why the coffee shop? Why not a fast food place? Why not a restaurant?
- Why a sandwich? Why not pizza?

The final situation in which that a leap of faith can occur is when the researcher begs the reader to simply take what has been said as fact. For example, a researcher might state, "Night clubs are successful because the music volume is very high." We can likely agree that one would expect loud music in a nightclub; however, we cannot say for certain that a nightclub's success or appeal is attributed to the loudness of the music. Hence the researcher has taken a leap of faith in the argument and is asking the reader to take the leap too. A researcher can avoid this leap of faith by reframing the statement; for example, "Nightclub goers voted 'Frogs' the best in the 'Loud Music' category." Most arguments that rely on leaps of faith are the result of theories that are supported with weak evidence or flawed reasoning. By refraining from making broad unsubstantiated statements, research can focus on a specific area and facts can be readily found to back up statements.

Overstating the Research

A common problem observed within research that comes from a Western cultural background is the **overstatement** of an idea or concept. This problem likely derives from a preference for quick delivery of information and a dependence on sound bites. Such research gravitates to a given concept and then overstates the concept beyond its ability to remain true. For example, research by Roger Ulrich and Rachael and Stephen Kaplan has revealed that being immersed within nature and having access to natural vistas has many beneficial qualities for humans. Some professionals have taken these results and oversimplified them to include pictures of natural scenes. And some contend that hospital privacy curtains with pictures of nature scenes yield the same kinds of benefits as actual natural vistas and as being physically immersed within a natural setting. These assumptions are an example of overstating the research because it is unknown whether it is simply the visual quality of a natural scene that has beneficial qualities or if it is the multisensory stimuli that causes the beneficial qualities, in which case scenic pictures or curtains would yield little to no value because they stimulate only the visual processing centers (see Figure 3.5).

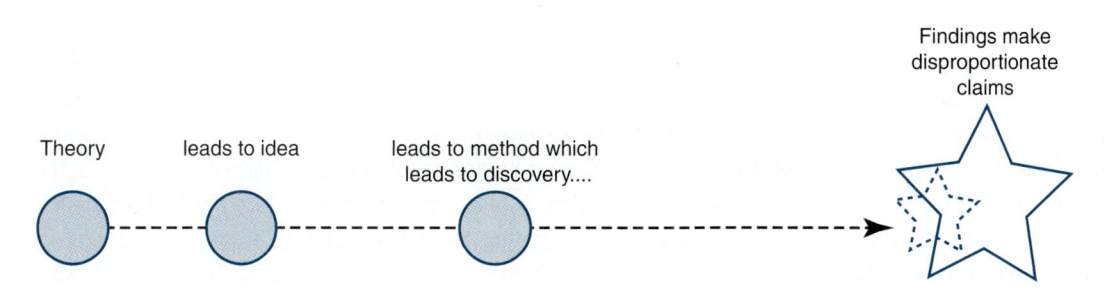

FIGURE 3.5 Overstating the Facts. Actual accounting of the findings is overshadowed by bold, exaggerated, or sensationalized claims that the evidence does not support.
Source: Sinclair, E. (2009).

The bottom line in research revolves around credibility, reliability, and validity. By and large, all researchers want their discoveries to be taken seriously by the academic community and perhaps to have other researchers pick up where they left off and continue an investigation of their subject. Therefore, it is crucial to reduce all issues that might jeopardize the work. The most basic rules of engagement are:

- Follow a clear and concise research statement or hypothesis.
- Gather sufficient data that is appropriate and relevant.
- Develop a technique to test research variables that will add to the knowledge.
- Analyze the data in a fashion that is organized and complete.
- Summarize the data and draw only conclusions that the results infer.

Summary

All theses and dissertations propose an idea, select a method, implement a method, and then analyze results; design students have to incorporate those results into a design. The stages of the research process—formation, development, and outcome—teach design students how to accurately and systematically collect data that will answer questions and logically justify their design approaches. In the professional world, these skills increase the worth of students and provide them with the expertise necessary to find and analyze any information that their future employers might require. Any research process—whether architectural, scientific, or even artistic—requires that systematic decisions be made prior to setting out.

Developing a thesis statement is much like wanting to paint a picture. The artist thinks, "What would I like to paint—a landscape, a portrait, or a mosaic?" For the researcher, the questions are: "Do I want to ask a question and explore for answers?" and "Do I want to make a statement and test it for results?" Developing an approach is much like *preparing* to create a work of art. The artist pauses to consider how to best capture the image on the canvas: from which angle or in what kind of light? This is the case with positivism and postpositivism. In what light does the student researcher want to "paint" the study? Positivism rejects intuition and demands scientific measurement. Postpositivism is participatory and collaborative with regard to the relationship between researcher and subject matter. It requires the voices and the interpretations of many people to offer the multifaceted discoveries that are prevalent with this position. Positivism provides results that have the ability to be "generalized" to other similar situations; postpositivism offers results that pinpoint one situation or group and remains true only for that scenario.

Selecting a method is much like the thought process of an artist who has decided on the subject and position of the image, but has yet to select the medium in which to create the work. The artist considers all of the available options: watercolor, ink, charcoal, or oil, knowing that any of these media will have an effect on the "look" of the end product. This metaphor is used to describe the developmental stage of research. Design researchers gather data from scientific literary sources best suited to be their "medium," knowing that if superior data is acquired it will be reflected in their final design. The next selection the artist makes prior to painting is the surface or substrate—the paper, canvas, or fabric. With a paintbrush in hand, the artist considers the implications for the perception of the final image imparted by the base material. Some materials absorb colors and others add to the colors. Such is the way with a line of reasoning. Deductive reasoning starts with a broad statement, and by continually removing data, it refines the statement. Inductive reasoning examines a situation from the inside and moves outward with each addition of data towards the conclusion.

Completing the thought process of an artist preparing to paint is the decision regarding interpretation. Some artists gravitate toward sublime single-line mathematically profound statements, and others offer resplendent mosaics conversant with metaphor and symbolic meaning—either way, the artist makes this interpretation choice prior to putting brush to canvas. It is similar with the quantitative and qualitative approaches. Quantitative approaches prove or disprove an assumption with numeric tables, graphs, and statistics that may not be immediately understood by the reader, but appear undeniably accurate. Qualitative approaches explore concepts with a vast array of supporting narratives, vignettes, and data to conclude in a rich dialogue explaining the conditions of the subject so fully as to hold the findings above reproach.

The outcome, the summation, the veritable "drum roll" of all the hard work and dedication to the pursuit of knowledge and a new way to design is not without hazards and roadblocks blocking the way to finishing the thesis or dissertation. Caution must therefore be exercised in any endeavor worthy of this academic caliber. Making any illogical statements, failing to provide sufficient data so as to cause readers to make leaps of faith in the research, or overstating the findings are all examples of things to avoid. If artists make mistakes in judgment, they stand to lose money and materials. If a student-researcher makes mistakes in judgments, the student stands to lose the one thing that cannot be reclaimed: *time*.

Glossary

Determinism—The view that every event or action is determined by a prior occurrence.

Formative—Research done to help create or improve a process or product.

Generalize—To extend a truth beyond the available data.

Hypothesis—A proposal intended to explain certain facts or observations.

Illogical argument—An argument that lacks sufficient data to support an outcome.

Invariance—A variable that is unaffected by a designated operation or transformation.

Leaps of faith—Asking another person to simply believe what another has to say without proof.

Logical thought process—A series of verifiable thoughts that are linked together to form a hypothesis or theory.

Mixed methods—More than one method is used simultaneously or at different stages within the research.

Operationalism—The process of specifying the extension of a concept.

Overstatement—An exaggeration that extends the truth beyond the facts.

Process—To address something according to programmed instructions in order to obtain a set of verifiable results.

Qualitative—A process that refers to the quality or characteristics of something being described, rather than an exact numeric measurement

Quantitative—Something that can be given meaning or value through a numeric representation.

Research question—A question that specifically states what the researcher will attempt to answer.

Review of literature (ROL)—An extensive literary examination of other scholar's work in order to develop a solid foundation of knowledge on a given topic of study.

Summative—A method of assessment at the end of a given set of activities.

CHAPTER 4
Formation of a Topic and Argument

chapter outline

Introduction

Identifying a Topic

Preparing a Thesis Statement

Forming a Research Question
Concept Mapping
Developing a Research Question

Beginning the Process
The Abstract
The Introduction

Dissecting an Argument
Logic Mapping

Selecting Research Objectives
Recognize Objectives
Specify Objectives
Organize Objectives
Define Objectives

Summary

> "Knowing where you're going is all you need to get there."
> —Frederick Frieseke

chapter objectives

By the end of this chapter, students should be able to:

- Identify the topic of their research.
- Conceptualize their topic in terms of a thesis statement, a research question, and argument.
- Select the initial typology or environment to apply the research.
- Assign specific research variables and objectives to begin preliminary review of the literature.

Introduction

The formation of a thesis topic generally weighs heavily on the minds of students pursuing a degree. Ideally, the exercises in Chapter 3 should have aided in the tentative discovery of a general subject of interest for the student. At the very least, the exercises should have formulated an understanding of what lies ahead. In this chapter, a narrowing and focusing of the topic as well as specific issues surrounding it will be addressed. Through the use of examples and activities that outline the step-by-step procedures of identifying a topic, preparing a thesis statement, forming a research question, forming an introduction, and outlining objectives to begin the review of literature, a sense of security should be imparted in the mind of the student. Any student who has reached the stage of writing a thesis within his or her academic program has exhibited the discipline and the skills necessary to successfully complete a thesis. With that being said, it is greatly suggested that the student take copious notes and utilize every activity within this chapter to ensure a solid start in the journey of writing a research document. To quote Carl Frieseke (1976), "Knowing where you're going is all you need to get there." (p. 68)

Identifying a Topic

Before the research process can begin, design students need to do two things: identify a topic and select a typology or space to research. The diversity of issues and typologies within the built environment affords researchers with an abundance of avenues and perspectives from which to pursue research. This is both a blessing and curse: a blessing because the student-researcher has many options, and a curse because many student-researchers find the process of narrowing down their ideas to be a daunting task.

The first step in evidence-based design research is to identify a topic also called an **area of inquiry**. It is important that the researcher be as specific as possible when defining this area of inquiry. To illustrate, the category of *sustainability* is much too large to analyze into a single research paper. Likewise, design buzzwords such as *experiential design* or *parasitic architecture* should be only a part of the design process, not the topic. For instance, *types and performance* criteria of materials can be the main topic of research: the *application* can be in sustainability, experiential, or parasitic design. Unless the student has many years to complete the research, it is imperative that thesis or dissertation candidates be as specific as possible when identifying a topic and typology. Note how the example in Box 4.1 took the broad topic of sustainability and narrowed it down to a specific subset (interior finishes labeled as sustainable versus unlabeled interior finishes).

Use Activity 4.1 as an opportunity to practice narrowing down a topic.

The second step when identifying a topic is to identify a building, a space, or a type of environment. Because each environment has its own unique set of circumstances, researchers must acquire a comprehensive understanding of how that environment functions, particularly in relation to the area of inquiry. To get a better understanding of how environments that appear to be alike have very different and unique needs, we will use the health-care environment

BOX 4.1 Narrowing the Topic

Topic Ideas	Steps
Sustainability	Topic too broad
Interior finish materials	Narrowed to category of sustainability
Sustainable vs. traditional materials	Narrowed to subset of category
(*sustainability label*) vs. (*no label*)	Qualifying aspect (Variable)
Cost/benefit ratio	Unit of analysis and goal

FINAL STATEMENT:
"What is the cost/benefit ratio of using sustainable interior finishes vs. traditional finishes?"

ACTIVITY 4.1 Narrowing the Topic

Starting from the broad topic of hotels and resorts, how can you refine this topic into something more narrow and manageable for a research topic?

Example

"How do people wayfind within large hotels or resorts?" *Wayfinding* is the topic of research that is applied to the typology of hotels and resorts. (Note: This particular statement is a deductive approach, which means to find out or deduce.)

Topic Ideas

Follow the steps to the right and fill in your ideas:

Hotels and Resorts

_____

_____

_____

_____

Steps

Broad topic
Narrow to a category
Narrow again to a subset
Find a qualifying definition
What will be used: a measurement or goal?

---

as an example. A broad definition of a health-care environment is one that "provides support and promotes health." In the United States, the myriad of health-care environments includes hospitals, rehabilitation centers, clinics, and nursing homes, to mention only a few. Each of these environments has different functions and caters to different populations with different needs and perspectives (e.g., patients vs. nurses), therefore requiring different design strategies. Therefore, the researcher's specific environment type needs to be clearly stated. A good beginning might look like this: "What is the cost-benefit ratio of sustainable interior finish materials versus traditional finishes used for a community clinic?" An opening statement such as this informs the reader about the nature of the document and what is to be expected from the research.

To get a better understanding of how a student might begin to identify a topic and explore a path of research, review the following four cases, which reflect the first stages of students brainstorming through a topic:

STUDENT A

This researcher has identified an interest in *music*. From this point, the researcher engaged in a brainstorming activity and hosted a focus group in order to identify all of the environments where music was a prominent feature of the environment. From this exercise the researcher identified concert halls, opera houses, churches, community parks, street corners, stadiums, schools, music stores, malls, department stores, nightclubs, and recording studios. The researcher then selected an environment type: an opera house. This is the environment that the student researched and thereby gained a thorough understanding of how it functioned. To get this understanding, the student engaged in another brainstorming session and formed another focus group in order to identify key factors or concerns within the selected environment. In this situation, the student further identified the following factors as key issues: acoustics, lighting, temperature control, perceptions of crowding, the ability to perform special effects on stage, accessibility, and number and conditions of restrooms. With this information, the student then began gathering literature related to auditoriums, theaters, and concert halls. Because each of these environments has similar situations and circumstances as an opera house, it was safe to conclude that these environments would be relevant. In this way, the student learned about the chosen environment by learning about the factors that effect similar environments.

The next phase of the design research process is to identify a question that leads to a research method. In researcher A's project, the student wanted to develop an open-air opera house but was unsure whether such a facility could achieve comparable acoustical variations to that of an enclosed opera house. The method chosen was a comparison study in which a sound meter was acquired to monitor the diversity and variation of sound quality in an actual opera house. That data was recorded and similar readings were taken at an outdoor amphitheater. The student then compared the diversity, range, and spectrum of sounds to determine which sounds or pitches became compromised in the outdoor theater. With this data and further literary review, the student put forth a prototype of an outdoor opera house that had specific features intended to preserve the purity of sound. Granted, this building may or may not function as intended, but the goal is to design based on verifiable evidence—hence the term "evidence-based."

STUDENT B

This student had an interest in Carl Jung. (Although Carl Jung is an interesting individual, unless the student planned to design a monument dedicated to Carl Jung, the first order of business would be to identify what it is about this historic figure that was admired.) Through a process of self-exploration, the student created a collage of all the aspects about Carl Jung that was interesting. Once this was done, the student analyzed the final product to determine common themes. The student identified the reoccurring theme of alchemy and mysticism. From this point the student identified environments where alchemy and mysticism are supported. Environments included a spiritual center, church, theme park, private club, and a private residence. Ultimately the student decided upon a spiritual center, but the student had to determine how the ideas and themes of alchemy and mysticism could be incorporated into the prototype of a spiritual center. This exploration process led to a method of inquiry. In this case, student B opted for a photo analysis to study numerous cases and situations where alchemy and mysticism were omnipresent. Through this comprehensive analysis and documentation of images, the student clustered the images according to themes that were further assessed for inclusion into the student's design of a spiritual center prototype.

STUDENT C

This student identified an interest in cars and other motorized vehicles. Because the student included "other motorized vehicles," some self-exploration was needed to determine exactly what was so fascinating about motorized vehicles. Similar to student B, student C prepared a collage of preferred images. The student then analyzed those images with friends and family. The common theme present in each of the images was determined as the way *power can be metaphorically represented* in motorized vehicles. The student identified custom paint shops, design centers, convention centers, and retail outlets as environments where images of power and vehicles could be seen together. From this point, the student engaged in a brainstorming session where common factors and attributes were identified that supported the function and operation of a custom paint shop. Included in this process was a desire identified by the student to make this paint shop more sustainable. The two predominate violators of sustainable practices identified were air pollution and ground water contamination. After the student combed through the literature, potential ways to vent harmful airborne containments from the shop and ways to reduce harmful fluids from accidentally seeping into the soil were identified. From this point, several exploratory models (experimental method) were developed to express enhanced sustainability. The student then selected the best model and proceeded to improve that model into the final prototype.

STUDENT D

This student expressed an interest in community-initiated participatory design. The first step for this student was a quick preliminary review of the literature available on this topic, for two reasons: first, to learn about the different types of community-initiated design and second, to identify the pros and cons of each type in order to justify the "community" process. Because much of what this student wanted to research was driven by external forces—that is, the community—the student needed to do some *preliminary* research to identify the community's desired building typology. As part of the initial review of the literature, the student also explored effective methods and biases for implementing a survey and conducting a community focus group. This student opted to conduct three separate focus groups. The proceedings were videotaped in order to analyze the results at a later date. Ultimately the results revealed a need for low-cost housing. The student then analyzed the pros and cons of past low-income housing models used throughout the United States. In addition, the student selected a building site to further research that community's demographics and unique behavioral patterns common to specific ethnicities. Part of this review of the literature evolved as a process to understand the cultural norms of the specific community. From this point, the student assembled several different prototypes of low-income housing designs to be presented at community forums, where participants were led through a series of design charrettes to identify the architectural elements that the community would embrace. Again, this process was videotaped for later analysis and thus developed a prototype of an ideal community-initiated design for the final portion of the research project.

ACTIVITY 4.2 Topic Collage

To help provide clarity to the overall research topic, create a presentation board with a collection of many images representing your ideas pasted to the surface. Follow these steps:

1. Identify a core area of interest.
2. Gather images depicting all of the manifestations of this core interest.
3. Arrange and affix them to a stiff board or heavyweight paper.
4. Ask friends and family to see if they can identify a common theme or pattern within the collage.
5. Write down their comments.
6. Reflect on the importance of those comments and in relation to your core topic develop a theme or concept.

These are only a few of the myriad of student processes that have been used to identify the thesis topic, as well as conceptualize the research. It is important that student-researchers engage in conversations about their topic and the processes they plan to use. By speaking to others about the process, they will be better able to conceptualize a research strategy. Likewise, *research* (methods) and *application* (design) are complex entities, and when a researcher merges the two, the end result is often manifested in a dynamic exchange of theory and practice. This means that students are likely to develop unique styles and techniques for their research project. However, one reoccurring theme within all research projects is the formation of an **argument** and a set of results. See Activity 4.2.

Preparing a Thesis Statement

Within physical and social sciences, a thesis statement provides the overarching theme, along with expected outcomes. The design researcher's thesis statement must also demonstrate a possible solution through the development of a prototype. Because of this additional component, the thesis or dissertation within design education often contains a specific typology from which this concept can be applied. To illustrate; in the previous example, Student C wanted to develop a sustainable automotive design center.

This information provides only the beginning of the thesis statement. The next component is a summary of the argument, which will serve as the crux of the researcher's entire thesis or dissertation. In the case of the automotive design center, one might expect that the student's argument will revolve around issues of:

- Air pollution
- Soil contamination
- Water contamination
- Noise pollution

Therefore, the student will need to conduct a preliminary review of the literature so that a basic understanding can be acquired of the many issues in relation to the human physiological responses to environmental toxins. Evidence to support an argument or claim that a sustainable automotive center is a good idea may include any provable claim, such as:

- Higher incidences of asthma rates among residents in close proximity to auto body shops
- Lower GPAs earned by neighborhood children due to excessive noise
- Negative drop in perceived local property values

The next part of the thesis statement should provide a compelling argument to support the crux of the overarching theme. A discussion of how and why the overarching theme is important contributes to the overall body of knowledge. Following the previous example, the student could make a statement such as, "Combustion engines are a quintessential part of American culture and can be found in many forms, such as boats, planes, dirt bikes, automobiles, and other essential forms of transportation. However, the customization and repair of such items result in many unsustainable byproducts that are concentrated in and around automotive design and repair centers. As such, greater research needs to be directed toward the identification of practices to create more sustainable automotive design and repair centers."

A thesis statement not only identifies an issue of concern, but also briefly explains how further information will be obtained to identify a potential remedy. Continuing with this example, the researcher might decide on experimental methods that call for the design and assembly of several different models from which the student could run simulations to assess indoor air quality and potential techniques to capture liquid byproducts prior to contaminating the soil. Another potential method that this student might use is a comparative analysis of material specifications as they pertain to noise abatement and containment. Therefore, the combined methods address the stated issues of sustainability: indoor air quality, ground contamination, and noise pollution. The final portion of the thesis statement—unique to the design student—is the development and assembly of a prototype environment.

Forming a Research Question

CONCEPT MAPPING

A concept, an idea, a hypothesis—they are all the same thing. They are abstract notions of the imagination that require something more substantial to give them life and credibility. A significant part of a designer's education is concept creation and the subsequent development of a tangible artifact. To communicate a concept to others, the design researcher must take an ethereal idea and represent it in a physical form. Without this physical manifestation, a concept is nothing more than the thought of one person. So too is a research topic: it is merely an individual insight until finely honed, proven, and shared with others. A concept or topic idea is likely to manifest differently depending on the specific typology of the environment. Consider the differences between a community clinic and a hospital. They are similar but different environments. Both provide health care, but the social status and physical size differ significantly between the two. Therefore, the concept—as well as the design—of these environments will be different. After working through a topic idea for a research paper, a student of design should select the environment that is the most relevant to that idea.

As researchers develop and begin to work through a concept, they must document and organize their thoughts. This part of a research paper involves the design and construction of a highly structured and detailed document. Design students are brilliant at representing their ideas three dimensionally. Whether it is a computer-generated model, an actual three-dimensional model, or renderings of a three-dimensional space, the connectivity between walls, floors, and furnishings can be seen and physically manipulated. Writing is similar, in that words and phrases also require connectivity. However, writing involves the ability to translate thoughts and ideas into words that come together in a way that carries a unified meaning. For example, one might say, "I see what you mean." But without more words to provide clarification, this could reflect an object that is actually being seen or it could indicate an understanding of an idea. Hence the assembly of words to create and convey an idea is much the same as the creation of a design in that it must properly and clearly convey the concept. In fact, American writer and journalist Ernest Hemingway (1932) once said, "Prose is architecture . . . ." (p. 153).

Concept mapping is a brainstorming tool that designers use to get all of their ideas down on paper to generate a topic to research. Students write down areas that are of interest to them, things they are curious about, or topics that they simply enjoy. The next step is to look for patterns among the major topic headings. For example, if a student had three "big ideas": issues of the female population, public spaces, and environmental behavior, then perhaps a connection could be posed in the form of a question: "What are the behavior manifestations of women in public spaces?" This could be followed by creating subordinate ideas branching off of each big idea, such as: women—societal changes since the beginning of the twentieth century; public spaces—more public spaces in urban environments than in suburbs; environmental behavior—I have observed people acting differently in various environments. It often helps to write questions off to the side of each main topic to further the quest for a topic that the student will enjoy studying for one or more years. Figure 4.1 illustrates an example of concept mapping and Activity 4.3 gives the student the opportunity to practice this technique with a few variations.

DEVELOPING A RESEARCH QUESTION

The design research paper requires students to articulate their thought processes in both the literal form (model, drawings, and sketches) and the figurative form, with the construction of the research paper (text, graphs, and images). The end result is a designer who can articulate *thought* in multiple mediums—cognitively, physically, verbally, and orthographically.

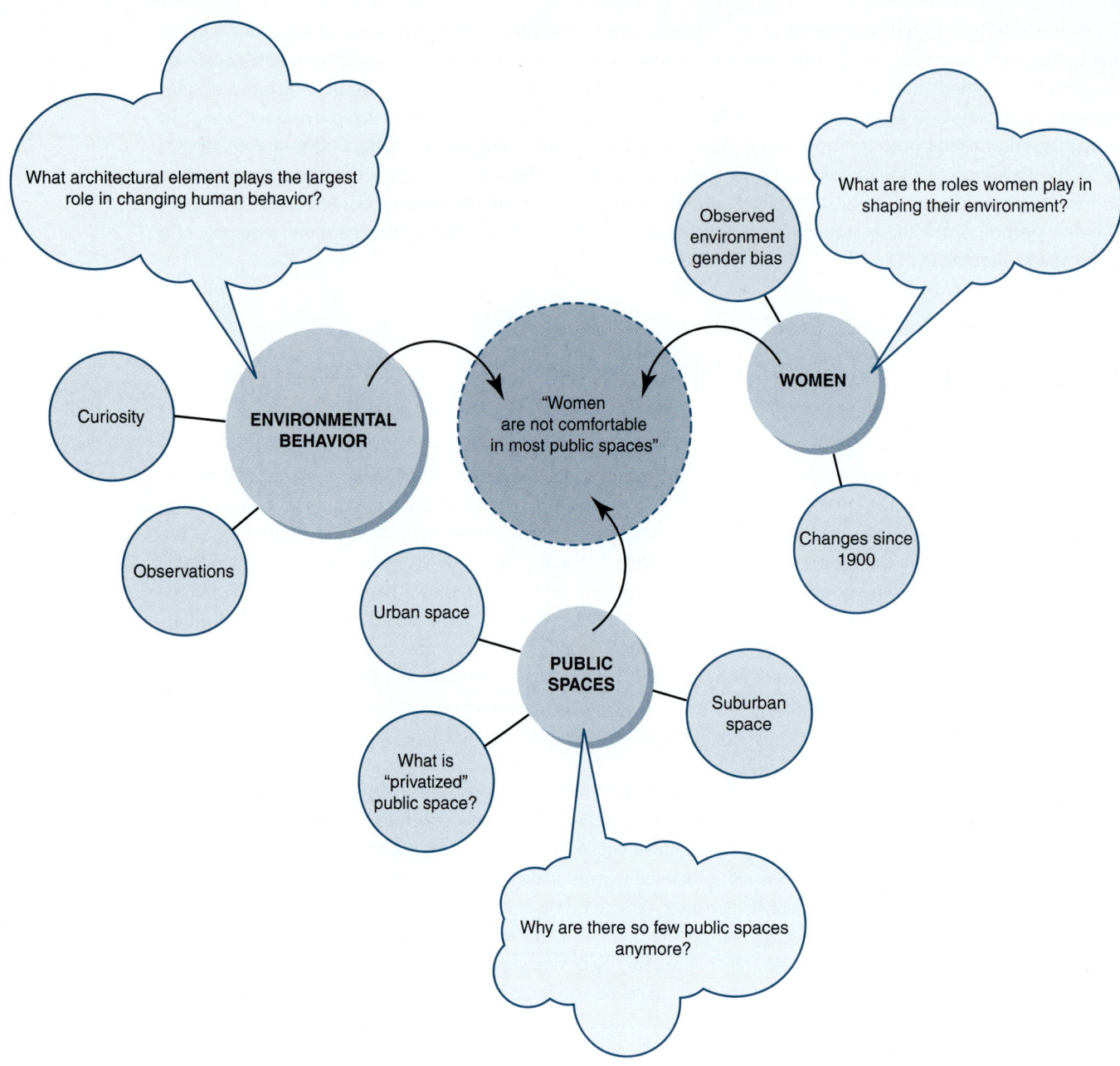

FIGURE 4.1 Concept Mapping. Concept mapping is a creative thinking process in which ideas feed into each other and the conceptual idea for the research is refined. *Source:* Sinclair, E. (2009).

Once a topic concept is identified, the researcher must identify either a typology or an environment—a space to *apply* the findings. To begin, the researcher should do some general reading related to the primary topic. This general reading is not meant to be included in the review of the literature (discussed in Chapter 5); it is meant only to provide the researcher with fundamental knowledge of the topic. For example, if the topic is autism, the researcher should gain an understanding of what autism is: what are the various spectrums of the condition, and how do symptoms manifest for those populations?

To gain this fundamental understanding, the researcher might access the Internet and read comments and articles on the subject matter. However, with regard to the initial information, only the information from the most credible sources should be used. During the first initial days of research, the student will conduct an exploratory of "down and dirty" information. This is considered preliminary inquiry and not a substitute for an intensive review of academic literature to be done later (the review of literature). However, from the first day of a thesis or dissertation, the researcher must take notes and make sure to record *all* pertinent information: the source of that information, the date that information was found, and any other attributes that would make it easier for the researcher to relocate that information at a later date (refer to the citation management discussion in Chapter 3).

ACTIVITY 4.3 Concept Mapping

Select the most comfortable format as a starting point: triangulation, question, or statement. Follow the instructions to conceptually map out an early form of the research question.

To reinforce the "brainstorming" nature of this task, take a large piece of paper, such as butcher wrap, or tear open and lay flat a brown paper bag. Write down ideas. They can be personal experiences, observation, interests, theories of others that you would like to investigate further, or perhaps something that you already know much about and for which you would like an opportunity to focus on a specific element. Here is a helpful hint: do not get too preoccupied with getting this right the first time—your idea is meant to evolve and change, so simply get as many ideas down as possible.

Triangulation	Question	Statement
Results in a rich yet complex thesis topic. (Beware of tangents.)	Results in an answer.	Results in a "prove or disprove" situation.
Leaving room in the center of the paper for culminating all your ideas into one statement or question, write down a few topics, interests, or things you are curious about. Then scribble down as many factors or elements about each topic that you can come up with. Next, look for connections or patterns among the topics; then write in the center your initial research question. See Figure 4.1.	Start in the center by posing a question, such as, "Does the use of concrete in city parks encourage skateboarding?" Surround this question with all the ways it could be answered or any additional thoughts regarding the subject. Continue to ask yourself: "Why is this?" or "Why would that . . .?"; for instance, "What if only wood and cobblestone were used in city parks?" Once you feel that you have sufficiently brainstormed, see if a few main areas emerge. Perhaps most answers were in the topics of building materials and public park policy. These are your points of departure for the next stage.	For example, "Since the inception of formaldehyde use in plywood, rates of Fragile-X autism have increased." This process is good for the student who already has an idea of two issues that are seemingly related or causing something. Causal is the research term for "causing something." Brainstorming around this central statement would include every possible way that you could prove or disprove this theory. This will end up looking much like a pros and cons list or pieces of information that you would need for evidence, such as statistics on autism rates or studies on the effects of formaldehyde exposure for children or pregnant women.

The next step in a research project is to identify a research question that will serve as the overarching theme throughout the document. One pitfall observed in many students' work is the desire to conceptualize from a holistic perspective. Seeing the "big picture" is admirable, but wanting to solve *all* the problems related to a subject rather than tackling only a small portion of the issue often results in the student taking on too much work and becoming overwhelmed later in the project. For instance, in the example of **idea mapping** in Figure 4.2, a resource center for autistic children is sufficient for one research paper because it is expected that the student will delve deep into the relationship of autism and the physical environment of a tutoring room within a community center. Hence if sustainability were also included into the statement—for example, "a resource center for autistic children that is sustainable"—then the topic would require the work of two research papers and therefore presents a multitude of problems for the student with regards to future research developments. Steps must be taken to resist the urge to research topics that are too broad or into areas that are too ambiguous. The goal for the researcher is to narrow down the search parameters to a manageable scope of study and complete an in depth and thorough investigation of the topic.

In order to convey the thought process shown in Figure 4.2, and to form a personal perspective, the researcher must develop a graphic representation of the steps of research development. See also Activity 4.4.

When conceptualizing a research question, the researcher might begin with words such as "how" or "why." For example:

- "How can a casino (the typology) be designed so that it can be a family vacation destination (idea or concept)?"
- "Why would a client want to incorporate sustainable practices (idea or concept) into an office space (typology)?"

Note that the framing of the question provides a clear direction for the student, and ultimately the reader. In the last example, the reader would not expect to learn about sustainability, but he or she might expect to learn

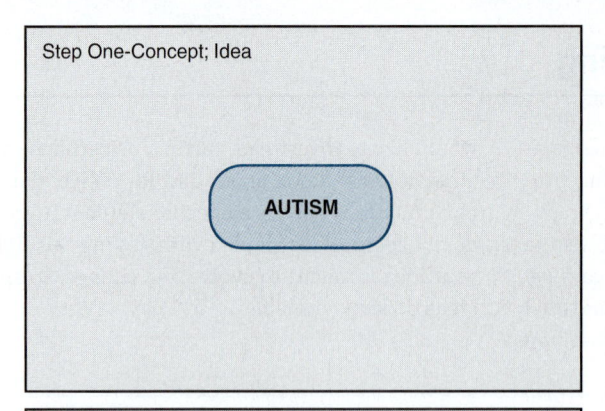

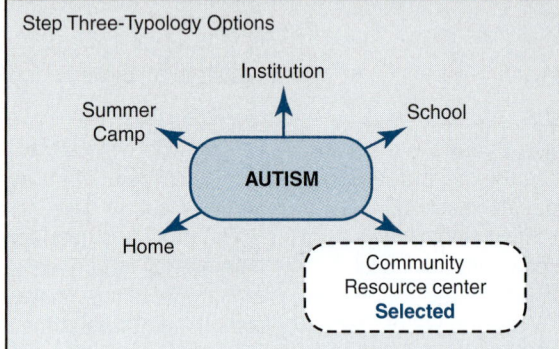

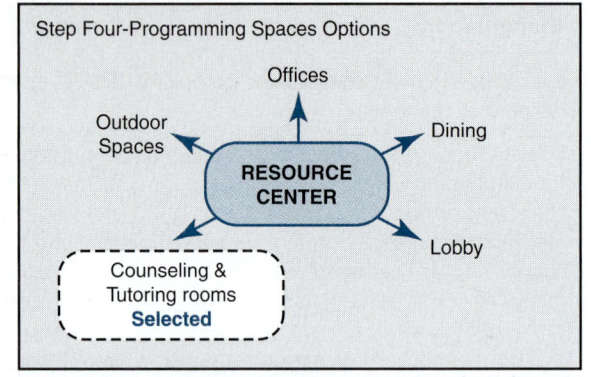

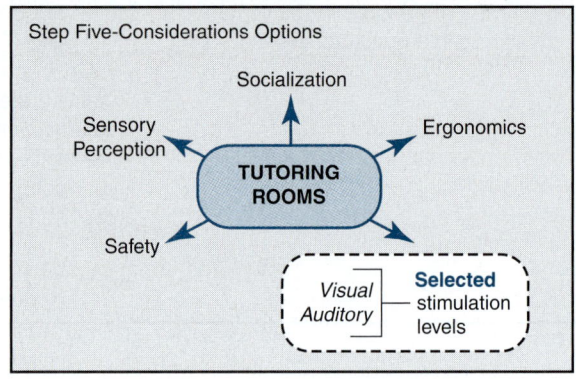

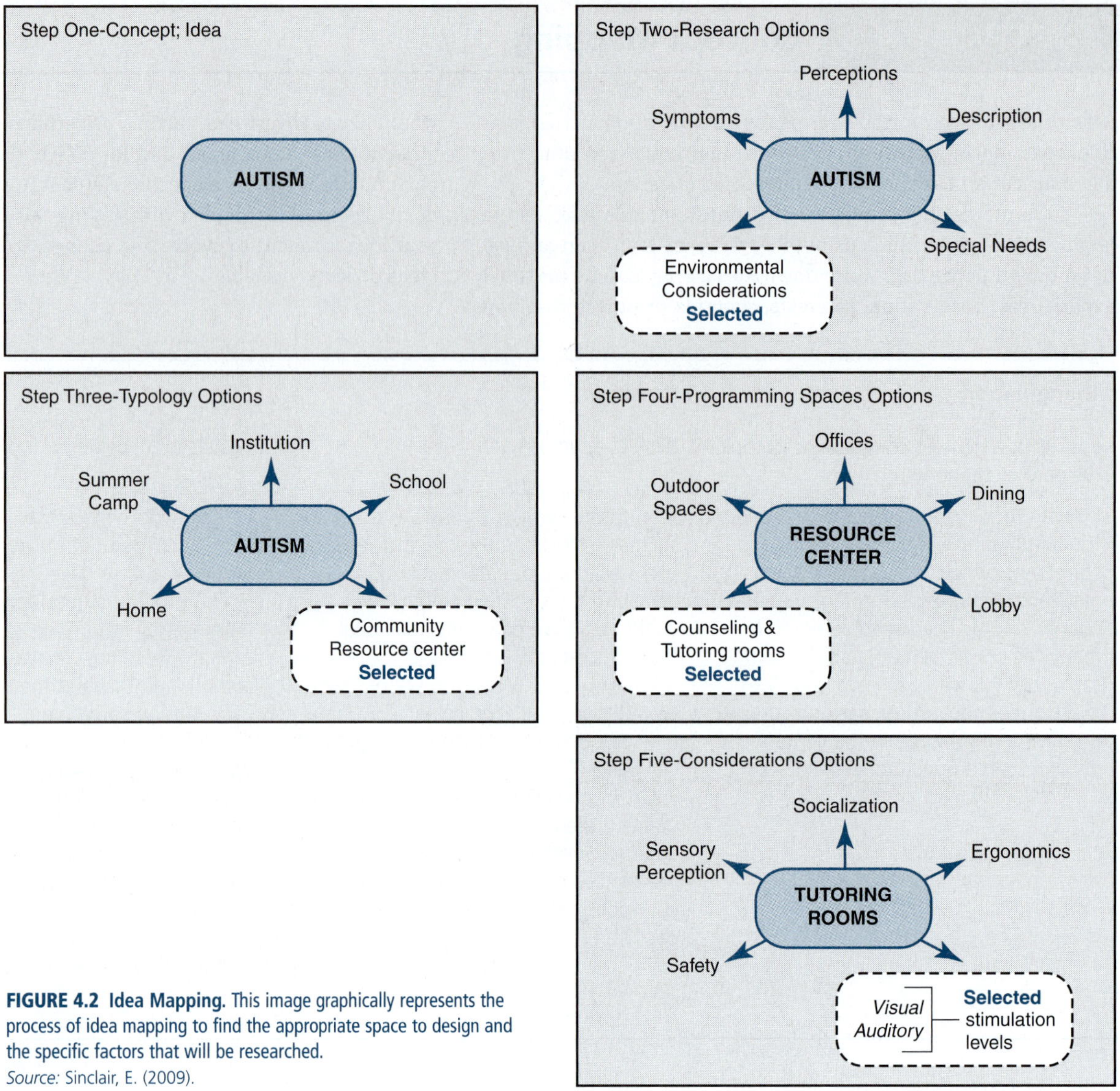

FIGURE 4.2 Idea Mapping. This image graphically represents the process of idea mapping to find the appropriate space to design and the specific factors that will be researched.
Source: Sinclair, E. (2009).

ACTIVITY 4.4 Conceptualization of the Research Question

Either recreate a graphic like the one in Figure 4.2 or fill in the table here to work through the options available for your research topic. The end result should be the framework for the research question or thesis statement.

Concept/ Idea	Topic Options	Typology/Environment	Specific Space	Objective/Perspective
Example from Figure 4.3 **Autism**	Perceptions Description Symptoms **Environmental Needs** Spec. Needs	School Summer camp Home **Resource center** Institution	**Tutoring rooms** Lobby Dining Office Outdoor spaces	Ergonomics Safety **Stimulation** Sensory Socialization
Idea #1				
Idea #2				

about the cost or employee health benefits of sustainable practices. Consider the research question as a type of road map that informs the researcher and the reader *where* the research is going. In an evidence-based design thesis, the researcher will always go from concept to typology, or from typology to concept. In research terms, the perspective of where a researcher begins depends upon whether he or she is following an inductive or deductive thought. To reiterate from Chapter 1, inductive reasoning goes from the specific to the general, always adding more to the information. This would begin with a specific typology from which an idea would be applied. Deductive reasoning, on the other hand, goes from the general to the specific, continually reducing the information down to the absolute core or solution. A researcher subscribing to this method of reasoning would likely begin with an idea and then apply that information directly to a specific typology. The research question should identify whether the researcher is approaching the project from a deductive (general) or inductive (particular) perspective.

"How" or "why" questions set the tone for the researcher to develop the argument. The question "How to develop an educational resource center for autistic children?" presupposes a need. Therefore, the researcher is also obligated to find information from reputable sources that support the assumption that an educational resource center is indeed needed for autistic children.

Beginning the Process

THE ABSTRACT

By understanding some of the fundamentals of the research process, the application of knowledge may be put into practice. The corner stones of research writing are brevity, specificity, clarity, and defensibility. This means that all written documents must be to the point, without personal opinions, emotions, judgments, or bias (prejudice). The writing should be detailed and clearly state the researcher's intentions and be heavily cited to substantiate all claims. There are no emotional or poetic statements in research writing; the work may result in profound conclusions, but the document is an artifact of the quest and a recording of the facts.

Initially, a thesis or dissertation identifies a problem, a solution, and an environmental design proposal. It is this incorporation that will form a preliminary **abstract** for the project. An abstract is generally written after the research is complete, though it is the item that is always read first. See Table 4.1.

Therefore, it is good practice to write a preliminary draft of the abstract to get a feel for correlating and summarizing the research and identifying the problem. The **problem** is the issue under investigation, and is typically the first sentence of an abstract. Here are some examples of a problem:

1. Soaring housing prices coupled with limited salary increases have led to increased portions of one's salary being allocated to the cost of housing.
2. Every year, thousands of terminally ill people are forced to live in excruciating physical pain in the name of humanity. However, when a sick animal is in the same terminal condition, it is considered "humane" to euthanize the animal.
3. The trends in health-care design are evolving from a purely clinical and singular approach to a more holistic practice that includes eastern traditions and environmental modification.

Table 4.1	*Writing an Abstract*
Purpose	The abstract summarizes the content of the research document and enables readers to quickly understand the purpose, methods findings.
Length	Typically, an abstract does not exceed 500 words, and contains at least 150 words. However, the word count for an abstract does not include the title, in-text citations, or references.
Content	The content usually includes the purpose or issue that is discussed or analyzed within the research document, the process or methods used to acquire new information, a summary that discusses core conclusions derived from the results, and an overall conclusion of the study.

The second sentence identifies a solution, which will serve as the underpinning premise of the entire research process. Building upon the previous examples, solutions might include:

1. In order to continue providing affordable housing in the United States, a new model will need to be devised.
2. If we are to agree that humans have free will and that we in the United States are free, then euthanasia should be an option for those seeking relief from chronic or terminal illnesses that negatively affect one's quality of life.
3. If health-care facilities are to remain competitive in the future, the practice and design of these facilities will need to adapt to the changing values and expectations of society.

The third step is unique to the design fields because the fundamental pedagogy of design curricula is the development of an end product—a building or an environment. However, society is increasingly demanding end products that are designed with the use of evidence-based procedures. Therefore, the design thesis is good practice because the final stage is the proposed environmental outcome of the research process. Using the same examples, the third phrase of the abstract might look something like this:

1. Through a review of past and present housing typologies, a new typology will be developed that will merge common successful attributes, while eliminating attributes that detract from affordability.
2. Given the current social aversion to euthanasia within the United States, steps will be taken to develop a facility that will provide not only the most peaceful end for a person who opts for euthanasia, but also security from those who seek to impose their moral values upon others.
3. To meet the diverse needs of a population seeking holistic and integrative medical treatments, the facility design will need to accommodate required equipment for various alternative therapies, as well as use environmental design to communicate a more evolved health-care system.

THE INTRODUCTION

When the pieces are put together, the writer ends up with a paragraph that clearly states the problem, solution, and proposal. This paragraph can then be expanded in order to form a *preliminary* introduction to the thesis. At this stage of the writing, it is important to remember that these sections are all *initial drafts* that will go into the final research paper. They will change, evolve, and improve as the student continues to search for, gather, and produce new information (see Chapter 7 for methods of producing new information). See Table 4.2.

This preliminary introduction paragraph can be reduced in size and used to form the thesis statement. The following example demonstrates the assembly of the problem, solution, and proposal from example 1:

> Soaring housing prices coupled with limited salary increases has led to <u>increased</u> portions of one's salary to be allocated to the <u>cost of housing</u>. In order to continue providing <u>affordable housing</u> in the United States <u>a</u>

Table 4.2 Writing an Introduction

The introduction provides the reader with an overview of the research. It includes information related the researcher's position and explains how this position is explored within the research. Following are some key points that should be included in the thesis introduction.

Statement of the problem	Succinctly identify the topic and relevant information about why the topic is important.
Background and need	Provide relevant literature to support the importance of the topic. The researcher should summarize what is already known about the topic, identify areas in which additional knowledge is needed, and specify how these gaps will be addressed.
Purpose of the project	Explain what the researcher hopes to accomplish with the study.
Research objectives	Identify the research objectives and how they will serve to prove valuable.
Methods	Briefly describe the methods that were used to acquire new knowledge.
Limitations	Discuss any limitations or restrictions of the research.

new model will need to be devised. Through a review of past and present housing typologies, a new typology will be developed that will merge common successful attributes while eliminating attributes that detract from affordability.

Once the paragraph has been assembled, the researcher will need to identify key words or phrases within the paragraph. This is demonstrated in the previous example by underlining the key words. These words and phrases are then taken out of the paragraph and assessed to see how they can be reassembled into one sentence. For example, the underlined words in the previous example include:

- Increased cost of housing
- Affordable housing
- New model
- New typology
- Merge successful attributes

From these key words and phrases, a thesis statement can be constructed: A new model and typology that merges the successful attributes of affordable housing needs to be identified in order to address the increased cost of housing in the United States. See Activities 4.5 and 4.6.

ACTIVITY 4.5 Thesis Statement Practice

For practice, read the following two paragraphs, identify key aspects from each of the three sentences, and construct one sentence that encapsulates all of the ideas.

Paragraph 1:

Every year, thousands of terminally ill people are forced to live in excruciating physical pain in the name of "humanity." However, when a sick animal is in the same terminal condition, it is considered "humane" to euthanize the animal. If we are to agree that humans have free will and that we in the United States are free, then euthanasia should be an option for those seeking relief from chronic or terminal illness that negatively effect one's quality of life. Given the current social aversion to euthanasia within the United States, steps will need to be taken to develop a facility that will provide not only the most peaceful end for a person who opts for euthanasia, but also security from those who seek to impose their moral values upon others.

Identify five words or phrases that are most important to the meaning being conveyed in this paragraph:

_____
_____
_____
_____

From these words or phrases, assemble one sentence that uses each of the words or phrases to convey the core thoughts contained within the original paragraph.

_____
_____
_____

Paragraph 2:

The trends in health-care design are evolving from a purely clinical and singular approach to a holistic practice that includes eastern traditions and environmental modification. If health-care facilities are to remain competitive in the future, the practice and design of these facilities will need to adapt to the changing values and expectations of society. To meet the diverse needs of a population seeking holistic and integrative medical treatments, the facility design will need to accommodate required equipment for various alternative therapies, as well as use environmental design to communicate a more evolved health-care system.

Identify five words or phrases that are most important to this paragraph:

_____
_____
_____
_____
_____

Now assemble one sentence that uses each of these words to convey the core thoughts contained within the original paragraph.

_____
_____
_____
_____

ACTIVITY 4.6 Thesis Statement Development

Follow the instructions to develop a preliminary thesis statement and continue this process using new sentences until you are satisfied with the result.

In one sentence, identify a single problem:

_____
_____
_____

In one sentence, identify a solution:

_____
_____
_____

In one sentence, identify a proposal:

_____
_____
_____

Now put the three sentences together to form one paragraph:

_____
_____
_____
_____
_____
_____
_____
_____
_____
_____
_____

Once the thesis or dissertation statement has been crafted, the researcher can begin to write the first draft of the introduction section. This can be accomplished by expanding upon the original paragraph by adding concrete details to each of the sentences, thereby transforming the sentence into a paragraph. Please note the following example. The original sentence said:

> Soaring housing prices coupled with limited salary increases has led to <u>increased</u> portions of one's salary to be allocated to the <u>cost of housing</u>.

From this sentence we are able to offer more clarity to the argument by simply expanding on the core thought. This expansion might look like this:

> During the past decades, population growth has had a negative effect on the economy in terms of the cost of housing and average annual salary increases for the labor force. This assumption is based on economic theories of supply and demand. Because of an increased population, the low supply of housing has caused values to increase substantially. Likewise, because of a larger labor pool, the demand for a given worker has decreased, which means that employees cannot command as much money for their services. Therefore, the increased cost of housing coupled with a decrease in salary translates to the average person allocating more of his or her monthly salary to housing. This condition is further exacerbated by the higher demand for affordable housing, although affordable housing currently has a limited availability throughout most of the United States.

In this paragraph, we have expanded the basic idea of increased housing cost, aligned it with decreases in wages, combined it with a shortage of affordable housing, and connected it to a basic economic theory of supply and demand. In other words:

- High supply of labor equals low wages
- Low supply of affordable housing equals high housing cost

The second part of our original paragraph stated:

> In order to continue providing affordable housing in the United States, a new model will need to be devised.

This sentence made a claim that a new model needed to be identified. Yet before a new model can be identified, the researcher would have to indicate that what other models have been brought to fruition and are now outdated. Consider how this is addressed in the following paragraph:

> The growing population trend continues to affect housing demands while negatively affecting the ability of individuals to meet those demands. This means that the need for affordable housing will continue to grow. One of the first ways in which Americans addressed increased housing costs was through the advent of dual-income households in the 1980s. Once multiple family members were contributing to household expenses (and in some cases still not being able to meet their financial demands), housing developers built cheap housing tracts in rural areas that many could afford. However, the increased transportation costs that resulted from living further away from employment centers led to these homeowners being back in the same financial condition. A new model of building or a new conceptualization of housing needs to be explored. Some of the social models might include co-ops, communal living or a modified version of time-shares. Some of the architectural models might include decreased square footage, decreased quality, or increased urban sprawl as a method to decrease capital investments for the initial housing development. Clearly, the architectural solutions mentioned are in conflict with current thoughts on sustainability and social ethics.

In this paragraph, the researcher puts forth social and architectural solutions and then introduces concepts of sustainability and ethics. Each of these topics will need to be identified as research objectives addressed within the review of the literature. This final sentence states:

> Through a review of past and present housing typologies, a new typology will be developed that will merge common successful attributes while eliminating attributes that detract from affordability.

Here the researcher begins to make the claim that by learning from past and present practices, a new model of housing can be devised that will be affordable. Look at the following paragraph, which is based on the researcher's original proposal:

> A possible solution for affordability may be found in the merging of social ideas for financial conservation and the practice of architecture and design. Before such a merging can take place, a thorough review of past and present housing typologies and ways of coexisting will need to be examined. Only from this base of knowledge can new typologies be explored and investigated for common successful attributes, as well as those factors or attributes that detract from affordability.

With the combination of all three paragraphs, the researcher now has the beginnings of the introduction section. This preliminary introduction will be added to the document once the methods (discussed in Chapter 7) are selected.

Dissecting an Argument

Every thesis needs an argument that encapsulates the entire research document. In many ways, it is the portion of the final document that captures a reader's curiosity. To gain a better understanding of how to develop an argument and what a reader expects to learn from the argument it is necessary to dissect the following. See Box 4.2.

To dissect this argument, start at the beginning:

> Many people experience greater learning retention when they learn through kinesthetic activities **(CITE)**.

This is a bold statement; although it might be self-evident to those in education, it will require support through the inclusion of an in-text citation or reference (see Chapter 2). Whenever the design student makes such a statement, it is advised that he or she write/type into the text "CITE" and highlight the word, thereby creating a highly visible reminder of what information needs to be found or facts that will require the support of credible sources. The next sentence:

> In the past, there were a myriad of vocational schools that catered to the kinesthetic learner, but since the 1980s, many of these schools have fallen victim to budget cuts **(CITE)** and litigation fears **(CITE)**.

also requires a citation from a reputable source because it is necessary to quantify the financial "losses" and to document the closing of numerous vocational schools. In this case, the reader would also expect the researcher to elaborate on *what* budget cuts and *what kind* of litigation affected vocational schools within the body of the document. Hence the reader might expect to see a section in the review of the literature related to the cause and result

BOX 4.2 Dissecting an Argument

Many people experience greater learning retention when they learn through kinesthetic activities. Therefore, to inspire students to learn, greater emphasis needs to be placed on the value of kinesthetic learning environments. In the past, there were a myriad of vocational schools that catered to the kinesthetic learner, but since the 1980s, many of these schools have fallen victim to budget cuts and litigation fears. } The Issue

For many young people, reintroducing vocational-style learning environments might be the only solution to combat the growing number of high school dropouts. This project will seek to address issues of high school dropout rates via the reintroduction of a vocational school model that specializes in art and design, and the role of the physical environment as an influence and support for instructional pedagogy. } The Solution

To support such a bold assertion, a comprehensive review of the literature was augmented with data obtained from key informant interviews conducted with young people residing in the proposed community and who have recently dropped out of school. This data was then combined with the data obtained from community brainstorming sessions that were intended to identify the desires of potential students, teachers, and administrators and three case studies that were analyzed for precedence as well as functional factors. The combined results of these methods were then triangulated and formed the basis for the design and development of a prototype vocational school. } The Proposal

---

of legislative policies that culminated in the loss of funding to public schools. The researcher needs to cross-reference this information with the subsequent higher operational costs associated with vocational schools. For example, the question of whether art or woodworking tools and equipment are more expensive to purchase, maintain, and secure than traditional school equipment should be addressed. In addition, the reader would expect the researcher to produce a few case studies identifying specific instances in which a school district was sued because a student was accidentally injured while using specialty equipment (refer to writing style manuals on how to cite legal documents). In essence, the researcher has put forth two arguments that he or she believes to have a direct bearing on why kinesthetic vocational learning continues to disappear from the educational system of the United States. However, with these arguments the reader is led to believe that the student-researcher will provide not only evidence, but also a solution:

> For many young people, reintroducing vocational style learning environments might be the only solution to combat the growing number of high school dropouts.

The difference between this argument and the prior statements is the complexity of the thought process. The arguments are based on fact and a one-to-one relationship. Within the researcher's review of the literature section of the research paper, the reader should be able to find statements that back up what the researcher has claimed. For example:

> In the 1980s, Massachusetts Proposition 2.5 resulted in dramatic budget cuts to public schools (Doe, 2010).

The one-to-one relationship means that the approved ballot measure MA Prop 2.5 *caused* public school budget cuts. This is a simple and easy-to-prove argument. However, the latter argument on reintroducing vocational-style learning environments is a much more complicated argument to prove and requires the researcher to extrapolate and infer causality based on a multitude of supporting facts. To clarify: it is impossible to state with absolute certainty that the reduction in vocational opportunities is the single cause for increased dropout rates.

However, one could say that students who are kinesthetic learners and whose learning styles are not being addressed in the public school system are less likely to experience academic success, which may lead students to conclude that they are not smart enough to be in school and subsequently adopt a futile perspective regarding their intellectual capabilities. Although this statement is full of assumptions and cause and effect relationships, it can be supported with a multitude of prior research findings. To show how this might work, consider the first part of the assumption:

> Students who are kinesthetic learners and whose learning styles are not being addressed in the public school system are less likely to experience academic success.

This statement might be partially supported through current trends of increased class sizes. It can also be partially supported through documentation of trends related to evaluation methods, such as multiple-choice exams versus demonstration-based exams. Next, the researcher might find additional supporting documentation showing that the most effective kinesthetic instructional methods also require low student/teacher ratios. Hence the argument could be restated:

> Increased classroom sizes often promote the use of more efficient grading techniques **(CITE)**, which has resulted in more multiple choice exams as the primary and often sole method for student evaluation **(CITE)**. Thus these trends cater to visual learners, who tend to have higher reading comprehension rates **(CITE)**, which then yield higher scores and learning outcomes.

By stating that current educational trends neglect the kinesthetic learner (who requires lower student/teacher ratios and project-based assignments) and including trustworthy sources, the researcher demonstrates the argument of learning outcomes with regard to "high school dropout rates" as a real and valid possibility worthy of design merit. In the next section, the researcher makes the following statement:

> This research will seek to address issues of high school dropout rates through the reintroduction of a vocational school that specializes in art and design, and the incorporation of the physical environment as an influence and support for instructional pedagogy.

The researcher alluded to the ability to reduce student dropout rates by developing a vocational school that specializes in art and design. Hence the reader would expect to see materials that support this conclusion, such as the results of community forums, focus groups, or surveys (refer to Chapter 9 for surveys, interviews, and observation methods). Also, because of the specific purpose of the school, the researcher must further defend his or her position that the vocational school should be for art and design and not for something else. Developing a profile of the community and the students of that community who have recently dropped out of school can justify the purpose of the school. A component of the profile might be photographs of graffiti commonly seen in that community or other creative uses of everyday materials suggesting a community invested in art and design. This particular research should also provide an indication, perhaps with a survey, that if the proposed vocational school were a viable option in their community, those whom had dropped out might have stayed in school.

The final portion of the argument informs the reader what the researcher will do in order to support such a bold assertion: perhaps a comprehensive review of the literature augmented with data obtained from key informant interviews conducted with young people who are residing in the proposed community and with young people who have dropped out of school. This data should then be combined with the information obtained from community brainstorming sessions that were intended to identify the desires of potential students, teachers, and administrators, as well as the three case studies that were analyzed for precedence. The review of the literature, in addition to the key informant interviews, will support not only a vocational school, but also a school that specializes in art and design, thereby determining whether such a need exists; this can then be regarded as the preliminary (formative) research.

Once a need has been verified, the researcher should then engage in predesign programming needs. This would be accomplished through one of the two researcher-identified methods: one that involves the thoughts of stakeholders (students, teachers, and administrators) and another that involves a case study analysis of other vocational schools. The results from these two methods should then be clearly identified and discussed as to how they informed the researcher's design of the prototype vocational school. In summation, the process of how the research argument is conceptualized, dissected, and implemented (how the data is interpreted and methods formulated) is easy to replicate when generated in a step-by-step manner as shown through these examples. To stay on track throughout the course of research, remain organized and stay on task.

LOGIC MAPPING

As the research progresses, students should from time to time take inventory of the facts they have collected and check for a logical connection to the statements made in the introduction and in the argument. **Logic mapping** is a tool that helps the student to stay focused and organized over the many months of writing a thesis. It is a graphic representation of the path that the research is taking; as a technique, it is especially beneficial to design students because they tend to be extremely visual people.

Each statement that is made serves as an independent point of contention that must be backed up with evidence (citations from reliable sources) to make connections to other issues. As a method for time management, this technique is best utilized outside of the computer, drawn by hand and displayed prominently within the study environment (such

FIGURE 4.3 Logic Mapping. This graphic shows a linear progression of a thesis idea and the documenting of the sources that will support or discuss them.
Source: Sinclair, E. (2009).

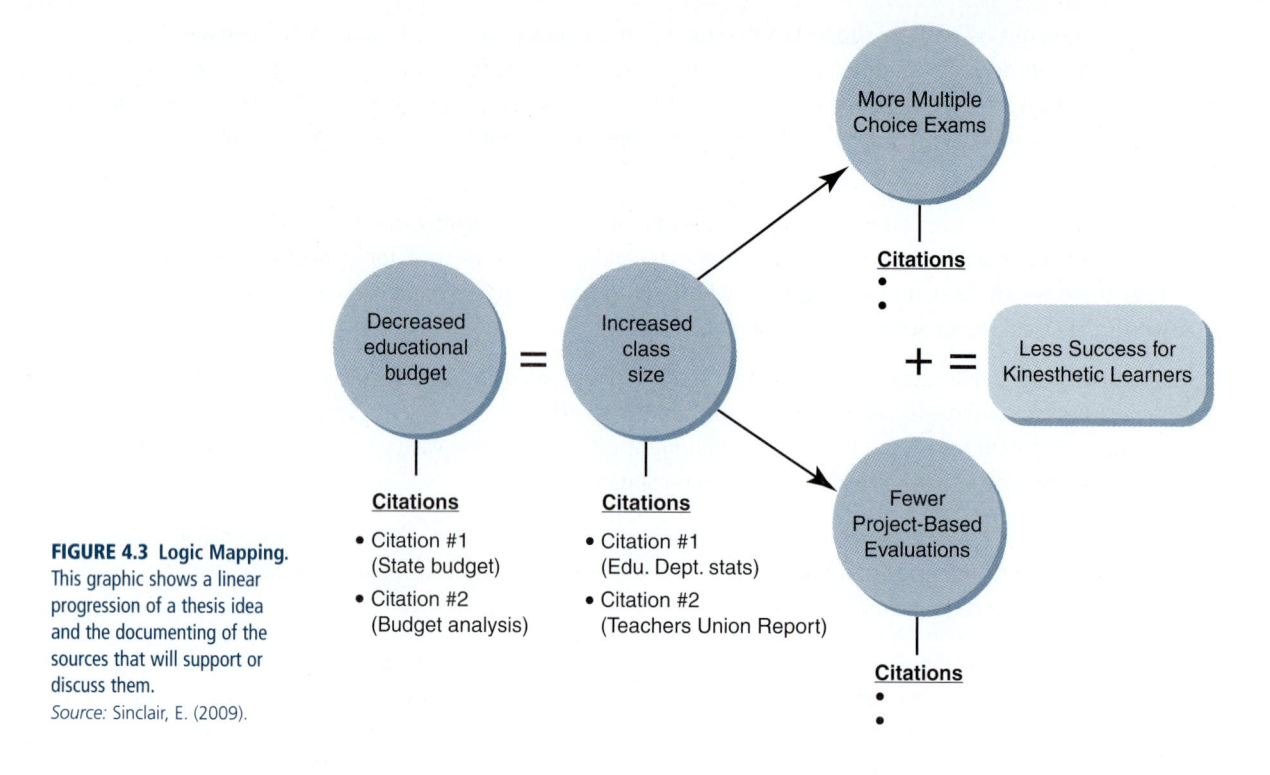

as on a chalkboard). When new information is acquired, it can be tracked immediately and areas that are "light" or lacking research evidence are very noticeable and can be attended to directly.

The procedure is straightforward: each statement or idea is written down in linear "equation form" and the citation supporting it (along with a brief description of the evidence) gets written directly beneath each item. As more and better citations are found, the logic map will grow and evolve—always serving as the road map for the research. It behooves students to occasionally take a photograph of the logic map for archiving. Use the format of Figure 4.3 to create a logic map.

Selecting Research Objectives

RECOGNIZE OBJECTIVES

The reason why a researcher should start the introduction at this point is because it will provide clear and defined objectives that will help guide the review of the literature. These **research objectives** are points within the three initial paragraphs of the preliminary introduction. Often, the premise of an argument is found in the first couple sentences, and much of the remaining statement suggests a path of logic that will be used to support the argument. Recall from previous sections that design research starts with an idea or concept and then moves toward an application. One way to identify research objectives is by looking for statements that need further clarification or arguments that need to be justified. To do this, a process similar to revealing the thesis statement is utilized. First, underline significant statements, isolate those statements, and put them into a bulleted list. Second, place an action verb in front of the statement in order to show the readers what they can expect to see in the review of the literature. To get a better idea of how this is done, analyze the first paragraph of the same fictional research project used in the beginning of this chapter:

> During the past decades, population growth has had a negative effect on the economy in terms of the cost of housing and average annual salary increases for the labor force. This assumption is based on economic theories of supply and demand. Because of an increased population, the supply of housing has caused values to increase substantially. Likewise, because of a larger labor pool, the demand for a given worker has decreased, which means that employees cannot command as much money for their services. Therefore, the increased cost of housing coupled with a decrease in salary translates to the average person allocating more of his or her monthly salary to housing. This condition is further exacerbated by the higher demand for affordable housing, although affordable housing currently has a limited availability throughout most of the United States.

The first paragraph of the introduction has the following underlined statements that require further discussion:

- During the past decades, population growth has had a negative effect on the economy in terms of the cost for housing and average annual salary increases.
- Economic theory of supply and demand.
- Average person must allocate more of his or her monthly salary to housing.
- Affordable housing is limited.

SPECIFY OBJECTIVES

The next step requires the student to put an action verb in front of each statement. This verb will indicate the depth and scope of the subject under investigation and provide a grocery list of sorts for the information the student must go find. The examples from the previous example are modified to show this technique in action:

- *Document* the population growth within the United States from the 1960s to present day.
- *Summarize* significant societal trends that has related to cost of living increases since the 1960s.
- *Review* the relationship between income and the average price of a house from the 1960s to the present.
- *Discuss* economic theory as it relates to human population and the ideas of supply and demand.
- *Track the changes* in average salary distribution for basic cost-of-living expenses from the 1960s to the present.
- *Define* affordable housing *and document* availability since the 1960s.

Note how each point is refined in the process: for instance, rather than "past decades," the choice was made to narrow it down to "1960 to present." This considerably reduces the amount of work and information that the student-researcher will have to analyze, thus reducing the chances for error or tangents. Without this parameter, the researcher would be obligated to secure data throughout all recorded U.S. history. However, these parameters must subsequently be reflected in the preliminary introduction. Note the changes made:

> Since the 1960s, population growth has had a negative effect on the economy in terms of the cost for housing and average annual salary increases. This assumption is based on the economic theory of supply and demand. Because of the increase in population that has taken place since the 1960s, the supply for housing has caused values to increase substantially. Likewise, because of a larger labor pool, the demand for a given worker is lower, which means that employees cannot command as much money for their services. Increased cost of housing coupled with a decrease in salary means that the average person must allocate more of his or her monthly salary to housing. This condition is further exacerbated by the higher demand for affordable housing, although affordable housing currently has limited availability throughout most of the United States

To some extent, the approach that a researcher takes in the research journey determines the areas where supporting data will need to be obtained. This information will be self-evident in the words the researcher chooses to describe the research topic, the way those words are assembled in the thesis, and the action verb used in the research objective. All words have meaning, and the combination of words can either enhance or alter a meaning. This is why it is important for researchers to select their words carefully. The words used to describe the researcher's approach to inquiry should be clearly articulated in the research objectives.

ORGANIZE OBJECTIVES

It is helpful for the researcher to list the research objectives in concise—one-sentence—statements. Each of these objectives should translate into specific areas of inquiry that help bring the student from concept to application. In order to see how this works in practice, consider the following fictional introduction paragraph and subsequent list of research objectives. The numbers that follow a sentence in these paragraphs coincide with an objective:

> *A society's culture and social depth are often evaluated through its art and science* **[1]**. Thus, one could argue with some certainty that all artifacts of design found in this world, serve as a type of historical record in which buildings, furniture, and other accessories and their stylistic attributes express the sociopolitical climate of an era. *However, with the advent of uncontrolled capitalism and a media-crazed "pop culture," design has become aesthetically sterile and a gross montage of fictional realities based on mass-reproduction* **[2 & 3]**. *This has led to a fracturing within the design professions between those who can design inexpensively and those who design for a temporary frivolous world.*

Design professionals have a social responsibility to provide society at large with aesthetically enriched and authentic environments. *This can be accomplished by employing greater creativity within the design process and the generation of aesthetically unique attributes that are true to their era [4]. One method to address the relative absence of authenticity within the design of the built environment is by drawing upon the human experience as it relates to experimentation, exploration, free association, spontaneity, unconscious expression, and spiritualism [5].*

The underlined sentence is the fundamental premise of the argument and implies a path of exploration and discovery. This is evidenced by the choice of the words "could argue" and "serve as a type of." These words imply the researcher's ideas and not the existing knowledge that the researcher wishes to test, experiment, or measure. Therefore, as the researcher explores the topic, new information and knowledge will be added (inductive approach) to the thesis, resulting in a document that thoroughly discusses the subject from the perspective of the stated objectives. As the previous statement was analyzed, the following research objectives were extracted:

1. *Discuss* the role of design as it represents the culture of a society.
2. *Analyze* the influence of capitalism on modern design practices.
3. *Assess* the influences of pop culture on society's expectations from design.
4. *Identify* ways to apply greater creativity that represents culture and society.
5. *Explore* the relationships between the creative processes associated with expressionistic art and the processes associated with the design of the built environment.

By using the method of adding an action verb, students can develop a clearer and more focused approach to their research. Consider the action verbs used in the previous objectives: discuss, analyze, assess, identify, and explore. *Discuss* infers greater informality and a bantering of ideas. *Analyze* takes the discussion to the next higher level, where the reader would expect the researcher to make deductions, identify strengths and weaknesses, and interject contrary arguments to ideas. *Assess* is much the same as *analyze*, but includes a dimension of viability and weighted measurement. Whereas *analyze* means to delve deep into an idea, *assess* means to make some kind of determination. *Identify* simply means to find and draw attention to something. *Explore* infers an organic process by which the student identifies a question of inquiry and gathers information from reading, observation, reviewing statistical data, and so on, all without predetermined expectations. The word *investigate* can be used synonymously with explore and assumes that the author will follow a stream of logic to see where it ends.

The action verb that affirms or declares a research objective guides the outcome and perspective from which a reader of the thesis would expect to see a line of logic in the document. This is evident by the order of the listed objectives and the desired goal the information is expected to provide, as in this example:

1. First: *Discuss* the role of design/society—to prove a connection or relationship exists.
2. Second: *Analyze* the influence of capitalism on design—to prove a problem exists.
3. Third: *Assess* the influences of pop culture on design—to measure the alleged damage.
4. Fourth: *Identify* ways to apply greater creativity to design—to suggest solution.
5. Fifth: *Explore* the relationships between the creative processes and the built environment—to tie-in to prototype development.

From the final objective, the researcher suggests an overall intention to pursue an exploratory study. When the purpose of research is to identify a phenomenon and there is little or no previous research, it is called an *exploratory study*. This type of study is undertaken to better comprehend the nature of a given problem. The ability to measure the relative importance and overall impacts of a design choice remains critical; in this situation, the researcher should produce a design that considers each of the objectives and justifies the specific characteristics and components from the list of research objectives.

DEFINE OBJECTIVES

Throughout the research process, there can be no substitute for clarity, specificity, and the use of a professional vocabulary. To truly understand the power in the meaning of the verbs, the researcher should experiment by using different verbs to clearly define the research objectives. For example, consider these statements:

"*Diagram* the movement patterns that are likely to occur within a given room."

"*Classify* the different movement patterns that are likely to occur within a given room."

ACTIVITY 4.7 Define the Objectives

Small group activity: Use your preliminary research objectives and insert a few different action verbs in front of that objective. Discuss with the group how the meaning changes.

Assess	A set of conditions from an action or phenomena can be compared. These conditions must be clearly described.
Classify	To place objects, words, or situations into categories according to a predetermined criteria.
Construct	Develop a drawing, model, or computer rendition that identifies an object or set of conditions.
Define	Generate a set of requirements used to describe an object, word, or situation.
Demonstrate	Perform a set of actions that show application in a document, model, or device.
Describe	To name all of the necessary components of an object or phenomena.
Diagram	Construct a visual representation of an idea, phenomena, or subject under investigation. Diagrams should be complete with labels.
Distinguish	Identify the difference between two aspects of an idea or phenomena under investigation.
Estimate	A probable assessment of an object or phenomena developed from extrapolation and correlation without the use of a standardized scale or measuring device.
Evaluate	A classification of objects, events, or phenomena as defined by a set of criterion.
Interpret	Translate information using verifiable and justified methods.
Measure	Apply a verifiable standard scale to an object, event, or phenomena.
Order	Arrange two or more objects, events, or variables according to a stated criterion.
Predict	Use a rule or principle to deduce an outcome or infer an outcome.
Reproduce	Imitate or copy an action or phenomena.
Translate	Transcribe one symbolic form to another.

In both sentences, the main idea is movement patterns as they relate to a given room. However, the first sentence simply requires a verbal or visual map (*diagram*), and the second sentence requires labeling (*classify*) of different movement patterns. It was the action verb that changed the meaning and expectation for the researcher and the reader. Typical tools for use when generating more action verbs are a dictionary, thesaurus, and the "synonym" function on a word processing program (for example, in Microsoft® Word, highlight the word and go to Tools → Language → Thesaurus). The following verbs and their associated definitions in Activity 4.7 may be helpful when composing the research objectives.

Once a set of research objectives has been identified and researchers are clear as to how the action verb will be manifested in the writing, they should begin reading books, journals, and other sources of academic literature. Assuming that the majority of students will be using computer word processors, to stay focused and on task the objectives should be inserted (in a different color) above each section as they are writing. Once all of the objectives have been satisfied, the researcher can delete the objectives and integrate the paragraphs so that the paper flows properly.

Summary

Much like any journey, the student-researcher needs to know where he or she wants to go before setting out. The research process is the same: identify a topic, a question to answer, and a typology—and head out. The diversity of issues and typologies within the built environment affords design researchers with an abundance of avenues and perspectives from which to research. However, any subject that is much too large to analyze in a single research paper should be avoided. An opening statement or thesis statement informs the reader about the nature of the document and what is to be expected from the research. The next statement identifies a question that leads to the research method selected to answer the question. Design studies include the physical and social sciences; the thesis statement of evidence-based design therefore provides overarching themes along with expected outcomes and possible solutions through the development of a prototype.

Design researchers can utilize multiple tools to "design" their thesis or dissertation. Concept mapping is a brainstorming tool that designers use to get all of their ideas down on paper in order to generate a topic to research. Idea mapping is useful when organizing the options available for selecting typology, spaces, and objectives. Engaging in conversations about their topic and the processes they plan to use within small group settings helps design students to better conceptualize their research strategy. In addition, to gain a preliminary understanding of their subject matter, the student may access the Internet to read relevant commentaries and articles. And finally, to stay focused and organized over the many months of thesis writing, a logic map allows the students to (from time to time) take inventory of the facts that they have collected and to check periodically for a logical connection to the statements made in the introduction and in the argument.

Once the research is underway, the ability to write scientifically must be practiced, vocabulary must be sharpened, and the final document must be succinct and devoid of any extra unnecessary words. It should clearly state the researcher's intentions and be heavily cited in order to substantiate all claims. The journey—the process of research, and the final project for many students—has an unintended consequence: it is a path toward a greater level of communication. For the design student, the end result can be nothing less than the rare designer who can articulate thought and communicate it in multiple modalities—cognitively, physically, verbally, and orthographically.

Glossary

Abstract—A summary of the main points of an argument or theory.

Area of inquiry—Theoretical approaches to a set of ideas or concepts.

Argument—A fact or assertion offered as evidence that something is true.

Concept mapping—The graphic formulation of ideas that lead to a concept.

Idea mapping—A graphic clustering of thoughts that lead to one or more ideas.

Logic mapping—The stringing together of ideas and concepts to form a logical thought process.

Problem—A question raised for consideration or solution.

Research objectives—A set of actions pertaining to a topic of research that helps the reader understand what the researcher intends to do.

Review of Literature

CHAPTER 5

> "The one and only substitute for experience which we have not ourselves had is literature."
>
> —Alexander Solzhenitsyn

chapter objectives

By the end of this chapter, researchers should be able to:

- Discern the factors of quality literature.
- Identify important attributes and the purpose of an ROL.
- Discern the difference between referencing an author and plagiarism.

chapter outline

Introduction

Assessing the Literature
What's in a Credential?
What's in a Title?
What's in a Publication?
Assessing Bias

Preparing an ROL
Stage 1: Define the Topic
Stage 2: Search and Organize
Stage 3: Evaluate and Assess
Stage 4: Analyze and Interpret

Assembling an ROL
The Introduction
The Body

Concerns and Considerations
An Invalid ROL
Plagiarism

Summary

Introduction

The next section of a thesis or dissertation is formally known as the **review of the literature or ROL**. This analysis is a critical part of the evidence-based design researcher's process. Researchers gain a thorough understanding of their subject through a comprehensive ROL. The ROL follows the abstract and the introduction in a thesis document. The purpose of an ROL is to broaden the perspectives and understandings of the thesis topic by reading as much relevant written material on the subject. Researchers often revisit and update their abstract and introduction on near completion of their study, but the ROL, once finished, should require very little revising. In the ROL, thesis students identify all relevant works and show a rational relationship between the past work of others and their own research. Isaac Newton once said, "If I have seen farther than others, it is because I stood on the shoulders of giants." To "stand on the shoulders of giants" means that the thesis student has learned and gained knowledge from the work of highly qualified scholars. The ROL is the most important part of the thesis because it demonstrates through the comprehensive evaluation of qualified scholarship that the student has a profound understanding of the subject given them by experts in their field. However, a paper without the critical evaluation within an ROL would be merely a book report.

Critical evaluation is accomplished by describing the topic in question, presenting an overview of the literature published on the topic, comparing the various authors' perspectives and findings, and then discussing the implications the information has on the thesis. This literary review also gives the researcher the opportunity to refine the topic being investigated. Generally, the ROL will go through three or four drafts before it is deemed complete. Because most thesis students are not yet experts in their area of study, the ROL also provides a perspective that

- identifies areas where research duplication can be avoided,
- exposes the student to alternative methods, and
- provides a platform from which findings can be related to the student's previous work.

The best research typically derives from an existing problem rather than simply the curiosity of an idea, a phenomenon, or a building type. In many instances, a phenomenon involves inadequate knowledge in existing research, an inconsistency or contradiction in existing knowledge, or an inadequate application of a theory. Therefore, it is best to reframe the question and state a precise problem. Through this conceptualization, the ROL can act as a lens from which the researcher focuses in on a specific subject matter. This lens limits peripheral vision, thereby limiting the effects of co-variables and tangents from distracting the student (see Figure 5.1).

FIGURE 5.1 Review of Literature. The review of the literature (ROL) gives the researcher substantial credibility by referencing the previous works and findings of authors with more expertise than themselves: "standing on the shoulders of giants."
Source: Sinclair, E. (2009).

Assessing the Literature

When beginning an ROL, consider devising a plan to evaluate all of the sources of information. In a free society, every person is entitled to his or her own opinion, yet many of these opinions appear in popular press articles. Examples are:

- Newspapers, magazines, books, flyers, advertisements, manuals, and periodicals
- Internet and radio interviews
- Television news broadcasts and film documentaries

Opinions, however, are not based on expert consensus, and as a result are deemed unreliable. In a research document, the ROL must be assembled from data that appears in peer-reviewed (also called "refereed") scholarly publications, such as:

- Journals
- Textbooks
- Government reports

A **peer-reviewed publication** can be defined as information that has gone through a blind review process in which a panel of subject-experts review (referee) the material and then combine the collective reviewer responses to either confirm or deny the claims made within the publication. Only when the independent reviewers reach a consensus regarding the material can the work be published. Table 5.1 contains a quick assessment tool to help researchers identify peer-reviewed material versus material for popular press.

Table 5.1 Scholarly Publication vs. Popular Press

Mechanics	Scholarly Publication	Popular Press
Length	Longer articles providing in-depth analyses of topics.	Shorter articles providing broader overviews of topics.
Authorship	Author usually an expert or specialist in the field; name and credentials always provided.	Author usually a staff writer or a journalist; name and credentials often not provided.
Language/Audience	Written in the technical or theoretical jargon of the field for scholarly readers (professors, researchers, or researchers).	Written in nontechnical language for anyone to understand.
Format/Structure	Articles usually more structured, may include these sections: abstract, literature review, methodology, results, conclusion, bibliography.	Articles do not necessarily follow a specific format or structure.
Special Features	Illustrations that support the text, such as tables of statistics, graphs, maps, or photographs.	Illustrations with glossy color photographs, usually for advertising purposes.
Editors	Articles usually reviewed and critically evaluated by a board of experts in the field (refereed).	Articles are not evaluated by experts in the field, but by editors on staff.
Serialization	Typically, volume and issue numbers are identified, and pagination of the articles in one issue pick up from the ending page number of the previous issue; there are usually four to six issues published per year, thus constituting a "volume," with each volume beginning on a new page 1.	Each new issue begins with page 1, and individual issues most likely referred to by month and day date, rather than volume and issue number.
Credits/Citations	A reference list (works cited) and/or footnotes are always provided to document research thoroughly.	A reference list (works cited) is usually not provided, although names of reports or references may be mentioned in the text.
Cost	Access to a single article can be purchased for up to $40.	Entire publication (all articles) can be purchased for under $15.
Perspective	Viewed as expert knowledge and valid information.	Viewed as casual opinion for entertainment value.

Textbooks are an excellent source of broad-based information; they often provide the researcher with a strong foundation, but when it comes to assembling the data needed for an ROL, textbooks are often too broad and take too long to read. This is not to say that they cannot be used, but that their use should be limited. Articles appearing in scholarly journals, on the other hand, often provide more detailed knowledge and are often written from a distinct perspective from which the researcher can analyze and select how the data might be integrated into the ROL. Also, students are typically able to read through several journal articles more quickly than a book. The more journal articles the student can review and the greater the diversity of perspectives the student can identify—the greater the likelihood that the research study will be viewed as reliable and authentic. A typical thesis should have at least 30 reviewed articles; a professionally published research document will generally have more than 100.

There are two limitations or concerns to be aware of with an ROL. The first involves the likelihood of identifying, securing, and reviewing publications that may have little or no value to the subject area. Researchers must be prepared to avoid those sources and the dreadful task of trying to fit useless information into the ROL. This section is intended to help the researcher identify good sources of literature. The second limitation is finding contemporary information. For example, information on health care written in 1953 may be obsolete in 2010; therefore, as a general rule of thumb, sources should not be less than ten years old unless the topic involves the humanities, history, or social sciences.

WHAT'S IN A CREDENTIAL?

When reviewing the content and quality of other authors' work, researchers need to consider the author's credentials. Academic research degrees generally take the form of:

- MS (Masters of Science)
- MA (Masters of Art)
- PhD (Doctor of Philosophy)

Authors who carry these credentials are more likely to have greater exposure and experience with the subject matter, as well as the research process. There are a host of equally valuable professional degrees, but these are not always rooted in research methods and practices. A few examples of professional degrees are:

- EdD (Doctor of Education)
- MBA (Masters of Business Administration)
- M.Arch, (Masters of Architecture)

It is important to differentiate between the credentials of an *academic* degree (which uses research methods) and a *professional* degree (which may not use research methods). Many professional degree programs culminate in a comprehensive portfolio often referred to as a "Capstone" or "Project Demonstrating Excellence," which differs greatly from the research methods of a design thesis or dissertation. Therefore, students should also evaluate the author's credentials from this perspective to warrant the addition of the publication into their ROL.

WHAT'S IN A TITLE?

After an initial assessment of the author's credentials, the researcher should examine the publication's title. From the title, a reader should be able to deduce the essence of the study. Unfortunately, some titles are geared toward increasing the volume of paid readership or creating sensation rather than portraying the article's substance. For example, the word "sustainable" is a buzzword commonly used in contemporary design vernacular. When it is included in a title, it may be targeting a popular reference to sustainability rather than specific examples of sustainable evidence-based designs. Another title issue is a lack of specificity or the detail needed to give a reader a thorough understanding of the subject. Consider this fictional title: *Schools and Design: The Autistic Child*. This title is so vague that it is unclear what information this paper will contain: the pros and cons of a school from the perspective of an autistic child or something entirely different. To limit the reader from reviewing a document with a preconceived expectation only to be disappointed, the abstract or book summary should be read first for an indication of its appropriateness for the ROL. In the spirit of completing an ROL in a timely manner, and as a note of caution to students as they write their own titles for their thesis document: remember that a vague title is often the cause of vague content.

WHAT'S IN A PUBLICATION?

There are different types of publications that may be obtained for an ROL. Through an understanding of these types, student researchers can better assess the value and merit of a publication in relation to their information needs. Of the different types of acceptable sources for a literature review, the following overview is what a reader can expect from a publication:

- Research journals often contain moderate detail regarding background information, questions or hypotheses, the methods used, and the results and conclusions. These publications are intended for academic scholars to review the work of their peers and to enable that work to be seen by a wider audience.
- Funding agency reports are often required as part of a research grant or fellowship. These documents tend to be very long and provide a detailed account of the subject, method, and results.
- Reports that inform policy makers and professional societies offer viable interventions based on research results and conclusions. These kinds of publications are likely to contain detailed information regarding an outcome and forecasted trends.

ASSESSING BIASES

Another criterion for evaluating the quality of literary work is an assessment of the author's arguments, as well as a balanced discussion of those arguments. The quality of literary works depends greatly on the author's ability to provide substantiated evidence to support his or her claims along with an objective portrayal of the evidence, which also includes data that may *not* support his or her position. For readers as well as writers, it comes down to fairness and honesty. **Bias** is a prejudiced viewpoint or the ability to influence an understanding in an unfair way. For readers this means that they might disregard or ignore what an author is saying simply because they refuse to think of a subject in any way other than *their* way. For authors, this means that they might choose to not include information that could shed a negative light on their research. In short, quality research literature depends on the author's ability to provide all convincing arguments and conclusions, as well as the reader's willingness to consider opposing thoughts. Another form of bias that a thesis student must be aware of is referred to as *performance-based funding* or *research funding bias*. The 2007 study of Chimonas et al. shows that research funded by pharmaceutical and food manufacturers is likely to report only results favorable to their industry. This is an example of the biggest conflict of interest within scientific research. Socrates taught his students to question everything in the pursuit of knowledge and understanding. So too must thesis students arm themselves with the **Socratic method** and *always* question the motives, methods, and especially the financial backers of literary sources. Like the students of Socrates, a design student must also exercise critical analysis skills and continue to inquire at every junction of the research process: Why? Who researched this? When was the study done? Is this unbiased and objective?

Preparing an ROL

When preparing an ROL, students must assemble and synthesize different perspectives to form a unified support system for their thesis argument. Researchers must be able to construct a compelling line of reasoning in order to support their work. To do this, the researcher must supply the reader with evidence that

- is based on reliable sources,
- is ordered in a logical and concise way, and
- establishes accurate connections to the core hypothesis of the paper.

One tool that might help beginning researchers organize their thoughts as they pertain to the review of literature is a chart with the first column stating what the researcher has learned along with his or her citation. The second column should indicate what it is that the literature means to the researcher's project. This column is unique to design prototyping. It is the implication to design that can be presented either as an asset or as a limitation to the invention. See Table 5.2.

This is an important step in the process because it can reveal factors previously unknown to the researcher. To illustrate this point, consider if a student found this fictional argument within the literature that they were reading:

> Coffee shops often serve as a "third place" for many young people. Third places are where people feel comfortable and enjoy being around other people. Perceptions of comfort are synonymous with interior spaces that are warm and cozy. Therefore, a coffee shop that serves as a third place must be warm and cozy.

Table 5.2 Organizing the Literature

Fact	Meaning	Implication
Views of nature facilitate faster healing within the healthcare environment (Ulrich, 1995).	Gaining a view from all hospital rooms is a lofty endeavor, but if it can be achieved, the people may begin to perceive hospitals more favorably.	Design Idea: Include window boxes outside of patient windows containing flowers and other elements commonly found in nature.
Common sounds found in the health-care setting can increase levels of patient stress (Doe, 2004).	Noise levels within the health-care environment negatively affects patient stress levels.	Design Idea: Install sound meters throughout health-care facilities that remain illuminated green when noise levels are low, but light up yellow when levels start getting too loud and red when there is too much noise.

The crux of this argument is that warm and cozy environments equal "comfortable," which is an overstatement and generalization that may be true only in colder climates or for certain people, but not true in warmer climates and other people. In the desert or humid climates, "comfortable" might consist of "cooler" and "harder" interior surfaces. An ROL done by the student relating to environmental perceptions could reveal other previously unknown or unconsidered differences in perceptions based on culture, gender, climate, and a host of other factors that the student must then find, add to, and discuss in the ROL.

In many respects, the ROL can be likened to a puzzle, because the researcher must review and gather copious amounts of information, then integrate it into one comprehensive section of the thesis. The ROL is about reviewing, analyzing, and assessing content written by other people. Directly quoting other authors is sometimes called "hiding behind giants" and is best avoided except to point out rare and profound statements made only by another expert author. Instead, students should demonstrate that they have critically analyzed the literature and that they understand the implications by rewriting or paraphrasing the information in their own words. When student researchers can consistently demonstrate such scholarship, they will truly be "standing on the shoulders of giants."

In order for researchers to produce a high-quality ROL, they must develop a strategy to find literature relevant to their subject and keep a record of vital ideas. Without such a strategy, a researcher might exhaust many hours in a library accumulating data that has no relevance to the subject matter. The ROL should be seen as an exponential process in four broad stages. The first stage is to define the study topic and the significant factors that exhibit a direct relationship to the topic. The second stage involves the organization and search for relevant literature. The third stage involves the evaluation and assessment of literary materials for significant contributions to the topic. The fourth stage is the analysis and interpretation of findings and relating them to the researcher's topic.

STAGE 1: DEFINE THE TOPIC

Defining the study topic and introducing the objectives indicates the depth and scope of the subject under investigation. Please review the section "Selecting Research Objectives" in Chapter 4. Once the topic and purpose of the research has been established, finding the appropriate literature is simplified (Figure 5.2).

STAGE 2: SEARCH AND ORGANIZE

By this time, students should already have a grasp of the topic and the typology that they will develop into a thesis. Recall from Chapter 4 the processes of identifying a topic (concept mapping), selecting a building or a type of environment (idea mapping), and the logical connection of the thesis statements to literary support (logic mapping). The direction the research will take was outlined in Chapter 4 under the "Specify Objectives" section. In addition to gaining a preliminary understanding of their subject matter, students by now would have also accessed the Internet and familiarized themselves with the general nature of their topic (see Figure 5.3 and Activity 5.1).

FIGURE 5.2 Step 1—Topic Identification. To identify the topics needing the information of a ROL, start by looking at your idea and how it relates to your designable space.
Source: Kopec, D. (2009).

APPLICATION — What information is needed about the concept or idea and its relationship to the application. — CONCEPT/IDEA

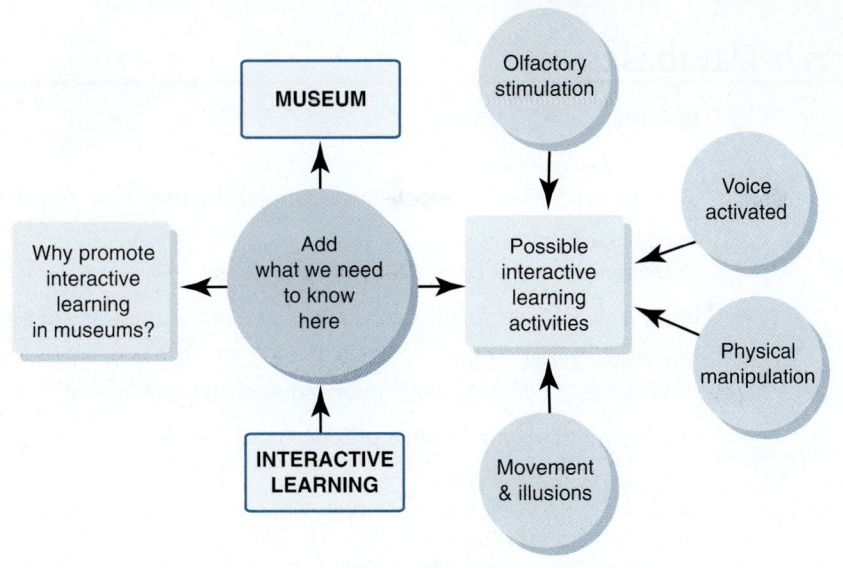

Figure 5.3 Step 2—Search and Organize. An organized search for information means outlining what the ROL needs to support thesis objectives, answer any questions readers might have, and validate the form or arrangement of the final designed space.
Source: Kopec, D. (2009).

Literature commonly falls into three major subject areas: life science, physical science, and social science. These areas can be broken down into minor categories such as:

- Art and language (history to technical aspects)
- Economics and business (infrastructure to organization)
- Community and human (urban planning to mental health)
- Cultural studies (communications to world views)
- Educational studies (learning technology to philosophy)
- Social science and human development (physiology to behavior)
- Social theory (issues: structure to processes)
- Science and technology (innovations to methodology)

ACTIVITY 5.1   Research Checklist

In order to proceed with the ROL, review this example and fill in the checklist with your thesis components to prepare for finding the appropriate literature.

	Research Component	Fill in item or statement
(example)	Topic	*Autism*
☐	Topic	
☐	Building Type or Environment	
☐	Thesis Statement	
☐	Thesis Objective #1	
☐	Thesis Objective #2	
☐	Thesis Objective #3	
☐	Thesis Objective #4	

Table 5.3 Research Databases

Category	Website
Art and Language	http://www.cpanda.org (Cultural Policy and the Arts National Data Archive from Princeton University)
Economics and Business	http://www.stat-usa.gov (A service of the U.S. Department of Commerce)
Community and Human Factors	http://www.informedesign.umn.edu (A service of the University of Minnesota)
Cultural Studies	http://www.questia.com (Online research library; subscription required after trial period)
Educational Studies	http://www.ies.ed.gov (Institute of Educational Sciences)
Social Science and Human Development	http://www.pubmed.gov (A service of the U.S. National Library of Medicine and the National Institutes of Health) http://www.ssrn.com (Social Science Research Network)
Social Theory	http://http://www.loc.gov/rr/ElectronicResources (Library of Congress database search and e-resources)
Science and Technology	http://www.adsabs.harvard.edu (SAO/NASA Astrophysics Data System)

Note: The Library of Congress offers a unified gateway into the catalogs of hundreds of other libraries worldwide at http://www.loc.gov/z3950. At http://www.scholar.google.com, quite an impressive array of titles can be found on subjects for a preliminary review (the advanced preferences tool allows you to narrow the search).

Note of Caution

(1) All online searches run the inherent risk of "forgetting" how the item was located; therefore, a list of searched words should be kept alongside the computer to maximize the search and minimize the chances of information getting lost. For the especially cautious researchers, there are also software programs available that record daily searches, phrases, and websites visited.

(2) Wikipedia is not a credible source! Read it, but do not cite it.

One of the best resources for information is still the library; the minor categories listed previously are also often how the stacks (bookshelves) of a library are organized. Therefore, if the topic of research were "advances in concrete construction," the student would most likely find the majority of his or her research sources in the "science and technology" section of the library. The next best resource for information is Internet databases. At the time of this writing, the more noteworthy databases for design students are listed in Table 5.3.

Organizing the literature can be done in many ways, and the three most popular approaches are: controversy, method, and position. Utilizing *controversy* as a way to organize the books, each source article or study that the student has reviewed must be put into one of two categories: authors that support the topic and authors that oppose the topic (see Figure 5.4).

By using *methods* as an organization tool, students put all the reviewed literature into groupings by the empirical method used to gather the data. For instance, perhaps previous research had been done with surveys, but new innovations with experimentation have opened the topic to new and compelling data. An example of this would be the study done in the 1970s on exterior pedestrian circulation. During this study, researchers asked college students for their perceptions and emotions regarding exterior pedestrian paths around their campus; the only method of data gathering was *questionnaires*. The results stated that women were afraid of small enclosed alleys and on certain pathways to parking. Nearly 30 years later, new "virtual environment" machines have been designed and built to measure a human's physical responses to an environment. A similar test was done with this new method, and the results were influential: they included findings that nearly *all* people are more cautious in alleys, not because of the shape (narrow) but because of the lack of escape routes—test participants' eye movements were recorded as looking for a way out of the environment. A similar test was done to monitor the stimulated path to the parking lot and again, different results emerged: nearly all people responded to the lack of visual information. Essentially, poor exterior path lighting and foliage that reduced the field of vision is what most people responded negatively to with the virtual paths—not the function or shape of the path. This is not to say that either study was wrong in the findings, simply that the information can be separated into different sections classified by technique or method: results by survey and results by experimentation.

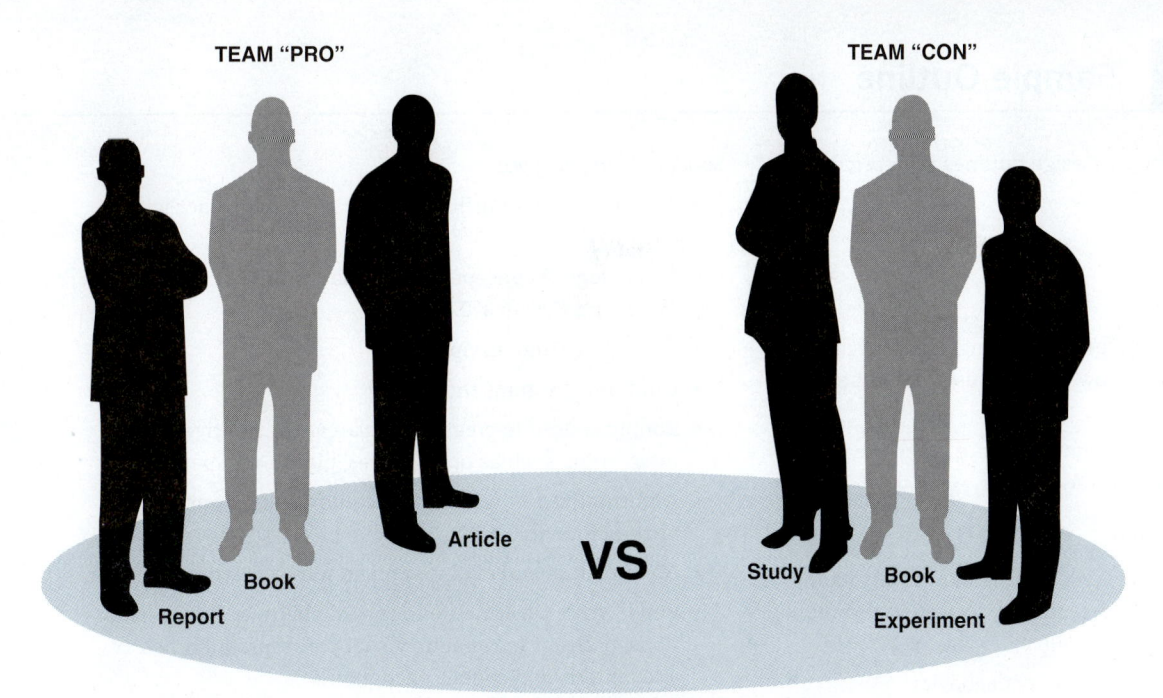

FIGURE 5.4 Organizing ROL by "Controversy". How to organize the literature by controversy within the field of study.
Source: Sinclair, E. (2009).

The next popular organizing theme is to cluster the authors by thesis *objective* or *position*. Every thesis has a position (objectives or points that they are trying to make); therefore, this chain of logic can also be used to sort out the data collected during the ROL. As the books are reviewed, they can be discussed under each new "objective" as a subheading of the ROL. In this way, the readers of the thesis will be able to keep all the background information for each point that the thesis author is trying to make topic-appropriate, thereby providing a logical path to follow as they read.

STAGE 3: EVALUATE AND ASSESS

The third part of an ROL has students evaluating and assessing each article, book, or study reviewed for a deeper more critical understanding of the literature. Questions that will help to keep the researcher focused during this stage might include:

- What are the counter-arguments to the author's points?
- What are the ideas put forth by the authors to explain a particular event or trend?
- What are the weaknesses in the authors' arguments?
- What other evidence is available to support alternative explanations?

STAGE 4: ANALYZE AND INTERPRET

Once researchers have assembled what they plan to use in the ROL, they should create an "outline" of each book, article, or material read. InformeDesign, a database developed as a joint venture between the American Society of Interior Designers and the University of Minnesota, uses a good "outline" method. In essence, what the website does is paraphrase important attributes of a scholarly piece of literature through the use of bulleted statements as they fall under the subheadings of Design Issues, Design Criteria, Key Concepts, and Research Methods. (For efficient record-keeping purposes, students choosing to mimic the InformeDesign format should also place an in-text citation and page number behind each of their bulleted statements.) For example, Box 5.1 is the extrapolated information from the article "How Architecture Regulates" written by Rajiv C. Shah and Jay P. Kesan and published in the *Journal of Architecture and Planning Research*. It is important to note that the verbiage the student uses in the outline must be an interpretation or paraphrasing and not a verbatim copy of the author's words. For details of how to paraphrase, see Chapter 2.

BOX 5.1 Sample Outline

Here is a sample of how InformeDesign outlines each piece of literature reviewed for easy access.

InformeDesign Article

Design Issues

- This review discusses the "understanding of how architecture affects behavior and how it can be used to influence particular behaviors."
- The categories by which design issues are synthesized are communication, interaction, and biases.

Author-Identified Design Criteria

- The power of architecture is recognized by scholars in architecture, geography, urban planning, sociology, anthropology, and law.
- Architecture can influence and affect behavior.
- Rejection of environmental determinism.
- School districts and parents should be cognizant of the legal standards as programs are designed and proposed for young children with autism.
- Focus on synthesizing the existing research to provide an insightful typology of the various ways architecture affects society.

Key Concepts

Communication

- Through choices of materials, colors, forms, sizes, furnishings, and landscaping for a building.
- Different cultural norms may view architecture as expressing a different communicative norm.
- How buildings symbolize and reproduce essential elements of cultural life.
- Aesthetic zoning.
- Copyright protection of architectural work leads to creative architecture. Buildings express a set of symbolic opposition and hierarchies that order societal divisions.
- Perception of organizations, institutions, and ideas.

Social ordering of space

- Architecture can influence how people interact with each other.
- Psychological concepts of personal space and territoriality (Shah and Kesan, 2007).
- Dominance and discipline.
- Land use planning and zoning.
- Zoning is used to create public areas for positive social interaction, such as open spaces, plazas, and parks.
- A normalized environment would evoke a normalized behavior.
- Architectural surveillance and architectural manipulation.
- Buildings can contribute to spatial ability by limiting locations, paths of movement, visual paths, programmed encounters, and chance encounters.
- Aspects of the physical environment including classroom density, noise, furniture arrangement, temperature, and lighting affect researcher performance.
- Crime prevention through environmental design and encourage consumer behavior.

Biased space

- Architecture is not neutral.
- Social engineering to achieve class or racial exclusion.
- Bias within the built environment can affect values such as reliability, efficiency, sanitation, environment, and safety.
- Accessibility bias, ADA.
- Building regulations affect where buildings are located, the materials used in their construction, the interior design, and the incorporation of smoke detectors and sprinklers.

Research Method

The authors synthesized existing research (Review) to provide insightful typology of the various ways architecture affects society.

Limitations

One of the difficulties this paper had to overcome was the varying different languages and disciplines used in discussing architecture.

Adapted from: Shah, R.C., and Kesan, J.P. (2007). How architecture regulates. *Journal of Architecture and Planning Research*, 24,4, 350–358.

Assembling an ROL

The purpose of the ROL is to broaden the perspectives and understanding of the thesis topic, not only for the thesis student, but also for the *reader*. Therefore, although writing a thesis may be in fact a highly individual and personal endeavor, the readers of the thesis must not be forgotten. Be kind to those who are not as familiar with the topic by formatting the thesis in such a way as to aid the reader in understanding all the complexities of the topic matter. Kurt Vonnegut (1985) said it bluntly: "Pity your readers" (p. 38). Though the format is rarely the same for any research paper, there are some general guidelines. Main sections are developed and then broken down further into subheadings

ACTIVITY 5.2 ROL Organizing

Using your selected thesis topic or objectives, write potential subheading titles for the ROL section. The objective format separates the literature into groupings that support the main points of the thesis. If a major controversy exists within your field of study, the pro/con format divides the literature reviewed into two opposing "teams." The methodology format is good when an area of research has gone through different ways of being measured. Students should be aware that these formats represent only *ideas* for how to organize their research. The information in the ROL should be written in the order best suited to get your point across to the readers.

Organizing Method	First ROL Section Subheading	Second ROL Section Subheading	Third ROL Section Subheading	Fourth ROL Section Subheading
Sample Topic: Urban Gardens *Objective format	"Foliage as Urban Climate Control" *Followed by all the literature found discussing this issue	"Vegetation as Urban Pantry" *Followed by all the literature supporting this objective	"Planters as Urban Water Filtration" *Followed by literature outlining this theory	"Vertical Garden Applications" • Followed by sources describing case-studies
Objective format				
Pro/Con format				
Methodology format				

to organize the vast amount of information the researcher has amassed into more manageable pieces. The overall objective is to as efficiently as possible explain all of the literature reviewed and discuss how it was significant to the thesis research. Nonetheless, the most basic of ROLs should include this information and follow this order:

1. *Introduce* the research question and explain how the literature was selected.
2. *Describe* how the ROL is organized and what the information intends to do or prove.
3. *Explain* each publication *thoroughly*.
4. *Combine* and compare all the reviewed sources.
5. *Discuss* the ideas and findings of all the authors and what consequences this information had on the thesis research.

How students decide to organize (sections and subheadings) the facts, study results, or authors' perspectives is entirely up to them. In order to help with this, Activity 5.2 provides a few suggestions of how to go about organizing the literature that was reviewed.

THE INTRODUCTION

The ROL is the "background information" of the entire thesis; therefore, the researcher must prepare an introduction for this section. First, the introduction should define the general topic and provide the reader with a perspective from which the literature was reviewed. Second, the researcher should point out common themes found within the body of work that was reviewed. Some of these themes or trends might include disagreements regarding the theory or method. The ROL may also highlight where previous work may have followed lines of logic that led to erroneous conclusions or identify existing gaps in the research. The third component of the introduction to an ROL is to establish the researcher's perspective by explaining the criteria used in analyzing and comparing the literature. See Box 5.2.

THE BODY

The next part of writing the review of literature is the *body*. Once several outlines have been compiled, researchers aggregate the data to prove and/or expand on their theory. Researchers can group the outlines in whatever way is most conducive to telling their story or getting their point across. Categories or subheadings can be developed according to

BOX 5.2 Sample ROL Introduction

"Relevant research established the suppression of public spaces over the last century. The unforeseen trend that stood out as the most striking was *the reduction of Americans exercising their freedom of speech*. Therefore, this research was redesigned to explore the correlation between the changes in public space and the changes in Americans "speaking up."

Several theoretical orientations or differing positions regarding the built environment and the connection to human behavioral adaptations have been identified in the analysis of the literature. This study includes looking at the changes in people, buildings and legislation while developing associations between the information gathered."

---

the method (such as reviews, theoretical, phenomenological, and case studies). Another way of clustering the information is according to conflict or controversy within the subject field. Authors and their work can be grouped by who is against a theory and who is in favor of a theory. Although the important thing to note is that the researcher needs to explain the rationale for the way in which the literature was organized. Though this rationale may have been derived from a personal motive, every desire to use informal, first-person, or vague phrases such as, "lots of," "I will describe," or "I feel" should be avoided. Utilizing specific headings even during the draft stage can help point out organization problems or problems with logic or perhaps gaps in the information necessary to prove the student's point.

Once the data has been gathered, the researcher summarizes each source's information with as much detail required to accurately convey the ideas. The tempo of the writing should be a brisk even pace, while avoiding abrupt leaps in the flow of information that might lose the reader (see "leaps of faith" in Chapter 3). The body section of the ROL provides the reader with the researcher's perspective and point of view. As such, the researcher must continually provide a **tie-back** to his or her perspective as the literature is analyzed. The example in Box 5.3 shows how the literature was used to tie back to and reiterate the thesis statement.

Like all other sections of the thesis, the ROL requires a conclusion. Here the researcher must summarize the contributions of each study reviewed and its relevance to the researcher's study. This includes contributions to the body of knowledge, weaknesses within the methodology, gaps in research, and any other issues discovered. This section should then be concluded with insight into the core hypothesis revealed from the literature and how that premise then applies to the discipline or practice of design. See Box 5.4.

BOX 5.3 Literature Summary Example

Within this sample section summarizing each book or article, the highlighted text reflects the thesis statement and closing tie-back to the thesis.

"In *Privately Owned Public Spaces: the New York Experience*, Kayden introduces evidence and examples in support of this thesis of 'private developers redefining society and the sociocultural environment' by interpreting zoning laws, policies, and incentives to best suit their financial interests. In many cases, the financial bonus these New York investors received was additional floor area, also known as Floor Area Ratio (FAR), in exchange for maintaining public spaces. Soon after construction, these developers enclosed the 'public spaces' with fences, thereby excluding the general population . . .

Further, in *Brave New Neighborhoods: The Privatization of Public Spaces*, Kohn states that because of the 'private' status of the few privately owned public spaces that still allow access to the general public, the First Amendment granting the right to Freedom of Speech is not applicable . . . thus hemming in the basic rights granted each American citizen . . . resulting in less people exercising their right to speak out against cultural injustices . . . thus private developers are effectively redefining American society."

BOX 5.4 Sample Excerpt of a ROL

"There seems to be a general agreement on housing in the United States since the 1950s being designed for economics and not for how people actually live and move within their homes (Brown 1981, Smith 1995, Jones 2003, Santos 2001), but in particular Smith (1995) sees design as a consequence of mortgage trends, while Brown (1981) puts cultural identity and zoning as main factors of a market-driven design. Although Brown's work has the limitation that it considers the data of only one city . . . its main importance lies in . . . ."

Concerns and Considerations

AN INVALID ROL

Invalid results can lead to misleading conclusions. These are sometimes caused by the researcher not being prepared to conduct the study or the researcher making careless yet honest mistakes. Other conditions that can bring about invalid results are an inaccessibility of scholarly literature or time constraints. However, the most egregious cause of invalidity is researchers skewing the data to suit his or her own preconceived ideas.

Providing solid research to a body of knowledge is important to enable the next person to build upon that work. However, if any of the research that is being built upon is flawed, then the entire body of knowledge within that stream of research comes into question. Much like a line of dominoes, once a single tile falls, a chain reaction is put into motion. Hence, we can liken each domino to various aspects of research, which include study background (ROL), conceptual framework, research objectives, overarching theme of the study, the study context, the study's methodology, the results and applications, and the conclusions. This is why the peer-review process was put into place, as an attempt to stop this chain of dominoes from falling.

PLAGIARISM

The ROL is a section of the research document that is assembled from a compilation of other authors' and researchers' work. Therefore it is imperative, that researchers work diligently to:

- Monitor and record the work of others.
- Remain vigilant and meticulous about separating the authors' evaluation of research from their own.
- Give credit to all authors by using references and citations

Giving credit not only increases the researcher's authority, but also prevents the researcher from plagiarizing. For a detailed discussion of plagiarism, see Chapter 2. For developing the bibliography section, Table 2.2 outlines both MLA and APA style.

Summary

The review of the literature is a critical part of the evidence-based design researcher's process. It is considered the background information on a subject and the foundation for the entire thesis or dissertation. Researchers gain a thorough understanding of their subject through a comprehensive reading of the experts' consensus, perspectives, discussions, and understandings on the topic. This critical evaluation describes the topic in question by presenting the literature published on the subject and comparing the various authors' perspectives and findings, while tying the information back to the student's theory. To use a metaphor, an ROL is much like the foundation of a building: without the support of literary giants, the entire structure is unstable.

Assessing and evaluating each source for the significance that it can provide the thesis is a skill in and of itself. Such is the same with the materials used for the structure of a physical foundation: poor quality materials and an untrustworthy manufacturer will jeopardize the integrity of the building. In this chapter, students learn the value of and difference between a peer-reviewed/refereed scholarly publication and a popular press piece by deciphering the mechanics of the two formats. Evaluating the author's credentials is shown to be a good litmus test of the author's experience and authority on the subject matter. The title of a book or article offers clues to the content of the literature. For purposes of filtering all of the books and articles a student will amass, a title may or may not be an accurate depiction of the content; therefore, a quick reading of the abstract or summary will guide the student as to whether to include it in the ROL. A note to students as they prepare titles for their own research paper: titles should as concisely as possible describe the nature of the research.

The ROL best serves the thesis document by being based on reliable sources, being ordered in a logical way, and by establishing accurate connections to the hypothesis. Developing a strategy to find literature relevant to the subject and keeping a record of vital ideas is the most practical way of tackling this section. Straightforward objectives and a solid topic can be researched online through databases and at libraries much more efficiently than ephemeral and ill-defined ideas. The four stages of reviewing literature are: define, search, assess, and analyze. These stages provide students with practical steps for completing a review of the literature. To explain all of the literature reviewed and discuss how it was significant to the thesis research is more easily accomplished by outlining each source in a bulleted format made popular by InformeDesign.

Continuing with the analogy of a building's foundation: masons (students) who haphazardly pile up bricks for the foundation rather than organize the bricks in such a way that they each connect and support each other is only wasting time (and such masons run the risk of never being hired again). Assembling an ROL to support the "story" or prove the thesis claims can be accomplished in a variety of ways. As each thesis has a different set of goals and objectives, students should allow enough time for reading, as well as for taking breaks from the rigors of the ROL. They should seriously consider their thesis and decide how best the literature they have read can connect and support their claims. Once the information has been laid out in such a way as to provide a sturdy and ample foundation for the topic, students can continue to build their thesis.

Glossary

Bias—Selective attention and interpretation of research or research variables the support a researcher's preconceived ideas or notions.

Invalid results—An inaccurate outcome of a study because errors or bias in the research process.

Peer-reviewed publication—Publications that have been examined by other scholars who all agree that the content accurate and has been portrayed appropriately.

Review of literature—An examination of other scholar's work in order to develop a solid foundation of knowledge on a given topic of study.

Socratic method—A form of problem-solving based on questioning and opposing viewpoints.

Tie-back—Relating new information back to the fundamental of the research inquiry.

Issues in Research

CHAPTER 6

> "The most important persuasion tool you have in your entire arsenal is integrity."
> —Zig Ziglar

chapter objectives

By the end of this chapter, students should be able to:

- Understand ethical research behavior.
- Talk openly about any bias they might have toward their research subject and offer techniques to remove this limitation.
- Have a clear understanding of which specific variables exist within their study.
- Recognize the different sampling types and the implications of each.

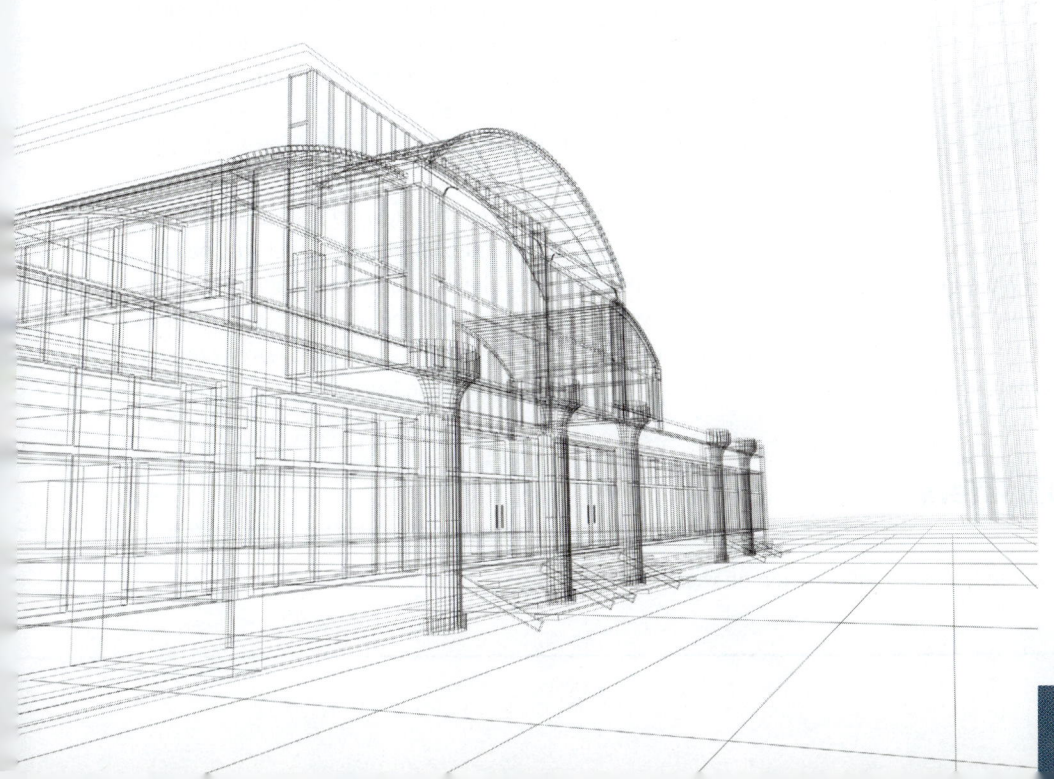

chapter outline

Introduction

Ethics

Variables

Biases

Sampling
Probability Sampling
　Simple Random Sampling
　Stratified Random Sampling
　Systematic Sampling
　Cluster Sampling
Non-Probability Sampling
　Availability Sampling
　Quota Sampling
　Purposive Sampling
　Snowball Sampling

Choosing a Sampling Method

Summary

Introduction

The review of literature allows researchers to understand their subject and to learn what others have written about that subject. The next section of the thesis or dissertation, "Methods," asks students to identify and secure information of their own. However, in order to be successful, researchers must be able to identify the boundaries of their research. Then the researcher must determine how he or she will acquire new information: in short, what method(s) will the researcher use to obtain new information? Before students begin to gather data, they should be aware of all factors that lead to greater validity, ensure greater control, and proactively mitigate any potential biases. Factors include but are not limited to ethics, variables, and biases.

To ensure validity, researchers must define and guarantee that a study will perform as intended. This can be accomplished through the control of variables that could affect the outcome. The ability of the researcher to control extraneous variables is an important part of the research process. One group of extraneous variables is researcher biases and ethics (more on this later in the chapter in the section on bias). This means that the researcher must take steps to ensure that the research and the researcher remain ethical and to limit research bias.

Ethics

The design of the built environment and the human experience is an interwoven symbiotic relationship. Just as the built environment affects behaviors, our behaviors in turn affect the built environment. Evidence-based design research examines both the design of the built environment and human behaviors so that a productive symbiotic relationship that promotes health and safety can be formed. Unfortunately, many past designs neglected the role of research, leading to catastrophic consequences (i.e., the Tacoma Narrows Bridge, the Massachusetts Registry of Motor Vehicles in Roxbury, Paris's Charles de Gaulle airport, and the Bellevue-Stratford Hotel in Philadelphia). As such, it becomes a matter of ethics to fail to conduct or pursue design research. See Box 6.1.

Within design, it has become common practice to conduct postoccupancy evaluations to determine the success or failures of a design. The intent is to identify areas for improvement, as opposed to the confirmation of predesign results. This practice uses the occupants as unknown test subjects, which can be interpreted by some (including these authors) as unethical. Following this line of logic, design without predesign research could be seen as *uninformed experimentation*, which is unethical. Of course, this is only one perspective. The rationale for this perspective is that occupants of the built environment expect the designer to know about and be able to mitigate health and safety concerns as part of the design process.

In many cases, a conundrum exists between the intended use of a building and design, and the actual way the building occupant's use that environment. A **conundrum** is a term used in research to describe an intricate and difficult problem, or a conclusion based on guessing. Conundrums can also be a result of failing to conduct predesign research. It is challenging, if not impossible, to factor in and control for every situation that might happen to a building over the course of its useful lifetime. One example of a conundrum is that buildings often have a life span much greater than that of humans. This means that we cannot accommodate through retrofits all of the advancements with regard to seismic engineering to all early twenty-first century buildings. Therefore, as much predesign research as possible is the most ethical design procedure. See Activity 6.1.

Another common conundrum within the design fields is that designers are often beholden to product manufacturers and are typically constrained by client budgets. For example, it has long been known that formaldehyde, benzene, and gases that form *volatile organic compounds* (VOCs) are harmful to human health, yet they continue to be used in new construction. This conflict is not new; the use of asbestos was a standard practice for years even with its known health risks. To illustrate, many class-action lawsuits have been brought forth recently by people who have contracted mesothelioma, a form of cancer associated with asbestos exposure. Similarly, class-action lawsuits have been made in

BOX 6.1   Design Disasters

Please refer to the following website if you would like more information on these and other design-related disasters:
http://www.matscieng.sunysb.edu/disaster

ACTIVITY 6.1 Postoccupancy Evaluation

Consider some of the implications of ethics in this example and continue the discussion to include site issues, due diligence in the profession, and other possible things that could be overlooked during the predesign phase.

Question

If someone were to conduct a *postoccupancy evaluation* in 2010 on the Chrysler Tower in New York City completed in 1930, in an attempt to identify ways to make the building perform better, would that be unethical?

Discussion

The building has been in use and people have been forced to conform to the building's idiosyncrasies for 80 years.

Answer

The answer to this question is "no."

Explanation

The term "postoccupancy" implies occupation of the building immediately (about 12 months) following its construction. Therefore, this evaluation of an existing building *for comparison or for greater analysis* is not a postoccupancy evaluation; it is a *case study*.

---

response to the uses of benzene because of its relationship to the onset of leukemia. In response, the state of California has recently mandated that disclosure notices be placed in car dealerships, gas stations, and other places where VOC gases tend to be high. Now that these chemicals are known to cause harm, how can researchers ethically conduct studies to ascertain the long-term effects? The answer is in *informed consent*. By educating employees at such establishments about the harm associated with the chemicals, if the employees opt to remain, researchers can then ask them to participate in a study to monitor the effects of prolonged exposure.

In recent years, language and guidelines have been developed to protect research participants, including **informed consent** and **voluntary participation**. This type of protection is especially relevant because researchers had previously relied on "captive audiences" for their subjects. These captive audiences were often part of workplaces, prisons, and universities. Informed consent is a process whereby individuals involved in the research process are educated about the research and any potential risks. As a matter of ethics, researchers cannot knowingly and willingly place participants in a situation in which they might be at risk of physical or psychological harm.

Even when ethical standards and principles are established, there may be instances in which the research process conflicts with the rights of participants. To help navigate the slippery slope of ethics while formulating a research method, many universities and institutions have formed **institutional review boards (IRB)**. These boards are composed of people who review thesis statements and research processes and methods to determine the ethical implications and measures, if any, that need to be included in order to ensure the safety and rights of the research subjects. IRBs are an important part of the research process because they provide a third, outside perspective, which helps to protect both the organization and the researcher against potential legal implications of neglecting important ethical issues.

Institutional Review Board

As stated previously, IRB is an acronym for Institutional Review Board. It is responsible for ensuring that all research conforms to established ethical protocols and regulations set forth by the United States Food and Drug Administration (FDA). It is composed of a group of individuals who have been formally charged with the task of reviewing and monitoring any and all research that involves human subjects. The purpose of this group is to protect humans from research that may result in physical or psychological harm, as well as to preserve the individual rights of human subjects used for research purposes. An IRB thus has the ability to approve, require modification of, or disapprove any research method that it deems as being contrary to the human condition.

Colleges and universities that engage in research often have an IRB to monitor research conducted by students and faculty. Schools engaged in limited research endeavors may opt to employ the services of an "outside" independent or institutional IRB as opposed to having their own in-house IRB. Many local hospitals have IRBs; smaller professional schools may form an arrangement with that IRB to examine the occasional research project that a student or faculty member may wish to embark on. When a school doesn't have an IRB or an agreement with a local IRB, the student or faculty member may seek the services of his or her own outside IRB.

Currently, some liberal arts and teaching colleges and all research universities require students who include human subjects in their research to first have their research method and implementation strategy reviewed and approved by an IRB. In most instances, IRB approval is required in all human-to-human situations, such as a researcher asking an individual or group of people to complete a survey, or the photographing or videotaping of people as part of an observational method. IRB approval should be obtained for research projects of any scope involving the collection or analysis of human data. The only categories of research that may not need to be submitted for IRB approval are literature reviews, hypothetical research designs, and some forms of design prototyping.

The fundamental purpose of an IRB is to review any and all informed consent forms, as well as privacy guarantees. Some IRBs have templates from which the student or faculty can work from; others require the researcher to draft his or her own informed consent and privacy statements. The IRB will vet (inspect) the verbiage and any situation in which an alternative meaning could be inferred. A signed informed consent document is evidence that the research participant knows of his or her rights, and what he or she may expect from the research process. It offers further proof that the person has agreed to participate in the research study. An IRB's review of informed consent and privacy documents also ensures that the institution has complied with applicable regulations that directly affect the institution. In total, the informed consent should:

- Explain in detail the study and its parameters.
- Allow the participant to opt out of the study.
- Provide a mechanism to respond to participant's questions.
- Ensure that the participant comprehends the informed consent document and research parameters.
- Confirm that the person voluntarily agrees to participate in the research study.
- Provide agreement that the researcher will continually inform the participant on any change that affects the research study or participant.

It is the IRB's responsibility to verify and guarantee that all study consent procedures comply with state and local laws.

Variables

Within any research project, there are factors that can influence results. These factors are called *variables*. Variables are measurable characteristics or properties of people or things that can take on different values. Variables can be defined by their nature: behavioral, stimulus, and organismic; or they can be defined by their use in research methods: independent, dependent, or constant. A **constant variable** is one that doesn't change. The **dependent variable** is the element that changes as a result of the independent variable. The **independent variable** is the factor or situation that is manipulated by the researcher. **Behavioral variables** are defined by their nature, which consists of the normal behavioral responses of an organism. For example, all life will seek out food and water when hungry or thirsty. The seeking out of food and water is a behavioral variable. Another variable defined by its nature are **stimulus variables.** These variables directly affect or have the potential to affect behavior. An example of this could be the sight of an advertisement for apple pie that causes a behavioral response such ordering a piece of pie. **Organismic variables** are characteristics of the research participant that include age, ethnicity, gender, and so on. See Table 6.1 and Box 6.2.

Table 6.1 Variables

Constant variable	A consideration or factor that doesn't change.
Dependent variable	A consideration or factor that changes in response to the independent variable.
Independent variable	The factor or situation that is manipulated by the researcher.
Behavioral variables	Defined by their nature, which consists of the normal behavioral responses.
Stimulus variables	Affect or have the potential to affect behavior.
Organismic variables	Characteristics of the research participant, including age, ethnicity, and gender.
Confounding variables	Instances or occurrences that alter the natural discourse of the experiment.
Extraneous variables	The undesirable variables that influence the relationship between the variables that an experimenter is examining.

BOX 6.2 Variables

Research Variables

By Nature	By Use
Behavioral	Dependent
Stimulus/Independent	Extraneous/Confounding
Organismic	Constant
Stimulus	

The next set of variables is defined by their use in research methods, such as experimentation. These include independent variables, which are factors manipulated by the researcher. Then there are dependent variables, which are factors measured by the researcher. The dependent variable is expected to change as a result of manipulating the independent variable. If there are no changes in the variable regardless of action, then the variable is deemed constant. To get a better idea of these variables, consider this situation. A researcher wants to understand the movement patterns of men when they first wake up in the morning. The *movement patterns* are the dependent variable. What would change the way they move might be *the means* by which they are woken up (alarm clock, earthquake, fire, pouncing child, etc.); this is the independent variable. What is constant in this situation is the floor plan of the home.

In order to establish a causal relationship between two variables, the researcher must establish that four conditions exist.

- Time order
- Covariation
- Rationale
- No other explanation for effect

The first, time order, states that the *cause* must exist before the *effect*. In the previous example, the cause is the reason the man is woken up. The effect is his subsequent movement pattern. The second is covariation: this is when a change in the cause produces a change in the effect. Hence if the man usually gets up by an alarm clock, would he bump into more walls than usual if he were to be awakened by an earthquake? The third condition is rationale, in which there must be a reasonable explanation of why the dependant and independent variables are related (i.e., an earthquake triggered a fight-or-flight response, thus making the man more aware of his surroundings). In the final condition, there are no nonspuriousness explanations. In other words, there can be no other explanation to satisfy the cause-and-effect relationship.

In addition to the aforementioned variables, there are a host of other variables that can affect research results. These are called **confounding** and **extraneous variables**. Confounding variables are instances or occurrences that alter the natural discourse of the experiment. For example, if a design student were studying into the wee hours of the night before a final exam, he or she might feel stressed and/or look unhealthy the following day. However, he or she might have also consumed coffee all night to stay awake and ate low-nutrient fast-food meals to save time. Hence, it would be hard to tell whether the stress and sickly appearance was caused by too much caffeine, poor diet, a lack of sleep, studying, or some combination of all of these factors. In most cases, confounding variables occur in situations that involve more than one explanation. In the example of the study measuring the morning movement patterns of men, a confounding variable might be one man's prior training in emergency response (as a firefighter, in the military, or as law enforcement) that causes him to respond differently than others. When humans are involved in research, there is a high probability that there will be more than one confounding variable because each of us brings diversity of experience to the research. The best approach is to eliminate as many confounding variables as possible. Hence, the results for the man who had emergency response training should be removed from the study in order to remove that confounding variable. However, it is not always possible to eliminate all confounding variables. The best way to address this sit-

BOX 6.3 Extraneous Variable Example

On the first day of phase 2, "field observations," of a research study, the weather changes suddenly for the worse, thus:

- Directly affecting the outcome or final result, or
- Indirectly affecting the outcome by adding another day or two between the first and second phases.

---

uation is to incorporate the confounding variables as **covariates,** which are factors that affect one or more of the population as a whole. Hence the student researcher would form clusters based on covariates such as occupation and training.

Another problematic feature of research is *extraneous variables*. These are the undesirable variables that influence the relationship between the variables that an experimenter is examining. An example of an extraneous variable might be the weather. See Box 6.3.

Extraneous variables are problematic because they influence the outcome of an experiment, even though they are not the variables that are actually of interest. Using the prior example, an extraneous variable might be an unforeseen thunderstorm that causes the man to wake up before the scheduled alarm clock is to sound. It should be a goal to decrease, or control, the influence of extraneous variables as much as possible, but this is not always possible because a researcher cannot control situations such as weather. See Activity 6.2.

ACTIVITY 6.2 Test Your Knowledge of Variables

This short quiz will allow students to gauge their understanding of the different types of variables.

1. A test subject's characteristics, such as sex, age, and cultural identity, are _____ variables.
   A. Constant
   B. Organismic
   C. Behavior
   D. Extraneous

   An experiment: three groups of college students are being fed different types of lunches each day for six weeks. Group 1 are all freshmen; they eat all carbohydrates (at 11:30 a.m.). Group 2, sophomores, eat all protein (at 12:30 p.m.). Group 3, juniors, eat a balanced meal (at 1:30 p.m.). After six weeks, the students will take the same literature exam and scores will be analyzed.

2. Which is the constant variable?
   A. Food type
   B. Time of lunch
   C. Year of student
   D. Time of study: 6 weeks

   During the literature exam, many of the students from Group 2 cannot seem to stay awake; it is discovered that the time between eating an all-protein lunch and the exam time is insufficient for digestive processing (four to six hours is required); therefore, the students' bodies were slowing down in order to work on breaking down the proteins.

3. How can this experiment be saved?
   A. Consider the digestive processing time as an extraneous variable and add a second exam for later in the same afternoon to see if Group 1 (carbs) have a similar digestive lag response.
   B. Remove all the results from Group 2.
   C. Assess the scores of each member of Group 2, cluster them into who has better digestion than the others, and consider them as stimulus variables.
   D. Do the whole experiment over again and make everyone eat lunch at the same time.

4. Field observational studies of how people arrange themselves on park benches throughout the day. Researchers will be looking at _____ variables.
   A. Responsive variables
   B. Sitting variables
   C. Behavioral variables
   D. Dependent variables

5. Temperature is the independent variable and water is the dependent variable; what is the situation?
   A. Water is changing the temperature.
   B. Temperature is changing the water.

Answers: 1.B, 2.D, 3.A, 4.C, 5.B

Biases

Bias is an unknown or unacknowledged variable, which can be present during any stage of research, such as during the design, measurement, sampling, or even in the choice of topics. Bias is common within research because most of us want to confirm our beliefs. Monitoring the biases in research should be a constant and ongoing process because once a bias is introduced into the research process, it has the potential of infecting the entire study. See Table 6.2.

There are two overarching biases that researchers should address in their study. The first are **internal biases,** which are typically associated with the researcher, the general setup of the methodology, or the fundamental premise of the study. The second set is called **external biases,** which result from sources that are generally outside of the researcher's control. How a student addresses bias will reveal the degree of validity of the research endeavor.

Because each person views the world from the perspective of his or her own familiarity and knowledge base, their assessment of what they experience—and how they interpret it—can result in a bias that could potentially compromise the study's internal validity. For example, a person with very strong beliefs regarding religion may not be objective when studying some phenomena (pro or con) pertaining to religion. Even if the researcher can detach himself or herself from the phenomena, the authenticity of the results will come into question. This situation is similar to the tobacco industry conducting its own research and saying that tobacco is completely safe. Most of us would not believe that research, simply because of the source of the study. A researcher should have a passion and interest in his or her study, but when the results of the study are to be used for validating a personal view, then he or she should refrain from research in that area.

Because all humans have beliefs and convictions, it is important to identify and acknowledge one's own biases towards the subject area. Of course, some biases may be founded on truth and high moral convictions, such as the relationship between sustainable design and global warming, but researchers have the responsibility to separate the *truth* of the research from their ideologies and remain objective throughout the process. Biases can result from racism, sexism, ageism, or ideologies such as politics or religion. Regardless of the source of the bias, it should be considered a *conflict of interest* and be resolved or removed.

One source of biases that threatens internal validity occurs during *selection*. In this situation, the study criteria or parameters selected are limited to those aspects that already fit into the researcher's comfort zone. For example, a researcher may decide to study a phenomenon only from a case study precedent (case studies are generally limited to one element: one person, one building, or one geographic site) and not from an empirical method (such as experimentation) simply because the researcher is unsure how to research in any other way. Likewise, the case study subject matter might come only from the referral of a friend or a site that is easily located, as opposed to researchers truly delving into the subject matter themselves to uncover quality data from different perspectives. For whatever reason, people have comfort zones and tend to avoid information and subject areas that are outside of their comfort zone. To illustrate this issue, consider these statements:

- Women may fear homeless men
- Adults may feel uncomfortable around teenagers

Table 6.2 Seven Deadly Sins of Research

If researchers anticipate or acknowledge any of the following conditions, steps must be taken immediately to resolve or remove the issues.

#	Sin	Description
1	History	Some type of traumatic event occurred that can affect results of the research (earthquake, terrorist activity, etc.).
2	Maturation/evolution	An excessive amount of time from the study to the implementation.
3	Testing	People start to anticipate answers they assume the researcher wants to hear.
4	Instrumentation	Leading verbiage or too many questions.
5	Selection biases	Selecting only those people who fit into your comfort zone.
6	Diffusion/imitation	Friends discussing or overhearing responses.
7	Compensation	Using a group of people rather than sampling one from each group.

- An ethnic group may be apprehensive around another ethnic group
- One culture may have an aversion to another culture's art

When an individual chooses to venture outside his or her comfort zone, the risk of conflict exists; therefore, care must be taken in order to avoid letting any fears or bias contaminate the results. Remember, bias is a two-way street. From the sample situations listed previously, although a woman might fear attack from a homeless man, the homeless man might fear institutionalization from the woman.

Other forms of selection bias occur as a result of data being gathered specifically from people through referral services or from volunteers. As suggested earlier, people tend to interact and use services and techniques that they are familiar with. For instance, if a team of researchers wants to entice homeless men to a shelter to study the men's level of medical and dental needs, the team must acquire data from homeless men who currently either do not use or refuse to go to the homeless shelters in their region. Data obtained from homeless men who currently use shelters will reveal only how existing medical services could be made better (because they already utilize the available services). **Volunteer** or **referral biases** also occur because people who volunteer or are referred (sent by someone who shares common interests) tend to be different from those people who never volunteer or come in contact with organizations where volunteers are needed. Likewise, there are groups of people who are more likely to volunteer their time for a research study than other people. The bias occurs because these volunteers might be more motivated and concerned about an issue at hand, or they simply have more free time in their lives to fill out long surveys or questionnaires. There is often monetary compensation for participating in a medical or drug research study. Therefore, researchers must acknowledge that the participants may not be the best candidates for the research if their motivation is money. Along with this are the differences between those who respond to research inquiries (surveys, etc.) versus those who do not, although it must be noted that those who *do* respond are generally more likely to have a greater interest in the outcome.

Many researchers have the potential to become emotionally involved in their work; this can result in **selection bias**. Often referred to as "cherry-picking," selection bias can occur with sampling techniques or the data obtained. In essence, researchers select data points that lead to outcomes that support only "their ideas." Hence, the results are invalid because the data has been compromised. Please note that the premeditated elimination of information that creates opposing views or that disproves a researcher's theory is unethical and dishonorable. A component of selection bias is **publication bias**. In a global environment, the importance of interdisciplinary exploration is paramount to the reliability of research findings. Thesis students often gain feelings of greater security by restricting their research parameters to their own discipline. Hence, if architecture, psychology, or medical students limit their review of the literature (ROL) to only their areas of specialty, they are also engaging in selection bias by not broadening their quest for information.

A form of selection bias often overlooked is called **spatial bias**. This occurs with the comparison of different subsegments. To illustrate: apartments and condominiums may look similar, but they are very different. These differences may influence the outcome. Consider the individual owners, for example, condominium owners are more likely to regard their residence with more "permanence," whereas apartment dwellers might consider their residence to be a more "temporary" living condition. Grouping these two segments together, as they are clearly "nonequivalent" clusters, leads to bias.

The criteria for selection of participants for a study is another significant source of bias that can lead to the corruption of data. One such source comes from ideas related to diffusion or imitation. This occurs when friends discuss or overhear responses made by others. Some people may be intimidated to share their ideas when their ideas differ from those of the mainstream or their peer group. Likewise, these same people may be prone to repeat responses made by other influential participants. In both situations, the responses are not reliable and can contaminate the data. Similarly, bias can occur when one or more subjects drop out of the study before it has ended, which is known as **withdrawal bias**. Not only is this likely to affect the remaining participants, but the results will also be incomplete.

Timing biases occur when the study hours conflict with specific clusters of people. For example, a focus group held on Tuesday afternoon at 3:00 p.m. might interfere with people who work 9–5 jobs; therefore, it is very likely that the study will lose a significant portion of a potential population because of scheduling. Another time-related bias is **maturation bias**, which occurs when a study extends over a prolonged period of time in which the subjects have ample opportunity to be exposed to a variety of factors that may influence the outcome. For example, a survey of hospital patients and employees might initially reveal a desire for greater cosmetic changes to their environment. But after an earthquake, the same group of people might shift their concern to greater environmental safety.

BOX 6.4 Sample Ambiguous Question

It is good practice to have several people preview a research survey prior to releasing it to study participants. This can mitigate errors by correcting them before they reach the sample audience.

"How does the room *feel*?"

One response might be:

    "hot" (*temperature*)

Another response might be:

    "hot" (*beautiful and trendy*)

The next bias is called **measurement bias.** The instrument researchers use to collect data and measure information can create problems in several ways:

- Tool may not be calibrated properly (scale, software, or hand calculations).
- Creates an ambiguous or confusing message for the participant (interview or questionnaire).
- Inappropriate tool for study purposes (thermal body scan to measure rainfall).
- Instrument contains spelling, grammar, or syntax errors (survey or questionnaire).

If researchers do not properly calibrate and maintain their measurement equipment, errors may be pervasive throughout the experiment. This also includes computer programs on which users can program equations to calculate data; one slight error while entering the data can invalidate all other results.

Ambiguous or misleading results can also occur from different interpretations of a question or line of inquiry. For example, an open-ended questionnaire might ask respondents to identify what they see when they look at a photograph of mud. One respondent might say "brown blob"; another might say "liquid milk chocolate"; and a third might say "death." Although the researcher might be able to deduce the origin of the first two responses, the third response is unclear. If the research tool had been a personal interview rather than a questionnaire, the researcher might have been able to glean more information from the subject, perhaps revealing that the subject's pet cocker spaniel died in a mud pit. See Box 6.4.

When using written instruments—whether interview questions that the researchers asks another person to administer or a survey/questionnaire—it is important to have that tool proofread for spelling or grammatical errors. An inappropriately spelled word or misplaced comma could change the entire meaning of the question and thus lead to erroneous responses. See Box 6.5.

Once the researcher is ready to implement the research tool, there are several issues that must be considered—or at the very least acknowledged. Researchers often have face-to-face interactions with lonely people that can lead to long conversations and the participants altering their responses in an attempt to please their "new friend," the researcher. On the other hand, some groups of people are highly distrustful of research, fearing that the research will be used against them in some fashion. These participants may also alter their responses in an attempt to influence the research results. Also, be aware that if the research tool is trying to ascertain incidents from the past that the participants

BOX 6.5 Sample Spelling Error Question

It is good practice to have several people preview and offer sample answers to each question in a research survey or questionnaire prior to releasing it to study participants. This can reduce errors and misunderstandings by addressing and rewording the questions before they reach the study participants.

"How do you like your *piers*?"

Researcher wanted to ask about:

    "How do you like your peers" (*as in friends*)

What the participant was actually asked:

    "How do you like your '*platform built on stilts that jettisons out over a body of water*'?"

are likely to recall *positive* events with greater precision than *negative* events. Researchers must also be aware that they may approach negative questions with greater force than other questions. This then leads to **expectation bias.** As researchers approach their study with preconceived expectations, these expectations can be transferred to the participant through facial expressions, tone of voice, or even word choices. As with any bias avoidance, the best action is to remain focused and objective and have trusted advisors review the research tools and process often.

Sampling

Sampling is a systematic process of selecting a representative group from a specified whole that possesses similar characteristics or attributes. On finding a suspicious mass or tumor on a patient, a doctor will take a small "sample" for testing; the diagnosis would be for the total mass, not just the "sample." To obtain research data on high-density housing developments, a researcher might include condominiums, apartments, and cooperatives as the same sampling. Ostensibly, this data can then be applied to designing for a greater variety of high-density developments. Data obtained from a sample is then used to draw conclusions about a subject area. There are various kinds of sampling procedures, and depending on the theoretical concerns and choice of method (observation survey, etc.), **probability** or **nonprobability sampling** designs can be appropriate in research.

PROBABILITY SAMPLING

Probability sampling consists of randomly selected elements (or people) that will be tested. The test results will then be considered the same as if the researchers tested everything (or everyone). Therefore, there is a *probability* that a small sample can represent the whole. The theory behind a probability sample is that an increase in sample size will lead to greater representation of the study's subject matter, thereby increasing the accuracy of data retrieved. Using a probability approach to select a sample can help prevent biases in the selection of study subjects, which then increases the ability for the findings to be generalized to cover the same subject on a larger scale. Although this method provides the greatest reliability, the ability to obtain a true probability sample can be time-consuming and costly. There are four types of probability samples:

- Simple random sampling
- Stratified random sampling
- Systematic sampling
- Cluster sampling

Simple Random Sampling

A simple random sample means that each element of the study is randomly selected from the total sample population (i.e., a study of iconic buildings would have to include every iconic building on the planet). Once the entire sample population has been identified, their names might be placed in a hat and ten randomly pulled out. It would be those ten buildings that would then be studied regardless of personal preference or beliefs pertaining to those buildings. See Figure 6.1.

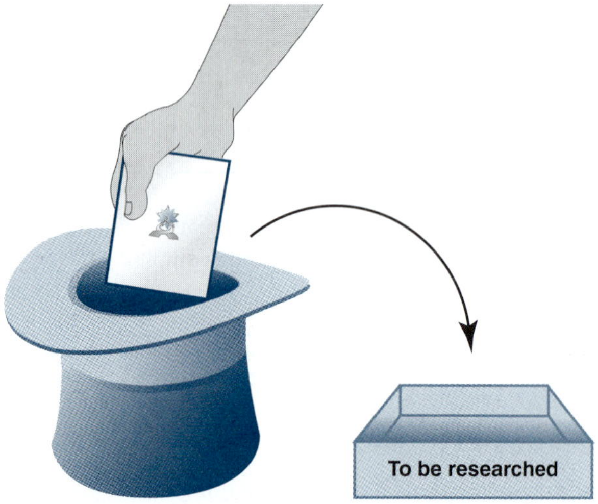

Stratified Random Sampling

The stratified sample is used when the samples require greater diversity. To get a better understanding of this, think about a researcher placing all of the folded photos of iconic buildings into a box and randomly selecting 25 photos: it is quite conceivable that all 25 photos will come from the early 1900s. (Why is it quite conceivable? Were only twentieth-century photos put in the box?) Clearly, early twentieth-century architecture is not a true representation of all iconic buildings. Likewise, early twentieth-century architecture makes up only a small percentage of all iconic buildings and therefore cannot be considered representative of the total population. To ensure a representative sample, homogeneous strata are created. In this case, each stratum (or layer) would include a single grouping such as: period, style, typology, and designer. Once these strata are formed, the researcher can then go about selecting a predetermined number from each stratum. See Figure 6.2.

FIGURE 6.1 Random Sampling. A simple random sample is much like pulling names out of a hat.
Source: Sinclair, E. (2009).

Stratum.... pick 3 from each

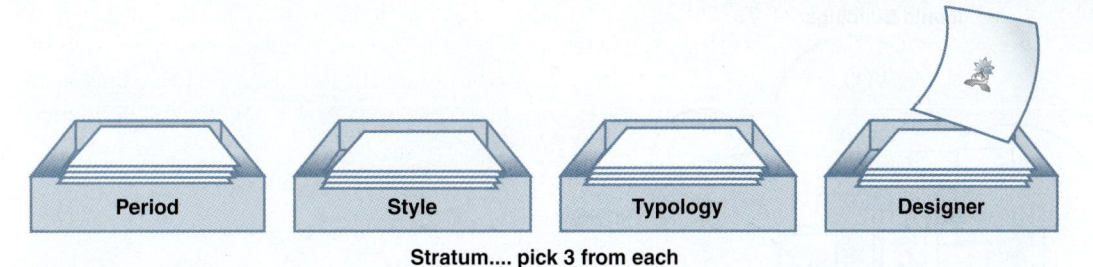

FIGURE 6.2 Stratified Sampling. A stratified random sample includes randomly selected items from presorted specified groupings.
Source: Sinclair, E. (2009).

Systematic Sampling

As the name implies, systematic sampling follows a system that selects subjects to be included in a study based on some pattern. This pattern is usually based on numbers (i.e., every other, every third, or multiples of three, all of which are noted here as "**kth**"). Following the previous example, the researcher randomly selects the first building to study. From that building, every *k*th (9th, 27th, 81st, etc.) building is then selected for study. It suffices to say that systematic sampling has the advantage of being more practical and often more efficient than simple random sampling. However, the selection of subjects for study may only appear to be random, but really still be organized. See Figure 6.3.

25 Buildings

= 8 Buildings to research

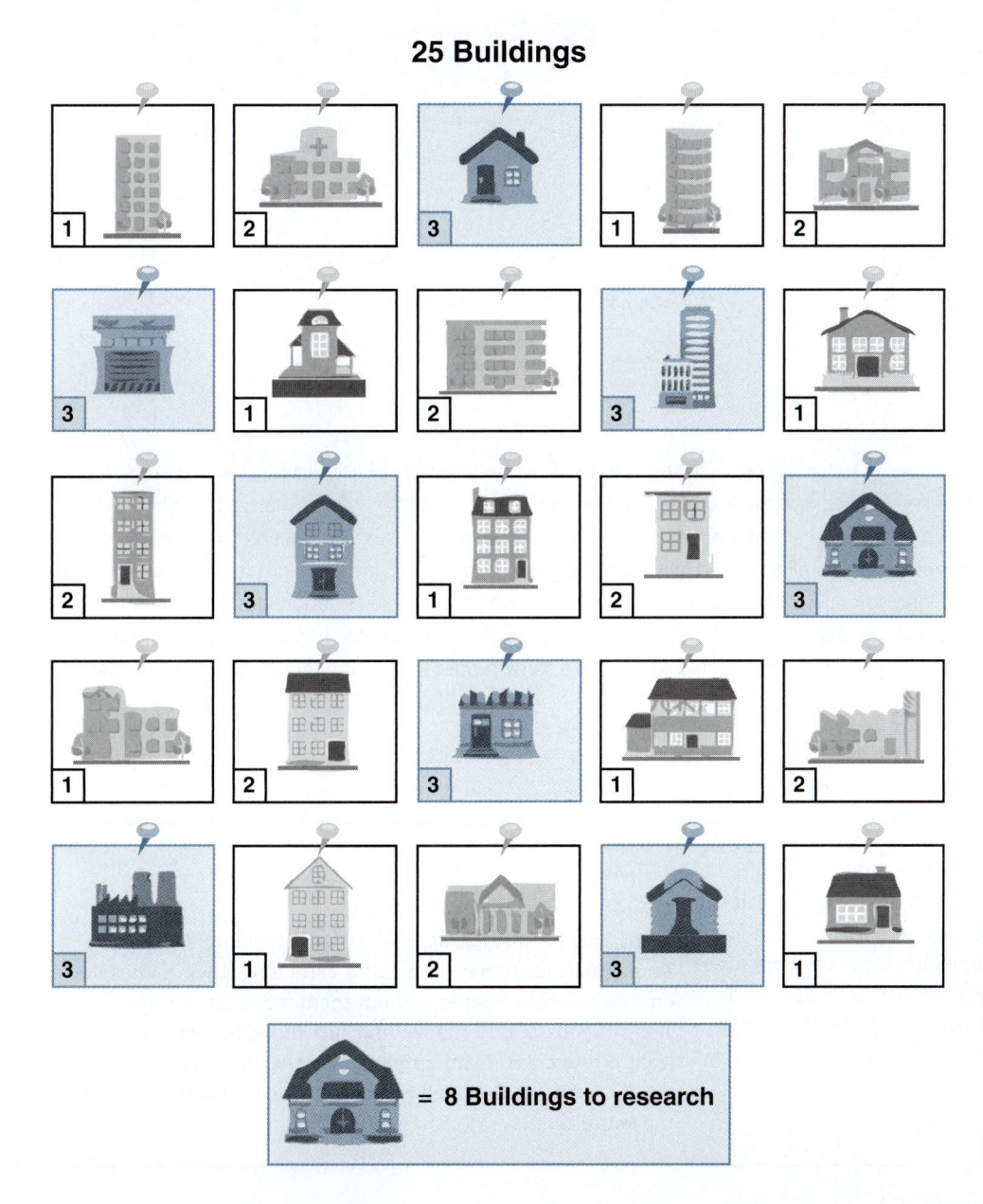

FIGURE 6.3 Systematic Sampling. A way to utilize a systematic sample. By pinning 25 building options to the wall and selecting every third one to research, the sample size becomes 8 buildings rather than 25. (You can pick: every other, first in the row, and so on.) This system works well when selecting people or specific houses to ask for an interview for your research project.
Source: Sinclair, E. (2009).

FIGURE 6.4 Cluster Sampling. Cluster sampling is a process that reduces each group to specific categories within that cluster.
Source: Sinclair, E. (2009).

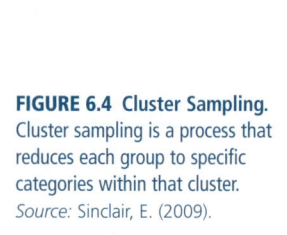

Cluster Sampling

Similar to stratified samples is cluster sampling. In short, a cluster is the assembly of like elements into groups. A cluster sample is often multileveled because the first level separates one attribute of the subject matter, but when that distinguishing attribute is removed and another appears, it leads to yet another clustering. For example, the first cluster might be iconic buildings, and then all the churches might be clustered together, which might lead to the clustering of churches by religion and so on. Hence there are always clusters within clusters. Although cluster sampling can be more efficient and provides the appearance of equal representation, the reality is that it is still possible that a representative from one of the clusters is never selected to be in the study group. Hence, the representation of the sample would be compromised. See Figure 6.4 and Activity 6.3.

ACTIVITY 6.3 Sampling Exercise

Using the sampling techniques of simple random sampling, stratified random sampling, systematic sampling, and cluster sampling, break the class into four groups of students, one for each sample type. Each group will sample the rest of the class for whatever goal they decide (where everyone was born, age, graduation year, neighborhood, etc.). The purpose is to get familiar with the process of sampling.

EXAMPLE:

The total class size is 40 people.
Team 1 (10 people) has simple random sampling.
Team 1 decides to have the entire class write their names down on small pieces of paper and put them into a bowl. A member of Team 1 pulls out 15 names and has those people come to the front of the class. Team 1 then states that the characteristics of the 15 people at the head of the class represent the makeup of the entire class.

NONPROBABILITY SAMPLING

Researchers cannot always use probability samples, due to subject, cost, or time constraints. For example, say that a research team wanted to study teen runaways. There are no records of these individuals, but obtaining a sample of respondents is necessary to conduct the research. However, the sample would likely have to be a nonprobability sample. The scientific value of nonprobability sampling revolves around *theoretical insight*. Nonprobability samples are a way to express an argument that may not have been conceived of before; researchers require a tool to better express their theoretical ideas. For example, when a researcher engages in field research, the desire may be to acquire a more comprehensive understanding of how factors might come together to influence an outcome. There are four types of nonprobability samples:

- Availability sampling
- Quota sampling
- Purposive sampling
- Snowball sampling

Availability Sampling

As the term states, availability sampling is assembled simply by the availability of elements or people in the vicinity. In this situation, a researcher has no real plan, but rather decides on elements to study at random. An important factor to remember with this tool is that the selection of samples is likely to be influenced by numerous factors that have the potential to negatively affect the reliability and validity of the results. If a college professor wanted to survey how many students would prefer turning in homework assignments via the Internet, simply walking down the hall and asking those available students is an example of an *availability sample*.

Quota Sampling

Quota sampling often uses a matrix that highlights attributes that are the same among the sample population. If we want to study important landmarks among different cities, one attribute that all landmarks in the study share might be size (i.e., the landmark building is taller, wider, or has the largest footprint compared with other buildings). Another part of the matrix would be the different known variables disbursed throughout the entire population. In the example of the landmark building, one variable might be weather conditions, because all buildings are subjected to weather in one form or another. Once the matrix is complete, the researcher reviews all the attributes and determines each attribute's representation in the total population. See Table 6.3.

Purposive Sampling

Another kind of nonprobability sample is called purposive sampling. In this situation, the researchers identify and select subjects to be included in the sample from using their "best judgment." Although this method has many flaws, it can be useful for exploration. For example, a researcher might select from various popular trends (television shows, fashion, and so on) in an effort to understand why certain designers' work resonates with society at a given point in time. Within these purposive samples, the researcher is in charge of selecting what or who will be included in the study. However, the results of studies using this sampling procedure are rarely applicable, but rather best serve as a launching pad for more research.

Snowball Sampling

The snowball sampling technique is often used when access to the population is impossible or the researcher is exploring a phenomenon that has not yet been revealed. With this form of sampling, the selection of one element leads

Table 6.3 *Quota Sampling Matrix Example*

Seventy percent of landmark buildings are tall	Twenty percent are wide	Ten percent are landmarks for some other attribute that makes them a landmark.

In a quota sample, the representative attributes must be a true reflection of what is real (i.e., 70 percent of all landmarks buildings in the world are indeed tall).

Table 6.4 — Sampling Techniques

Simple random sampling	Randomly selecting people throughout the population; it is hard to obtain a truly random sample.
Purposive sampling	The researcher uses their judgment in the selection of sample members.
Systematic sampling	Involves the selection of every *k*th member of the population.
Quota sampling	The researched develops a quota matrix (25 percent African, 25 percent Asian, etc.), then select subjects based on the quota.
Availability sampling	Takes in the responses of any available person at any given time. One drawback is that the researcher rarely can know if the respondents share any characteristics with the targeted "whole" group.
Stratification sampling	Grouping members of a population into relatively homogeneous strata before sampling. This process is good because it increases representation and reduces sampling error.
Cluster sampling	An initial sample of group members is selected first. Then, all members of the selected cluster are listed. Finally, the members listed in each of the selected clusters are sub sampled, which provides the final sample of members.

to the identification and selection of others and these in turn to others, and so on. For example, the researcher might have revealed a sociocultural development that contributed to society's embracing of the Eiffel Tower as an iconic structure. Initially, the French people hated the tower, threatened lawsuits if it was built, and called it an "odious column of bolted metal." However, within several months of its completion, it was considered the "spirit of the French." The researcher might then look at those same factors to see if they, or a variation of them, were in play when the Sydney Opera house entered the world stage and subsequently became an iconic building, and again when the Petronas Towers were completed. It is important to understand that through the study of the Sydney Opera House the researcher may have uncovered another contributing variable that cross-references with other iconic buildings designed around the same time. Hence a building or typology that would not have been ordinarily included in the sample was added because of the additional information derived from the previous. However, the time and cost can vary depending on the type of probability sample. Table 6.4 details the different types of probability sampling along with the potential obstacles.

Choosing a Sampling Method

Selecting between a probability and nonprobability sampling procedure depends on the theoretical premise of the research study and the intended tool to acquire new information. To recap, the main differences between probability sampling and nonprobability sampling are that:

- With probability, there is a chance of the sample representing the whole.
- With nonprobability; there is a chance of the sample *not* representing the whole.

A nonprobability sample is the least reliable because not everything pertaining to the subject matter can be sampled, and it lacks a true representation for the wider population. This type of sample, however, tends to be the least expensive to implement and thus can provide some preliminary data to justify further research. The following examples should aid in the decision-making process for a student considering sampling to collect data or research direction. See Box 6.6.

In Box 6.6, Example 3, the student makes the argument that a landmark should serve to represent the "identity" of the city. The first action of the student was to identify what aspects of the city that the residents of San Diego identified with. To answer this question, the student randomly asked pedestrians how or what they identified with San Diego. Although the researcher may have randomly selected who was asked, this endeavor was limited to the downtown area, thus, making this sample a *randomized availability sample*. This particular technique caused bias within the results because the beach community of Ocean Beach or the art communities of Hillcrest or the suburban communities of Del Cerro (to name only a few) may have had different responses. However, the researcher conducted the sample

BOX 6.6 Sampling Examples

Example 1: There are significantly fewer religious buildings that serve as icons as opposed to commercial towers; the researcher may use the nonprobability method of quota sampling as part of his or her simple random selection process. This might take the form of randomly selecting five commercial towers because this typology represents 50 percent of all the iconic buildings in the sample and only three monuments because these only represent 30 percent of the total sample.

Example 2: Subject matter: Iconic buildings throughout the world.

Investigation: Develop an understanding of whether social factors or design elements bring about an *iconic status*.

Sample type:
1. Using the book *Iconic Architecture of the Twentieth Century*, the researcher cuts out all of the photographs of iconic buildings along with their location and description. He or she then folds the photos and place them into an empty box. The researcher then asks a friend to randomly select 25 folded photos from the box. This first stage is called a simple random sample.
2. Because there are too many buildings in the sample, the researcher decides to narrow down the pool by using a systematic sampling approach to clusters. To do this, the researcher clusters the 25 photos according to typology, beginning with a tourist site such as the Seattle Space Needle or Eiffel Tower, continues to office buildings such as the Chrysler Tower or Tai Pai 101, and then cultural centers such as the Sydney Opera House or the Disney Concert Hall. Note that these clusters are not exhaustive and can also include religious centers such as Saint Basil's Cathedral and Notre Dame, and government buildings such as Buckingham Palace and the White House.
3. From these clusters, the researcher decides whether his or her next selection will come from a systematic sample based on the odd or even placement of a structure in a line. To ensure a degree of randomness, the researcher selects the odd or even placements based on the toss of a coin (heads odd/tails even). In this example, presuming that the coin landed on heads means that the researcher goes through the line of clustered photos and picks up the first, third, fifth, and so on.
4. The researcher then stratifies the remaining 13 photos into clusters according to continent. He or she then randomly selects one building from each continent to include in the final study sample. Note that although there may be 7 continents on the planet, there have been only 3 continents represented from the 13 photos that came from the systematic cluster sample.

Example 3: To offer a greater understanding of how sampling might work from a design perspective, the following is from a student thesis:

"World-class cities throughout the world have significant landmarks that serve as a unifying identity (e.g., Eiffel Tower, Seattle Space Needle, Patronis Towers). However, many would-be world-class cities such as San Diego lack an omnipresent landmark that serves to unify and solidify a single identity. This project, therefore, proposes the design and development of such a landmark structure that will be placed in the heart of downtown San Diego."

---

within one small area—downtown. Each of these communities mentioned should have been included in some small percentage. To expedite the process the student could have compiled a list or matrix of the characteristics of San Diego's identity, the researcher then could cluster into themes: structures, places, lifestyle, sociopolitical, and environmental. This list acts as a tool for the responses to be documented under each theme. See Table 6.5 for an example. From this point, the researcher can take photographs of objects, events, and concepts that were identified from each cluster of people representing each community. The student could then analyze those images for common attributes

Table 6.5 Examples of Responses Placed into Clusters

Landmark	Places	Lifestyle	Sociopolitical	Environmental
↓	↓	[Sample participant responses] ↓	↓	↓
The Hotel Del Coronado	Balboa Park	Laid Back	Religious Conservative	Canyons
Coronado Bridge	San Diego Zoo	Surfing	Retired Individual–Centric	Beaches
Museum of Man Steeple	Sea World	Military	Multicultural Liberal	Chaparral

and traits. Once they have been identified, the concept could be integrated into a single structure that the majority of San Diego residents would in all likelihood be able to identify with.

Another way in which this researcher can accomplish his or her goal of identifying an inspirational landmark might be to randomly select several cities throughout the world and analyze those cities for their significant landmarks. Then, through a critical analysis of this sample pool, the researcher starts to identify significant attributes of each landmark in an attempt to identify similar attributes that could apply to a San Diego landmark. Again, the researcher could cluster his or her sample pools by perhaps clustering two landmarks in Latin America, two in Asia, two in Europe, and so on.

Summary

Ethical considerations throughout the research process must be closely monitored and continually assessed. The general population expects designers to know about and be able to mitigate all health and safety concerns within the built environment as part of the design process. Likewise, the research community expects the same due diligence from researchers. As a matter of ethics, researchers cannot knowingly and willingly place participants in a situation in which they might be at risk of physical or psychological harm. Student-researchers should always get informed consent prior to testing or observing people in conditions that are outside of their normal daily activities for the sake of ethics and their research results.

Variables are measurable characteristics or properties of people or things that can take on different values. Bias is an unknown or unacknowledged variable that can present itself during any stage of research, such as during the design, measurement, sampling, procedure, or even in the choice of topics. Internal biases that are researcher-based and external biases that are outside of the researcher's control are either prejudiced or preconceived notions that may cause the research to lose credibility and the information gathered will be considered invalid. As researchers approach their study with preconceived expectations, these expectations can be transferred to the participant through facial expressions, tone of voice, or even word choices. As with any bias avoidance, the best action is to remain focused, objective, and to have trusted advisors frequently review the research tools and the process.

Sampling is a systematic process of selecting a small representative group from a specified whole that possesses similar characteristics or attributes. Therefore, there is a probability that a small sample can represent the whole. The use of sampling techniques within research is generally related to human participants and their responses. Examples include surveys, interviews and focus groups. However, the idea of sampling may be much broader and may include a sampling of cases to be analyzed as part of a case study analysis. Other examples include a sample of materials to be used to develop a cost analysis or to determine the degree of energy efficiency obtained from different materials deemed sustainable, or perhaps a sampling of different cultural icons. Hence it is important to understand that sampling is not a method, but rather a tool for securing information.

Glossary

Behavioral variables—Any elements of a research process that can be changed or are influenced by human behaviors.

Confounding—Inability to distinguish the separate impacts of two or more individual variables on a single outcome.

Constant variable—A variable that always stays the same in the experiment; it never changes.

Conundrum—An intricate and difficult problem, or in research a word used to explain a conclusion based on guessing.

Covariates—A variable that occurs at the same time as the primary variable.

Dependent variable—A variable in an experiment that is altered by a change in the independent variable.

Expectation bias—Bias towards an anticipated result by the experimenter.

External biases—An external agent that have a negative effect on the research.

Extraneous variables—An uncontrollable variable that offers an alternative explanation of the results.

Independent variable—A variable whose values are independent of changes in the values of other variables.

Informed consent—A legal condition where a person has given consent based on a clear appreciation and understanding of the facts of the research.

Institutional review boards (IRB)—A group or committee that is given the responsibility by an institution to review that institution's research projects involving human subjects.

Internal biases—Preformed ideas and preferences built into the research study.

kth—A sampling interval, also known as a skip, this system is the distance between an unknown participant or object of study and the next.

Maturation bias—When the results of a study change because of repeated exposure to the study.

Measurement bias—When information collected for use as a study variable is counted or measured inaccurately.

Nonprobability sampling—A sampling procedure in which the selection of population elements is based in part on the judgment of the researcher.

Organismic variables—Characteristics of the research participant that include age, ethnicity, and gender.

Probability—The chance, or likelihood, that a certain event will occur.

Publication bias—Reporting study results that are favorable and positive, and for publicity reasons, either not reporting or downplaying results that are negative or inconclusive.

Referral biases—Identifying participants for a research study based on participants likely to join and stay throughout the entire research process.

Selection bias—A bias in the assignment variables rather than assignment by chance.

Spatial bias—An asymmetry of perception and/or representation of spatial information.

Stimulus variables—Variables that will initiate some reaction.

Timing biases—Elements and variables that are selected and implemented based on probability of a certain outcome.

Variable—A variable is a feature, quality, or condition that can be measured.

Voluntary participation—Participation in a study or research program based on one's own free will.

Volunteer—A person who participates and/or performs work without the expectation of compensation.

Withdrawal bias—When a group of test subjects or research elements are suddenly removed from a study thereby affecting the outcome.

CHAPTER 7

Methods

chapter outline

Introduction

Formatting the Methods Section

Data Gathering and Analysis
Quantitative and Qualitative Approaches

Phenomenology and Design

Ethnography

Other Research Approaches
Mixed-Methods

Summary

> "Method is much, technique is much, but inspiration is even more."
> —Benjamin Cardozo

chapter objectives

By the end of this chapter, students should be able to:

- Define the difference between qualitative and quantitative approaches.
- Discuss the pros and cons of the various methods.
- Identify bias and other common research problems to avoid.
- Analyze and select the best method for their project.

Introduction

During the past few decades, there has been a trend within the design fields to move away from art and philosophy and toward evidence-based design. What delineates evidence-based designers from many of their contemporaries is the decision-making process. A fundamental tenet of evidence-based design is research and evaluation. The designer is thus required to be a critical thinker and arrive at design conclusions from data obtained from a formal inquiry. Evidence-based design is not about using research to simply substantiate a preconceived idea; rather, the research data should be used to assist the designer in developing more thoughtful designs. Traditional design can be summed up as "design intent," but evidence-based design strives for "intentional designs."

Because evidence-based design is becoming more commonplace in the design industry, design education must be proactive if it is to provide students with the necessary tools that will allow students to be effective professionals. Hence design education must incorporate studies similar to those that revealed how to incorporate antimicrobial characteristics into carpet fibers, optimal lighting levels for neonates, and the effects of noise on critical-care patients. To fill this need in design education, some schools and universities have begun to ask for comprehensive research projects or to include research methods into a design thesis.

To date, evidence-based design is largely used for the design of hospitals and clinics. The use of scientific and justifiable methods to reach important design conclusions often appeals to physicians and administrators who frequently demand facts, scientific rationale, statistics, and spread sheets to justify design related expenses. Evidence-based design has proven effective in justifying expenses to hospital boards. Furthermore, the outcomes of evidence-based design have been shown to positively contribute to the experiential quality of patients and their families, as well as providing more effective and lower-cost health care. In order to bring about good evidence-based design, the designer must understand the principles of research methods. As the name implies, **research** (the gathering of information) **methods** (a calculated and well-thought-out plan) are highly structured. There are many methods that a researcher can use to gather information. Careful planning and controls are needed to prevent biases and contamination of the results. There are many types of methods, and a few of them are discussed in detail within this chapter. In essence, the goal of any method selected must be reliable and the data obtained from those methods must be valid. See Figure 7.1.

Current Information: Extensive review of literature

Methods: Further testing by researcher

Discussion & Conclusion: Analysis of literature and research findings

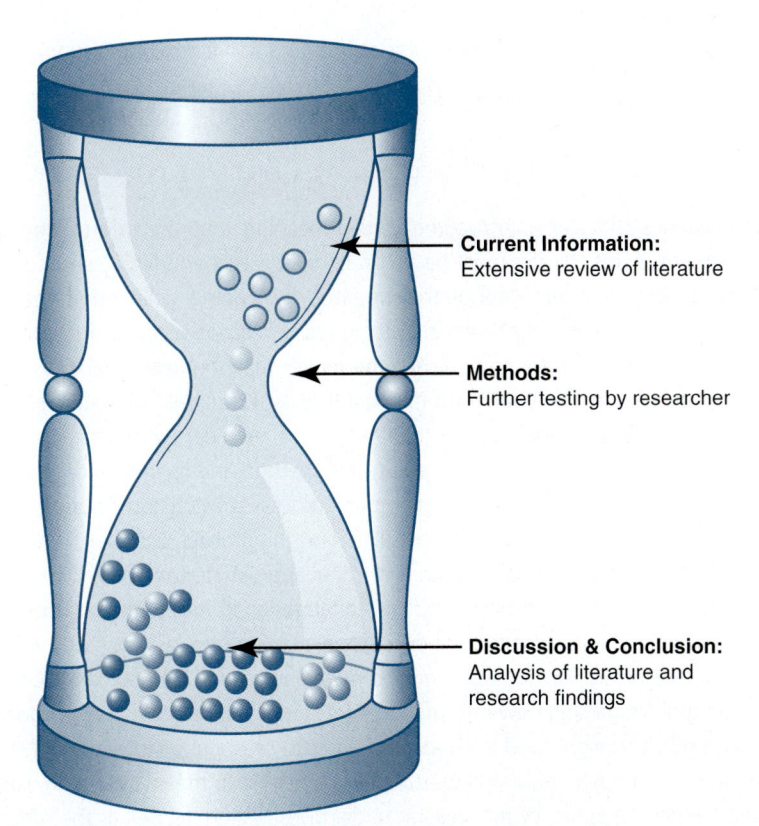

FIGURE 7.1 The Research Process. Research is much like the sand in an hourglass. Information found in an extensive review of the literature trickles down through the methods phase, where it is tested or filtered to gain a deeper insight, and finally all the information flows and mixes into the discussion and conclusion portion of the research document.
Source: Sinclair, E., (2009).

Formatting the Methods Section

The methods (also called *methodology*) section within a thesis or dissertation follows the ROL section. The proper sequencing of sections or chapters allows for a logical flow of information. The introduction establishes the reason (rationale) and basis for the research, the ROL gathers and outlines all of the preexisting credible information, and the methods chapter delineates a path and plan for adding new data. The methodology chapter allows researchers to move on, in order, to focus in on their research, as opposed to the studies of others. Simply put: it is expected that the researcher will do *something* (experiment, observation, etc.) to add to the greater body of knowledge. The result of the method then produces a set of conditions that guides the project design. The research document therefore represents the acquisition and organization of a topic's background, known facts, and new data into a format that is meaningful to the reader and the design process. The basic arrangement of the methods chapter typically follows this ordering of informational sections or paragraph headings:

1. Introductory:

    Justify the approach (*qualitative or quantitative*)

    Describe and justify the method selected (*experiment or phenomenological*)

    Explain each variable, parameter or criteria (*goal, subjects, and location*)

2. Implementation:

    Thoroughly describe how the tool was selected (*survey, double-blind trial, GIS analysis*)

    Outline controls for eliminating bias and errors

    Explain the procedure for analysis

3. Discussion:

    Explain the results of the research tool

    Discuss the limitations and strengths of the tool

    Outline possible extraneous variables and peripheral details

4. Site analysis (see Chapter 8 for details):

    (*only for theses and dissertations requiring a geographic location for design application*)

    Site: Legal description, physical characteristics, climatic survey, sociocultural perspective, neighborhood context, and environmental dynamics

    Analysis: Site constraints/strengths, site circulation, massing, connections, public/private, and so on

In order to eliminate situations that can confuse the **data**—meaning that the information gathered would lack **reliability** or **validity**—the methods chapter must be accurate, systematic, and highly structured. To help avoid possible contamination, researchers must learn about their method by reading what others have already discovered. Therefore the introductory section of the methods chapter gives a description of and justification for the selected method. The fundamental purpose of this is to convince the reader that the researcher truly understands his or her methods and is able to implement that method with minimal threats to the reliability and validity of the data. Much like the ROL, this section also requires the researcher to stand on the shoulders of giants, which means that citations are required to substantiate any claims made with regard to the method and its implementation.

The second part of a methods chapter is the implementation process. This section describes the technique (tool) the researcher used to acquire new knowledge. In order to shed light on this process, consider the following example. A design student wanting to research and design a psychiatric hospital appropriate for Doha, Qatar, selects a case study as the data gathering tool. The case study is of a psychiatric hospital designed for Southern California. Within the implementation section of the methods chapter, the student discusses why this particular case study was selected and utilized. The student illustrates that because San Diego has a similar climate and natural lighting conditions as in Doha, it was an appropriate and justifiable tool for gaining new information. The student then elaborated on how both locations have arid climates, both receive much sunlight, and both are subjected to seasonal wind patterns (Santa Ana and Sirocco, respectively). The student was thorough in giving important details related to the investigation, such as the time of day, weather conditions, and the demographics of the location under investigation, as well as the other factors that have influenced the data or analysis. However, there were limitations to using this case study. The student wrote about how Southern California has much more greenery, which decreases the volume of airborne dust (an important factor when designing a hospital) and is located farther from the equator than Doha, thus effecting natural lighting patterns and

ACTIVITY 7.1 Preliminary Method Outline

Use the following example as a guide to completing the activity with your own research parameters.

Research Variables	Method Design (Plan)
(example)	**Subjects:** Find a preexisting group (natural)—preschool class and exclude results of female subjects.
1. Male; 3–5 yrs. old (subjects)	
2. Lighting levels (cause)	**Document:** Levels of light during school hours.
3. Attention level (effect)	**Test & measure:** Attention level with picture-matching games.
4. Tucson, Arizona (location)	**Compare:** With past experiments (ROL) to rule out possible geographic differences.
1.	
2.	
3.	
4.	

intensity. Accordingly, the student outlined the controls he or she put into place during the analysis of the case study to minimize these discrepancies. Therefore the student had provided as much detail about how he or she intended to acquire the new knowledge on psychiatric hospital design for a similar geographic climate as Doha. Further, the section clearly explained how the new research differs from previous psychiatric hospital design research as outlined in his or her ROL chapter. In this way, the implementation section validates the researcher's knowledge and ability to do research.

The third part of the methods section discusses and explains in detail the results of the tool (survey, interviews, etc.). Included in this section should be a brief description of the criteria that the researcher set forth in the early stages of his or her research. In short, a paragraph or two should be written on the exact information that the researcher seeks and the criteria used to evaluate that information. To illustrate this, consider the parameters and study criteria of a design student's thesis:

Method:	Experimental (*quantitative approach*)
Tool:	Natural experiment (see Chapter 11)
Goal:	Measure lighting (cause) on attention level (effect)
Cohort/ Subjects:	Males, 3–5 years old (preschooler)
Location:	Tucson, Arizona (United States)

What gives research results validity and reliability is the act of holding steadfast to the absolute word of what the researcher says he or she will do and then accurately reporting what did happen. See Activity 7.1.

Data Gathering and Analysis

QUANTITATIVE AND QUALITATIVE APPROACHES

Quantitative research generally involves the use of numeric representations such as percentiles or whole numbers. Simply put, quantitative results are reflective in *quantities*. The data is then demonstrated with the use of graphs, tables, or charts. Quantitative approaches tend to be rigid and demand strict adherence to the facts. Because of these tight controls, the method tends to be **replicable**. This means that multiple researchers can conduct the same research method based on the same factors and arrive at the same results. Likewise, because of the numeric representation, there is little room for subjectivity or misinterpretation of the data. Instead, if a researcher felt that any limitations with this method existed, he or she would discuss and offer criticisms in the section outlining the research tool (the third part of the methods section) or within the explanation of his or her process for data gathering techniques (the second part of the methods section).

An example of research using quantitative methods is longevity studies. If a hypothetical research theory states that "a single brick will last between 200 and 250 years in a harsh climate," then one can safely assume that a building in Fairbanks, Alaska, that is constructed of brick will last between 200 and 250 years, not including other factors such as earthquakes, and shoddy construction practices. Therefore, it is important to remember that the quantitative approach provides results for certain parameters that carries only a certain probability of being true in every case and for every situation.

In contrast, a **qualitative** approach is often deemed by the "hard" sciences of chemistry and biology as being "soft," because qualitative studies are often based on self-reported data or through interpretive observations that are then reinforced and substantiated with the reviewed literature. Qualitative approaches seek a greater understanding of a given research problem or topic from the perspectives of the local population and provide context to experience. Qualitative results are in the *quality* of the information derived from study participants' responses. It is also useful when a researcher wants to identify the relative influence of intangible factors that may not be readily apparent in graphs and charts, such as social norms, socioeconomic status, gender roles, ethnicity, culture, and religion. Although findings from qualitative data can often be extended to other similar situations, the fundamental premise is to gain a rich and in-depth understanding of a specific situation or phenomenon. To illustrate, consider this statement: "Bricks influence design." The use of a qualitative method such as gathering self-reported data from a small focus group of designers and architects would be an appropriate technique/tool to analyze this statement. Analysis of their responses might identify a related theme that could be used to suggest *how* the use of brick influences design. The distinguishing factor in this example is that in the qualitative method, the synthesis of the data comes from the researchers' own interpretation and analysis of the open-ended responses, instead of from data recorded numerically, as in the case of the quantitative example. Table 7.1 is a systematic representation illustrating the differences between quantitative and qualitative approaches in research.

Table 7.1 Quantitative vs. Qualitative

	Quantitative	Qualitative
General framework	Seeks to *confirm or deny* hypotheses about phenomena. Instruments are rigid and elicit responses through a predetermined categorization. Tools generally consist of close-ended questions, surveys, and structured observations. Responses do not influence or determine how or which questions will follow (questions and ordering are predetermined).	Seeks to *explore* phenomena. Instruments tend to be open and flexible. Data is often identified as reoccurring threads contained within the responses to a series of questions. Tools tend to consist of loosely formed questions designed to evoke additional questions similar to that of an organic conversational format. A set of data will affect and influence the next phases of data gathering. Data collection and research questions are adjusted according to what is learned.
Question format	Closed-ended	Open-ended
Analytic process	To identify a numeric representation to show variation. To predict relationships. To develop a numeric description of a situation or population.	To identify with words similarities and differences. To provide a verbal description and explanation for various relationships. To describe with words and individual's experiences or the norms of a group.
Data recording	Ascribing a numeric value to various responses or observed occurrences, and using those numbers to describe a situation or phenomena. Results often lead to statistical assumptions and conditions.	Audiotapes, videotapes, and field notes are used to record conversations and events. These items are then reviewed multiple times to identify common themes. Results are often in-depth and come in the form of long narratives.

Adapted from: Family Health International (2009). *Qualitative Research Methods: A Data Collector's Field Guide. Module 1: Qualitative Research Methods Overview.* Research Triangle Park, NC: Family Health International.

Phenomenology and Design

Phenomenology is a research method that began with the philosophical reflections of Edmund Husserl during the mid-1890s and is one of the most significant philosophical movements of the twentieth century. A basic definition of **phenomenology** is the "interpretive study of human experience with the goal to study and elucidate human situations, events, meanings, and experience as they occur" given by von Eckartsberg in 1998. Within research, phenomenology is popular among artisans, designers, and philosophers because of its applicability to abstract metaphorical representations of the world. The study of phenomenology attempts to extract essential features of subjective and intuitive experiences. According to Holl (2000) phenomenology ascribes essence to experience. He believes that the complete perception of architecture and design depends on the joint nature of the material and detail that are experienced within the **haptic realm**. Because architecture and interior design have firm foundations in the arts, it is not surprising that many people within these fields gravitate to phenomenology as the premise of their research.

Haptic sensation is the information that arrives to the brain while one touches tactile surfaces. However, feeling a surface alone may not allow for an object to be completely identified; therefore, a visual confirmation gives the individual a cognitive agreement—the *whole picture*. Therefore, to the human mind, touch, sight, and experience together constitute *meaning*. The haptic realm is a core concept of phenomenology as it relates to the design of the built environment. Holl describes the haptic realm as being similar to the taste of foods being different and dependent on the combined flavors of its independent ingredients. For example, some say many meats "taste like chicken," but depending on how the chef prepared and seasoned the chicken, the taste of that meat will always vary. Holl further suggests that if a person has access to only artificially flavored foods, that person might as a consequence eventually find naturally flavored foods unappealing. Then he relates this back to architecture: if the general population gets used to being in environments constructed of fake, pressed-wood products and plastic-simulated stone, then perhaps spaces of natural materials of real wood and authentic stone might one day become unappealing. He speaks of an overall deprivation of the essence of a *holistic experience*: one of texture, material, scent, and temperature all wrapped up into one experience (Holl, 2000). However, one could argue that the built environment itself is artificial and if we were to live in caves as our distant ancestors, we would then only live in dwellings provided by nature.

Phenomena can be anything and it can be everything. As a qualitative research method, phenomenology has been shown to have great value within the various fields of psychology and social sciences. This is because the method can document the experiences of a person or a group of people in their past or present situations. In essence, the built environment has no meaning without the interpretations and experiences of the people who occupy the spaces and interact with the structures. Phenomenological descriptions of past or present feelings are often obtained through interviews, which provide for the description and discussion of meaning. By understanding phenomenology, professionals in the design fields can better understand how a client perceives space and what meaning the client gains from the environment. In this way, phenomenology can be important to the design professions because it allows the researcher to document and record people's experiences and their interpretations of space.

Perhaps the greatest strength of phenomenology is its ability to explore the interconnection between the meaning of space and objects within the cultural context by allowing language to be the vehicle of information gathering. However, the researcher must yield to the reality that language itself can be an inaccurate form of data gathering and it may be the video documentation of facial expressions, body language, and vocal tones that provides the necessary richness to the phenomenological process. Though the method has been discussed a great deal and used as a platform to engage in philosophical discussions, only a few have put the method into practice to see if indeed the design professions can benefit from phenomenology as a research method. Figure 7.2 diagrams an example of the phenomenological approach. The core variables are place and people, seen on top and bottom, respectively. For clarity no specific place or group of people are indicated—unlike a research project, in which these variables would be absolutely explained in detail. The main sources of existing information on this subject come from previous journal articles and interview results to establish precedence and/or guide the researcher. The primary types of new information will be attained by the researcher via video documentary and photo documentary (both forms of interviewing or observing). Note how the objectives overlap the information from various sources to include measuring spatial awareness, material language potentiality, and interpretation of body and facial expressions. The study will analyze the data gathered in effort to define symbology of building typology with regard to modern culture. The final goal will be the accumulation of ample data to support a

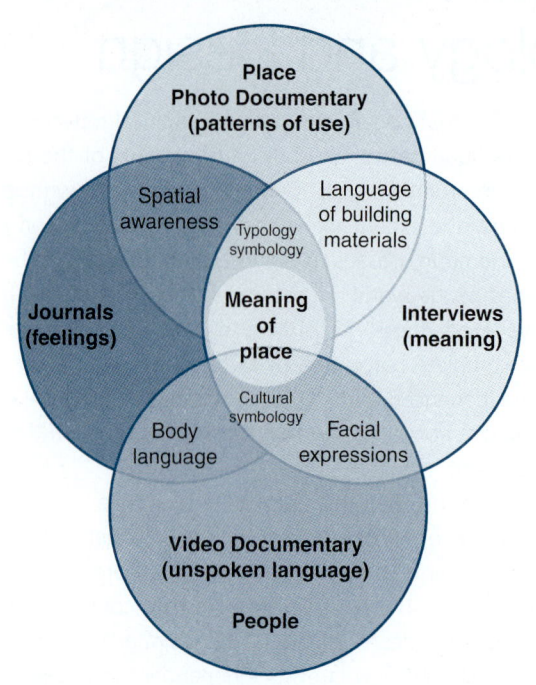

FIGURE 7.2 Phenomenological Approach. Graphic representation of a phenomenological approach, showing the overlay of information, interpretation, and meanings from several sources, all combining to develop one holistic definition of meaning of place.
Source: Sinclair, E. (2009).

relevant and valid theoretical definition of the *meaning of place*. The designer/researcher would then provide a physical representation of the thesis by developing a design project reflecting all the findings of what *people* require of *place*. See Figure 7.2.

Ethnography

An **ethnographic study** seeks to understand communication and meaning as well as behaviors and beliefs as the foundation for building a testable theory. Applying the literal ideas of *ethno*, meaning "people," and *graphic*, meaning "to write," the definition of "ethnographic" is the "writing of people." It is an ideal method for the study of people in a natural setting because it allows for the exploration of situations or events within the social context. As a research method, ethnographic studies can be descriptive or **analytical**, meaning that they can either describe a social situation resulting from some event, or analyze the individual variables leading to an event. For example, communist-style architecture can be studied ethnographically to identify the effects of architecture in supporting social control, or it can be broken into individual pieces such as the heavy masonry (language of materials) that contributes to ideological communication.

Some areas of interest for ethnographers include the use of **symbols**, **cultural patterns**, and the unspoken knowledge of family and community. Symbols are the material artifacts of a given culture, such as the art, clothing, buildings, or even technology. Ethnographic research strives to understand the unique cultural connotations associated with symbols. Cultural patterning is a relationship between two or more symbols. In ethnographic studies, symbols and beliefs need to be understood as elements of a whole. This relationship might include how members relate to various symbols and whether this relationship changes with context. Another relationship might be how the symbols contribute to learning and the passage of knowledge from one generation to the next. A third relationship might be of relative importance. In this case, the symbols might be ranked according to cultural importance. For example, the U.S. Capitol building is a significant cultural symbol. Unspoken knowledge is a culture's way of perceiving and navigating the world; it is the mysterious and profound understandings often deeply embedded in cultural beliefs. This knowledge just *is* and is rarely discussed or even consciously acknowledged by people.

Ethnographic studies are typically conducted within communities at either a macro or micro level. At a macro level, a researcher might study a broadly defined cultural group such as San Diegans or New Yorkers. At a micro level, a researcher might study a particular neighborhood or condominium association. In the design fields, ethnography can inform the designer of common uses, practices, and needs of people within given spaces. It is a method that allows designers to discover what a group of people do and why. One key component to ethnographic studies is the continual evolution of the researcher's initial theory. As a research process, authors Schensul and Le Compte identify the most common uses of ethnographic studies, including the following

1. Definition of an issue or problem when it is not clear
2. Identification and scope of the problem, including
   - settings,
   - people, and
   - predominant stakeholders.
3. Exploration of factors contributing or associated with an issue or problem
4. Description or explanation of unexpected or unanticipated outcomes
5. Identification of common characteristics that compare with a target population

For example, consider a mixed-used development that remains vacant after a year of being opened. The conclusion is that no one wants to purchase the condominiums or rent out the commercial space. In this situation, an ethnographic study may be used to analyze why the community is resisting the new development or why the development is not attracting new people or businesses into the community.

The primary tools used to collect ethnographic data are **interviews** and **observations**. Interviews are formal documented discussions between people for the purpose of asking questions and recording responses. They are often conducted several times with an established group of people who have been selected because they are known and respected residents within the community. Repeated interviews are used to compare information obtained from previous interviews or interviews done with other members of the community. This data is then cross-referenced with other data obtained from a ROL pertaining to the population and to the situation under investigation, and related to the variables of interest. This cross-referencing is done to elucidate an idea or bring greater clarity to an issue of interest.

When using interviews to acquire information, the researcher must first explore the topic in detail so that he or she can obtain a solid background on the issues at hand. This information will aid in the development of appropriate and probing questions. The interviews should be audio- or video-recorded for ethical and legal reasons, and it is good practice for the researcher to get the respondent's approval prior to being recorded. In an ethnographic study, the use of open-ended questions is preferred so that further exploration can be conducted in an area of interest. See Box 7.1.

Another method of gaining knowledge for an ethnographic study is observation. This method often involves a researcher watching or participating in a community or family for an extended period of time. Within observation studies (also discussed in Chapter 9), there are two primary modes of information gathering. One is **direct observation**, in which the researcher simply becomes part of the background while observing and recording actions and behaviors. The second is **participant observation**, in which the researcher becomes involved in and records the activities being investigated over an extended period of time. It is not unusual for an ethnographic researcher to live in the community or with a family for months or even years before gaining an accurate perspective of the different situations and events. From this immersion, the researcher is able to gain access to information and experiences that might be available only from within the community. The longer a researcher observes, the more in-depth information he or she will

BOX 7.1 Close-ended vs. Open-ended Questions

	Close-ended question (measuring)	*Open-ended question* (analyzing)
	What color is your car? Did you have a good day? When did you move here?	What do you *think* about the new building? *Tell* me about your day. How do you *feel* about this street?
Goal:	Single-word or short responses	Full and meaningful responses

BOX 7.2 Journal Excerpts

Person 1	Person 2	Person 3
On Saturday I woke up at 8:30 a.m. I turned on the coffee maker, booted up my laptop, and proceeded to feed the dog and load the dishwasher with dirty dishes from the night before. Once the coffee finished brewing, I poured myself a cup, grabbed my laptop, and got back into bed, where I drank my coffee and read the daily news . . .	Today, Saturday, I started my day early. At 7:00 a.m., I made a quick cup of coffee. I drink instant coffee, so I heated up the water in the microwave and made my coffee. Then I threw on an old sweatshirt and pair of jeans, and went out to the garden. I sat on the edge of garden drinking my coffee and admiring my tomatoes. When I was done . . .	The darn neighbors woke me up early today (9:00 a.m.) by playing their rap music too loud. Knowing that I couldn't go back to sleep, I got up and threw on some clothes that didn't smell too bad and went downstairs to the coffee shop. The line wasn't too long, so I got my latte fast. I sat down at a curbside table and watched people walk by as I drank my latte. I noticed . . .

Commonalities: Sitting and drinking coffee.
Differences: Person 3 got his coffee somewhere other than home. There are suggestions that Person 3 lives in a high-density residential complex. There is no evidence in statements from Persons 1 and 2 as what kind of housing they reside in.

---

glean for the research. However, a common issue with participant observation is the loss of objectivity. **Scientific objectivity** maintains that researchers must remain impartial and unprejudiced when reporting their findings without drawing any assumptions or casting their beliefs onto the conclusions. The researcher must state the facts, and only the facts. Interpreting and documenting the results can be problematic with an increasingly personal connection to a group of people or to a design solution. Hence in an ethnographic study, the acquisition of data is obtained from:

- Watching what happens
- Listening to what people say
- Asking many strategic questions

Another approach to gathering ethnographic research is the process of **self-report journaling**. This method requires that the participants keep a journal of comments regarding a variety of events for a predetermined period of time. A benefit to this approach is that it allows for the recording of the participant's expressions of emotion, which may not otherwise be detectable through external observation. When participants are journaling, a source of concern is that they can censor, omit, or lie about what they include in their journals. At the end of a predetermined time, the researcher collects the journals and reads through them to identify common themes. See Box 7.2 for an example of a common theme.

The process of analyzing an ethnographic method includes the researcher's initial interpretations, preliminary analysis, reflection, and the development of new questions to be explored. First, the data should be organized around a conceptual framework of the questions that arose at the beginning of the study. Second, the data should be inserted into a framework from which the researcher can support the analysis and thus draw conclusions. A technique to do this includes separating the data into conceptual categories. Examples might include the use of water, recycling practices, and energy uses. To see how this might look, consider the following: "The subject begins his day by brushing his teeth. Despite repeated efforts to get the subject to turn the water off while brushing his teeth, all efforts fail and the water runs constantly for five minutes every morning." From this standpoint (water conservation), the researcher could also catalog other water-related habits: toilet flushing, laundry, dish washing, and watering the yard. This data can then be compared with other categories to determine an overall predisposition for conservation, as well as integrated and/or supported with results from other methods (i.e., surveys or experimentation).

Data analysis and theory development come at the end of the research. From the acquired data, the researcher develops theories from the perspectives of the members to avoid theoretical preconceptions. When writing the analysis and discussion of the information obtained from ethnographic studies, researchers must assemble an analytical narrative that discusses the information obtained, along with its implications. This narrative may include written vignettes similar to the one described previously or detailed descriptions of events or situations. The databases for ethnography usually consist of extensive descriptions of the details of social life or cultural phenomena in a small number of cases. A common flaw for beginning researchers is the failure to provide a level of

ACTIVITY 7.2 Match the Terms and Ideas

Term	Idea
Descriptive ethnographic approach	Material artifacts of a given culture
Analytical ethnographic approach	Stating the facts without personal opinion
Cultural patterning	Watching people for a period of time
Symbols	Analyzes individual variables
Interviews	Researcher's presence affect subject's behavior
Observation	Researcher observes and participants
Direct observation	Describes a social situation
Scientific objectivity	Formal discussions
Participant observation	Researcher observes in the background
Self-report journaling	Relationship between two or more symbols

extensive detail within the narrative that is required for analysis. At this juncture, the researcher should take a moment to test his or her understanding of the basic ideas of each research term outlined so far. See Activity 7.2.

Other Research Approaches

There are many different ways to pursue research. How students approach their research depends on their goals. Some of the more common research approaches include descriptive, correlation, causal–comparative, and experimental methods. The supporting premise for each of these approaches is the idea of quantitative or qualitative analysis. Once researchers decide on a research approach, they should decide how the data will be analyzed and discussed.

A **descriptive approach** to research strives to describe a situation or phenomena statistically (quantitative) with numbers or through detailed narratives (qualitative). What is important about descriptive research is that it does not attempt to identify causes or solutions. It only describes. This method is ideal when developing occupant profiles or gaining a deeper understanding into a situation or phenomena. A designer might engage in descriptive research in order to gain a better understanding—for example, of what the daily job duties of a nurse consists of, as well as identify the common concerns within that profession.

When researchers are attempting to identify the relationship between two variables, such as the level of lighting and a nurse's behavior, they are engaging in a **correlational research** approach. However, caution should be exercised when highlighting a relationship between two variables because the apparent relationship may not be in response to a change in the other observed variable. For example, anger displayed by a nurse may have occurred when the lighting conditions were bright, but the lighting may not be related to the anger. Once a relationship has been established, such as low levels of lighting and the incidences of patient chart errors, then further predictions can be made. A prediction from this correlation might state, "Low levels of lighting negatively affect the review of contracts in a law office." Note that the correlation implies predictions and potential relationships—not causation.

Another type of research is **causal–comparative**. This form of study looks for direct cause-effect relationships between the study's variables in an extremely static manner. Typically, the variables are events in the past and the researcher has no control over either. This approach demands the identification of a **causal–comparative independent variable** and the recording of its effect on another identified **causal–comparative dependent variable**. The causal–comparative study, however, differs from experimental approaches because the independent variable is *not* under the experimenter's control and the researcher must accept the values of the independent variable as they come. If a researcher had power to control the independent variable, then this research would be an *experimental research*, which is defined in the next paragraph. To emphasize this difference between independent variables of the causal–comparative approach and the experimental approach, see Box 7.3. Considering one's desire to study the socioeconomic status of a group (an independent variable, because the researcher cannot change who these people are) and how it

BOX 7.3 — Causal–Comparative Research vs. Experimental Research

Causal–Comparative		Experimental	
Independent Variable	Dependent Variable	Independent Variable	Dependent Variable
(Input)	(Output)	(Input)	(Output)
Not controlled		**Controlled**	
Socioeconomic status	Student GPAs	Time watching television	Student GPAs

affects the GPA of the group's students (dependent variable, because we can document only the end results). In comparison, if a researcher wanted to experiment, he or she would choose a variable that could be changed and controlled, such as the amount of time kids watch television and how it affects their grades in school. See Box 7.3.

Experimental research studies or measures the effect of one variable on another variable, which in this case means that the outcome will be tested. One of the main advantages of experimental methods is that it allows the researcher to detect a cause-and-effect relationship by manipulating the input and measuring the output, because the researcher can isolate one or more variables in order to identify and measure its relative importance. In this way, experimental designs work well for research projects that have a clearly defined concept and hypothesis. They also tend to have a high degree of reliability because the process and circumstances can be repeated. This reliability is, however, contingent on the degree of external validity or transferability. **External validity** is when the study findings are of such a high quality that they are deemed relevant and the results can be transferred and applied to other geographic locations and populations.

A disadvantage of experimental research is the degree of artificiality, meaning that the variables are often so tightly controlled that they may not occur naturally anywhere outside of the laboratory. This could lead to issues of internal validity. **Internal validity** is when a study has properly proven that one thing causes something else to happen. This is usually the goal with clinical drug trials. A drug is introduced to a test subject, behavior and biological changes are monitored, modifications are made to the drug dosage to predict outcomes, other factors are then systematically ruled out as peripheral causes, and finally conclusions are drawn. As a side note: there are ethical considerations to using biological organisms for experimental purposes. For many decades, humans have used animals and other humans for experimentation, but in an enlightened society, one has to question the ethics of those acts. It is also important to the researcher to know that when experimenting with humans we must first obtain informed consent. See Box 7.4.

When conducting experiments such as the effect of a variable (such as lighting) on human behaviors or performance, it is best to study two groups concurrently. The first group is the *experimental group*, which receives the intervention or changes. The second group is called the *controlled group*. This group receives no intervention and is not

BOX 7.4 — Experimental Variables

(Sample)

Thesis or dissertation statement: "Through the use of new technologies that can harness human energy output from a variety of exercises, it is feasible to develop a fitness center that functions completely off the electrical power grid."

Independent variables

- Necessary energy requirements to power a 1,000 sq. ft. fitness facility.
  [The size of the fitness facility is an important variable because larger facilities would require greater energy and smaller facilities should require less energy.]

Dependent variables

- Number, type of, and energy output of different technologies that produce energy.

In this situation, the researcher would need to obtain a group of people who would utilize the different pieces of equipment for a given duration and at a moderate intensity. He or she would then record the kilowatts generated and compare that number with the total kilowatts that would be needed to power the facility for a 24-hour period.

exposed to any changes. If both groups show improvement, then the results cannot be attributed to the intervention or change. A **placebo effect** is an improvement that cannot be attributable to the intervention or change. Therefore, only when the experimental group shows improvement can this be attributed to the intervention or change.

A couple of issues can occur with experiments, including the **Hawthorne effect** and **experimenter bias**. The Hawthorne effect occurs when, through the research process, participants begin to feel "special" because the researchers are giving attention to the group, which then affects the group's behavior. Experimenter bias occurs when the researcher gives either more or less attention to particular set of variables, thus influencing the outcome.

MIXED METHODS

Depending on the subject matter, a mixed method can often be an appropriate way to research. The **mixed method** is a formal research process designed to give the researcher both qualitative and quantitative data to examine. One type of mixed method involves the collection of statistical and narrative information. The researcher analyzes the two types of data simultaneously or concurrently. An example of a concurrent mixed-method use might be a survey that uses a numeric response system (also called *weighted response*) along with open-ended questions that allow for individual written comments. Another form of a mixed-method approach is a *sequential mixed method*. This approach requires researchers to analyze one type of data in order to determine how to analyze the next set of data. This method might be manifested as the development of survey questions derived from the aggregate discussions obtained from a series of focus groups. In this case, the focus group discussions guided the researchers toward a particular set of variables from which they opted to focus more closely on. The researcher then takes those variables and morphs them into survey questions to get a statistical representation. The ability to mix or combine hard (numerical) and soft (narrative) data can offer a sophisticated and organized tool for developing a reliable theory. The following activity can be used to explore and evaluate a thesis research project from the standpoint of each of the most common research methods. See Activity 7.3.

ACTIVITY 7.3 Methods of Research

In the rightmost column, enter the variables of your research project that would be benefited most by the attributes of each method.

Research Goal	Method	Tools	Qualitative (Qual) or Quantitative (Quan)	Your Project Variable
Describe a situation or group.	Descriptive **statistically**	☐ Measure ☐ Record ☐ Profiles	Quan. #	
Describe a situation or group.	Descriptive **narrative**	☐ Interviews ☐ Videos ☐ Observation	Qual.	
Extract essential features of subjective and intuitive experiences.	Phenomenology	☐ Interviews ☐ Videos ☐ Audio	Qual.	
Study people—describe a social situation.	Ethnography **descriptive**	☐ Observations ☐ Interviews ☐ Journals	Qual.	
Study people—analyze individual variables.	Ethnography **analytical**	☐ Observations ☐ Surveys ☐ Census/Statistics	Quan. #	
Study and test variables for cause/effect.	Experimental	☐ Testing ☐ Measure ☐ Experiment	Quan. #	
Combine methods: numbers and written description to prove theory.	Mixed method	Any applicable	Qual./Quan. #	

Summary

Just as there are different techniques to holding a golf club and there are various procedures that are used to sculpt marble or ways to render a drawing, so too are there multiple methods of research. Evidence-based design follows this path: research, evaluate, document, and design. Methods are the tools evidence-based designers add to their "design palette" alongside their graphic pens, markers, rulers, and trace paper. Methods provide the calculated techniques and structured processes that add a high degree of scientific sophistication to each project. There are many different ways to pursue research. How students approach their research will depend on their goals. The first step for all research is the extensive ROL on a subject, followed by methods, which evaluate and test a given theory. Early in the research process, the researcher must describe and clearly demonstrate a deep understanding of the method selected for the investigation. This chapter outlined the organization of the methods section and some of the most common methods used within design research.

The organization of the methods section is essentially broken into three sections: introduction, implementation, and methodology criteria. The introduction reiterates how the study was initially designed and planned out. The following section details how the researcher gathered the new information on each factor that influenced the outcome. The last section discusses and explains what tools were used to gain additional information, as well as the criteria used to analyze the new data. Although the length and format of the methods section is as unique as each research project and can be modified to fit the study, every research project will be either quantitative or qualitative in nature.

A quantitative research approach analyzes data that results in quantities. This numeric data is then represented in the form of graphs, tables, or charts and informs design conclusions. The raw data tends to be rigid and is regarded as "hard" facts. In contrast, qualitative research approaches results in quality data that inspires a design in subtle yet poignant ways. Through the extensive documentation of narratives and the symbolic interpretation of language, a rich and in-depth understanding of a specific situation or phenomenon emerges.

The ability to interpret data is a skill that can be developed. This skill offers the designer the critical thinking and abstract thought processes that add a complex intellectual organizing tool for developing reliable theories and profound designs. The voice of the researcher and the style of writing in the document are important factors in a successful thesis. However, mitigating issues that arise with gathering data and reporting findings may be more important. These issues are all easily avoided with a clear-cut method, only a few variables, and resisting the temptation to go off on research tangents. Therefore, with dedication, organization, and timely documentation, writing your methods (methodology) section is by far the most straightforward of all the sections of the research document.

Glossary

Analytical—A detailed examination of an idea, concept, or phenomena.

Causal–comparative studies—Research that seeks to identify associations among variables.

Causal–comparative dependent variable—The effect in the cause-and-effect relationship.

Causal–comparative independent variable—The purported cause in the cause-and-effect relationship.

Correlational research—Involves relationships between two variables in which one is a predictor and the other a criterion.

Cultural patterns—A set of behaviors and interactions, cognitive constructs, and affective understanding that are learned through socialization.

Data—A collection of facts from which conclusions can be drawn.

Descriptive approach—Data and characteristics used to describe populations or phenomenon under investigation.

Direct observation—Behavior or events are observed while in action.

Ethnographic study—The systematic collection of data derived from direct observation of the everyday life of a particular society, group, or subculture.

Experimental—A method of investigating causal relationships among variables.

Experimenter bias—Any effect in which the beliefs and expectations of the researcher affect the measurement and recording of the dependent variable.

External validity—The ability of a study's results to apply to the general population in real world circumstances.

Haptic realm—Exclusively related to the sensation of touch.

Haptic sensation—The understanding of something through stimulus and the information passed through the skin.

Hawthorne effect—When research subjects act differently because they are aware that they being studied.

Internal validity—The degree of accuracy among the study findings because of the controls of bias.

Interviews—A conversation between two or more people for the purpose of obtaining information from the interviewee.

Method—A systematic way of arriving at a set of conclusions.

Mixed method—More than one research method used simultaneously or at different stages to arrive at a set of conclusions.

Observations—A systematic way of watching and analyzing something in an effort to draw conclusions.

Participant observation—When a researcher is an active participant in the events and situations that he or she is studying.

Phenomenology—A body of knowledge derived from empirical observations of events that are not grounded in any fundamental theory.

Placebo effect—A measurable or observable improvement that cannot be attributed to the intervention.

Qualitative—A process that refers to the quality or characteristics of something being described, rather than an exact numeric measurement.

Quantitative—The results or meaning of a study explained or described through numeric representation.

Reliability—Consistency in measurements, or the degree to which an instrument measures the same way each time.

Replicable—The ability of others to repeat the study in some other place and arrive at the same conclusions.

Research—A systematic investigation of a subject or phenomena in an efforts to establish and identify pertinent facts.

Scientific objectivity—An attempt to capture the nature of some subject under investigation in a way that does not depend on any other variable.

Self-report journaling—A process in which subjects keep and write down their thoughts, feelings, and reactions to specific events or circumstances.

Symbols—Expressions of ideas and concepts through the use of single images or a combination of graphic markings.

Validity—Grounded or justifiable facts or conclusions.

CHAPTER 8

Site Analysis and Case Studies

chapter outline

Introduction

Site Analysis
Implications and Purpose
Tools and Diagramming
Process and Procedure
Analysis and Interpretation
Presentation of Findings

Case Study
Technique and Process
Resources
Building Typology Study

Summary

> "If a building is to meet the needs of all the people, the architect must look for some common ground of understanding and experience."
>
> —John Portman

chapter objectives

By the end of this chapter, students should be able to:

- Explain the purpose of the site analysis and case study.
- Understand the implications of the site analysis and case study.
- Know principles and tools of observation.
- Recognize what to examine and how to implement the data into the design process.
- Become adept at graphically communicating data that supports and justifies the design.

Introduction

Historically, many artists and designers have drawn upon their own practical experiences and intuition to create designs appropriate and responsive to a particular site, user, or environment. Because it can take years for a designer to acquire the vast amount of experiences and

Table 8.1   Subsections of a Site Analysis

Presite analysis	Remotely gathering information regarding the site; preparation.
Site visit	Physically being on a site to document features/conditions.
Comparative site analysis	A means for comparing and evaluating two or more sites.
Contextual analysis	Assessment of personality of the site and community character.
Postevaluation	Process and prepare information for presentation.

the knowledge base necessary to address the multitude of probable issues within design, research can be a way for a younger designer to hit the ground running. In ancient China, the seasoned feng shui masters relied on a process called xiangdi (philosophy of observation and orientation appraisal) as they assessed a site and other buildings for their feng shui qualities. In many ways, one can argue that seasoned designers have engaged in similar observation and appraisal processes, which is how their "intuition" became so well developed. For the younger professional beginning his or her career, active and focused forms of observation and appraisal can lead to a significant knowledge base much sooner than the more organic method often relied upon in the past.

Design schools often include **site analysis** and **case study** precedence as predominant or traditional methods for research. Both methods are deeply rooted in the notions of observation and appraisal, and can bring an organizing rationale to the often complex and competing priorities of design. A *site analysis* is the observation and documentation of conditions on the property of a proposed project. A *case study* is the design equivalent of "standing on the shoulders of giants"; this type of study investigates comparable projects (buildings, uses, styles, etc.) in order to develop a strategy for understanding the complexities of a project for paradigmatic information. A site analysis is an excellent tool for understanding the environmental and contextual impacts on a design proposal. For the purposes of this book, using a site analysis and case study as traditional research tools will be explained as systematic processes of organized discovery. Admittedly, there are many ways to go about a site analysis, but for the sake of brevity only one generalized method will be discussed in this chapter. Table 8.1 reflects the general phases of the site analysis process.

With feng shui, for example, one would not build a home at the bottom of a valley where flooding might occur, or at the top of a hill where it would bear the full force of wind and other environmental conditions. Modern site analysis is more sophisticated in both process and technological methods. Consider a designer of a school. In order to select the appropriate soundproofing for an optimal learning environment, the sound pressure of a nearby busy road would need to be measured (magnitude of noise in decibels, or dB). Likewise, a case study can be utilized in this same example to determine, by way of studying a previous school design, the best amount, location, and quality of natural light sources to promote learning and stimulate students and teachers alike. Thus, assessing the opportunities and constraints of a site (site analysis) and similar designs (case study) often inspires, and always benefits, the design process.

Site Analysis

A **site** is a unique place; it is a slice of the landscape, and nothing about it can be oversimplified. A **landscape** by its very nature is very nearly everything around it, including the associations that people bestow upon it, the emotions it inspires, and the character a design can evoke once integrated into the landscape. A landscape is never "just the land" or its natural or arbitrary boundaries. To use an analogy, if the landscape is an epic novel of an entire civilization, then a site is a chapter on the personality of only one person. The purpose of a site analysis is to gain a profound respect and understanding of the character and personality of the environment prior to designing for it, on it, in it, or around it.

If a site analysis is completed properly, all of the documented information reaches the design in some fashion. Consider for a moment what it is to *analyze* something. Here are five synonyms for the word "analyze": examine, study, scrutinize, consider, and explore. To provide clarification to the process of a site analysis, consider each of these synonyms as used in the following sentences. If a site lacks trees or other naturally occurring shade and the southern sun presents a considerable amount of heat in that specific climatic zone, then the designer might *examine* multiple ways (designs) to correct this deficit, such as insulating devices, shade structures, or perhaps a design that includes built-in shade. If the site is extremely dark at night due to a lack of sufficient street lighting, the designer might *study* the need for more lighting, the night-time crime rates and perhaps the efficiency of photovoltaic lighting to add to the project. If the community in which the site is located has proposed a new development to be built within the next five years, designers might *scrutinize* the implications this future development would have on their project by attending community meetings and gathering as much information as possible on the proposed development. Perhaps a wonderful view of the ocean or mountains can be seen from the site, in which case it is likely that the designer would *consider* this information and use it to implement a "design answer" such as framing the view with walls or windows or perhaps adding an above-grade deck for users to enjoy the view. If, during the initial gathering of information, the designer (who is not native to the area) discovered that the majority of the population surrounding the site shares one cultural background, the designer would *explore* and learn everything possible about the residents and their cultural traditions in an effort to bring the project into line with the identity of the community. Thus, each piece of information represents an action the designer can take and defines a problem that can be answered with design.

The information from the site is recorded on a project base map. A **project base map** is created prior to going to the site. Information on the map includes: the outline of the legal property boundaries, streets, building setbacks, and the location of adjacent buildings, and is an extremely helpful tool at the site. On returning from a site visit and preparing to analyze the information on the project base map, the best piece of advice for the researcher would be to ask the following questions of every mark, note, or diagram that they drew on their base map:

- "What should be done about this?"
- "Why is this important to the project?"
- "Will the building become an asset or a liability for this _____?"
- "How can this _____ be integrated into the design?"

By asking these questions, the answers become the *analysis*, the first steps toward applying the information to a design. But how do students know if they have analyzed a site accurately and implemented the information correctly? Students will know they have properly analyzed and applied the site's information to their design if the space or building that they have created is suitable and fitting only on that specific site and would not work anywhere else in the world.

The reason for a site analysis is to gain a profound understanding of all the challenges and opportunities—the qualities a property has to offer, in addition to the qualities of the site within its surrounding landscape. This is sometimes referred to as the quest for "spirit of place." This level of understanding can come only from the total immersion to the site; designers have been known to live on a site for months to truly understand what design interventions would work best and be the most ethical for the location. Most thesis students will not have this luxury; therefore, visiting a site several times and at various hours to observe and document should be sufficient. The best way to do this is to develop a log in which the researcher can document the different dates, times, and experiences encountered. Figure 8.1 is an

Site Analysis Log		
Location of Site: 31-193 Hawaiian Belt Road (mile marker 16), Hilo HI. _____		
Date	**Time**	**Observations**
09.21.09	5:32a.m.	As the sun raised a shadow was cast from a distant mountain onto the site causing a small sliver of the site to become brightly illuminated while the majority of the site was cast in darkness.
09.21.09	5:37p.m.	A group of young teens were hanging out on the site. Some were playing with materials found on the site (sticks) while most were standing or sitting on rocks. A couple seemed to be talking about me and snickering as if I was invading their space.
09.30.09	11:38a.m.	The site is very warm and bright. I received unobstructed sunlight during the middle of the day. I am struck by the absence of a breeze I felt earlier. I think the elevation to the west blocks the breeze from this site. I am also struck by the silence of the site. As I sit here I feel so peaceful, tranquil and hot.

FIGURE 8.1 Site Analysis Log.

example of a log used by an architecture student that can easily be adapted and applied for a site analysis that an urban planner, a landscape designer, or an interior designer might use.

The site analysis is a process of researching, observing, and taking inventory of a select space within a larger system of its **context**—its landscape. For the architect, this process is integral to the design of a building. For the interior designer, the site analysis is a way to bring unity between the exterior and interior environments. The architect looks at ways to extend or incorporate a building within the landscape, whereas the interior designer or landscape designer must analyze the landscape in order to create a seamless transition between the exterior and interior, and vice versa. There are specific tools and techniques to document the elements of a site, as well as a particular set of means to analyze the data in preparation for a site analysis.

IMPLICATIONS AND PURPOSE

The overriding purpose of the site analysis is to gain a level of respect for and an understanding of the physical properties and the associative and emotive qualities of a site. The ideal development of a design, whether it is the building itself or the interior qualities, is one in harmony with its site. If the design conflicts with the environment to the detriment of the users, then an assumption can be made that the designer was similarly inattentive and thoughtless with the rest of the design. To illustrate: in a hot desert climate, a building designed with large roof overhangs for shade, along with thick walls and specific areas that are partially earth-sheltered for protection from the heat, would be considered appropriate for the environment. In this scenario, a proper site analysis provided the information a designer needed to protect the design and the people from the harsh climate.

Interestingly, today's technologies can greatly enrich a site analysis. Consider the previous example, in which earthen materials are conducive to dry desert areas; perhaps further into a site analysis, a satellite image or GIS data set reveals a fault line fairly close to the site. In this situation, earthen materials would need to be reinforced and flexible interior finishes would be advantageous. Within these interiors, flooring considerations might include selecting ceramic tiles rather than single-slab granite or polished concrete, because single tiles could be replaced more readily, should an earthquake cause floor damage.

A *comparative site analysis* is generally used in the professional environment as a means for comparing and evaluating the benefits of two or more sites for the selection and purchase of one for a project. Students can use this type of analysis to compare sites prior to selecting one for their thesis. Combined with a case study approach, buildings from similar climates yet with differing stylist leanings can be contrasted; for example, Iran and Iraq have climates similar to that of Palm Springs, California, and also have periodic seismic activity. A comparative analysis, combined with a case study, might reveal alternate design solutions or lead to the discovery of new hybrid designs appropriate to the site. As with any research, it is important to develop a list of criteria to provide structure and order to the analysis. Generally, the site analysis for an academic project includes, but is not limited to:

Legal aspects (zoning, building codes, property boundaries)

Architects: Building size relationships, future potential adjacencies, and governing restraints that affect the design.

Interior designers: Potential compromises of interior-to-exterior views and natural lighting patterns, and unique restrictions of materials to be incorporated into the design.

Physical characteristics (site features, topography, views)

Architects: Building orientation, form and materials, potential drainage issues, and relative effects of existing or future buildings on view corridors and neighborhood context.

Interior designers: Identification and enhancements of natural views, mimicking exterior visual characteristics with interior design features, and capitalizing on natural elements to be incorporated into a design.

Climatic surveys (solar survey, wind rose, snow, or rainfall)

Architects: Identification of appropriate materials, environmental stressors, and maximizing passive design principles (i.e., thermal mass, roof slope, space planning).

Interior designers: Heat gain, effects of weather on interior finishes, interior space planning (i.e., closet/coat room near the ingress/egress in cold climates).

Sociocultural perspectives (demographics, history, pedestrian patterns)

Architects: Vernacular norms, connections to the community and circulation requirements.

FIGURE 8.2 Site Analysis Criteria.

	Site Analysis Criteria	
Location of Site: 123 Boylston Ave, Boston MA.		
Criterion	**Observations**	**Implications**
Legal aspects (zoning, building codes, property boundaries)	Zero property lines	View corridors obscured, limited natural light.
Physical characteristics (site features, topography, views)	Abuts a front (West facing) sidewalk, 7-story building to the south, 8-story building to the north, and a 7-story building to the east. Across the street on the west side is a 5-story parking garage.	Parking garage can accommodate parking. Interior features will not be enhanced by the exterior, they must therefore stand on their own.
Climatic surveys (solar survey, wind rose, rain or, snowfall)	Coldest weather comes from northeast. Building will be somewhat blocked from the full force of weather. Snow and icy conditions in the winter, heavy use of salt on roads and sidewalks.	Front entry will require a transition zone containing a hard surface where smaller area carpeting can be placed to absorb excess water and salt dragged inside during the winter.
Sociocultural perspectives (demographics, history, pedestrian patterns)	Walking/public transportation community. Strong sense of history, traditional design preferences with liberal social ideals.	Requires personal space for storage (coats, bags, umbrellas), bring in traditional more ornate designs, strong need for integration of accessibility features.

Interior designers: Appropriate use of display items (i.e., cultural customs). Social patterns of communication, seating proximity, and recreation.

Environmental "dynamics" (noises, smells, "neighborhood vibe")

Architects: Identification of design solutions that will be embraced by the community and will celebrate the opportunities and minimize the challenges of the site.

Interior designers: Use of appropriate ventilation systems to diffuse odors, as well as finishes and materials for sound dampening.

Researchers must first identify the criteria by which they will analyze a site. Then, as the site is visited, they should record the findings and identify the implication of those observations to the design. Figure 8.2 provides an example of this process in a written format. Again, it may be approached differently from all the individual and unique perspectives of design (architect, interior or landscape design); as designers are typically visual people and communicate graphically, this example illustrates that this information can be formatted to any individual communication style: written, graphic, or tactile.

The site analysis may also include a brief overview of the context of the surrounding neighborhoods. Imagine surveying a site in a community in which all the surrounding buildings are constructed of brick in the vintage mercantile style (see Figure 8.3). The project can then be designed to "fit in" with the scale and character of the community, or the designer could contrast the design with the context of the community. The main purpose of context, a subsection of a site analysis (called *contextual analysis*), is to become familiar with the ambiance of the community. Whether designers decide to accentuate or differentiate their design from the community at large is not the critical issue here—what is critical is being cognizant of what already exists. The process and results of site and contextual analyses ultimately offers a means of validating the thesis design.

TOOLS AND DIAGRAMMING

The tools used for a site analysis fall into the categories of their intended use: presite, site visit, and postevaluation. *Presite analysis* is information that must be acquired prior to visiting a site, which includes:

- Maps (of the region, city, area, neighborhood, and property or planimetric map or "plat map" for short)
- Aerial photos (for building locations, mass, and orientation)
- Reference information (history of area, present zoning, and proposed changes)

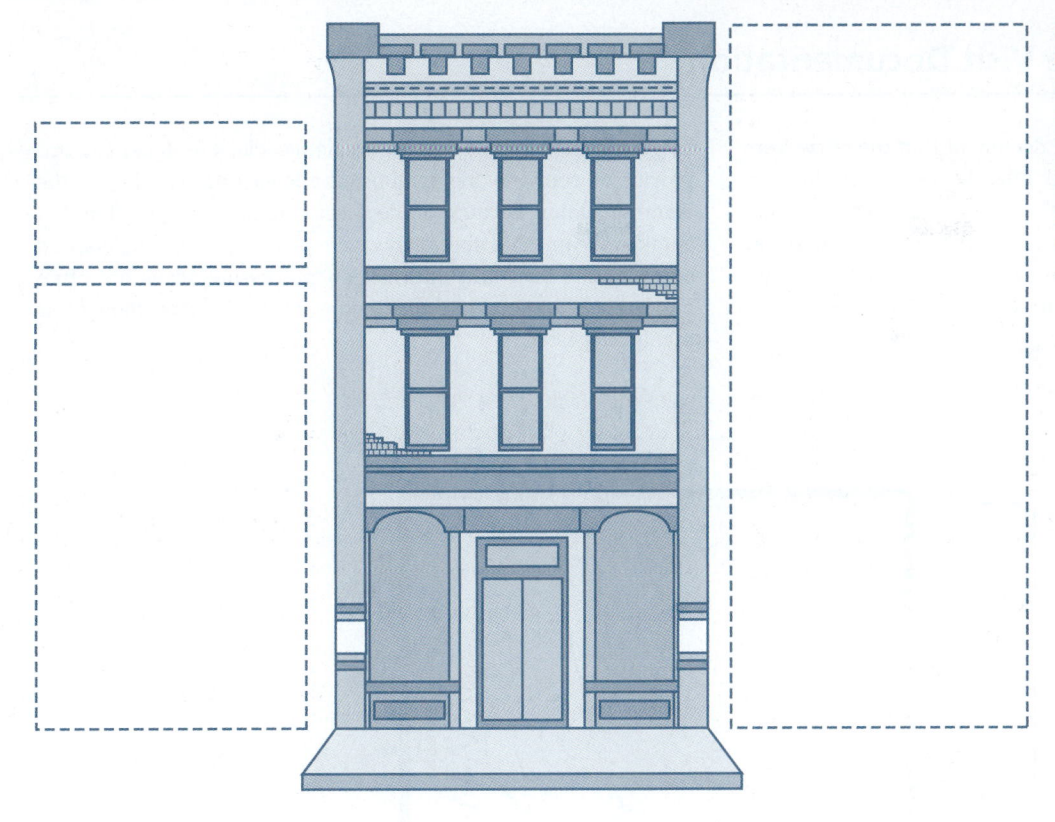

FIGURE 8.3 The dashed boxes illustrate an important concept: what a designer ultimately designs is not a greater factor than the understanding of what else has already been designed around the site. Bigger, smaller, higher or multi-leveled, these considerations should be made along with the knowledge of what the neighborhood "context" is."
Source: Sinclair, E., (2009)

Tools needed for the actual site analysis are specific to each project, but every site analysis requires that the researcher take the following with them:

- A project base map
- Measuring tape (greater than 16′ length)
- A camera and/or sketchbook

Additional tools to bring to the site might include an audio recorder if the "sounds" as well as the "sights" are important to the design process, and a laser level tool (a "clinometer") for measuring elevation changes on a site or a shovel to provide access to a preliminary assessment of the soil type on the site. During the site analysis, student researchers need to be able to employ the greatest tool of design—diagramming. Diagramming can be considered a form of "design shorthand." Over time, designers develop their own shorthand symbols; Figure 8.4 illustrates the most commonly used symbols during the survey of a site. Each diagram, if not entirely obvious to the student would also need a one or two word description or "note-to-self". See Box 8.1.

Though many schools of architecture have incorporated these tools into the curriculum, interior design programs can also benefit from a site analysis. By charting sun angles in relation to window placement, the amount of light and radiant heat entering a building can be calculated. This can inform the designer as to what types of window treatments will best serve each of the spaces. Likewise, knowing where and the approximate distance a structure is from a roadway, airport, or railway will help the interior designer better understand ambient noise conditions, which can be mitigated or exacerbated by interior finishes and accoutrements. See Activity 8.1.

Postsite analysis tools aid in the understanding of the implications of the data gathered. These tools help convert the data from the site visit into "design information," which in turn will result in a "design response." Tools include, but are not limited to:

- Clear plastic "write-on" transparency film (used with overhead projectors)
- Physical site models
- Photo collages
- Computer-generated or -abstracted model

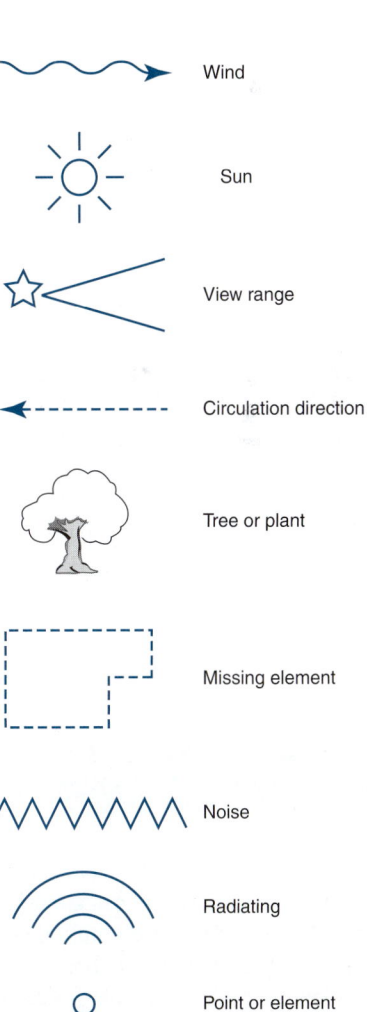

N	North
∿→	Wind
☼	Sun
☆◁	View range
←-----	Circulation direction
🌳	Tree or plant
⌐ ¬ (dashed)	Missing element
/\/\/\/\	Noise
)))	Radiating
○	Point or element

FIGURE 8.4 Examples of typical diagramming symbols used in a site analysis."
Source: Sinclair, E., (2009)

BOX 8.1 Site Visit Documentation

During a site visit, a student must document that the noise from the nearby freeway extends well into the center of the site. Therefore, the symbols for "noise" and "radiating" can be combined. The diagram for "noise" represents the location line to say "noise comes from here" and the symbol for "radiating" is included to say "and doesn't stop until here." See Figure 8.5.

Then the added note might be a design intervention: "Add noise barrier here: water fountain?"

Or a measurement note:
"90dB (Decibels)"

Diagramming symbols are not unchangeable; a designer can improvise or combine the symbols to increase the quality of the communication. Because of the sheer volume of information that is taken in during a site analysis coupled with the time elapsed between site visit and information processing, ideas are often forgotten. Therefore jotting down a quick note or thought is highly suggested.

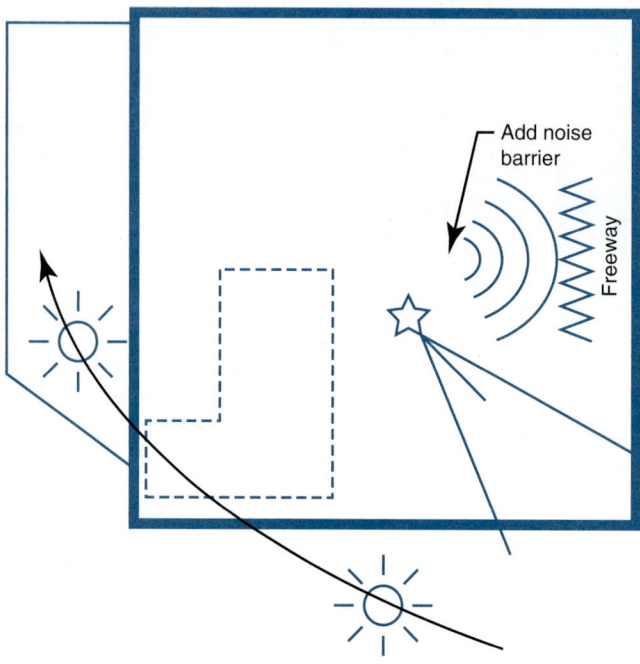

FIGURE 8.5 Site Elements in the Plan View
Source: Sinclair, E. (2009).

The idea is for the students to arrange their data in such a way as to provide guidelines from which to proceed with their project. In other words, everyone has a different way in which they "process" information. So, if 20 students did the same site analysis, there will most likely be 20 different and unique ways of interpreting the same information. A good site analysis should work effectively for the student and, like other research methods, must integrate other research findings. To create an example of this, consider a student thesis project on the subject of office environment optimization. The student, through his or her ROL, learns that glare from large expanses of unprotected window glazing is a source of migraines in office employees working on computers, but during the site

ACTIVITY 8.1 Criteria Evaluation

The fields of design include architecture, interior design, industrial design, landscape design, and urban planning, among others. These fields offer on multiple perspectives from which to research and gather information regarding a site. Thesis students of design from any discipline can use this activity to practice developing a list of criteria to begin a site analysis.

Step 1: Identify a typology (type of use: bank, gas station, house, school, etc.).

Step 2: Identify what is important to know about a site and its surrounding community.

Step 3: Identify what design ideas take into account a site and the characteristics of the community.

BOX 8.2   Postsite Analysis

The following examples show the different ways in which the same information can be arranged for better analysis on the basis of student learning preference.

Student A	Prefers to see information in isolation	Student A chooses to redraw each piece of information onto transparencies and label them (i.e., wind, solar access, and so on); these are then overlaid onto the project base map. The student addresses each issue independently with a design solution. One at a time, the layers of information cause the design to evolve in response to every opportunity or challenge documented during the site analysis.
Student B	Prefers to see information all at the same time	Student B opts to build a site model at 1/8" scale and abstractly represent, with objects such as wire, tubes, and string, all the site constraints and positive features. The student then adds in various conceptual models of his or her design, adjusting the architectural/design response to each object representing a data point (such as solar gain, freeway noise or odors).
Student C	Prefers to piece the information together to create a narrative	Student C creates from the many photographs taken at the site a collage of images and views that is affixed to the project base map. The student uses the imagery to communicate proper building orientation, door and window openings, and circulation paths. The images create a story, a pattern, and a path that the student can respond to through design.
Student D	Prefers to reinterpret the information into another format	Student D theorizes that having a computer decipher the information collected during the site analysis would be the most objective process. The student enters the information into a computer-generated graphic modeling program as points or in matrix form as numeric values and sets the modeling parameters, and the program builds an abstract representational model of the site issues as points of "go/no go." The design evolves out of the student's interpretation of the computerized theoretical abstraction.

analysis decides to capture the breathtaking ocean views by adding a wall of windows into the project design. Thus, this fictional student used the site information appropriately as a *design* tool, but did not analyze it correctly as a *research* tool. Evidence-based design is about seamlessly integrating what is known (evidence) with what is felt (design). Design students are cautioned to gather site data and analyze it as any other research method or tool. Researchers must *use* the site analysis information and not simply present the information as a chore that has been dutifully completed. Thoreau warns of this phenomenon when he said, "Men have become the tools of their tools" (Thoreau, 1854, p. 61). Box 8.2 provides examples for creating an effective tool for processing site data and conditions for analysis.

PROCESS AND PROCEDURE

The actual site analysis is a multiphase process of collecting, documenting, filtering, and analyzing information pertaining to a site. Although the overriding premise of the endeavor is to do the following:

- Document and diagram site features.
- Interpret and filter data.
- Outline and display findings.

The first step is to collect as much preliminary information as possible before going to the site. Prior to going to the site create a project base map for field measurements and observational surveys. As mentioned earlier, the project base map includes the outline of the legal property boundaries, streets, building setbacks, and the location of adjacent buildings. The base map can be computer-aided design (CAD) or hand-drawn, though it is important to go to the site with several photocopies of the project base map, a camera, and a measuring tape to document, observe, and record site features.

The second step is to go to the site to record information. This should be done at least four times: once by day, once by night, once on a weekday, and once on a weekend. Walking to the site from a distance, as well as driving to the site, can further the research exploration process because both activities provide a different experiential perspective from which analysis may be drawn and both have different meanings for the interior and exterior design.

The third step is to document as many features as possible by diagramming them onto the base map, followed by measuring driveways, tree bases, sidewalks, and other features, and finally by photographing inside and outside of the site. The fourth step is to record and arrange the information into a format from which designing can begin. The purpose for this is to address present day views and shading, and projections for future views and shading, as well as to assess privacy and noise considerations. The final step is to render the completed site analysis with recommendations and conclusions into a layout conducive for presentation and addition to the thesis document.

ANALYSIS AND INTERPRETATION

The investigation of a site happens on several levels. It might be easiest to understand this concept by borrowing the design terms *title*, *elevation*, *plan*, and *section* for a moment. Much like the title page for a set of architectural drawings, the term "title" can represent the initial level of a site analysis in which the student must look up all the legal aspects of the property:

- Who owns it
- Boundaries locations
- The property setbacks (areas of a property that cannot legally be built upon)
- Zoning information
- History of the site

Similar to the elevation drawings of a project showing all the elements that rise up from the ground plane, the "elevation" level of a site analysis examines all physical features in the vertical plane. While the site analysis is in progress, it is good practice to document the features found in and around the site by quickly hand drawing them in an elevation (face-forward from the ground up) flat view. See Figure 8.6.

If the term "plan" is used to describe all the elements of a site that move or cut through the horizontal plane, then the site analysis must also document the following (see Figure 8.5 inside Box 8.1):

- Sights
- Smells
- Plants or animals
- People (circulation or traffic patterns)
- Climatic zone or other sensory features

The term "section" is used here to represent attributes that *cut through* vertical levels or volumes. Again, this is best-recorded or illustrated in section whenever possible. See Figure 8.7.

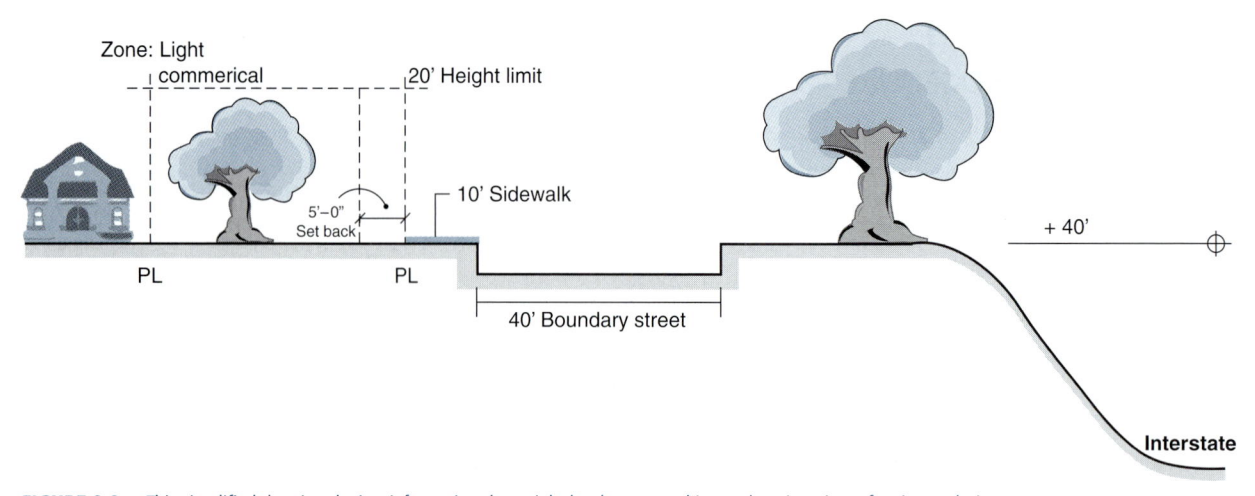

FIGURE 8.6 This simplified drawing depicts information that might be documented in an elevation view of a site analysis.
Source: Sinclair, E., (2009)

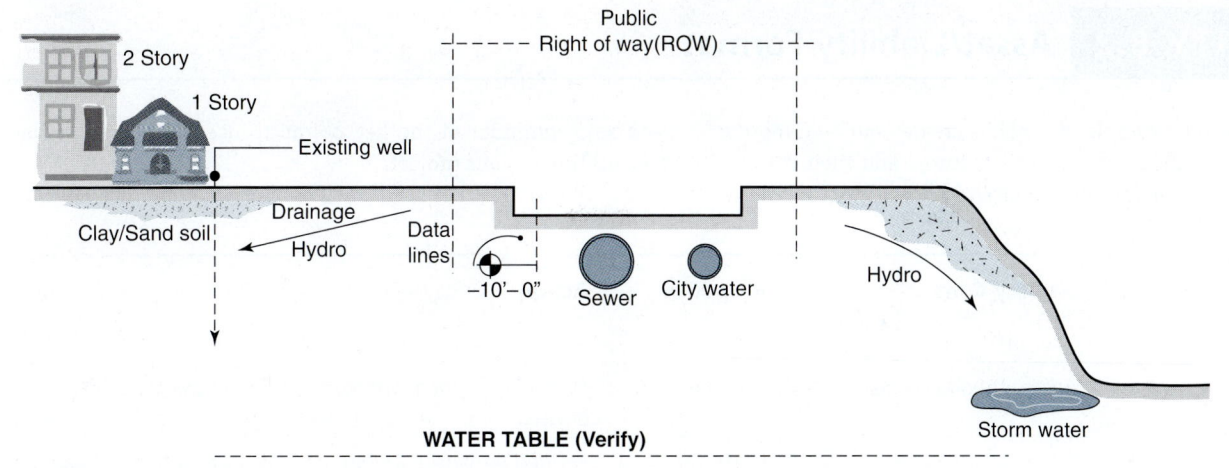

FIGURE 8.7 This simplified drawing depicts information that might be documented in a sectional view of a site analysis.
Source: Sinclair, E., (2009)

A plethora of information can become part of a site analysis; the student alone decides what it is that he or she *needs* to know. Table 8.2 contains a checklist of sample features and aspects that might be sought out while analyzing a site.

PRESENTATION OF FINDINGS

Analyzing the information gathered from a site can be a daunting task. The graphic presentation of the findings is as open for debate, as is any discussion within the world of design. Each designer has a *voice*—their own style of communicating that is comfortable and familiar to them. Therefore, this next segment addresses only the issue of information and not specific graphic format or presentation style.

Table 8.2 Site Analysis Checklist

This table lists some of the features to be documented during a site analysis. How this information will be later translated into a design solution is dependent on the discipline (i.e., architecture, interior design, landscape architecture).

Title	Elevation	Plan	Section
☐ Owner	☐ Other buildings (measure and photograph)	☐ Locate north	☐ Mass of adjacent buildings
☐ Legal property description	☐ Trees and vegetation	☐ Street names	☐ Underground utilities
☐ Setbacks	☐ Sidewalks and fences	☐ Sights, smells, sounds	☐ Earthquake zones
☐ Legal easements	☐ Topography	☐ Wildlife	☐ Hydrogeology of the site
☐ Zone	☐ Elevation changes	☐ People (users, visitors, and neighbors): who are they?	☐ Stormwater
☐ History	☐ Aboveground util.	☐ Traffic and circulation loads (car, bus, train, bike, skateboard, and people)	☐ Soil type
☐ F.A.R.	☐ View corridors		☐ Watershed/water table
☐ Dedicated use	☐ Materials tradition within area (brick, stucco, etc.)		☐ Wells
☐ Future land use planning (any new developments coming soon?)	☐ Reflection/glare from surrounding buildings?	☐ Handicapped (ADA) features	☐ Septic tank/leach fields
☐ Archaeological significance	☐ Width of streets	☐ Solar path and shade from other structures	☐ Foundations/basements
☐ Municipal overlay zones	☐ Height restrictions	☐ Prevailing wind	☐ Underground structures
		☐ Climatic zone	
		☐ Services (trash, communications, alleys, etc.)	

Other Considerations

☐ Spatial relationships ("5 min. walk to grocery store"; get a feel for the neighborhood)
☐ Threshold of security (local crime rate, general condition and attitude of area, proximity to emergency services)
☐ Amount of local public space? What service or other features does the community need to become self-sustaining?
☐ Any natural resources on the site? (e.g., cobblestones can be used for site walls or great solar access for PV electricity.)
☐ What are the local activities and customs? (parades, farmers markets)

ACTIVITY 8.2 — Asset/Liability Format

Using the following example as a guide, create your own matrix and fill in the columns with the site features and their results. This information filter can be formatted into a display or simply used as a reminder of the key points to use during the verbal presentation of your project.

Asset Pros	Liability Cons	Response	Action
Example:			
	Adjacent building glare	Eliminate	Designed a green wall and used mechanical louver devices
Wonderful lake views to east		Celebrate	Framed employee lounge windows to capture morning views
	City-mandated trash pickup at property entry	Avoid	Built underground trash bin elevator
Large granite boulders on site		Modify & use	Relocated to front for use as entry fountain

The presentation of data for design use is a tricky subject. First, who will be in the audience? Are they knowledgeable or comfortable reading the abstract graphic plans utilized by design professionals: plans, sections, and elevations? Will the presentation be viewed from afar (more than 15' away) or close up, such as is the case with the thesis document? The answer to each of these questions creates a different presentation scenario, as does the formatting of the information to be brought forward by the site analysis. The student must be able to articulate exactly how the site analysis data translated directly into the final design.

Filtering the site analysis data for presentation is vital to getting important concepts across quickly to the audience or reader. In this section, several information formats will be suggested, although they are rudimentary at best and students are advised to develop and exercise their own unique formats. The general idea is to be selective with the information that is presented. All the information is vital for the design, although only particular pieces of data are necessary when portraying the validity of a project with regard to its site, audience, and time constraints. The first suggested format for organizing the site analysis for presentation will be called the *asset/liability* format—a list of pros and cons of site factors. As with all formats, the data should be displayed in graphic and text form, as most people take in information on various levels. Students should begin by assembling a list of the assets the site offers the project, as well as the liabilities that will be corrected by the project. See Activity 8.2.

The second format is the *needs* format. If the student has a strong grasp of the needs of the project, the site information that fills those needs are the elements that should be highlighted or brought to the forefront. For example, when designing a fire station, defining the needs criteria of the fire station staff is extremely helpful when selecting and analyzing the site—in other words, a comprehensive **program** will inform the designer what is needed from a site for its users. See Activity 8.3.

The third format is the *overlay* format. There are situations in which the building type will not be assigned; much like in a thesis, the student decides what to design. To avoid becoming overwhelmed by the vast array of design options that could be exercised, it is ideal for the site to "tell" the designer what to create. For example, actions and decisions must be made based on the results of a comprehensive site analysis. Students should start with the macro and move toward the micro: region, county, community, neighborhood, and finally site, building, or space. The components of this type of analysis are overlaid, layer by layer resulting in the ideal location with the best use, and concludes with the final decision. Consider the concept in Box 8.3 by way of example.

There are some general practices for the presentation of a site analysis:

- Highlight the most important information.
- North arrow is always pointing up.
- Use large and sparse text.

ACTIVITY 8.3 Program Needs Format

Using the following example as a guide, recreate your own matrix and fill in the columns with the site features and their results. This information filter can be formatted into a display or simply used as a reminder of the key points to use during the verbal presentation of the project.

Need	Site Condition	Objective	Action
Example:			
Architectural Program: Mixed-use complex: community center, senior housing, and ground-level medical clinic			
Mixed-use zone	City requires two low-income housing units in this mixed-use zone.	Maintain housing element.	Reconfigured housing units to include mandated low-income housing.
Site within one block (100' of public transportation)	Train and trolley within two blocks. Bus within one block.	Reduce parking needs and support local pedestrian lifestyle.	Site spans last 75' of block, trees planted to shade the longer walk to train, and front entry pull-out added for taxi pickup.
Existing building to renovate	Existing building would require seismic retrofit; rear lot sufficient for additional structure.	To not disrupt the personality or scale of the neighborhood with a new mixed-use model.	Structural exterior skin was designed to support upper building addition without altering original exterior facade.
Alley access	Alley paving is in poor condition and is a narrow drive aisle.	For resident or patient entry and rehabilitation garden.	Permeable pavers are extended beyond rear yard and garden to widen and repair alley access while mitigating site runoff.

- Label the drawing.
- Color code data and use a legend.
- Use photo examples for complex situations.
- For purposes of legibility and clarity, apply arrows and leader lines to the drawing and use the project base map consistently and always at the same size and orientation.

Case Study

A case study is defined by the Merriam-Webster Online Dictionary (http://m-w.com) as "an intensive analysis of an individual unit stressing developmental factors in relation to the environment." It is the same as "standing on the shoulders of giants" and learning from a prior project. Case studies are used by many other disciplines and are not exclusive to the design field. By and large, case studies include the researching of plans, details, and materials used on or in a particular type of building to help identify good and bad examples of design, use of space, or construction. Case studies assist in the learning from the successes and failures of similar scenarios—for example, learning about hospital design through the success of other models. Case studies can also be used to investigate peripheral implications, such as design scenarios (hypothetical prototyping), methods or materials of construction (technology and innovations), or client specific aspects (universal design or live/work). There is also a subcategory of case study referred to as the **building typology study**. Typically, a building typology study classifies and illuminates trends evolving within the physical appearance and symbolic meaning of a building type; for instance, typology asks the question, "What does a hospital look like in urban America?" and then answers it with location-specific graphic examples. This process also has applicability to an interior designer, who may ask

BOX 8.3 Overlay Format Example

The following fictional thesis project is an example of filtering the site analysis data to provide answers to designing the final project.

The thesis question is: "Where will an aging U.S. population live in 2050?"

First, the thesis student develops a set of data requirements that will outline the site search.

1. Locate area of highest projected population of people over age 65 for the year 2050 in the United States. [This information is plotted onto a U.S. map.]
2. Isolate the state with the highest projected sample population. [This information is outlined in bold lines on the first map.]
3. Narrow the state population down to the highest estimate on a county scale [The county is now outlined within the state map.]
4. The information search must shift directions, as cities do not always have this forecasted; therefore, the student must look at the current population and extrapolate the people aging-in-place and select the city most likely to have the highest aged population in 2050.
5. Once the city is selected, a base map can be created of the area.
6. Overlays are created one by one to represent the following information:
    a. Transportation. [Draw all major roads with load capacity, bus/trolley routes, etc.]
    b. Housing. [Draw or block out housing areas from zoning maps.]
    c. Health and medical services. [Draw a symbol for each location, add to legend.]
    d. Food and supply. [Diagram the locations of markets and services.]
    e. Cultural and entertainment. [Delineate zones, areas, or individual buildings.]
    f. Exercise and outdoor public space. [Mark areas where these resources are found.]
    g. Spiritual and community centers. [Diagram and note these locations.]
    h. Emergency services. [Use a symbol for all locations.]
    i. Spatial density. [Distance between all important elements: people vs. commerce.]
    j. Zoning [color code areas where zoning and land use patterns]
7. After all this data is gathered and mapped out on overlays, the process of site selection begins. Each overlaid data set will show up as points or areas within the city (color-coding or labeling the overlays is a good idea at this point). Once all the overlays are stacked on each other, blank areas generally emerge. Areas where the zoning changes or areas of opportunity may present themselves. Depending on the goals or programmed requirements of the project, researchers will find their thesis project site surface.

---

the question, "What do people expect from the interior design of a hospital?" Again, the question is answered with graphics. A wealth of knowledge can come from investigating similar building types and the designs used.

There is a saying within the design world: "There are no new designs." When faced with a new project type within a professional office environment, the firm will most likely have a staff member who has some experience with the particular building type. If not, the design team would develop a list of questions such as the following and set an intern to the task of quickly finding the answers:

- What has been done before?
- Has this building type been improved on with recent technological advances?
- What should be the design voice (style) or material language (symbolic meaning)?
- What structural systems have worked best in this climate or for this soil type?
- What obstacles have others run up against and which must be avoided?

A case study is also called a *precedent study*, meaning a study of a design that has preceded or come before. Consider, for example, the design of a health spa. If the designer had never worked on a health spa, he or she would need to identify some sort of starting point. A starting point might be information and images of health spas designed in the past. The examples (case studies) provide the designers with guidance and/or inspiration with their own design.

To research health spas designed in the past, the designer can first search broadly by "use" (health spas). He or she would then continue to refine the search to ideal designs that have been developed and excel at addressing the intended purpose. Some of the criteria that a researcher might include as part of the search for a case study are:

- Climate compatibility
- Environmental similarities (rural, urban, and other types)

- Reflective demographics
- Compatible floor plan arrangement
- Similar site constraints (if any)

The Internet is an excellent place to begin the search. It should be noted that a case study might vary in scale from a specific small element up to larger more complex system. Researchers should ensure as much compatibility as possible between the intended design and the case studies—in short, compare "apples to apples." Using case studies is not about copying another designer's work; it is about becoming informed and inspired.

TECHNIQUE AND PROCESS

The purpose of a case study depends on the needs of the researcher. For example, a case study might be researched from the perspective of analyzing the lighting of an interior environment. Such a study would be beneficial only to someone studying artificial lighting or daylighting (i.e., "apples to apples"). Because the scope of what is to be analyzed should be limited, students should resist the urge to use this case study to compare "energy usage," because that would be an entirely different case study ("apples to oranges"). A case study can explore an issue, a building type, an abstract concept, or even record the interrelationships between any combination of factors that affect design. For example, the relationships between the public, mixed-group, semiprivate, and private areas within an urban environment might be analyzed. A case study could also be used to recognize the boundaries of a design or to honor the successes of individual designers.

The case study process involves finding an ideal project. and researching that project through books, journal articles, or monographs, or perhaps through an interview with the original designer. If students were to outline their parameters, in the order shown in Activity 8.4 prior to searching, the whole process could be greatly accelerated. At this point in the thesis process, students should be accustomed to asking themselves, "What do I want to find?" As a helpful tip and to optimize any Internet search for a potential case study, students should type into the Internet browser search bar their query followed by the words "case study." (For example: "building energy use + case study".) The results should offer insight into case studies that have been completed or generate a new direction in the search for a project to evaluate.

ACTIVITY 8.4 Outlining Case Study Parameters

Use this format to outline your case study, including only the information that is applicable and adding factors and considerations that are specific to your thesis or dissertation project.

Find the Case Study	Examples
1. Search parameters (identify what it is that you want to find or examples that you wish to see)	Energy usage, circulation patterns, structural systems, indigenous plants, shading devices. cultural appropriateness, transit options, etc.
2. Building use (identify the main function or refer to its "type")	Libraries, hospitals, multiple-family housing, gas stations, bus stations, churches, dog houses, barns, recreation centers, museums, post offices, entertainment, etc.
3. Similar location or climate (i.e., Köppen-Geiger World Climate Classification Map)	Urban, suburban, exurban, rural. Desert, coastal, tropical, arctic, temperate rainforest, arid, etc.
4. User-specific type (identify the user group that relates most to the project)	Senior citizens, children, disabled, women, men, college students, homeless, single-parents, skateboarders, etc.
5. Architectural style (select a "design voice" to investigate)	Contemporary, bungalow, cabin, federal, craftsman, saltbox, functionalism, arcology, Queen Anne, etc.
6. Architect or designer (if the case study is to involve a compare and contrast of design voices)	Frank Lloyd Wright, Zaha Hadid, Rem Koolhaas, Alvar Aalto, Leonardo DaVinci, Marion Mahony Griffin, Le Corbusier, Antoni Gaudi, Bruce Goff, Julia Morgan, Peter Zumthor, etc.

Once an appropriate project case study has been identified and a significant amount of data has been acquired, the next step is to analyze the material and seek additional facts or images to provide a concise and complete evaluation of the project. The goal of the analysis is to draw out information that can be applied to the thesis project. As is the case for nearly all phases of research, the student must answer the most basic questions—who, what, when, where, and why. They should strive to raise the bar and also answer—what if . . . , what will . . . , and so what . . . . The answers to these questions will demonstrate to the reader that the student-researcher has taken action, cognitively challenged the theories, and come away with invaluable lessons that can come only from the experiences of designers who have come before them. For example, Student A is interested in critically analyzing the adjacencies between the transitional spaces of a large resort using three case studies. When the distance and arrangement of furniture between the check-in desk and the elevators has been examined and compared to the analysis of the case studies, an outline for the optimal distance and arrangement of transitional spaces for resorts is provided (this is sometimes referred to as a *space study*). Thus, in the thesis document, the student-researcher now has additional information to authenticate and validate the decisions made during the design process.

The final step in creating a case study is to format the information and add it to the thesis document. The format of a case study is commonly set up with succinct headings and bulleted facts. They can be in the form of a brief two-page synopsis or a ten-page comprehensive narrative. The first page frequently contains an image of the project and its basic information on use, location, design team, and so on. A case study should include a concise abstract of the project outlining: the project goals, the challenges, and the background of the design team. There is typically a summary illustrating the perspectives, analysis, and conclusions drawn from the issues that arose during the process of designing the case study project. See Box 8.4.

BOX 8.4 Sample Case Study Cover Page Format

The cover page of a case study should be as concise as possible while containing the basic information of the project. The following pages can elaborate in great detail the elements of the project that have been examined and implemented into the thesis project.

Image

Project Title

Use:
Location:
Year Built:
Owner:
Architect:

- Fact
- Fact
- Fact
- Fact
- Fact

Analysis:

Discussion:

Image

BOX 8.5 Case Study Resources

Here are a few of the "gems" on the Internet for locating projects to conduct a case study for a design project. These sites are a good place to start. A note of caution: verify all data before using the information in a case study, the majority of these websites are user-generated: *caveat emptor* (buyer beware).

Format and Examples	http://www.aia.org/education/AIAS075232 The AIA Case Studies Initiative. See the "Case Study Development Guidelines" for details and "Selected Case Studies" for examples.
Building Type	http://www.architypereview.com Architype Review is a comprehensive design forum on building types, designers and sustainable issues.
Project Type	http://www.mimoa.eu *Mi Modern Architecture* or MIMOA is a free online database of modern architecture around the globe.
Designers	http://www.egodesign.ca *EgoDesign* is a Canadian Internet magazine with global examples of architecture, design, fashion, and art.

RESOURCES

There are many good books on notable design projects throughout the world. However, students should expand their search to include any major stakeholder or agency that would have an interest in publicizing information on their projects. To illustrate, Student B is interested in finding a project that has successfully implemented geothermal heating and cooling into a commercial building application as the basis for his or her thesis investigation. The answer to "Who is a stakeholder in geothermal systems?" (energy companies) provides additional resources for the student to go find specific examples of projects that have already been successfully implemented. See Box 8.5.

BUILDING TYPOLOGY STUDY

The process of design and the practice of design are bound to a seemingly endless stream of information. The sources a designer can draw from are limitless: philosophy, physics, biology, ecology, art, geology, metaphysics, codes, or building methods. The sheer magnitude of information to comprehend opens the door for professionals, researchers, and students to learn from each other through a symbiotic relationship.

Through a building typology study a researcher can find answers to basic aspects of the function of a project, such as its type, symbolism, or configuration. In order to begin a building typology study, researchers must first know what it is that they would like to discover. Activity 8.5 should help get the process underway.

The study can be used to examine the evolution of a specific type of use or function (such as a bank, library, or house). In this situation, early questions for this analysis might be, "What does a bank look like?" "What is the meaning of a bank?" and "What does a bank need to communicate to draw customers?" During the last 50 years, building types have diverged from assumptions that have developed over time. Today, churches and libraries can be found in single-story strip malls. Additionally, many government agencies are found housed in prefabricated metal structures instead of the archetypical wide staircase rising to plinth and entry doors within the shadows of stately columns standing guard along the portico, classified as "Federal style".

Symbolic gestures have long been part of design language. Symbolism can communicate an unspoken ideology of the occupants, or the image the owners would like to portray. For example, many of the elements common to ancient Greek architecture have come to stand for democracy and knowledge. Likewise, many elements of Roman architecture are commonly understood to symbolize ethical principles and forthright justice. Thus, government buildings, libraries, and even banks have capitalized on these design elements to convey the same symbolic values to the general public. Therefore, society has come to recognize the patterns of what the look of a church should be or the proper arrangement of a library. For theoretical questions that can help focus the typology analyses will sound something like this:

- What does a library look like?
- What is it in a building's shape that communicates "church"?
- Are banks always made of stone to convey stability and permanence?

ACTIVITY 8.5 Building Typology Study Outline

Start the activity by writing at least five questions about the building type to be studied. Use the list of categories that can be investigated with a typology study. Select the issues that are pertinent to the project and add others that should be included along the way.

Examples:	"Do hospitals require special ventilation systems?"
	"What are the security protocols for a cruise ship terminal?"
	"What shape should the inside of an opera house be?"

Question 1:

Question 2:

Question 3:

Question 4:

Question 5:

Categories to Investigate

Use	Entry orientation	Square footage
Project	Massing of building	Height
Hours of operation	Spatial transitions	Budget
Location	Geometry	Building materials
Environment	Significant	Redefine neighborhood
Owner	Relationships	Reuse/restoration
Architect	Planning process	Ventilation
Physical expression	Lighting techniques	High-performance building
Mission	Energy systems	Cultural aspects
Goal	Structural systems	Historical aspects
Concept	User profile	Experiential qualities
Innovations in space arrangements	Public/private	
Organizing principle	Adjacencies	
Parking	Circulation	
	Location on site	

In many ways, designers are continually pushing the envelope with regard to site-specific design and the application of technology to create thoughtful designs that cannot be categorized broadly. As designers must continue to adhere to the principles of art (proportions, balance, etc.) and do so within the constraints of science (cantilevers, loads, etc.). Perhaps an analysis and documentation of the evolution of a specific building type could be utilized to add legitimacy to a thesis or dissertation project.

Recently, the term "building typology," when used by municipalities, indicates a specific building configuration on a property. Within this discourse, developers are offered a "menu" of possible ways in which buildings can legally be arranged on a piece of land. In this way, the city maintains control of the mass and scale of its neighborhoods, while designers strive to be creative within the confines of the prescribed envelope. Therefore, in this scenario a building typology study might be used to investigate and compare past configurations in terms of public acclaim and/or low tenant turnover.

The format of a building typology study is the same as a case study, with one exception: it compares different projects by only *functional* (use) and/or *spatial* aspects (massing). The presentation of information includes images that are reduced to their diagrammatic parts, location information, and general project parameters. How the information should be managed is dictated by the information requirements of the researcher. See Box 8.6 for an example of a typology study.

BOX 8.6 Sample Building Typology Study

A building typology study seeks to quickly access the benefits of the spatial aspects or look of a building, depending on its type. The following example compares three scenarios of urban multiple-family housing (two bedrooms with two bathrooms) built over ground-floor retail. The parameters of the study were to evaluate and determine appropriate massing and private exterior space for a similar program. (Please bear in mind this is a *brief* example.)

Project: The A Building **Location:** Tampa Bay, FL **Units:** (2) 2/2 + 1 retail **Firm:** Associates Arch	**Project:** The B Building **Location:** Los Angeles, CA **Units:** (2) 2/2 + 1 retail **Firm:** Architects R' Us	**Project:** The C Building **Location:** Portland, OR **Units:** (2) 2/2 + 1 retail **Firm:** Firm Design
<u>Housing Units (ea.):</u> **Interior Sq. Ft.:** 900 **Exterior Sq. Ft.:** 240	<u>Housing Units (ea.):</u> **Interior Sq. Ft.:** 800 **Exterior Sq. Ft.:** 400	<u>Housing Units (ea.):</u> **Interior Sq. Ft.:** 1080 **Exterior Sq. Ft.:** 120
Section and Elevation	Section and Elevation	Section and Elevation
Unit Arrangement — Horizontal—Stepped back	**Unit Arrangement** — Horizontal—In same plane	**Unit Arrangement** — Vertical—In same plane
Private Exterior Space Configuration: Narrow street front width of unit	**Private Exterior Space Configuration:** Opposing sides length of unit	**Private Exterior Space Configuration:** Opposing sides street front
Benefits: Street views, good interior light	**Benefits:** Most outdoor private space	**Benefits:** Largest living units
Limits: Reduced privacy, heat gain	**Limits:** Reduced daylight to outdoor space	**Limits:** Smallest outdoor private space
Discussion: This arrangement offers good views of street activity, though little privacy. Units are nearly identical and overall appearance of the project is one of uniformity. Large amount of glazing may increase loads on heating/cooling systems. The exterior spaces are both off of the main living areas and are afforded daylight, which extends well into the living quarters.	**Discussion:** This arrangement is an interesting application of exterior space, as several rooms within the units have access to the outdoor space, though without light wells, the spaces tend to be dark. The smaller units serve as live/work units in an art district. Nice use of stucco joints as decoration.	**Discussion:** This project marries the entrances for residents with clients of the retail space. The higher solid patio walls offer more privacy to a street presentation. The units are two-level vertical spaces; each level has a bedroom/bathroom. This spatial separation offers more opportunities for resident compositions: live/work, married with children, or roommates.

Source: Sinclair, E., (2009)

Summary

The purpose of these traditional design research methods is to provide designers with information specific to the region and unique site appropriateness of their design interventions, as well as a point of departure from which to design. The research goal for professional designers is always to gain a deeper understanding of the interrelationships between the environment and design. The research goal for professional developers is to limit legal, regulatory, and ethical issues. The goal for thesis students is to acquire valid information that will support their arguments or theories. Therefore, it behooves the designer, student, or practitioner to be cognizant of *all* the factors affecting their design scenario. Site analyses, case studies, and building typology studies all offer the experiences of observation, data collection, and analysis that can support and justify their design decisions.

Glossary

Building Typology Study—A group of buildings that share significant common features that are then clustered into a type conducive for studying as a whole.

Case Study—An in-depth investigation of an individual subject of interest, dedicated to imparting "lessons learned".

Context—A set of situations that continually change the way in which a subject of interest is perceived.

Electronic Surveys—Surveys that are either hosted on a website so that anyone can answer the questions or one that is developed and delivered via email to select individuals.

Landscape—Natural spaces viewed through cultural perspectives and exclusive to all that which the eye can see.

Program—A clearly written and organized document outlining the design project in terms of: space requirements, quality and quantity of spaces, systems, and other requirements. It succinctly summarizes the project's statement, mission, objectives and design philosophy.

Project Base Map—A map of the project site, which includes property lines, location of site features and other pertinent information to aid with a site analysis.

Site—A specific place of interest: unique piece of land/property used for a design project.

Site Analysis—An examination of a location for the purpose of deciding the most appropriate use and design for the site.

CHAPTER 9

Surveys, Interviews, and Observations

> " Genius is one percent inspiration and ninety-nine percent perspiration."
> —Thomas Edison

chapter objectives

By the end of this chapter, students should be able to:

- Discern the differences among surveys, interviews, and observational research methods.
- Identify the strengths and weaknesses of surveys, interviews, and observational research methods.
- Compare and contrast the appropriateness of surveys, interviews, and observational methods for their thesis project.
- Develop a basic framework from which to implement a survey, interview, or observational research method.

chapter outline

Introduction

Developing Questions

Surveys
Survey Construction
Survey Dissemination

Interviews
Initiating Interviews
Face-to-Face Interviews
Community Forums and Focus Groups
Electronic Media

Observations

Summary

Introduction

The systematic gathering and analysis of data is one of the most important aspects of a thesis or dissertation. Although there are many methods for acquiring data, one can stratify these methods accordingly: self-report, observation, document review, and experimentation. This chapter will discuss the different means of obtaining self-report data and how a researcher might go about gathering that information. The first question researchers must ask in regard to such data is whether to acquire the data directly or indirectly. The next pertinent step is to decide the breadth of the research. Self-report research methods can be applied to a large group of subjects to get a generalized scope of a situation, or to only a few people. In this way, the researcher is able to ask deep probing questions in order to gain a deeper understanding of a situation.

Included within the self-report research methods are a variety of direct and indirect data gathering methods. A **survey**, for example, is an indirect data-gathering method because the administration of a survey does not require the presence of the researcher. Data can be obtained, the results put into a statistical database and then the researcher can analyze and interpret that data. **Interviews**, on the other hand, require direct data gathering because an important part of the research is the vocal tones, body language, and interactions of the participants. However, a common component of both indirect and direct data gathering techniques is the use of questions. Researchers must therefore have a very clear idea of:

- What information they seek from each question.
- The type of questions they will be asking.

Developing Questions

In order to obtain relevant and informative self-report data, it is fundamental to acquire the ability to ask good questions. To do this, the researcher should either review or develop a list of very specific research objectives. To develop this list, the researcher should reexamine the fundamental premise of his or her thesis or dissertation. For example, if the researcher's fundamental premise is to develop a residential environment that enhances the sensory experience, the questions developed by the researcher should be written to elicit information related only to sensation in a residential environment, not sensation experienced in other buildings or in the natural environment. Through a clear understanding of the subject matter, the researcher can then draft the objectives. Three possible objectives from the previous example might include:

- Identify reactions to different levels of natural light entering the home.
- Discuss the different associative meanings attributed to different residential flooring materials.
- Compare initial reactions to two different furniture styles used in a living room.

From these objectives, the researcher can develop probing questions. It is important for the researcher to consider the breadth and depth of each objective in order to develop appropriate questions. To get an idea of this, consider the first objective, "Identify reactions to different levels of natural light entering the home." Is the objective speaking about lighting that enters the home first thing in the morning? Those who naturally wake up early might perceive this morning light favorably, but those who are "night owls" might view being woken up by the light negatively. Other nuances related to lighting are the presence of direct versus diffused, natural versus artificial, and real and perceived heat contributions. Hence a researcher could easily develop ten or more questions from just this one research objective.

Once questions have been formed, they need to be checked for spelling and grammar, as well as interpretation. Researchers should never assume that a participant will know the meaning of specific terms, words, or acronyms. As such, it is important to eliminate all jargon, slang, and regional colloquiums from the questions. Researchers should also avoid the use of questions that can be interpreted in more than one way. It is best for questions to be similarly phrased, so that a uniform understanding occurs, rather than several individual opinions made by different participants. From this uniformity, a profile of the larger population can emerge. Although this might seem easy to do, it is much more difficult than one would realize. Consider the question in Box 9.1, which appeared in a survey for an undergraduate architectural thesis. The researcher's intention for this question was to gauge how people perceived boundaries between public and private spaces. However, when the researcher received the answers, it became clear that the question was faulty. On further investigation, it was revealed that the participants conjured up different

BOX 9.1 Example of Misinterpreted Question

QUESTION: *With regard to meeting and visiting with neighbors, I prefer . . .*

	On the Street	At Entrance	In Property Boundaries	Home Entry/Porch	Inside House
Regular community events and unlimited opportunities to meet people (12 or more times per year)	☐	☐	☐	☐	☐
Occasional community events and infrequent visitors (more than 6 times per year)	☐	☐	☐	☐	☐
Complete privacy and limited visitors	☐	☐	☐	☐	☐

mental images of neighborhoods. Some related the question to a neighborhood where they lived in fear of their neighbors. Another group of participants related the question to a neighborhood where they are only temporary residents. Other participants related the question to a neighborhood where they do not perceive themselves as part of the neighborhood community. The result lacked collective meaning and a way to assess the results from the question. This problem could have been addressed with a series of questions that led up to this question. However, because this did not happen, the researcher ended up discarding all of the responses related to this question, which may have affected the overall results.

When test-piloting questions, the researcher should have several different people read the questions out loud. These people should not only answer the researcher's questions, as they understand the question, but also provide comments on how they interpreted the question. By hearing how the participant interpreted and answered the question, the researcher can gain additional insight into the actual question. In order for this process to be effective, the researcher cannot add clarity or offer any assistance to the participant. He or she can only listen. Only once **interpretation uniformity** has been achieved between all test pilot participants can the questions be considered ready for dissemination.

Surveys

Surveys are a nonexperimental method, intended for a descriptive study based on self-report data. They cannot offer explanations for phenomena or provide insight into cause-and-effect relationships. They are a means of collecting information from one or more sample groups in order to gain a broad overview of a specific subject matter. Surveys are most useful when researchers want to collect data related to the personal opinions or beliefs about a specific instance or phenomena. They are often directed toward a sample population that has been scientifically determined (see "sampling" in Chapter 6) so that the results represent the larger population; information is collected through a standardized process. The purpose is often to collect data about attitudes, values, beliefs, and past behaviors.

Surveys can use one of two predominant response mechanisms or a combination of both. The first response mechanism consists of predetermined closed-ended response categories. These can include anything from a list of words that participants select to a list of numbers that participants use to measure their opinions. See Figure 9.1 in Box 9.2.

Another response mechanism is the open-ended question. This approach offers the participants the opportunity to expand on their thoughts. Using the image and question in Box 9.2 as an example, a participant might say, "I think the room looks comfortable, but I don't like the flooring—it looks cold and uninviting." As you can begin to see, predetermined categories are much easier to quantify and analyze, but obtaining specifics is almost impossible. Likewise, the open-ended question allows for details, but subjective inconsistencies can confound the data. Consider the response example with an open-ended question. The participant said that it looks comfortable, but then said that it looks uninviting. Logically, how can an uninviting space also be comfortable? Analyzing such results can be very difficult and time-consuming.

BOX 9.2 Survey Question Format Example

When you look at this patient room, which word best describes what you think about it? Choose only one word.

a. Clean
b. Sterile
c. Boring
d. Cold
e. Average

———————————— OR ————————————

On a scale of 1–5 (5 being the most), how comfortable would you feel staying in a patient room that looks like this?

1   2   3   4   5

FIGURE 9.1

Source: Drawing produced by Hon, L. In Kopec, D., & Hon, L. (2008). Islam and the healthcare environment: Designing patient rooms. *Health Environments Research & Design Journal*, 1, 4, 111–121.

With predetermined response categories, either numbers or words can be used that are later assigned a numeric representation. However, numbers in and of themselves cannot be interpreted without an understanding of the assumptions that underlie them. For example, consider a simple 1-to-5 assigned rating value. In one situation, the number 1 can represent the best, and in another the number 5 can be the best. However, once the researcher chooses to assign value of one number to the "best," the value must be consistent for all questions.

In general, surveys can be useful when researchers are interested in gathering information on subject matter that is difficult to observe, such as beliefs, values, and interpretations. When a researcher wants to gain information from large sample sizes, surveys are an excellent method because they allow for standardization and assure that everyone receives the same information. Furthermore, the results can be aggregated and depicted statistically.

A disadvantage of surveys is that they rely on self-report data and thus must assume that the participants responded truthfully and accurately. In some cases, a participant might commit "honest" errors by either omitting certain information, experiencing confusion about what a question is truly asking, accidentally marking the wrong answer, or recalling something inaccurately. Assuming that most participants will be truthful, surveys can be fairly easy to distribute and collect. However, the mere fact that most surveys rely on the written word and established databases for the identification of potential participants and dissemination means that many subgroups within the general population may be inadvertently omitted, thus influencing the sample. These subgroups include, but are not limited to: those who do not read English, those who are illiterate, and those who live off the "grid."

SURVEY CONSTRUCTION

Once a researcher has decided to use a survey, also known as a *research instrument* or *tool*, then it must be constructed. The survey process includes the following steps:

- Outlining the objectives and goals of the survey.
- Writing a rough draft of the survey questions.
- Developing a plan for dissemination of getting the surveys to participants.
- Retrieving the instrument for analysis.

In many ways, the odds of getting the completed surveys back are directly related to the construction and wording used in the survey questions. A poorly designed survey often ends up in the trash, and if it is returned it most likely contains meaningless and inaccurate data. First, it is important to determine the participants' satisfaction with the selection of answers available to them for each question. One option is to provide the participants with alternate selections such as "Not applicable" or "Other." When people are revealing aspects of themselves, they often become aggravated or frustrated because they interpret the predetermined responses to be coercive or manipulative by offering only answers that do not accurately represent the response they would like to give. Therefore, neutral responses need to be included. See Box 9.3.

BOX 9.3 Coercive Question Example

Q. Indicate your cultural identity (select only one):

1. Deaf culture
2. Latino culture
3. Bisexual culture
4. Black culture
5. European culture
6. Female culture

This fictional question has the potential to aggravate and upset many survey participants, because identity is a multifaceted, highly personal, and unique expression of oneself. Therefore, were this question to be one of the first questions in a survey, participants are highly likely to stop taking the survey at this question, for the simple reason that they might consider their "identity" to be missing from the list of possible answers. Therefore, nothing within the survey would pertain to them. Researchers are encouraged to include in the selection of answers "Add Comment Here" lines, as well as "Other" or "Not Applicable" options.

When designing a survey, the researcher should first consider categorizing and arranging questions on the basis of how essential, useful, or simply convenient the data is to the overall research question. Questions providing essential data should appear first, so that if the participant encounters **survey fatigue** and fails to answer the final questions, the researcher will still obtain some of the most important responses. The order of questions also needs to be carefully thought out because certain questions may affect how the participant responds to subsequent questions. Furthermore, specific survey questions can either aggravate or encourage a participant to complete the survey. Questions that may seem difficult or sensitive should be ordered toward the end of the survey. This allows the participant to establish a rapport with the survey during the earlier questioning, so that when the more difficult questions appear, the participant is more likely to answer.

When composing the questions to be included in the survey, a decision must be made as to which of the three predominant response categories will be used. These response categories are:

- Multiple choice (close-ended)
- Open-ended
- Numeric open-end

Multiple-choice questions offer a list of possible answers, with the only choices for response being the few that are listed. Open-ended questions can be filled in with a short answer at the participants' own discretion. Numeric open-ended questions are used mostly to scale or rate the subject matter. Interestingly, many participants seem to appreciate scales or rating that use odd numbers. See Activity 9.1.

SURVEY DISSEMINATION

To maximize return rates, surveys should include a brief introduction that tells the participant about the research and the purpose of the survey. The method of survey dissemination often has a direct effect on the data, because all people have a preferred method of being approached, and if the target population's primary approach method is not used, the data results will be limited. By and large, surveys are administered either orally, with a person reading a question to the participant and marking down the response, or in written form, in which participant reads the questions and responds accordingly.

ACTIVITY 9.1 Develop and Deliver a Survey

In small groups, develop a quick three-question survey to deliver to other classroom members:

1. Outline a topic to investigate.
2. Develop objectives.
3. Focus questions on stated objectives.
4. Phrase the wording of questions to obtain accurate information.
5. Survey the class by hand count to each possible response.
6. Return to the group setting to formulate survey data into results and conclusions.
7. After all groups have completed their surveys, present the group's findings.
8. Explain the goal/purpose of each of the group's three questions and ask the class if anyone answered the questions because they understood the questions differently than the intended meaning.

Oral modes of survey dissemination involve a person attempting to engage another person in dialogue. This can happen face to face, such as outside of a mall, on a street corner, or in some kind of group gathering. Oral surveys can also be delivered over the telephone. There are many pros and cons to the oral survey. One advantage is the immediacy of acquiring the results. Having the questions read aloud allows the researcher to gather that data relatively quickly after it has been obtained. However, a significant disadvantage with oral surveys is that they require the participants to stop what they are doing in order to answer the questions. Another negative effect is related to an increased volume of telemarketers calling people's homes and an increased number of solicitors asking for signatures outside of grocery stores and shopping centers; as a result of such actions, many people are less receptive to oral surveys. An exception to this result may occur when the oral surveys are given in a group setting. However, the results obtained from groups are likely to be skewed because groups, especially if they have come together naturally (design students, club members, etc.) often share common attributes.

A second way to disseminate surveys is as a written document. These documents can be mailed, dropped off at select organizations, emailed, or placed on a website. A significant advantage to this method is that people can complete the form at their convenience. A disadvantage is that response rate tends to be very low. In terms of the mailed survey, these can be very expensive because the researcher is expected to send the initial document and expected to pay for the return of it by including a self-addressed, stamped envelope.

The lowest return rate comes from surveys dropped off at different organizations, and the best response rates come from **electronic surveys**. However, when using electronic data via the Web, the researcher must be careful of confounding variables related to the participant's geographic location. For example, out of 1,000 survey responses, 5 might have come from the Ukraine, whereas the remaining 995 all came from the United States. Hence, those 5, because of cultural differences, could skew the data, so they should be removed from the sample pool. To get a better idea of the strengths and weaknesses of different survey dissemination methods, see Table 9.1.

Table 9.1 Survey Approaches

Mode of Dissemination	Strength/"Pro"	Weakness/"Con"
Paper Documents		
Mail	Convenience Eliminate researcher bias Larger sample size	Cost Low response rate
Group	High rate of response Target population–specific	Lower number in sample size Scheduling
Drop-off	Convenience Tend to have good response	Need more time for returns Sample size is limited
Oral Dissemination		
Group	High response rates Ability to offer specificity	Small sample size Scheduling
Phone	High response rates Ability to offer specificity	Small sample size Participant inconvenience/irritation
Person-to-person	High response rates Ability to offer specificity	Small sample size Researcher bias (participants may or may not respond to researchers' looks)
Email	Cost Ease of editing Response rates Candid responses	Demographic limitations Lower confidentiality Presentation issues Instruction issues (technical problems)
Website	Cost Ease of editing Response rates Candid responses	Demographic limitations Lower confidentiality Presentation issues Instruction issues (technical problems)

The sample size for survey dissemination is dependent on the statistical results desired from the findings. In many situations, the sample population is determined through the availability of participants as well as the funds and resources for those conducting the survey. Unfortunately, the reality of resources and funding presents a strong potential for biases. Although it is impossible to eliminate all bias, precautions can be taken to limit their effects on the research. Please refer to Chapter 6 for the discussion on sampling. A note to researchers: response rates are about 25 percent of all surveys sent out.

ELECTRONIC SURVEYS

As mentioned, one way to disseminate surveys is to email them or place them on a website. In recent years, many online survey organizations have been created. Organizations such as Key Survey, Survey Monkey, and Zoomerang have made data analysis fairly easy, and allow the researcher to see multiple patterns. They are also sophisticated enough to allow the researcher to identify phenomena through cross-referencing and filtering key data points (individual questions). A couple of important factors that must be taken into consideration when developing an online survey, however, are the survey length and the potential for one person to respond multiple times, thereby biasing the results.

Survey length is a universal concern. On the one hand, a researcher wants to incorporate checks and balances into his or her survey, in order to ensure the authenticity of his or her results. Likewise, more questions help to form a better picture of the subject matter. However, people who use the Internet are used to quick actions and seem to be more susceptible to survey fatigue. If the survey is too long, the individual may just exit the survey before completing it, thereby causing the researcher to lose all of the data. One way to address this issue is through the formation of multiple short surveys. The first survey, maybe 20 questions, could provide some general information. The results of that survey can then inform the questions of the next survey. As an incentive to the recipients, the results of the first survey can be shown to the recipients. At the conclusion of the three short surveys, the researcher would have 60 questions answered, would be able to incorporate checks and balances to ensure validity, and would be able to make modifications that allow him or her to zero in on the subject of interest.

The second concern is the person who attempts to bias the results by answering more than once. The burden here will be placed on the researcher to install controls prohibiting responses from the same IP address. However, multiple people may use the same computer to respond to the survey, so the appearance of the same IP address multiple times may just be a coincidence. Until this issue can be resolved, it may behoove the researcher to simply delete all surveys that come from a single IP address.

Interviews

One way of implementing a survey is to read questions orally to a participant. The difference between this method and interviewing is that participants must select from a predetermined list of responses that best match their beliefs. Surveys that use orally implemented open-ended questions require the researcher to read the question to one or more people without offering any elaboration or clarification. These parameters, however, are not present with interviews because the premise of an interview is to obtain unbiased detailed and in-depth information from a participant about a subject of interest. It is best to identify 15 to 20 broad-based questions, which should be ranked in order of importance and designed to initiate discussion. If the participant's time is cut short, the researcher will at least have the answers to the most valued questions. Unlike orally implemented surveys, interviews allow the researcher to offer clarification or ask different questions to explore a participant's comment. Interviews can be acquired from:

- **Community forums**
- **Focus groups**
- **One-on-one discussions**
  - In person
  - On a video conference (web-based: Skype, Yahoo, Jajah, and Lycos)

The common factor between each of these methods is the verbal exchange between the researcher and the participant. In order to be effective as an interviewer, researchers must understand their target audience and draft a list of discussion questions that are appropriate for that target group. Issues of concern might include how the researcher presents him- or herself, the words used to establish trust and initiate discussion, or the setting where the interview is to take place. In addition, researchers should draft the questions differently for one-on-one interviews versus community forums or focus groups.

Understanding the population that a researcher wants to interview is an important part of building trust, which helps the participant freely offer information. Because everyone is judged by the first impression that they make, it is important to make a positive first impression by dressing appropriately. The way one dresses communicates volumes to the receiver. It may seem unusual to suggest to researchers use appropriate "image" generators, such as clothing options, but research shows that neglecting to adhere to a professional appearance negatively affects study participation. Hence it is important to gain participant's respect by avoiding inappropriate clothing such as a low-cut tops, baseball caps, short skirts, board shorts, and the like, making sure to wear nylons or socks and avoid open-toed shoes, including sandals. Clothing intended to highlight one's sexuality shows a lack of professionalism and may be viewed by the participant as vulgar. But it's best to scout out the environs and observe potential interviewees prior to the interview/survey date. For example, suits, ties, and high-fashion garments will alienate certain people. Such attire may be perceived as symbols of ego, power, and conspicuous consumption. Hence if the researcher is interviewing groups of people who have limited power or financial resources, then these symbols may be received negatively and the interview results may be unsatisfactory. In these situations, jeans, T-shirts, and sneakers are probably the most suitable; the goal is to make the interviewees comfortable, and to be one of them. As such, if the audience to be interviewed is made up of professionals, then professional attire is required. It is important to remember that a researcher's clothing should not be the focus of the interview, or distract from the participant's attention; apparel should make the participants feel comfortable and not intimidate them.

When developing questions and conducting an interview, researchers should pay special attention to word choice. Poorly worded questions can lead to double entendres and other forms of confusion, causing the participant to misunderstand the question or to interpret the question differently than what was intended. Slang, colloquialisms, jargon, and acronyms can all be alienating to a person. An example of a slang phrase might be "crash course" or "humongous"; colloquialism might be some regional word or phrase such as "sweet" or "cute." Although slang and colloquialisms infer a level of casualness, jargon and acronyms are often equated with professional language and can be intimidating. Jargon is a set of industry-specific words that are not used in mainstream language. Examples of jargon include a "building envelope" (that which surrounds the building) or "BIM" (Building Information Modeling) or "PING" (Packet Internet Groper), which is a testing protocol to verify that a computer is connected to the Internet—which now colloquially means to communicate with someone. When just the first letter of each word within a title is used, it becomes an acronym. Examples of acronyms can be found throughout American society: ADA, APA, or ACSA. A significant problem with acronyms is that the meaning is not uniform. For example, ADA could mean the Americans with Disabilities Act, the American Diabetics Association, or the American Dietetic Association; APA could mean the American Planning Association or the American Psychological Association; ACSA could mean the Association of California School Administrators, an Apple Certified Systems Administrator, or the Association of Collegiate Schools of Architecture. Therefore, it is highly advisable to refrain from the use of slang, colloquialisms, jargon, and acronyms when engaging in an interview.

The setting in which an interview is conducted can also have a significant effect on a person's level of trust and willingness to disclose information freely. For instance, interviews that occur at the participant's home or workplace tend to yield the best results because the participant tends to feel calm and secure in these environments. Conversely, interviews that take place in an institution, such as a homeless shelter, school, or even the researcher's workplace, often yield responses that the participant believes the researcher wants to hear. In many instances, a participant may feel powerless within unfamiliar environments, resulting in participants censoring their responses. A third environment where an interview might take place is a public setting. Restaurants, coffee shops, and malls are all examples of public environments. These public environments should be neutral, meaning that they appeal to both the researcher and the participant. For example, if participants who live in a lower socioeconomic neighborhood meet a researcher at a coffee shop in a wealthy neighborhood, this would likely make them feel uncomfortable and cautious with their responses.

The primary difference between participant response methods is the amount of time spent probing for data, and the number of people addressed with a single question. Interviews, for example, require one-on-one interaction and can consume one or more hours per interview. Surveys, on the other hand, can be sent to thousands of people at one time. Analysis of the data is also different. Surveys need to be quantified and thus require much data entry (unless web-based services are used), which often manifests as charts, graphs, and statistical descriptions. Interviews, on the other hand, tend to be more qualitative and require the researcher to be an astute observer. This is because the words provide only an answer to the question—body language and vocal tones provide another dimension to the data analysis that cannot be obtained from written surveys. This is because communication can be categorized into four types (verbal, nonverbal, visual, and symbolic); humans gain infor-

FIGURE 9.2 Human Communication Types. Communication is a vehicle for information that is composed of 60 percent body language, 30 percent tone of voice, and 10 percent word selection. This illustration depicts communicating a "greeting." A wave is a nearly universal body language symbol indicating a greeting; by following tone, inflection, and quality of word choice, a person hearing a foreign language can therefore understand a "greeting" by the delivery of the sounds. Ten percent of communication comes through word selection; a more formal greeting will be understood to mean that the setting requires the receiving person to conduct themselves in a proper and formal manner, whereas a casual greeting is a cue that the setting is a relaxed and informal one.
Source: Sinclair, E. (2009).

mation from each type at roughly the following percentages: 60 percent body language, 30 percent tone of voice, and 10 percent word selection. Hence face-to-face research affords an added dimension of analysis that enriches the data. See Figure 9.2.

INITIATING INTERVIEWS

Once a researcher has decided to use interviews as the primary source for collecting new data, a list of people who may be able to provide valuable information must be developed. These people should then be contacted via telephone, mail, or email. One way for the researcher to ease into the process and prepare is to create a "request to participate" postcard that includes a brief description of the research project and a formal request. Figure 9.3 is an example of such a query letter. It is important, however, that the researcher follow up with the people who indicate a willingness to participate within five to seven days. At this time, the researcher should provide the participant with possible dates, times, and locations of a community forum, focus group, or interview.

Once the researcher has identified a pool of potential participants, a list should be made of possible locations to conduct the interviews. In most cases, several options are available. Focus groups and community forums can be held in banquet rooms of restaurants and hotels, community centers, city-owned libraries, or even local parks.

I am a researcher at _____, and conducting research related to the developmental needs of autistic children. As parents of an autistic child I would like to invite you to participate in a small group discussion.

It is anticipated that the discussion would take about one hour, and it will be videotaped only for research purposes. Please indicate by checking the appropriate box for your willingness to participate in this discussion.

☐ Yes ☐ No

If you answered YES, please provide your contact information so that I can schedule a time and date.
Name_____ Phone Number_____
Email Address_____
THANK YOU

Figure 9.3 Sample Query letter.
Source: Kopec, D. (2009).

Locations for face-to-face interviews can be very informal, such as a bus stop, lobby of a hotel, or a park bench. What is important about selecting a site is that the location must have easy access to parking and be relatively easy to find.

Once the location has been identified, the next issue of concern is the necessary equipment. Because body language and tone of voice often provide a wealth of information, it is highly recommended that the researcher videotape the session for later review and analysis. However, it important that researchers obtain consent forms from each participant prior to video or audio recording. An advantage of videotaping interviews is that it allows the researcher to easily note at what point of the session important quotes and comments were made and allows the researcher to quickly locate comments for exact quotes. Within focus groups and community forums, videotaping the sessions allows the researcher to watch the facial expressions and body language of and between various members throughout the interview.

For community forums and focus groups, it is appropriate to provide some kind of incentive for the participants. Most people understand that most researchers have limited budgets, and hence do not expect much by way of incentives; however, a small token gift, personal thank-you card, or finger foods are appropriate gestures. Having snacks is also a great icebreaker and often facilitates greater discussion. If refreshments are served, they should be placed away from the table or primary area where the discussion will be held. For one-on-one interviews, it is appropriate for the researcher to pay for a participant's beverage if such services are offered at the interview location (as in a coffee shop or café).

With regard to community forums and focus groups, it is often best to prepare nametags so that people do not have to fumble around as they try to recall an individual's name. Also, the use of nametags can be beneficial for the researcher who desires greater clarification from a single participant or to single out a participant for a possible one-on-one interview at a later date.

FACE-TO-FACE INTERVIEWS

Once researchers have decided to use a face-to-face method to acquire further information, several logistical issues must be considered. Nonverbal communication is a two-way street, which means that while the researcher is assessing the participants, the participants are also assessing the researcher. See Figure 9.4.

The outcome of these assessments will likely influence how the participant responds. One of the first considerations is who conducts the community forum, focus group, or interview. Presumably, this should be the researcher because gaining control over personal biases and personal opinions is the first order of business: it is absolutely imperative that the person conducting the interviews be neutral. This means that the researcher cannot communicate beliefs or opinions by way of vocal tone or body language (i.e., should not lean or step back when a person says something shocking or inflammatory or expresses an opinion that is not shared). See Table 9.2.

Likewise, some participants may not like a topic being discussed; therefore, researchers need to be prepared for these participants to freely voice their opinions. It should be noted that it is the participants' verbal and nonverbal comments and behavior that are of interest—not the researchers'.

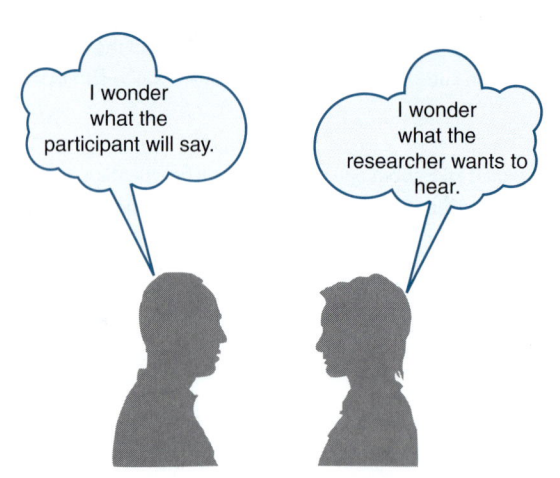

FIGURE 9.4 Nonverbal Assessment. Nonverbal assessment between interviewer and study participant. Controls should be put into place to minimize things such as periods of silence in which the interview may stray off course, as individuals then have the time to mentally assess each other, possibly affecting the responses.
Source: Sinclair, E. (2009).

Table 9.2   Body Language Guide

Sitting or standing straight	Person is seen as confident and secure with himself or herself.
Hands on hips	Person is seen as defensive; possible verbal aggression.
Eye contact	Person is seen as trustworthy; allows for greater interpersonal connections.
Playing with hair or tugging ear	Person is seen as nervous, distracted, or fearful.
Crossed arms	Person perceived suspiciously, "closed" to other people's ideas and unwilling to compromise.
Hands in pockets	Person is seen as meek and untrustworthy.
Open hands	Person is seen as open-minded and willing to listen to new ideas and concepts.
Hands in steeple	Person is seen as confident and trustworthy.

FIGURE 9.5
Source: Sinclair, E., (2009)

COMMUNITY FORUMS AND FOCUS GROUPS

There are numerous pros and cons to the use of community forums, focus groups, and interviews. Community forums or focus groups for example, are subject to **groupthink**, which is a distortion of reality and temporary cessation of critical thinking among highly cohesive groups of people. For example, if a group of neighbors come together to discuss the issue of a new housing development in their neighborhood, the overwhelming majority—without regard to the potential benefits to the neighborhood—might reject the development outright; this is known as a "not in my back yard" (NIMBY) response. The group wants something so badly that they cease to think logically, objectively, or as individuals, and merely "react" as a whole. Once groupthink begins, it may be hard for the facilitator to redirect the group. Once the facilitator loses the ability to keep the group focused, the session should be terminated. Other problematic issues with community forums, focus groups, or interviews are that they are time-consuming and the data obtained is often limited. However, community forums, focus groups, and interviews provide the perfect venue for people to express their thoughts. They are also well suited for an exploration of attitudes, thoughts, and perceptions of a group of people, providing the researcher with in-depth information. Another benefit of community forums, focus groups, and interviews for the design researcher is the ability and space to use visual aids and other presentation materials to a larger audience. See Table 9.3 and Activity 9.2.

Table 9.3   Community Forum, Focus Groups, and Interviews

Advantages	Disadvantages
Provides in-depth information and allows people to talk about their attitudes, thoughts, and perceptions.	Subject to groupthink and tangents: this can complicate the data gathering efforts.
Participants can hear what others are saying and thus become motivated to participate.	Provides limited information related to the attitudes, thoughts, and perceptions of individuals or smaller groups.
Visual aids can be used.	Facilitator must be able to keep the group focused, or the results could become contaminated.

ACTIVITY 9.2 Interview Practice

Select a partner to practice interviewing skills. Use one of your thesis topics, if possible. Develop the intended path of the conversation. Document the interview process and afterward discuss the implications, distractions, and positive features of the interviewing process. Switch places with your partner and play the opposite role.

In most situations, researchers will be the moderator of a community forum or focus group. It will be their role to plan out and prepare for the event, and they carry the responsibility to set the overall tone and atmosphere of openness from the onset of the session. This includes:

- Identifying appropriate questions
- Developing a clear perspective of the scope and purpose

The researcher should prepare 10 to 15 highly provocative questions in order to initiate and facilitate continuous dialogue. They should also be prepared for the occasions when the discussion goes off track or when someone contributes something unintended yet interesting—using it to the benefit of the research. In this way, the researchers moderate and analyze what is being said "on-the-spot," facilitating the communication while avoiding topics that stray from the research goals. See Table 9.4. To enable the researcher to compare and contrast responses, and thus develop more accurate results, multiple community forums or focus group sessions should be planned. However, because of the increased potential for confounding variables occurring from multiple sessions, the results—along with any differences in location, time of day, and participant characteristics—should be carefully documented. More often than not, the participants of the discussion session dictate the length of the discussion based on the amount of information they have and their willingness to participate.

Whether it is a community forum, focus group, or interview, an important aspect of face-to-face research methods is the ability to moderate the discussions. In short, the moderator has the authority and obligation to stop inappropriate behaviors and ensure that all members get an opportunity to express their thoughts. Depending on the group and the topic, people can hold strong convictions and passions, which can present as irrational thoughts and aggressive behaviors. Therefore, moderators must be skilled observers so that they can detect when participants are getting too emotional in their response(s) concerning the subject. When this occurs, the moderator needs to shift the group's focus to another question and let those who were becoming upset have an opportunity to calm down or redirect their attention. People who become overly emotional at community forums, focus groups, or even interviews often respond in one of three ways:

- Hostility
- Ceasing to participate
- Leaving the group

Any of these responses will likely confound the data and must be addressed when analyzing the results. It is also important to realize that moderators have the responsibility to remain sensitive to each participant's emotional experience, while retaining the mental agility to maintain control of their research group.

Table 9.4 Typical Group Settings Attendance

It is a reality when working with groups that those who say they will attend do not always attend. Here is a typical "invited/attendance" guide on the basis of the experiences of the authors.

Group Format	Participants Invited	Participants in Attendance
Community forum	20–30 participants	9–18 people will generally show up
Focus group	12–15 participants	6–9 will typically show up
Interviews	8–10 participants should be selected	5–6 will actually follow through

ELECTRONIC MEDIA

Traditionally, community forums, focus groups, and interviews were done in person. However, technological advances have now made it possible to conduct community forums, focus groups and interviews through **electronic media**, such the Internet's virtual spaces (including Linden Labs' Second Life), instant messaging, webcam interactions, and video conference websites. These methods of data gathering have the advantage of participants being able to remain in the comfort of their own home or office and allow for a degree of autonomy. Interestingly, people often disclose more personal information about themselves over the Internet as opposed to in person. There is a degree of artificiality and separateness that occurs from discussions held remotely that may make participants less likely to form bonds. Consequently, this may decrease groupthink and make expanded and deeper discussions more likely.

The greatest weakness of electronic media is that not everyone is comfortable with this medium. Therefore, the people who opt for this method are likely to share many of the same characteristics. The researcher does, however, have the potential of turning this negative into a positive, but doing so requires time and additional analysis, because more sessions will need to take place both in person and online, and the participant profile between the different groups will need to be carefully cross-referenced.

Researchers opting for electronic community forums, focus groups, or interviews need to gain an understanding of the best way for implementation. This includes selecting and recruiting a diverse array of participants, the media on which the discussion will be hosted (a virtual reality, formal conferencing center, etc.), and how to elicit deeper and more meaningful information. Like any other method, this process and its plan should be documented and described in detail within the methods chapter of the thesis or dissertation.

Observations

Observations are a field-study approach to nonexperimental research. It is a qualitative method with strong ties to traditional ethnography. An observation involves the monitoring and careful recording of some event or phenomenon. This monitoring and recording generally occurs in a natural setting and can take place over a prolonged period of time. The goal of researchers in an observational study is to develop a thorough understanding of an event or phenomena under investigation. Observation can be conducted from a distance or by participating and interacting with the subject or group. There are different ways to implement observational studies, each with its own advantage and disadvantage. These methods include:

- **Observing participant**
- **Participant-observer**
- **Neutral observer**

It is very important for the researcher to select the most appropriate method for the research.

An observing participant is one who will simply observe the sequence of events or situations as they unfold. In this situation, the researcher may opt to "shadow" a person throughout the course of one or more days, or he or she could simply sit at an adjacent desk, cafeteria table, or nearby chair in a meeting. The people are aware of the observer and the observer is present throughout many of the activities, but the observer does not actually engage the person(s) being observed. A clear disadvantage of this method is that people are aware that they are being watched and may alter their behaviors. An advantage of this method is that it is fairly easy to implement and the observations generally do not last longer than a couple of weeks. See Table 9.5.

A participant observer also approaches participants in their own environment and will often observe while participating in activities. In this situation, the observer actually becomes part of the scene. For example, if someone wanted to know how an office environment functioned, a researcher might get a job at an office. During the course of daily duties, he or she also records observations of how the office functions. The participant observer's role is to act as an "undercover investigator" to identify situations and events from an insider perspective, but without influencing the situation. Hence, researchers will need to be careful of the following:

- What they say to others
- The degree of gossip they participate in
- Avoid giving advice or offering opinions

Researchers must mitigate and limit these actions, as they may lead to an undesirable change in the outcome of the research. A disadvantage of this process is that when the truth is revealed, people often feel betrayed. This method is

Table 9.5   Observation Types

Type	Description	Advantage	Disadvantage	Locations
Observing participant	People are aware of the observer, and the observer merely watches and records the actions/interactions throughout a period of time.	Very ethical. Does not take much time. Easy to implement.	People often alter their behaviors and censor their words. Provides only a snapshot in time.	Observing actions/interactions in public service environments such as waiting rooms, airports, museums, and the like. The management is aware of the observer.
Participant-observer	The observer blends in and becomes a member of the team or community	Excellent for obtaining insightful information about thoughts and behaviors.	Low ethics; people often feel deceived. Requires longer period of time.	Observing actions/interactions within organization of structured environment such as offices, schools, prisons, and so on.
Neutral observer	The observer watches the action/interactions of people in public settings.	Very ethical. Doesn't take much time. Easy to implement.	Limited to public spaces. Provides only a snapshot in time.	Observing actions/interactions in public spaces such in or around bus stops, in a mall, hotel lobby, public park, and so on.

also time-consuming because it must continue for an extended period of time to produce valid and relevant results. However, it is an excellent way to obtain information that might not be achieved in any other way.

A neutral observer is one who sits quietly and tries to blend into the background and merely watch events and situations as they unfold. Much like in "people-watching," the subjects are often unaware that they are being observed. This is an excellent method to identify wayfinding practices or to establish social norms and adherence to rules. Researchers engaging in this type of observation need to be aware of any preconceptions they may have and take steps to limit such influences on the documentation and subsequent findings. A weakness of neutral observation is that access and availability to certain areas of interest is often restricted to researchers. For example, a researcher could not be in a doctor's waiting room all day, sitting alone and taking notes, without attracting some attention from staff and/or security.

When conducting observational methods, the researchers must take careful objective notes about behaviors, events, and situations that have been observed. These observations can come from visual actions, informal conversations, and body language or observing changes in noise levels or odor. Oftentimes researchers will engage in purposeful interactions, such as introducing a new object into the environment to gauge people's reactions. For example, a researcher might place a personal item on the chair next to him or her and wait for a person to ask the researcher to remove the item or simply go sit somewhere else. It is important for the researcher to record with as much detail as possible the actions and reactions of all subjects being observed. This includes the perspectives and judgments of the researcher/observer as well.

Observational studies are an excellent way for researchers to observe behavior in a natural setting. However, there are many limitations, which include the inability to ascribe causation. Although observations can describe events and situations, they are limited in their ability to say for certain that one event will lead to another event. Observations also tend to be time-consuming and require numerous and detailed notes of the event or situation being observed. The results of observations are often depicted as a narrative that synthesizes the interpreted data into an understandable and enlightening piece of writing. See Activity 9.3.

ACTIVITY 9.3   Observation Exercise

Observe and document a human behavior with regard to an environmental factor. For example, at crosswalks, people generally do not make eye contact. Write a four-paragraph document with the following headings:

Paragraph 1: Purpose of the observation

Paragraph 2: Environment and subject's description

Paragraph 3: Findings and conclusions

Paragraph 4: What I learned by observing

Summary

The systematic gathering and analyzing of data is one of the most important aspects of a thesis or dissertation. Obtaining data with the self-reporting methods of surveys, interviews, and observation can be done directly or indirectly—that is, face-to-face or from afar. It is important for researchers to consider the scope and purpose of each objective of their thesis in order to develop appropriate questions. Therefore, it becomes fundamental for researchers to acquire the ability to ask good questions.

Surveys rely on the written word, a large pool of participants, and an effective way to get the information to the people selected. The process of creating a survey includes outlining the objectives, writing a draft of the questions, getting the surveys to participants, retrieving their answers, and analyzing and interpreting the data. The major factors of a survey's success have to do with all of the participants understanding the questions and having an appropriate answer to select. There are two types of surveys: oral and written. The desired amount of raw data is an indication of the type a researcher might select. If 100 responses is the research goal, then 400 people should be surveyed—a general rule of thumb is that only 25 percent of the participant pool will respond to a survey request.

Interviewing subjects is a research method to obtain detailed and in-depth information. Factors key to the success of an interview include a setting that is comfortable to the individual being interviewed, questions that are worded in a concise and easily understood fashion, and making sure that the interviewer does not intimidate or distract the subject by way of appearance or body language. Researchers must be cognizant of nonverbal communication and gain control over their personal biases and opinions prior to interviewing any subjects. Similar factors are indicated with the moderating of large-group interviews, also known as community forums and focus groups.

Community forums or focus groups are subject to groupthink—a phenomenon occurring in large groups of people in which members begin to conform to a perceived majority view and stop thinking as individuals. Once groupthink begins, it may be hard for the facilitator to redirect the group; therefore, researchers must become adept at focusing the discussion and controlling departures from the topic. Researchers can predict the tipping points and the triggers that cause the discussion group to fall off track by observing the groups' activity and interactions.

Being a skilled observer is an important aspect of face-to-face research as well as field research. Observation is the monitoring and recording of subject-to-environment behaviors. The goal of researchers in an observational study is to develop a thorough understanding of an event or phenomena under investigation. Observations can be conducted from a distance or by participating and interacting with the subject or group. The main types are observing participant, participant-observer, and neutral observer. The main benefit of the observational study from a design research perspective is the understanding that the researcher comes away with, that the physical environment does affect behavior—and thus that what is designed for people will influence people.

Glossary

Community forum—When a group of individuals come together at a site to share information related to a subject of concern.

Electronic media—A form of communication that relies on electricity and electromechanical equipment to transmit.

Focus group—An assembled group of people who are asked to comment about a product, service, or concept.

Groupthink—The suspension of critical thinking and the formation of a distorted perception of reality that can occur within highly cohesive groups of people.

Interpretation uniformity—When a group of people interprets a set of results or outcomes the same way.

Interviews—A conversation between two or more people where questions are asked with the intention of obtaining information.

Neutral observer—A person who can observe a set of situations or circumstances without any opinion about the events.

Observations—A systematic way of watching and analyzing something in an effort to draw conclusions.

Participant-observer—A person who watches and records a series of actions while participating in the activity.

Survey—A tool used to collect quantitative information about opinions or phenomena within a population.

Survey fatigue—When a participant either answers questions without reading the question or fails to answer questions because the survey instrument is too long.

CHAPTER 10

Historical Analysis Method and Photo Analysis Method

chapter outline

Introduction

Historical Analysis Method
Areas of Research
Historic Documents
　Popular Media
　History Books
　Census Data
　Public Records
Data Analysis

Photo Analysis Method
Process
Approaches
Analysis Criteria
Photo Modification

Summary

> "Research is to see what everybody else has seen and to think what nobody else has thought."
>
> —Albert Szent-Gyorgyi

chapter objectives

By the end of this chapter, students should be able to:

- Evaluate historic material, including government documents, for their possible contributions to research.
- Identify the different ways in which a researcher could conduct a photo analysis.
- From a visual perspective, discuss why photo analysis might be an ideal research method for design research.

144

Introduction

This chapter discusses two methods of scientific inquiry: **historical analysis** and **photo analysis.** The primary difference between these two types of inquiry and other methods is that these studies limit the direct contact between the researcher and other people, subjects, or objects. Historical analysis reviews a host of documents published in the past. Researchers opting to use historical analysis as a research method might decide to include the following:

- Case law, to analyze trends in court rulings related to design practices.
- **Census data**, to understand changes in wealth and family structure or ethnographic history books to gain longitudinal perspectives.
- Historical analysis, which includes the observation and analysis of change over time as a way to understand contemporary designs.

Photo analysis is similar to the historic approach. This method requires the researcher to gather a series of images and analyze them from a given perspective. Perspectives may include any of the following:

- The photographer's sociocultural predispositions.
- The image's content, which can demonstrate precedence or archetype.
- Chronicling the evolution of a design style.
- Analyzing details in isolation.

When engaging in this method, the goal of the researcher is to document clearly how the photos will be analyzed and to make certain that all photos are analyzed in an identical and systematic manner.

Historical Analysis Method

Historical analysis is a research method requiring multiple sources to discover the situations or events that led to an occurrence of interest, which include, but are not limited to:

- History books
- Archived records
- Statistical reports
- Eyewitness accounts

To illustrate the need for this multiplicity, consider the following theoretical statement: "The changes in design styles often follow changes in technology, which then affect the evolution of culture." This chain of logic would require several pieces of evidence to substantiate each claim throughout a series of events. The historical analysis then becomes a systematic and objective examination for the purposes of reconstructing or conceptualizing a given situation. Therefore, the study should begin with a predetermined set of variables identified as having particular importance or significance to the research. The researcher will then need to collect, verify, evaluate, and synthesize the multiple datasets in order to establish a defensible conclusion.

Outlining the historical process is much like the process for all research methods: the first important step is to clearly identify the purpose of the study. The second step is to identify the relevance of the study to the reader. Using this information, the researcher can then formulate the central question and describe how the project will ultimately manifest, thus affecting the kind of resources to be obtained. See Box 10.1.

BOX 10.1 Historical Documentation Process

Step 1: Identify the purpose of the study.
Step 2: Identify the relevance of the study.
Step 3: Formulate the central question of the study.
Step 4: Describe how the project will reveal facts.
Step 5: Describe the kind and type of sources (books, photos, maps, census, etc).

For example, a researcher might wish to record the history of architectural designs developed under the Union of Soviet Socialist Republics (USSR). The central question might be "How did Soviet-style architecture differ from western-style architecture in terms of ideological communication?" The second step would be to identify the relevance to the reader. Hence, the researcher might fall back on a quote from George Santayana, "Those who cannot remember the past are condemned to repeat it." (Santayana, 1905, p. 284). The relevance then becomes this statement: "To learn from past Soviet architectural practices in order to prevent the consequences of those practices from repeating." Of course, this argument is predicated on the belief that architecture serves as an instigator and reflection of the sociocultural time. Only through historical analysis can the complex set of social interactions between society, time, events, environment, and cultural beliefs begin to be defined.

Historical analysis is an ideal process for learning procedures for students wishing to pursue careers in history or preservation. Other advantages to the historical analysis include, but are not limited to:

- Researchers cannot accidentally affect variables (the variables occurred in the past).
- Never one right answer, fact, or authoritative interpretation (history is for those who like a variety of research options).
- Process resists straight lines: between cause and effect and between past and present (history is a conversation with people, their opinions, places, and times;—it can only be interpreted—and it rarely predicts destiny).

A research study based on historical documentation can satisfy a study's central question using information found in old documents such as newspapers, magazines, and census data. Other information may be found in history books, birth and death records, and photographs, or in the actual physical environment (archeology). Once the researcher has outlined the plan of action needed in answering the central question, the next issue of importance is to describe how the information will be uncovered, along with an explanation of the subsequent value of the information.

Because historical research utilizes multiple sources, the process of gathering and analyzing data can become overwhelming. To help keep things clear, the researcher must develop a research plan that includes a list of sources, phenomena, and artifacts to be examined. As a time-management tool, this list should be sequenced according to when each portion of the research is to be completed. Although it is likely that this list will shift in priority and evolve along with the research, it will help to think ahead and identify potential pitfalls. It further behooves the researcher to periodically review the research gathered to assess if there is too much on one given topic or if additional research is needed in order to continue moving forward. See Activity 10.1.

AREAS OF RESEARCH

Designers specifically use historical analysis to study particular aspects belonging to four broad areas of research:

1. User group or behavior (person)
2. Site or community (place)
3. Building or artifact (thing)
4. Style or theme (typology)

Design and personalization are becoming increasingly popular. Anticipating this trend challenges the design field to address the following question: can a group of people, a user group, be defined by their environments, or vice versa? It has been theorized that the floorplan or functional use of a building will be used differently predicated on culture identification and age groups, among other factors. Therefore, historical analysis would be an excellent way to research a user group for cultural cues and an evolution toward preferences in spatial arrangement. A demographic survey, such as the U.S. Census, is conducted in the United States once every ten years, though similar surveys are conducted on the city level more often. Ideally, the researcher should exhaust all resources of **public records** to gain the most contemporary data when addressing the research and documentation of human beings.

The research of a site or community is extremely relevant to design. The inquiry is part and parcel of a site analysis (please refer to Chapter 8). Without the history and background of a landscape, its people and the dynamics (social and economic) of its evolution, a design could be deemed irrelevant on an academic level and a disrespectful intrusion on a public community level. Therefore, design researchers wishing to delve into the history of a community as a whole or just a particular site would be wise to use the results of a historical analysis to expand their design parameters and to refine their design programs to be more culturally competent.

ACTIVITY 10.1 Historical Research Plan

Follow these examples to develop a plan of action to document the historical data related to your research variables. To avoid problems or lost information at a later date, create an additional document for archiving the recorded references and sources used.

Variable	Source (APA Citation)	Key Facts or Ideas	Refined Variable	Notes
Phenomena (Event or Observation)	*(Example #1)*			
Suburban socializing	*Jones, A. (1996). History of Neighborhoods. Acme Publishing: Yourtown, WA.*	*Social behaviors expressed through consumerism.*	*The "mall" is a dominate social arena.*	*Find census data on area around local mall.*
Artifact (Object or Design)	*(Example #2)*			
Front porches	*Smith, A. (2002). ABC's of Historic Blueprints. Acme Publishing: Mytown, AL.*	*The iconic American front porch nearly disappears by the 1980s.*	*Record the "disappearance of the front porch."*	*Compare historic trends in which garages became attached to homes and the front porch diminished.*

    The historic analysis of a building is critical to the sustainability of the environment; often, it is the emotional connection a community has towards its older buildings that should be documented and analyzed. In many communities, old buildings captivate the hearts of the residents because of the history, cultural identity, architectural details and even the materials of the building. Therefore, speaking with long-time residents and questioning them about the building's symbolic meaning or sociocultural message is also warranted and applicable to designs that incorporate architectural adaptive-reuse techniques. A researcher should include an analysis of original documents, photographs, or blueprints. Investigations of this nature may include a visit to the local historical society, library archives, and/or museums, as these places are treasure troves of information. In order to effectively analyze these items, the researcher should establish some guidelines:

- What is the importance of the subject being studied?
- Does the design style conform to the theme of the era or did it propose a new way of thinking?
- What attributes of the design separated it from other designs of the same time period?
- Was the design altered either intentionally or unintentionally throughout any point in time and why?
- Besides dates, what other clues are offered that reveal developments of the time period in which it was designed (new industry or transportation advances)?

    A style can be studied to identify reoccurring themes embedded in design to avoid reinventing a design that already exists or to establish a solid foundation on a subject. The idea of incorporating a historical analysis into the design process is something that leading design firms such as IDEO already incorporate as part of the formative stages of design. The evolution of styles and architectural trends has been a hotly debated subject in the philosophical architectural circles for some time; therefore, the design researcher is duly cautioned to bring to the discussion as much historic data as possible, cross-referenced with facts of the generational culture of the time. For example, if the central question of a study was, "Did modern architecture disenfranchise 1960s youth?" three issues are immediately apparent. First, the study will have to bring forth documentation of what "modern architecture" is; second, the researcher will have to prove with historic data that the youth of this time period displayed behaviors of a group forgotten or neglected by society; and third, some factual data will be required to satisfy the subcontext of the entire question, "Does architecture or design affect human behavior?" **Cross-referencing** is the linking or layering of the similar information from different sources. As an analogy, in CAD programs cross-referencing is known as an "xref," in which one drawing supports another without influencing the function of either. In the research domain, in any given year, census figures can be cross-referenced with occupational data and housing starts to formulate a story depicting why and how particular communities started or grew. Thus, cross-referencing serves to verify and support the data (without manipulating the results) to provide the study with the logic and critical analysis that validates the entire research and subsequent document.

Often a research project will contain two or more areas to be considered simultaneously, such as a site and a building, or a building and an interior space. A researcher might want to understand how a site contributed to a building versus how the building has affected the surrounding environment. To illustrate this concept, the Chrysler Tower in New York City was once the tallest building in the world. During the unveiling of the building, it stood with prominence and served as a landmark within the city. Today, however, this same building has lost much of its prominence within the city because other buildings have dwarfed its height and much has been built up around it, diminishing its engineering marvels. Through a review and cataloging of background images within the older photos and by comparing similar views and changes over a period of time, a researcher might be able to arrive at conclusions that would have otherwise gone unnoticed. (See more in the section "Photo Analysis Method.")

Despite the many benefits of historical analysis, the process has limitations:

- The depiction of history
- The accuracy of historical records/recollections

Both variables are not culturally universal. The events of the Cold War, for example, lack a universal description between the United States and Russia. In other words, in both countries the events of the times would be recorded differently to match the country's perspectives. Another limitation with historical writings is that their recordings are subject to human error and that all authors have a perspective and thus a bias. As much as a writer attempts to write facts and facts alone, life experiences and personal points of view make their way onto the page. So it is recommended that the student, the designer, and the researcher always use several sources describing the same subject to gauge historic interpretations. In the event that multiple views are expressed, it is important to present and discuss *all* of these perspectives in order to give the results greater validity and legitimacy.

HISTORIC DOCUMENTS

Popular Media

Old newspapers, catalogs, and magazines often provide insight into the culture of a given period of time. Word choices, clothing, and hairstyles, as well as design styles and floorplan layouts, can provide clues into a society's norms and values. Regardless of the supposition, the demographic characteristics of the historic timeframe in question must be clearly identified so that overgeneralizations are avoided. For example, researchers wanting to analyze trends of social change in the United States throughout the twentieth century might look at the average wealth, political, and religious influence by using information found in popular media as a comparison.

In the scenario in Box 10.2, the thesis states that increases in wealth lead to changes in society's beliefs, and result in social reactions from religious groups., The first flaw in this argument is the association between wealth and change, such that, for example, both the French and Russian revolutions were caused by poverty and oppression, not wealth, and both led to significant social changes. Hence, the researcher will need to figure out how to delineate social change from political change. From this argument, the researcher may be speaking of social policy changes, as opposed to the overthrow of a government and the formation of a new political governing body. Once the researcher has developed the comparison, a chain of logic (refer to Chapter 3) must be created and the

BOX 10.2   Example Historic Supposition via Comparison

"Twentieth-century trends: with increased wealth comes social reform concerning equity, followed by reactions from religious groups."

To support this supposition, the researcher will need to draw comparisons.

For example:

Newspapers: In 1848, public policy changed to allow married women to legally keep and manage their own money, wages, and property.

Catalogs: In 1870, women are shown in long multilayered dresses and tight constricting corsets. By the 1920s, women were purchasing loose-fitting "flapper"-style dresses.

Magazines: In 1920, due in part to the correlation between alcohol-abuse and domestic violence, the religious and social movement (known as *temperance*) prompted Prohibition.

Newspapers: The 1950s and 1960s after WWII was another affluent period in U.S. history.

Newspapers: In the 1950s and 1960s, significant strides were made in civil rights of minority groups.

Magazines and television: In the 1950s, with the advent of mainstream access to television and radio, followed the formation of televangelists.

Newspapers and television: In the last half of the 1990s, with the "dot com" explosion, America saw another increase in wealth.

Internet: In 2001, the Harris Poll stated that 58 percent of surveyed adults were in favor of a federal law outlawing job discrimination based on sexual orientation, and 42% thought a law such as this already existed.

Newspapers and Internet: In 2008, members of the Mormon Church are alleged to have contributed to the defeat of California's bill to allow gay and lesbian marriage.

---

researcher must prove the statement with multiple pieces of evidence. With any investigation or type of study, a chain of logic is an excellent diagramming tool to chart the progress of the research. Figure 10.1 graphically represents the suppositions expressed and researched in this example.

History Books

To a researcher, history books are an invaluable tool when attempting to gain an overview of the conditions, circumstances, and practices of a given era. However, researchers must make sure that they incorporate a generous array of books: each book will be written from the perspective of the author, and as mentioned earlier, it is impossible to chronicle history without bias. These perspectives, though seemingly accurate, will be only one way of interpreting the subject in question. Hence, it is best to get a diverse array of opinions and thoughts related to the subject.

By understanding the historical context and the social norms and values of an era, a designer can better prepare for future designs. For example, photos of a home in the early 1950s might show wall-to-wall carpeting. By reading history books, a researcher can learn that wall-to-wall carpeting was not the norm in this era. Thus the researcher can deduce that the presence of wall-to-wall carpeting in the photo indicates that the home may have belonged to a forward-thinking or wealthy person. By conducting a historical analysis, the researcher is able to engage in **post-diction**, whereby he or she analyzes a series of variables to draw probable conclusions.

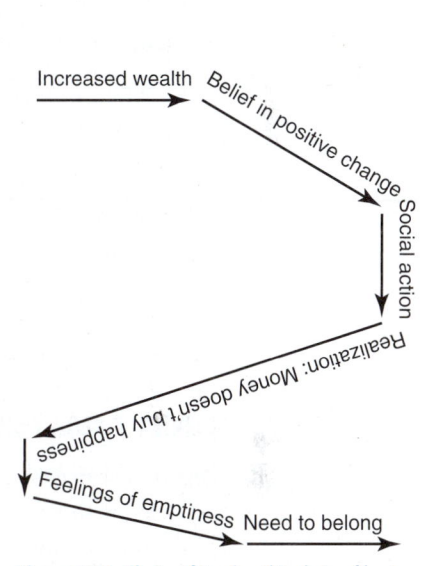

Figure 10.1 Chain of Logic. This chain of logic was developed to show how thoughts proceed to the next level of research inquiry. Along the way, all aspects are researched and documented. The chain of logic is an excellent diagramming tool to chart the progress during your research.
Source: Kopec, D. (2009).

Chain: Increased wealth → Belief in positive change → Social action → Realization: Money doesn't buy happiness → Feelings of emptiness → Need to belong

Census Data

Census data is another form of historic documentation that can be used to supplement other forms of historic information or as standalone demographic reports. An analysis of this data can reveal population shifts such as changes in ethnicity, single households versus couples, presence and number of children, and income and educational levels within a given area. An aggregation and analysis of this data can be invaluable for predicting future trends that can be used for the purpose of developing designs for a specific demographic. For example, census data might reveal that 20- to 30-year-olds congregate in high-density urban areas, but young families (28- to 38-year-olds) are more often found in low-density suburban environments. This data can then be compared throughout the decades to see whether this trend is reoccurring or is an anomaly. With this example, extraneous variables (see the experimental method discussion in Chapter 11) would have to be discussed—perhaps a lack of elementary schools in urban areas caused the young families to relocate.

Census data is considered a *public record* (that is, it is open for the public to view), though the typical format of the raw data (datasets) is in tabular form and analysis is time-consuming. It is suggested that U.S. Census Bureau Reports (which are analyzed and interpreted by Census Bureau researchers) be used first to establish whether analyzing individual datasets is warranted. Reports generally take three years after a census to be analyzed, compiled, and published. The reports contain the analysis of a specific subject written by a highly trained member of the bureau's staff and often include graphs, profiles, and predictions of future trends. An alphabetical listing of report subjects can be found at http://www.census.gov/main/www/a2z. Census information is used to gain an advantage by making it possible to glimpse into the past and gauge the future. It is valuable information for preemptively designing environments to support the needs of a changing community.

Public Records

Other public records that can be used for analysis are laws, codes, and zoning policies. One aspect that might be of interest is whether the date from which a law, code, or policy was drafted or changed affects its relevance to a modern society. The amendments or changes to these documents are readily available via municipal databases and public libraries. More often than not, the original document is shown with "~~strike through~~" text when a portion of the law is removed and [bracketed] when text is added to a law. Zoning or parcel maps generally have an amendment box in the upper right-hand corner documenting changes and dates occurring within the property tract area. Public domain records available to researchers provide a wealth of information. Most of the agencies listed here have divisions or bureaus within their organizations that are not intuitively linked. For example, information on "Oceans" can be found on all of these federal websites:

- U.S. Department of Commerce (NOAA) National Oceanic and Atmospheric Administration
- Department of Agriculture, under the Natural Resources Conservation Service
- Department of Defense, under the Office of Naval Research and Army Corps of Engineers
- Department of Energy, under the Office of Biological and Environmental Research

Each agency has historic records and reports available to the public. Most searches can be expedited by entering the words archive, report, or history (using quotation marks for an exact phrase) either in a general search engine (Bing, Firefox, Google, Yahoo, etc.) or within the search line of the specific agency. The best resource is the librarian at any library: librarians are highly trained experts with the knowledge to execute complex searches and a plethora of informational resources at his or her fingertips. Table 10.1 lists some agencies and the public record data they offer that would be useful to designers and/or researchers.

DATA ANALYSIS

Once researchers have outlined all of the information that they need to collect, they then identify a *systematic* way of analyzing that data. If a researcher wants to discover how a certain design style reflects the sociocultural conditions of a given era, the first step would be to identify how that information will be obtained—books, census, popular media, or other sources. Consider the following subject: the sociocultural norms of the late 1950s through the 1960s.

Table 10.1 Public Records and Data

Agency	Data Available
Law enforcement agencies:	Crime maps and trend reports
Registrar of voters:	Political party affiliation and voter mobility (no personal info.)
Department of Human Services:	Social needs
State Department of Finance:	Demographic, economic, and public finance projections
US Department of Commerce:	Trade and technological advances
US Department of Housing:	Community development and housing trends
US Department of Transportation:	Infrastructure and transportation policy and history

Table 10.2 Example of Multiple Historical Sources

This table represents one possible way of organizing the multiple sources of a historical analysis.
Investigating: "The sociocultural norms of the late 1950s through the 1960s."

Source	Document Type	Time Frame	Trend Identified
1.	History Books		
	(insert titles/ references here)	1950–1970	Transportation and futurism
2.	Magazines (vehicle ads)		
	Mercury Comet	1960–1977	Space travel and speed
	Ford Galaxy	1959–1974	
	Oldsmobile Jetstar	1964–1965	
	Oldsmobile Starfire	1954–1980	
3.	Television shows		
	The Jetsons	1962–1963	Intergalactic travel and cultural differences
	Star Trek	1966–1969	
	Dr. Who	1963–1989	
	Lost in Space	1965–1968	
4.	Department of Transportation statistics	1950–1960	Vehicle purchase and air Travel increases

One trend that a researcher might find from history books (first source) is that the mid-twenty-first century was notable for its transportation and futurism. This is echoed in popular media with automobile names (second source) such as the Mercury Comet, Ford Galaxy, and Oldsmobile Jetstar and Starfire. This trend is also revealed by the introduction and popularization of television shows (third source) such as the *Jetsons*, *Star Trek*, *Dr. Who*, and *Lost in Space*, which were futurist shows based on space travel. Through these and other trends of the time, sociocultural predisposition can be seen that is likely to have driven the spaceship-like design of the Seattle Space Needle, which was designed and constructed for the 1962 World's Fair. Then the final source might be the Transportation Department's statistics (fourth source) reflecting the dramatic increase in vehicle purchases during this time period, as well as the development of air travel. Through this example of systematically analyzing various forms of historical components, we see the building up of historical accounts, all supporting the refined thesis that "the sociocultural time period of 1959–1969 can be defined by its transportation and futurism." See Table 10.2.

Another way that history can be analyzed is through a causal–comparative study. A causal-comparative study is the ultimate "vs." (versus) scenario: a historic design researcher might use this method to ask, "What were the differences between brick vs. wood buildings during the 1920s?" With regard to a historic analysis, a causal–comparative study has to do with comparing elements of the past: it begins with an effect and ends with a cause. This type of study looks at static information—it compares and reports the findings. The key to a causal–comparative study is to understand that the researcher cannot manipulate variables, which is not a problem when exploring things that have happened in the past. For example, if a student-researcher were to analyze three university textbooks—one from the 1960s, one from the 1980s, and one from the 2000s—he or she would see that the textbooks written and printed in the 1960s consisted predominantly of words. By the 1980s, the viewer starts to see images supporting the text dispersed throughout the book. Finally, by the 2000s, textbooks begin looking more like a series of snippets that consist of boxes, tables, charts, graphs, and figures all interwoven into the text. Thus, a working hypothesis might state, "Throughout the years, textbooks have adapted to the prevalence of attention deficit disorder (ADD) and the reduced attention span of the undergraduate college student." This is just one simple example of a causal–comparative hypothesis, although it might be susceptible to **post-hoc fallacy**, for there are so many other contributing factors that may have led to the inclusion of more images into textbooks. Therefore, it is the researcher's responsibility to link the factor of changes in textbook format compared with reduced attention spans (which occurs in people with ADD). The researcher would need to first investigate the potential cause of reduced attention, such as the number of undergraduate students diagnosed with ADD in the years of 1960, 1980, and 2000. If the records show a progressive increase of confirmed cases of ADD within undergraduate programs throughout the given time period, this information supports the hypothesis. The researcher would then supply that information alongside the data collected regarding the textbook format. It would behoove the researcher to confirm that the publishers were aware of the changing condition of their demographic group, thus requiring them to revamp their format. Nonetheless, using the causal–comparative study to compare and understand phenomena is a beneficial way in which researchers can interpret and analyze events of the past, while being firmly and objectively in the present.

When analyzing past designs, researchers will often perform a photo analysis. This type of historical recording can be of tremendous value for designers because the researcher may want to study a particular architectural style or to track the evolution of a particular style. Recall the earlier example of the Chrysler Tower in New York City having a very different visual impact when it was originally constructed versus today. In other instances, a photo allows access to an object or area that might otherwise be unavailable. For example, a researcher might want to study the effects of cement that has been exposed to nuclear radiation. An ideal location to study this would be the site of the Chernobyl nuclear reactor meltdown in Ukraine. To stop high concentrations of radiation from entering the atmosphere, the former Soviet Union encased the building in a concrete sarcophagus. The effects of radiation on this concrete sarcophagus would be an ideal study, but the site poses too great of a health threat. As such, the researcher could study photographs of the various forms of concrete that would have been exposed to the high levels of radiation. This type of **remote sensing** provides a unique opportunity to focus and study the past within a real context and without the influences of modern elements, as well as researching objects from a physical distance. Other types of contemporary remote sensing images are satellite imagery, infrared thermo-scans, geographic information systems (GIS), magnetic resonance imaging (MRI), and positron emission tomography (PET).

Photo Analysis Method

Photo analysis is a method that enables a researcher to work with a primary source (the photo) in a nontraditional way. The process of analyzing photographic images is often done for one of three reasons:

- The researcher doesn't have access to a scene.
- The scene no longer exists.
- The researcher is physically unable to visit a scene firsthand.

Some researchers select a photo analysis because the goal is to gain a select perspective without the surrounding environment influencing their perceptions. Most often, a photo analysis allows a researcher to study a design that does not exist anymore. For example, a researcher may want to study 1970s architecture, of which New York City's Twin Towers were iconic. However, the Twin Towers no longer exist; hence, photos are one viable means for studying the building. Like other research methods, photo analysis requires an ability to critically identify and analyze various aspects within an image. Researchers can then study images in isolation, formulate questions related to similarities and differences, and make interpretations based on information revealed through a review of the literature—all without bias.

As designers are largely visual communicators, this research method is an ideal way to incorporate visual aids to document and present complex design-related inquiries. Thus, researchers choosing a photo analysis to convey information by comparing and contrasting images must be aware beforehand that there are many factors that influence how a photo is understood. These factors include:

- Purpose of the photo (was it taken to sell something or was it taken to simply document something?)
- Context of the image within the photo (does the photo include people or were there only objects in the photograph?)
- Framing of the object within the photo (is the object made larger or smaller by the surrounding elements—conveying hierarchy or were certain aspects of the image omitted by the photographer?)

Please see Activity 10.2 for a complete listing of many of the factors of a photo analysis. To keep the data consistent, it is imperative that the variables within each photograph are identified and compared for similar attributes. For instance, a researcher may want to study shadows: formation, size, and shape. Therefore, to study these effects of light and shadow, only photos taken at a similar time of day and season should be utilized. Thus, all photographs collected must have the same variables, attributes, and elements to ensure that the study is valid and relevant.

Other ways in which a photo analysis has been used as a method is to study symbolic meaning in an attempt to interpret the messages conveyed by a particular culture, such as hieroglyphics and sculptures. It has also been used to study a site in an attempt to understand a culture's language, mythology, and important symbols used to represent concepts. Within the fields of archaeology, anthropology, architecture, and urban planning, photos and videos have been used to study streetscapes, human travel patterns, and interrelationships between adjacencies, and to better understand the meanings people associate with place.

| BOX 10.3 | **Controlling the Environment of Analysis** |

All photos should be analyzed:

    With ample time (not rushed)

    Within a similar environment

    Within a similar state of mind

PROCESS

Once a researcher has decided to incorporate a photo analysis into a research project, he or she can take the photos or gather photos from other sources. When researchers decide to take their own photographs, certain controls must be established to maintain continuity, including angle, elevation, lighting conditions, and social interactions. Furthermore, if the research does not involve the human condition in any way then omitting or avoiding people in the photos is highly recommended. For scenes in which social activity cannot be avoided, the researcher might use computer software to remove people from the image during the postproduction process.

After gathering all the appropriate images, the next step is to analyze them. Included in the control of this next phase is the place in which a photo will be analyzed by the researcher. This includes the time of day, allotment of time dedicated to the analysis, and even weather conditions. Consider for a moment how a night person versus a morning person might view the same image at 8:00 a.m. Add to this scenario that it has been raining for several days, and it is likely that a photo with a sunny cheerful scene would be perceived more favorably than that same photo being viewed on a sunny day by either person. In the same way, the actual environment where a photo is analyzed is likely to influence how the researcher will perceive the photo. A photo being analyzed in a coffee shop versus a library will most likely be interpreted differently. It is crucial that the researcher control these nuances for as many influencing variables as possible. When this is not possible, he or she will need to discuss the possible influences of each variable in the overall analysis and discussion sections. See Box 10.3.

Once the photos have been analyzed, the results can be ranked according to a variety of criteria. The presentation of the analyzed photos might include modifying and/or diagramming the images for purposes of clarity using photo-editing software in the postproduction process. Postproduction includes any activity the researcher deems appropriate to illustrate his or her findings. For example, an element within the photo may be highlighted to identify and expedite discussion for its importance and relevance to the research (see Figure 10.3). The outlined process for this method, as described in the following section is the same for each of the three predominant approaches to photo analysis.

APPROACHES

The first of the three approaches to photo analysis is through **formal contextual**, the second is **intertextual**, and the third is **contextual.** A formal contextual analysis occurs when the primary image under investigation has been isolated from all other context. This means that the researcher would need to use software to remove the image from its background and let the primary image float on a page in isolation. This approach is an excellent way to get very pure ideas about a design without influences from its surroundings. A negative aspect to this approach is that all designs are positively or negatively influenced by their surroundings; therefore, this factor should be discussed in the limitations and conclusion sections of the research document.

An intertextual approach is an analysis of the photographer and his or her biases. This method is ideal for a researcher wanting to gain insights into a particular ideology. Because a photo can limit what is seen within a frame and can be taken within different lighting conditions, the photographer has the ability to capture an image either favorably or unfavorably. For example, many images of Los Angeles might portray the city in a negative manner, but when similar images are used to draw tourists to the city, they can be photographed in a way that creates a very positive portrayal. This kind of analysis might be beneficial when looking at how designs are perceived, such as Arab nations versus Western, communist ideology versus democracy, or even the differences between suburban and urban environments. Another illustration of how this method could be used is the chronicling of certain design styles throughout time. The Chrysler Tower was photographed as a shining beacon at one time; by the 1970s and 1980s, it was being photographed as an old decrepit building that should be replaced, and in the late 1990s and 2000s the building was once again being photographed favorably as an example of early American architecture.

A third analysis is contextual. This approach is often done to understand the relative importance of background: that is, surroundings, perspectives, and conditions on the interpretation of a design. When using this approach, the researcher should be aware of what is important and what is unimportant in an image. Imagine a photo of a hotel lobby; the presence of a taxicab (in the background) just outside the front entry may not have any importance, but the presence of a *covered* driveway to bring guests to the door may be very important. Another consideration to remember is the aspect of an image fostering conflicting "perspectives" or affiliations by the viewers, Visualize an image of a man playing with a young boy. Although this might evoke feelings of happiness and joy in some viewers (they "see" father and son playing), other people might view the same image with disgust and dismay (they "see" pedophile and potential victim). Therefore, the main objective with the contextual approach is to clearly understand the difference between the *interpretations* of the image. Once the researcher has a good idea of which approach the photo analysis should follow, the next step is to establish the criteria for the analysis.

ANALYSIS CRITERIA

Analysis of photographs follows three main sets of criteria:

- Factual data
- Symbolic message
- Emotional reaction

First, analyze what is factual, and then proceed to verifying those facts. For example, a fact is: "The Sears Tower in Chicago was the first to be built incorporating units of nine steel square tubes into a design" (keep in mind that all facts must be substantiated with citations). The next level of analysis is the identification of symbolism: "The Patronis Towers in Kuala Lumpur have a footprint that resembles the eight-sided star of Islam. This symbolic representation signifies the power of Islam within that nation." Again, this symbolism needs to be documented and verified with references. The third level of analysis is emotional reactions. Different people have different emotional reactions, but the majority of reactions can often be established within given aggregates of people. See Figure 10.2.

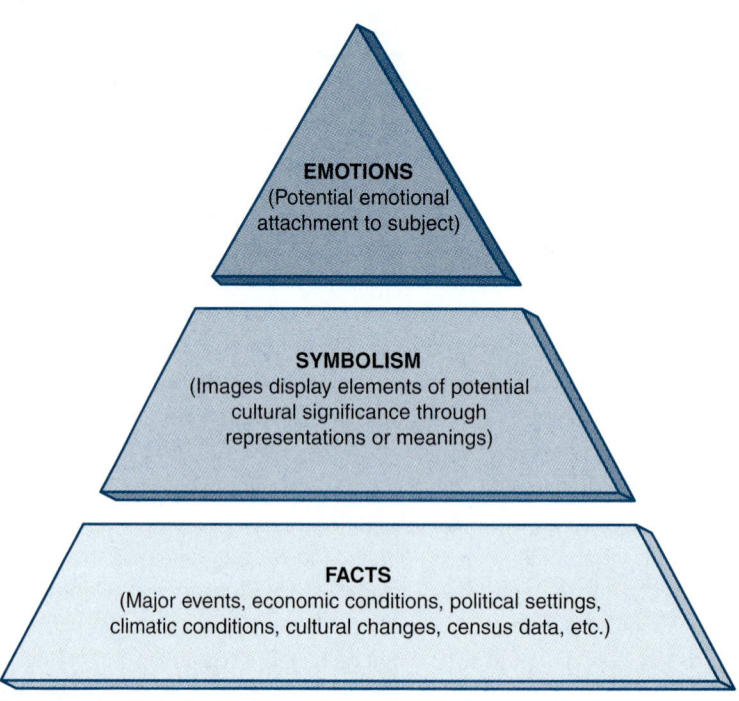

EMOTIONS
(Potential emotional attachment to subject)

SYMBOLISM
(Images display elements of potential cultural significance through representations or meanings)

FACTS
(Major events, economic conditions, political settings, climatic conditions, cultural changes, census data, etc.)

FIGURE 10.2 Levels of Photo Analysis. The levels of a photo analysis are facts, symbolism, and emotions. Each level builds upon the previous to result in a photo that has been thoroughly analyzed for all possible information.
Source: Sinclair, E. (2009).

When discussing the facts regarding a photographed image, the following data must be included in the discussion of the analysis:

- Important sociopolitical activities and major events (demonstrations, social movements, and important judicial decisions of the times).
- Economic conditions, including unemployment rates, new inventions, significant businesses, types of work, and various services offered and utilized (a thriving house-cleaning service industry might indicate a degree of wealth).
- Trends within culture and society (fashion styles, food preferences, architectural styles, manners and customs, recreational activities and public celebrations).
- Climatic conditions (seasons that are dry or moist, or catastrophic events, such as earthquake or flood).

When discussing symbolic meanings captured within a photo, the analysis must include the time that the object was photographed, the actual designer of the building or object, and/or perhaps the gauging of a well-defined user-group. Symbolic or metaphorical meanings often involve an understanding or a "social knowledge" shared by cultures, religions, or whole societies. To illuminate, if rhetoric is the art of using verbal language, then the visual metaphor is the language of visual art. Take the relationship between church and state, for example: if an ancient church were the largest building in a town or city or it was built on a hill overlooking the primary government building, this may have been an intentional visual metaphor, meaning that the church was the "higher power" in the community during that era. This level of analysis also looks to see how various artifacts and graphics are utilized and the meanings they convey. Symbols, their meanings, and their connotations change over time and from place to place. For example, the swastika can be seen as anti-Semitic or as good luck depending on its orientation, when and where the symbol is found, and of course, who is viewing it. Additionally, the use of color can also be revealing—the researcher must ask the question, "Are the colors vibrant and exciting or subdued and monochromatic?" Even the arrangement or number of elements visually communicates—this holds true for art, architecture, and even modern graphic design, which all employ this ancient symbolic language. (See Table 10.3 for several illustrations.)

As emotional reactions are often more difficult to analyze and understand, the researcher must learn as much as possible about the cultural norms, ethnic concerns, gender preferences, and professional biases to gain a deeper insight into the personal emotions of either the photographer or the person providing the feedback. To double-check for appropriate analysis, the researcher should put together a brief survey utilizing the study's photographs to gauge or gain insight into the emotional aspects of the images from other people. Please review Chapter 9 for a discussion on interviews and survey procedures. Activity 10.2 is a helpful guide to visualize all the criteria, as well as an aid in the successful completion of a photo analysis.

PHOTO MODIFICATION

Factors affecting an interpretation and/or understanding of a photograph can either contribute to or bias the results. For example, when the viewer is physically present to view a scene, he or she is influenced by the surrounding context (noises, scents, moods, and other people). By looking at a photograph of the same scene, the viewer can remove these external factors and bring a level of purity to the image, thereby adding focus to the subsequent research. In the event that further isolation of an element is required, software can be used. Once the photos have been analyzed, the results can be ranked according to a variety of criteria, including: the evolution of growth, cause and effect, and overt or subtle design features. The analyzed photos should then be modified and/or diagrammed with software to select specific portions of the photo to delineate and discuss. Diagramming an image using arrows, lines, or labels (such as "A," "B," or "C") to draw the reader's attention to the text discussing that particular element is preferred by most audiences and readers. Each area of importance within the photo needs to be highlighted, identified, and discussed for its relative value to the research. There are many ways to graphically draw attention to an element within an image. Diagramming or modifying a photo is limited only by the creativity of the design researcher. Figure 10.3 is merely one possibility. The photo was modified by cropping the special element out of the image, reducing the vibrancy of the original, returning the element to the photo, and finally inserting the commentary about the feature.

Every method has some limitations. The perspective in which a photo was taken can either enhance or diminish features of a design. Just as everyone has favorable and unfavorable photos of himself or herself, the same holds true for designs that have been photographed. Another limitation is the context. Though this can bring a level of purity to the research, it may be the interaction of a design with its surroundings that brings out the best in the design.

Table 10.3 — Symbolism and Visual Metaphors

Element	Symbolic Message	Example of the Visual Metaphor
An element on top	Better, more powerful or on top	
An element in front	More recent, modern, final product in an evolution	
Bigger element	More important, dominant	
Circle	Unity, wholesome, cyclical	
Square	Logical, honest, upright	
Two elements side by side	Equal, pair	
Four elements on corners	Boundaries, control, cardinal points, nature's elements	
Row of elements (in a line)	Path, journey, procession	

For example, Frank Lloyd Wright's Fallingwater House in Pennsylvania evokes a much greater emotional reaction when the sight, smell, and sound of the forest are added to the scene. Like other methods, the photo analysis is subjected to researcher bias, especially when comparing two or more design styles. Most designers gravitate toward a particular design style. As such, they may not be able to fully appreciate a design style contrary to their preference.

The human mind has the ability to perceive more than is actually present. It does this because of association and sets of rules that are used to help the mind make sense of the world around it. To get a better idea of how this

ACTIVITY 10.2 Data Collection Table

Use the format of this table as an organizing tool for collecting the most data from each of the photographs you are analyzing. Document your progression and references and record the date, time, and conditions of your analysis. Duplicate and file each analysis for future presentation of raw data.

Photo	Facts	Symbolism	Emotional	Notes
Analysis: 6/7/2010				
ATTACHED PHOTO HERE *(Example)* Photo #101				
DATE	*1932 (built and finished)*			
LOCALE	*Los Angeles, 6th St. Bridge*			
SUBJECT	*Bridge design—steel arches and concrete towers*			
EVENTS	*Olympic games*	*The Coliseum built to "American Proportions"*	*Local pride*	*In 1932, L.A. was considered geographically "isolated"*
PURPOSE (of photo)		*Found in a steel trade magazine— denoting innovations*		
Context (surroundings around element)			*Barren concrete viaduct—bridge looks good in contrast*	
Framing (how was element set up in the frame)	*Bridge centered in frame = most important No people/cars = scale difficult to determine*			
POLITICAL	*Radio broadcaster Pastor Robert P. Shuler highlights corruption in city government*	*"Power of the media"*		
JUDICIAL	*Raids on "female impersonators" and clubs*			
SOCIAL	*"Prohibition"*			
ECONOMIC	*Great Depression*			
CLIMATE	*Jan, 1932: 2" snow downtown* Los Angeles Times *October 7, 1932: "Fifth Ice Age Is on the Way"*			
INNOVATIONS	*Silicon polymers invented*			
TRENDS	*Reform (social, economic, feminist, labor, etc.)*	*Architectural— Egyptian*		
HEALTH	*TB scare, city limits visitors*			

FIGURE 10.3 Photo Modification. One technique of the postproduction photo modification for diagramming or highlighting information within the image and its relative value to the research.
Source: Sinclair, E. (2009).

situation can affect a photo analysis, consider that all images exist outside of a photo frame. However, the photo itself limits the viewer from accessing the information contained just outside of the frame. The information has only a certain probability of being congruent with what the perceiver believes is beyond the boundaries of the frame. From a literal sense, all photographs are symbols, but when they are representing an object that is not actually the "real" object, they may become more metaphorical than representational. For example, imagine a magazine photograph of a tempting slice of cherry pie. It is possible that such an image may stimulate the appetite of the viewer and perhaps the desire for cherry pie or something sweet. However, what if the slice of cherry pie were not a cherry pie at all but rather a rubber mold painted by an artist to mimic the real thing? In this scenario, the viewer may have experienced a psychological and physical response (appetite) via technology (art mold captured photographically and printed in a magazine on colored paper); thus, it is possible that the viewer responded to past experiences of the real object rather than the representational (or, in this case, metaphorical) object captured in the photograph, unless of course the viewer likes to eat rubber and paint. The researcher needs to be aware of altered photos or objects and avoid significant photo alterations during analysis. Furthermore, the researcher needs to focus only on the content within the photo that is being analyzed and not one's belief or perceptions of what is happening outside of the photo, because this would hinder the research. For example, person 1 likes the design of a recycling outlet. However, person 2 does not like the design and is adamant about this. When probed further, the researcher finds out that person 2 associates recycling outlets with homeless colonies. Hence person 2 would not like *any* design of a recycling center because of the tendency to impose a variable (homelessness) not contained within the photo.

Ultimately, photo analysis is an excellent way for the design researcher to study a design within a point in time, communicate visually, and emphasize complex cultural-visual language all within the boundaries of scientific rigor.

Summary

Historical research and photo analysis methods both limit the researcher's direct contact in location and time with the subject of their research. Both techniques offer the researcher a high level of objectivity and neutrality.

Historical documentation offers a systematic and objective-based analysis used to reconstruct or understand a given situation. The past is researched, documented, and interpreted by cross-referencing multiple sources of supporting data. Multiple views must corroborate the findings because individuals who have agendas of their own may have also written historical accounts. Therefore, to further substantiate the evidence, additional literature must be obtained from history books, census data, or public records. A designer can prepare for future designs through the historical research process by understanding historical context, social norms, and the values of an era.

The photo analysis method provides a "visual notebook" for researchers to record aspects of human material and culture produced in a time long gone or by a remote society. What would have been challenges in the past to researchers have been resolved by photography and historic records. Photos that are not significantly altered or enhanced have been shown to "legitimize" information. For example, if someone views a photograph of something, he or she may lose the ability to doubt its existence—hence the saying, "seeing is believing." The process of examining a photograph involves observing the facts, inferring peripheral meanings, accessing what new questions need to be answered, and finally the disciplined documentation of all findings.

Glossary

Census data—Demographic information gathered and used to describe populations and make social pattern predictions.

Contextual—A set of facts or circumstances that surround a situation or event.

Cross-referencing—An instance or circumstance that refers to related or synonymous information elsewhere.

Formal contextual—Pure facts pertaining to a situation or event.

Historical analysis—The aspect of history and of semiotics that considers how knowledge of the past has been developed and influences the future.

Intertextual—Referencing one author by another.

Photo analysis—Uncovering a story or facts that are found within photos.

Post-diction—An effect of hindsight bias that explains claimed predictions of events.

Post-hoc fallacy—An idea based upon the mistaken notion that simply because one thing happens after another, the first event was a cause of the second event.

Public records—Documents that are available for public viewing without restriction.

Remote sensing—Gaining information about an object or event without physically or directly experiencing it.

CHAPTER 11
Experimentation and Computer Modeling

chapter outline

Introduction

Experimental Methods
Types of Experiments
Control and Experimental Groups
Variables
Analysis

Computer-Related Methods
BIM
Analysis
GIS
Analysis

Summary

> "Intellectual freedom is the right of every individual to both seek and receive information from all points of view without restriction. It provides for free access of all expressions of ideas through which any and all sides of a question, a cause or movement may be explored."
>
> —American Library Association

chapter objectives

By the end of this chapter, students should be able to:

- Identify the benefits that can be obtained from an experimental method.
- Discuss the roles of dependent and independent variables for an experimental method.
- Identify the BIM type programs that can be used for research.
- Analyze the capability of BIM-type programs as a research methodology.
- List the different capabilities of GIS as a research tool.
- Compare and contrast the benefits of BIM and GIS as a research tool for architects and interior designers.

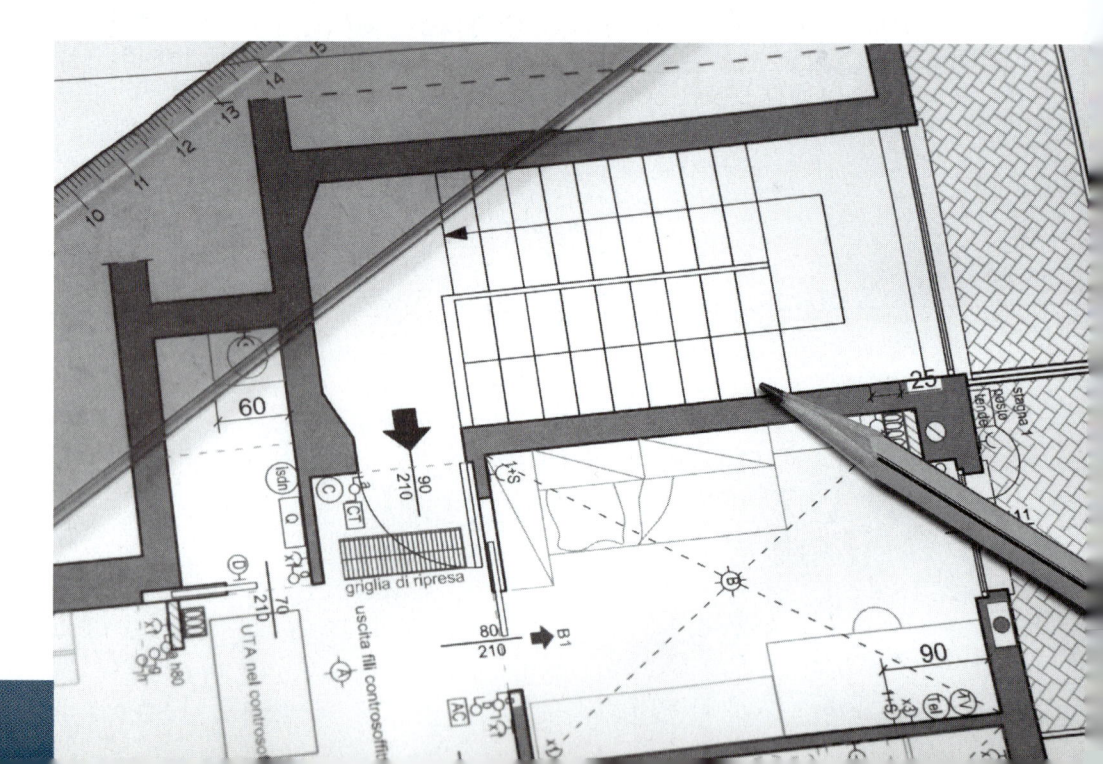

Introduction

When conjuring images of experimental methods, most think of a chemist mixing different solutions. Although this is one way to conduct experimental methods, it is just that—only one way. In design, researchers can conduct experimental research in a variety of ways. One way is to assess a material's properties or capability of harboring some other substance that might affect the environment negatively. For example, one researcher might conduct experiments on the feasibility of carpeting serving as a reservoir for bacteria in the healthcare environment. Other researchers might conduct experiments on the behaviors of a material in radiant heat levels in different climates throughout the course of a day, and/or direct versus indirect light exposure. Many lighting designers, for example, conduct experiments on natural lighting levels within a built structure during different times of the year, different hours of the day, or when the presence of ancillary materials are in a room (furnishings, window treatments, and so on). Some interior designers conduct experiments on human navigational behaviors for the purposes of space planning. In this instance, the experiment can tell the researcher how a subject finds his or her way around a space and what would happen if a subject were to enter a foreign environment or if any building features such as pillars or pieces of furniture were to impede direct movement patterns.

Most designers are simultaneously conducting experiments as they design. Interestingly, most design students continually conduct rudimentary experiments via their design process. Take a physical model of a space that a design student might take outside to survey how sunlight moves through the space, which causes the student to modify the design to achieve the desired lighting goal. Much of this research, however, lacks documentation, which is all that separates the design researcher from the traditional academic researcher. To give added value to the work of designers, one needs only to use the vocabulary of research along with a structured process for detailed recording of findings, and a systematic portrayal of results. From this slight alteration in the process, a design can be transformed from a conceptual abstraction to something designed with intent. The difference is twofold: **reliability** and **replicability**.

In today's high-tech environment, advanced experimentation can be conducted to inform and validate design. Computer-related experimental methods include the numerous applications afforded through **building information modeling (BIM)** and **geographic information systems (GIS)**. These types of computer applications have become a significant asset to the design researcher, leading to the development of tools that can be used to analyze and predict the performance aspects of a given design. These performance measures include, but are not limited to, lighting, ventilation, acoustics, structures, thermal flow, and energy use/expenditure. For instance, the Department of Energy (DOE) has developed its own set of energy-related tools to assess a building's energy performance. These software tools have the capacity to simulate a building's performance in relation to orientation, engineering, construction, and operation. With such software tools available, a design researcher has the ability to insert data points relative to his or her design. The software then produces a set of results that are then analyzed, interpreted, and applied to the project design.

Two software tools that have had a tremendous influence on design research are BIM and GIS. BIM is a valuable application because it can analyze multiple variables that range from the effects of weather patterns on the exterior of a building to the interior and the probable fading patterns that might occur in carpeting as a result of direct exposure to daylight. BIM can be seen as a tool that allows for the analysis of facts related to a given set of variables within one building: a micro system. The current trend within design is a shift in the use of these tools from simple analysis to analysis and synthesis (i.e., integrating the findings into the design process). This focus on research through experimentation with computer modeling has the ability to push the boundaries of what might be considered optimal building performance, as well as to produce greater accuracy when cost estimating, performing cost/benefit analysis, providing virtual three-dimensional scenes from which people can visually assess the aesthetics and/or functionality of a space.

GIS is a program that enables designers to see big-picture views of data sets on a region, city, or neighborhood in an effort to identify the needs and the consequences of the built environment: a macro system. Often referred to as *geodesign*, the implications of GIS as a research tool for designers include the identification of unique variables of an area that will impact a building's use, performance and design. This information on the small scale can help an interior designer with the selection of finish materials and furniture, and on a larger scale illuminate a plan for achieving carbon neutrality for an entire city for the urban planner. For example, in an area where there is high crime (including theft), a designer might specify heavy outdoor furniture to prevent it from being stolen or assess the situation for advocating for more street lights or landscaping for better visual surveillance. Likewise, areas where there are high vandalism rates may lead an architectural designer to specify that the exterior skin of a building be smooth and flat so that graffiti can be easily removed.

Experimental Methods

Experimental methods are highly systematic approaches to identifying "cause and effect" relationships. Like many data gathering techniques and processes, experimentation requires tightly controlled procedures. These procedures provide the researcher with a high degree of reliability, as the conclusion is a direct result of a controlled action. If the experimental method and controls are properly documented, the experiment can be replicated repeatedly by researchers who will achieve the same results, thereby increasing the validity. Each time an experiment is replicated and yields the same results, the study is said to have valid results, and thus a reliability of data. However, life itself (human or animal) serves as a confounding or perplexing variable because behaviors have only a certain degree of reliability. In other words, an experiment involving people is extremely difficult to replicate because we are all so diverse. In many cases, a laboratory is used to control as many factors as possible to ensure a high level of purity for the research. However, a laboratory environment is in itself an artificial environment and the results may not be indicative of what would happen in the real world.

Although experimental studies are an excellent method for gaining reliable data, their application to the design fields is limited, unless building simulation techniques and modeling evolve to a level that a building's performance can be more accurately predicted and positive identification of a cause-and-effect relationship can be determined. Current building simulation tools draw on experimental methods through the use of virtual situations in which the user, or building occupant, is placed in spaces that do not physically exist. Then, by conducting a series of analysis and synthesis procedures based on the participants' responses the researcher is able to arrive at design conclusions. BIM analysis of only building materials and not human response to the space, inspire optimum performance outcomes because direct one-to-one relationships of objects and the behavior of building materials are more congruent and applicable to the field of structures and physical science. Adding people, with all their personality quirks and emotional uniqueness, to an experiment brings a level of complexity to issues of validity and reliability. Therefore, experienced research scientists are better suited to handle these types of research endeavors.

Consider work being done at a few universities where researchers study the biological responses to conditions within the built environment that can be measured with **functional magnetic resonance imaging** (fMRI). This technology measures and maps the responses of the human brain to various stimuli. Neuroscientists from around the world are currently conducting this type of research. fMRI machines are extremely costly and prohibitive to the designer's realm, though the results of these studies can be available to the designer who has a membership to a good research library. At the time of this writing, the U.S. National Library of Medicine offers a free service called PubMed. PubMed is one of the most used databases of biomedical and social science research. Researchers opting for a serious exercise with the experimental methods and results of others with regard to applying this research to design will find this a challenging and rewarding endeavor. With regard to limitations, the human experience, metaphoric meanings, symbolic associations, or emotional qualities, the application of experimental methods are inadequate. This is not to say that experimental methods cannot be applied to these levels of inquiry. However, when they are, researchers should be cautioned that the results only have a probability of being accurate.

TYPES OF EXPERIMENTS

There are four types of experiments:

- **True experiment**
- **Quasi experiment**
- **Single-subject experiment**
- **Double-blind, placebo-controlled experiment**

A true experiment is when one type of subject is exposed to one type of condition. It is used to show a direct cause-and-effect relationship. It is considered the simplest of all experiments, as one type of subject(s), randomly selected, would have only a slim chance of providing extraneous variables in such minimal conditions. A simple example: say a design researcher needs to test the effectiveness of using the color red on the walls of an exercise room. The researcher randomly selects only 10 people from a very specific group of 100 people who have been evaluated as the type of person to use an exercise room. Then the researcher would divide the two groups equally, and have one group go into the red room and the other go into a white room. Once the subjects have spent the predetermined amount of time in the space, doing a predetermined activity, they leave the room and have the inside of their mouths swabbed to measure the stress hormones present in the saliva (DHEA, or dehydroepiandrosterone, and cortisol). The researcher then compares the stress results of the red room subjects (experiment group) versus the white room subjects (control group).

A quasi experiment is also referred to as a natural experiment. In this scenario, the researcher quite literally controls *nothing*. The quasi experiment is most like an observational study (discussed in Chapter 9). The biggest difference is that the subject(s) are not selected—randomly or otherwise. The subjects are already in the "box" and their responses to the stimulus is observed and recorded, then compared with the results of other similar experiments. An example of a quasi experiment that a design researcher might conduct would be to compare subject behavior at a revolving door in a department store versus subject behavior at a sliding door in a department store. By comparing performance and operational success, the researcher can perhaps extrapolate the best door option for a department store design.

In a single-subject experiment, a single case or subject is studied over a long period. This experiment is most like a longitudinal study (discussed in Chapter 1). One subject (person or thing) is exposed to a stimulus or condition repeatedly and at varying levels for a period of time to record change. A good example of this would be investigating what conditions various metals require to acquire a patina (texture and color changes due to weathering). To scientifically document the changes, researchers would be required to maintain a control group of the same types of metals to validate their results as being directly "caused" by the experimented conditions.

CONTROL AND EXPERIMENTAL GROUPS

To increase the reliability of experimental methods, the researcher should conduct a double-blind, placebo-controlled experiment. This simply means that two groups are studied and no one knows who is being studied—not even faculty, research assistants, or the test subjects. Only the person administrating the changes (having no contact with the subjects) knows which group is actually receiving the experimented stimulus. The **control group** in this case is given the experimental agent. The **placebo-controlled group** thinks they are being exposed to the experimental agent, but they are not. The differences between the two groups are measured. The double-blind, placebo-controlled experiment is always held to a higher standard of scientific detail and accuracy.

Another way that a researcher could perform an experiment is through **simulations** that use rapid prototyping, versus virtual-simulation tools and models, which might include **computational fluid dynamics (CFD)**. For a more hands-on approach, the student-researcher could develop model prototypes in an effort to identify preliminary data that can then be fed into a computer modeling program. For example, if the researcher wanted to study air movement patterns through a hotel lobby, he or she might build a scaled model. Then, using dry ice or water, he or she could gently blow the water vapor through the model to watch how movement occurs through the space, as well as where circulation is impeded. Ideally, the researcher would videotape this experiment so that he or she could play it back in slow motion to better investigate the results. Likewise, the researcher would be expected to develop a couple of different configurations of the proposed lobby arrangement in order to identify the best configuration for optimal air movement. There are many ways in which a designer could set up simulations to conduct experiments, but a key component to the validity of the experiment is the control of variables and the ability to reproduce the results. Experimental methods that use simulations are well suited for a design studio simply because the researcher/designer is probably already trained to build models, so subjecting the models to different conditions would be second nature. Therefore, if the researcher has the ability and wherewithal to accurately and efficiently assemble a research project utilizing an experimental method, he or she would be wise to do so. Results obtained from good experimental methods are lacking in the design fields; this is an approach that can offer much to the profession and fields of design. See Figure 11.1.

VARIABLES

If the student chooses experimentation as his or her research method, the first step is to identify the **independent variable**, the **dependent variable**, the **control variable**, and **extraneous variables** in order to understand what input leads to what output. For example, researchers studying human circulation patterns within a hotel lobby would look at (1) furniture placement, (2) the position of structural supports, and (3) the arrangement of the reception area, concierge, and restaurants if the theory is that "human movement patterns vary depending on the arrangement of the interior environment." Thus, the human movement patterns are the dependent variables. The arrangement of the furniture is then called the independent variable because we can manipulate the furniture to document the movement of guests. In short, an experimental independent variable will cause a change in the dependent variable. Within experimental research, it should be noted that it is not possible for a dependent variable to change or effect the independent variable. The final step in an experimental design is setting up two groups for comparison. The first is the experimental group, who will be the one to be "experimented on." The second group is the control group, who will

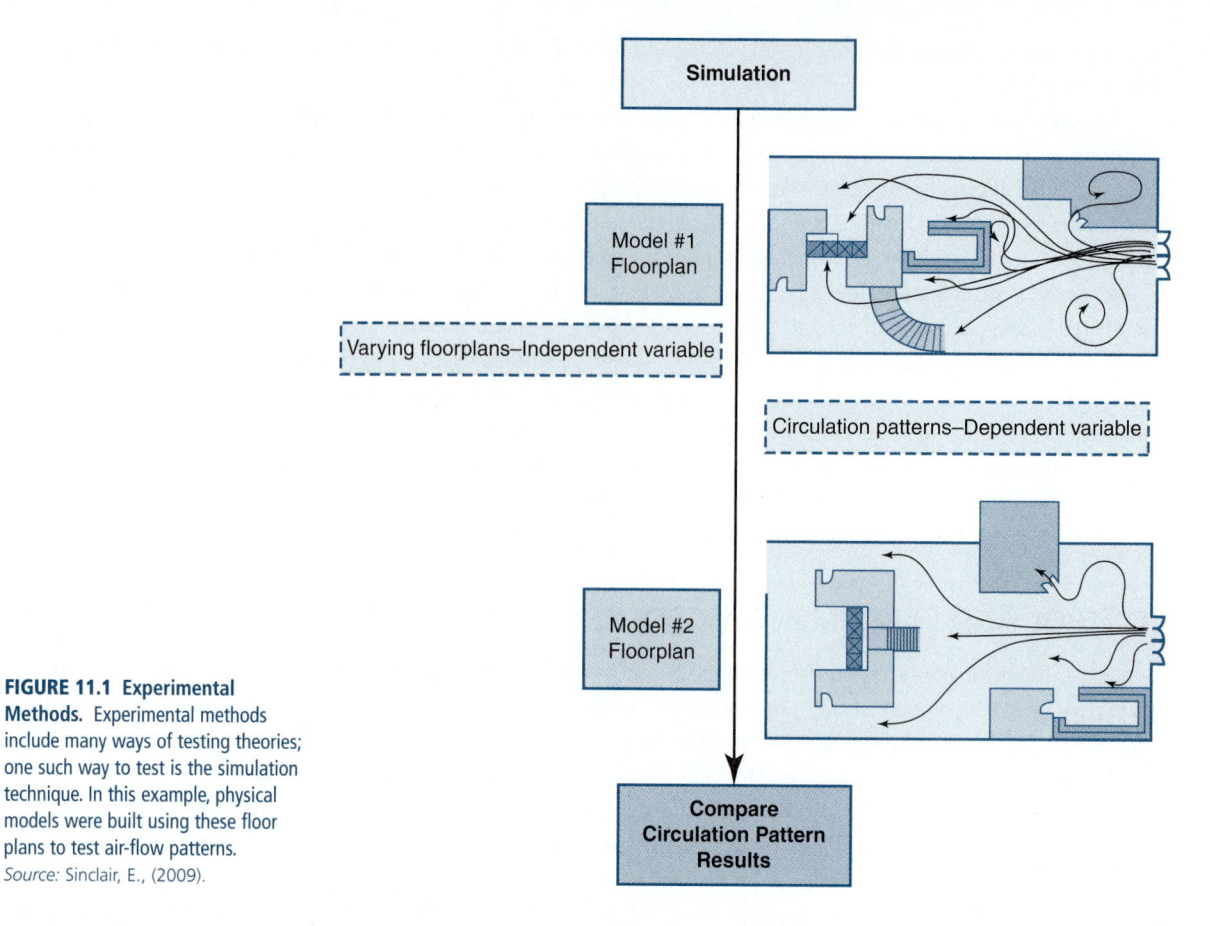

FIGURE 11.1 Experimental Methods. Experimental methods include many ways of testing theories; one such way to test is the simulation technique. In this example, physical models were built using these floor plans to test air-flow patterns.
Source: Sinclair, E., (2009).

represent the status quo—nothing will happen to them. The following is an example of designing an experiment that tests and measures the effects of lighting on the reading comprehension of students. See Box 11.1.

With an experimental method, the researcher manipulates the independent variables in order to determine whether and how much *or* how and to what degree it affects something else. The dependent variable is not controllable (that is, we can not control where a person will walk; we can only make routes more or less convenient). Another variable type is called a control variable. These are factors that remain constant. The control variable is

---

BOX 11.1 Experimental Example

The hypothesis: "Lower lighting levels allow for greater reading comprehension among sixth-grade students."

Independent Variable	Different lighting levels
Dependent Variable	Reading comprehension

Design of Experiment

To set up the experiment, the researcher must identify two classroom environments in which the sixth-grade students are fairly comparable. Comparability means that the class is similar in size (19–21 students), the gender breakdown is similar (within 47–53% ratios), the schools' socioeconomic characteristics are similar, and the classroom environment is the same in every way except the variable being tested (lighting). The type of light must also be identical; fluorescent, incandescent, and so on. (Note: if one classroom has hard-surface flooring, then the other must have hard surfaces, this is the control variable.)

Once the two rooms have been identified along with the sixth-grade students who will serve as the subjects, the next step is the identification of the control and experimental group. In the control group, the lighting levels will remain the same, but in the experimental group the lighting levels will be changed.

Because the experiment is measuring the children's reading comprehension, both groups will be given the same page to read, along with a series of questions to answer related to the content of that page.

The answers from both groups will then be compared to see whether the lighting levels had any affect on the accuracy of the answers. This kind of test would be done for a minimum of five sequential days to rule out any probable intervening anomalies (extraneous and confounding variables).

Table 11.1 Experimental Variables

Independent	The variable manipulated by the experimenter.
Dependent	The variable altered by the change.
Control	Variable whose effects must be neutralized or controlled.
Extraneous	Extraneous variables are unaccounted for variables that might affect the results.
Confounding	Unforeseen and unaccounted-for variables that adversely affect reliability and validity of an experiment.

later removed to more clearly see relationships without interference. To illustrate this variable, consider the example from Box 11.1. The type of flooring used in the environment will be used as a control variable. If the classrooms both have hard cement floors, then noise reverberation might influence concentration and perhaps reduce a child's reading comprehension. Therefore, the two groups must be tested in rooms, both having cement floors. In that way, a researcher can more accurately test the affects of lighting on reading, not the effects of noise reverberation on reading. Therefore, the researcher has effectively removed a potential confounding variable by making sure that both classrooms have the same flooring. In other words, the researcher has leveled the playing field for the experiment. Every experiment has control variables that must be addressed; otherwise, the results of the experiment will be distorted. The idea is to identify *one* independent variable that causes a change in *one* dependent variable (see Table 11.1).

Experimental methods are necessary to understand direct cause-and-effect relationships. However, when conducted in a real-world setting (such as a quasi experiment) experiments can be subject to **confounding variables**, which are instances or occurrences that can alter the natural course of the experiment. For example, if a researcher were studying the circulation patterns of a hotel lobby and the electrical power suddenly failed during one of the observation times, the loss of power would be considered a confounding variable. If there are more than one confounding variables present during an experiment, the researcher might opt to start the study over or continue the investigation and discuss the confounding variables in the conclusion chapter of the research document.

Other undesirable variables that can interfere with the action of the things the researchers are attempting to study are called extraneous variables. These are variables that influence the outcome of an experiment, though they are not the variables of interest. These variables are undesirable because they add error to an experiment. An example of this might be a test subject dropping out of the study before the test was complete. The change in research subject distribution patterns or the disruption to other research subjects may alter the results. The results might also be skewed with the loss of a participant, but the study itself is not affected by the change. Therefore, it becomes the responsibility of the researcher to document the change and rationally discuss without bias the affects of the change on the overall study.

ANALYSIS

A major goal of research design is to decrease the influence of extraneous variables as much as possible. Figure 11.2 reflects the process of the double-blind, placebo-controlled experiment using the earlier scenario of classroom lighting levels and the resulting reading comprehension of the students. To begin the analysis portion of an experimental method, the student-researcher should compile all of the experiment data into a format that allows the information to be easily compared: matrices, spreadsheets, or tables. The measurements of each response must then be organized into a sequence that promotes an analysis of like variables. For example, if an experiment were seeking to compare a stimulus at different times of the day, then responses should be organized in a chronological fashion. The next phase of the process would be the academic and scientific detailing of the information presented. If the example from Figure 11.2 were used to illustrate this, the reading scores of the children would first be detailed by classroom, and then the same information would be detailed to reflect the reading scores by each day of the experiment. Another way the information could be detailed to show reading scores is by gender. Ultimately, detailing is up to the researcher and is subject to whatever information is crucial and needed for the study. As the data is being processed and detailed into an organized configuration, the analysis or implications of the experiment should begin to reveal a

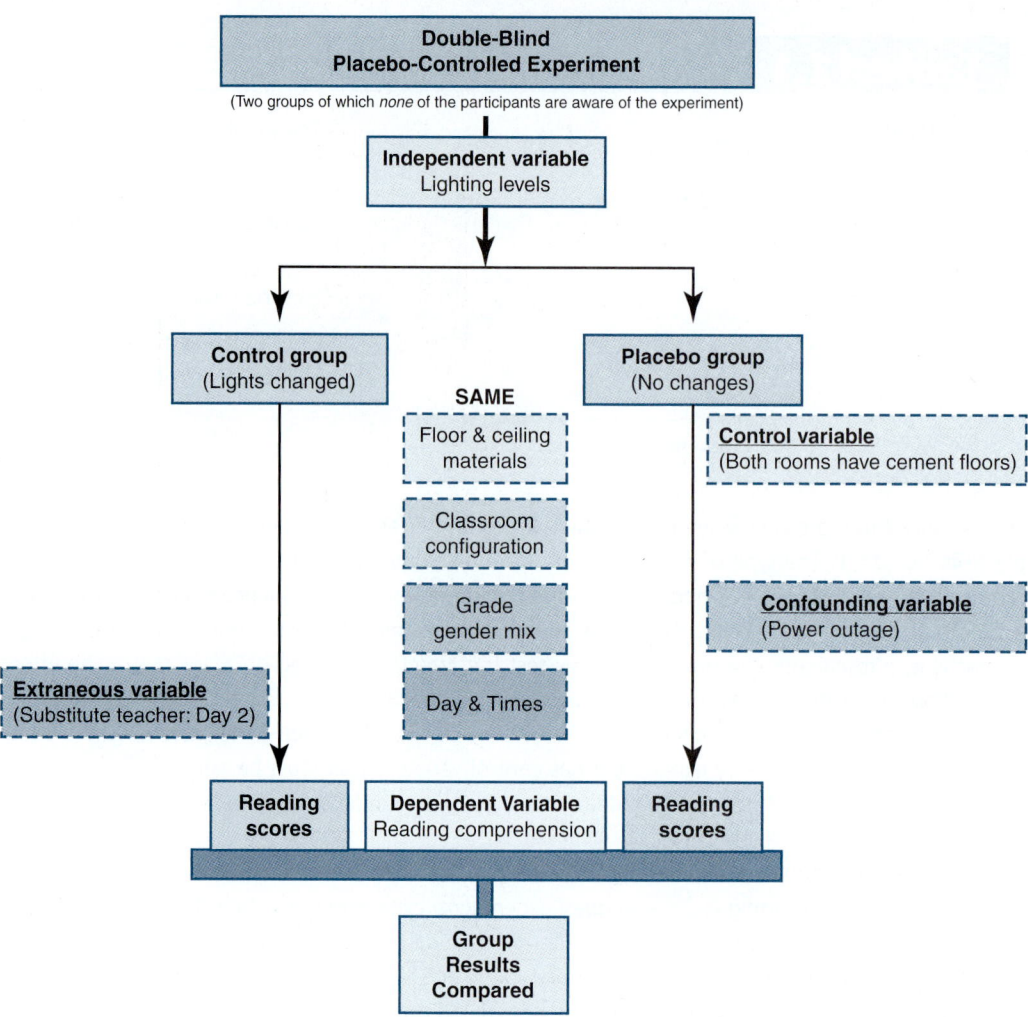

FIGURE 11.2 Double-Blind Placebo-Controlled Experiment. This image reflects the process of the double-blind placebo-controlled experiment using a scenario of classroom lighting levels and its effects on the reading comprehension of sixth-grade students.
Source: Sinclair, E., (2009).

pattern. During this process, the researcher may decide to back up the results with a secondary method. By way of illustration, if the children's reading scores were all lower than expected, the researcher might opt to return to the classrooms and interview the students to validate the findings; during the process of speaking with the students, it might be discovered that the children could not understand the questions of the written test. Thus, if the way in which the researcher chose to gauge the students' comprehension (i.e., a written test rather than a verbal questioning) was problematic, then the issue is a confounding variable and the student/researcher is obligated to document it as such within the limitations portion of the research paper. If time allowed and another experiment could be performed to measure the student's reading scores by way of verbal questioning, then the results of the two different experiments could be evaluated together. The interpretation of this scenario may be that the classroom lighting does have an effect on student reading comprehension scores, but the *method* of testing sixth-grade student reading comprehension has an even greater affect.

Computer-Related Methods

The late 1990s and early 2000s brought about an explosion of computer applications. Much of this software has proven to be a vital asset to the design industry in terms of design and research. Two applications that have contributed to design research are BIM (building information modeling) and GIS (geographic information systems). BIM is an overarching term used to describe software applications that have the ability to produce three-dimensional building images. Used widely by designers, these proprietary software applications include Bentley Architecture, Graphisoft, ArchiCAD, VectorWorks ARCHITECT, and Autodesk's Revit and Architectural Desktop, among others (see Figure 11.3).

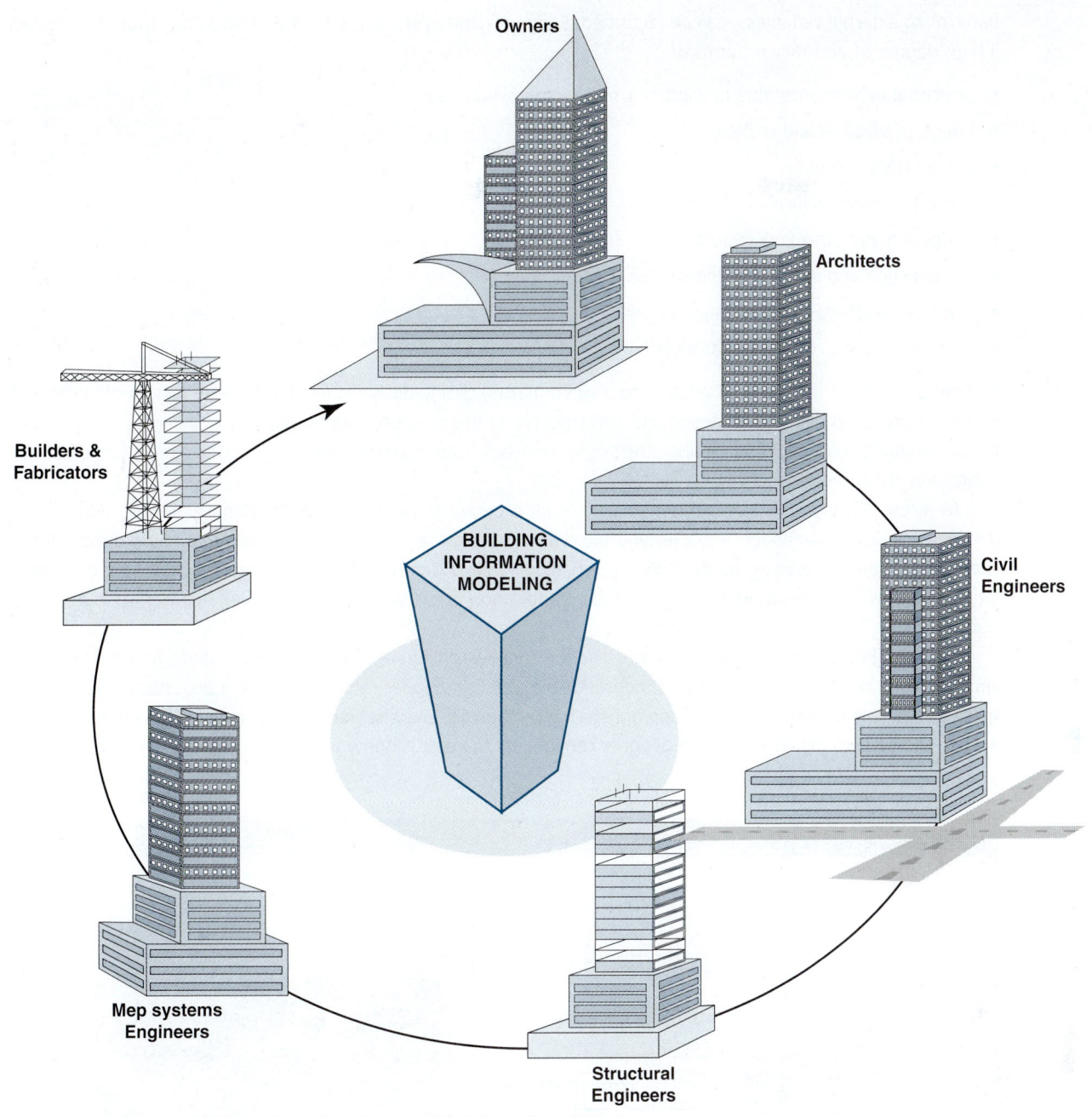

FIGURE 11.3 Uses of BIM. This graphic explores the range of disciplines utilizing BIM software.

GIS is often, but not exclusively, used by geographers, urban planners, and landscape designers to gain valuable data-rich insights into various relationships, patterns, and trends. Maps, reports, and charts are often the manifestations of the data obtained from GIS. Both BIM and GIS can be valuable tools in the pre- and post-design process.

BIM

The strength of BIM as a research tool is in the well coordinated and highly consistent information it can provide about a project. This group of software applications has the ability to provide continuous and immediate data pertaining to the direct consequences of design scope, schedule, and cost. As a research tool, it is well positioned to evaluate each of the three major phases in a building's lifecycle: design, construction, and management. It can further offer access to data that pertains to design, schedule, and budget information; construction quality, schedule, and cost information; and management performance, utilization, and costs. By inputting select vector calculations into a software application, a digital representation of a building—along with its projected response patterns to external variables—can be identified. Early pre- and postanalysis of BIM projects has thus far revealed a high degree of accuracy in terms of:

- Structural performance (due to wind, seismic, and dead/live loads)
- Effects of weather and climate
- Energy costs and usage
- Scheduled maintenance
- Budgeting and other cost factors
- Construction and delivery timelines
- The relative affects of coordination efforts
- Overall costs and cost/benefit analysis

BIM has also proven itself to be a valuable tool when making design decisions related to the reduction of waste and inefficient processes endemic to design and construction. In this way, BIM can be thought of as an effective tool in the sustainability movement. BIM is also effective in processes related to time and money savings, reduction of design errors, and enhanced productivity.

As a research tool, BIM can be used as part of an experimental process whereby climate, seismic, and natural lighting serve as the dependent variables and the different design factors such as orientation, material specification, and structural design serve as the independent variables. What is important for the research process is the documentation of the different results identified from each modification of independent variable (i.e., building attributes). See Figure 11.4.

Although BIM seems most appropriate for architectural research, it also has many applications for interior design and landscape design research. Through modeling, the interior designer can determine the acoustical qualities of a space as a means to specify the most appropriate finish materials. Likewise, radiant heat and sun trajectory inside of a space can be determined so that the designer can identify the best window treatment (if any are needed), whereas

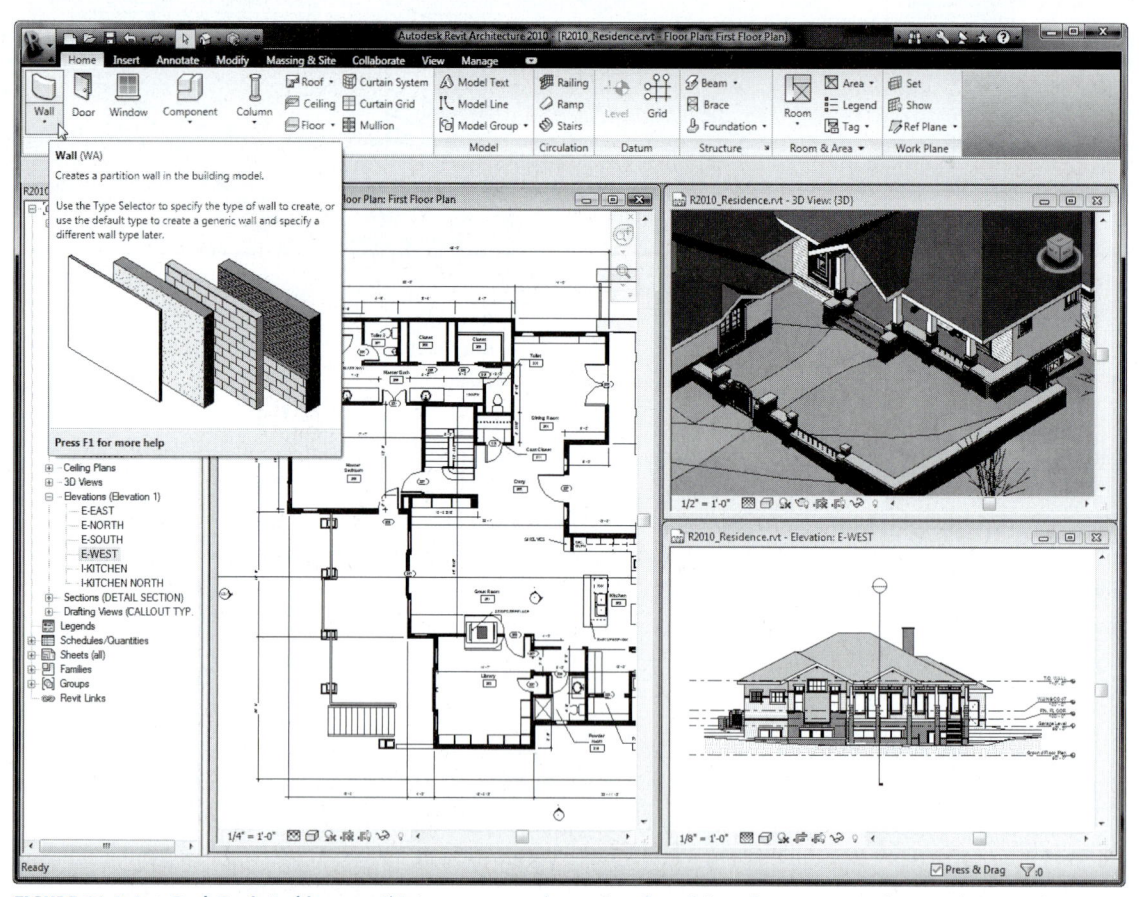

FIGURE 11.4 AutoDesk Revit Architecture. This image captures the user interface of the software capacity of AutoDesk Revit Architecture, which is just one of the many BIM products available.

Source: Autodesk with permission.

Table 11.2 Variables

Independent Variable	Dependent Variable	Effects
Wood frame structure	Category 5 hurricane (>150 mph)	
Wood frame structure	60 percent average humidity during the day	
Steel frame structure	Category 5 hurricane (>150 mph)	
Steel frame structure	60 percent average humidity during the day	

the landscape designer could evaluate the changing conditions of plant growth, ecological systems, and site integration. Another valuable tool for designers is the development of three-dimensional imagery, which can then be shown to individuals or focus groups for self-report data and insight into user preferences.

ANALYSIS

As with all research methods; details, documentation, and absolute clarity of intent are key factors. To best use BIM as a research tool, the researcher will likely develop a list of independent variables in order to identify the theorized effect on the dependent variable. See Table 11.2 for an example.

The results can then be seen in the chart as the effect. Once all of the independent variables have been assessed in their singularity, the researcher can then analyze the aggregate effects. In the previous example, the data might reveal that a wood frame structure would not hold together as well as steel, and that wood would be more susceptible to moisture damage than steel. Though this example produced the conclusion that steel is the obvious building choice, there will be many instances in which agreement will not be found and the researcher will have to analyze the results carefully in order to draw the best conclusions.

To use BIM as a research tool, the researcher would have to document projected effects of various designs (i.e., a building at a certain orientation will yield interior natural lighting equivalent to a certain number of foot-candles, etc.). This lighting can then be cross-referenced with a type of glazing used to determine the approximate radiant heat. See Figure 11.5.

FIGURE 11.5 Interior BIM Application. This image shows an interior space created with Autodesk Architecture that could be analyzed for various lighting techniques.
Source: Autodesk with permission.

Further calculations related to occupancy load and movement, along with the number and type of electronic devices, can be made to identify projected interior temperature highs and lows. This highlights a significant flaw with BIM as a research tool. The resulting data yielded by BIM programs is only as accurate as the data points inserted by the researcher. Ergo, faulty data points produce faulty results. However, through careful data entry, and the documentation of how the researcher manipulated the independent variables, he or she can thus produce a sound and logical argument that would be conveyed in the conclusion. Along with the presentation of results, the researcher should include his or her data points in a chart for peer review. For example, a student studying what the best building design is for high-wind conditions, should develop figures (images) that represent important concepts such as the wind force striking the building from first a "straight on" position, and then from an angled position in order to show the reader the differences in impact velocity on different building shapes. These charts and figures help the reader to better understand the perspective of the researcher.

GIS

GIS is a computer mapping system that allows variables to be seen, analyzed, and manipulated from a plan view. These maps often appear as layers that contain individual features. Each layer is linked to a specific feature, which is then depicted within a specific geographical boundary. The aggregation of all the layers allows the researcher to cross-analyze and consider a multitude of variables, leading to informed choices. The richness of GIS is its ability to pictorially demonstrate what might otherwise be considered disparate variables within a common geographical boundary. This process has the ability to reveal hidden patterns, relationships, and trends that may not be apparent with other data gathering and reporting tools. Here are only a few of the mapping capabilities of data and information available with GIS:

- Animal migration patterns
- Consumer patterns (service and/or shopping)
- Crime patterns and municipal property location
- Density levels for residential areas
- Pollution levels and pathways through a city
- Recreation and educational needs
- Soil and rock composition
- Types of business within a district

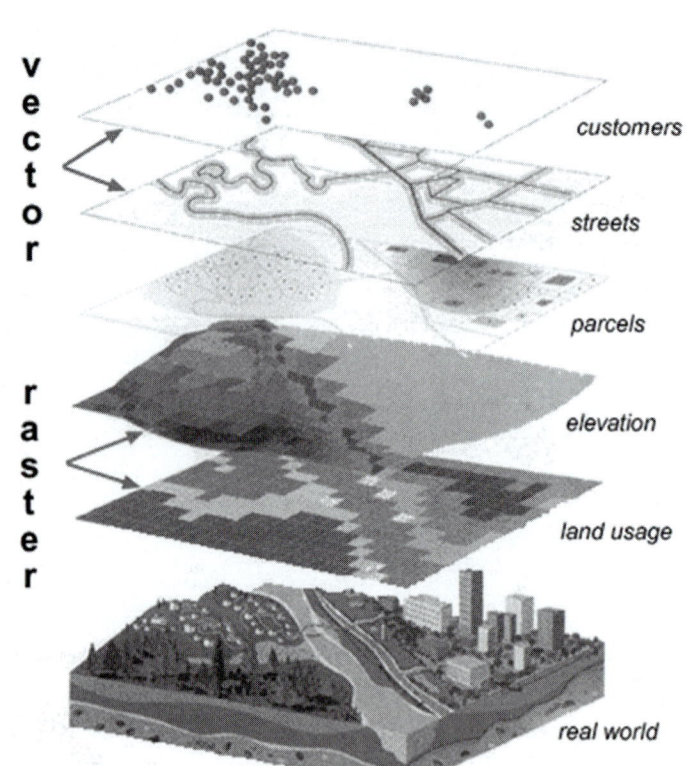

See Figure 11.6.

FIGURE 11.6 GIS Layering. This image shows an example of the layering capability of data sets available with GIS software.
Source: National Coastal Data Development Centre (NCDDC), National Oceanic and Atmospheric Administration (NOAA), USA

ANALYSIS

GIS has the ability to map where things are in an effort to take some kind of design action. This includes the ability to find a specific feature of interest in order to see its relative effect on the immediate environment, or to see the distribution of features on the map in order to see whether and what kinds of patterns emerge within a community. These patterns might take the form of quantities, densities, frequencies of some phenomena within a particular area; nearby elements and features such as rivers, mountain ranges, or a coal factory; or the evolutionary changes of a given area. Stanford University (2006) identifies five basic steps to a successful GIS project:

1. As is the case for all research methods, the researcher must identify the purpose of the project as well as the value of GIS as a research tool. Once this has been established, the researcher will then need to identify the total area to be studied as well as the level of detail shown in the map. (That is, is it important to show individual building characteristics? This question is answered when the student identifies the information needed for the research project.)

2. The researcher should then develop a logical flow chart that details the spatial analysis and necessary steps, including the types of analyses that need to be performed, content and number of overlays, and a spatial flow diagram that contains an outline of the procedures required for the data, a logical sequence of procedures to be performed, and a list of all the data required for each step.

3. The next significant step is an inventory of data requirements and sources of information. This is an important step because like with BIM, faulty data can lead to faulty results.

4. As is the case with many research methods, once a student embarks on his or her investigation, there may be a need to revise the procedures. It is acceptable to do this during the onset of the investigation, but it should not be done midway through the investigation unless the researcher has the time to begin the data collection from scratch. Once the data has been gathered and the analysis is complete, the researcher will want to evaluate the accuracy and validity of the results.

5. The final step is the presentation of results. It is important to understand any presentation restrictions, such as paper size and type of overlays. The researcher will want to keep his or her audience in mind when deciding to present the results. After all, the goal is to inform the reader—not to conceal meaning within long words, complicated jargon or confusing images.

Mapping quantities can be important for designers because it allows the designer to know important facts about the current or intended user group. To illustrate, mapping quantities can tell the designer how many children aged 8–12 live within an area as well as the quantity and dispersion patterns of parks, playgrounds, and school yards. From this data, the researcher might find that the parks, playgrounds, and schoolyards are located in areas where the fewest children are found. Another discovery that can be obtained from quantities and distributions might be the presence of barriers, such as freeways, between the clusters of children and the locations of the parks, playgrounds, and schoolyards. Though this example is fairly simple, mapping quantities can reveal very specific information about the people within a given geographic area. For example, a researcher could identify the frequency and distributions of boys aged 8–13 who have asthma and are diagnosed as clinically obese. A designer might want to know this information as part of his or her research and proposal for a more "walkable community." Another example might be to identify areas where dubious activities occur and which might thus benefit from redevelopment.

Of greater use to the designer is the mapping of densities. Density levels are often hard to fully appreciate without a big picture view. For example, a community may be composed of detached single-family homes, which should yield low-density levels. But through density level GIS mapping, the researcher may instead be able to identify high-density levels in that area because the measurement is based on the ratio of persons to acreage. On further investigation, the researcher learns that several families live communally under one roof. Therefore a project in that area would need to look at different rather than traditional definitions of high-density development and perhaps include multigenerational household design. For the interior designer, space planning would be very important because they would have to find a balance between private, semiprivate, and communal spaces within the home.

Understanding density levels has numerous implications, including adjacencies. It is not prudent to place an airport near a high-density residential area, for numerous reasons, including noise and air pollution. Likewise, it is important to know the position of tall buildings and large mountains when identifying sites for a proposed airport because these bodies can affect wind patterns. Hence, a mixed-use development with sidewalk cafés will never do well if the sidewalk café is frequently affected by air traffic, smells of a nearby tire factory, or is on a trucking route.

For researchers who wish to incorporate history or evolutionary trends into their research, the use of GIS mapping to track changes over a period of time can significantly enrich the historical data by marking and mapping when and where the changes occurred. Also known as *forecasting*, the researcher uses the historic information of a community to estimate and predict its future. This information assists designers in determining the most appropriate course of action or the most conducive design for that community's future. Consider this example: an interior design student's thesis on "Continuing Care Retirement Community Design" conducted a study on the historic evolution of carpeting use in residential versus commercial settings within the city of Toronto. Through GIS mapping, the designer identified the number of homes with wall-to-wall carpeting in 1950, 1960, 1970, 1980, 1990, and 2000. Then he or she cross-referenced that data with the presence of wall-to-wall carpeting in commercial settings during the same years. The results revealed that wall-to-wall carpeting was most used in commercial buildings, and its use began to decline in the 1970s. Therefore, the designer hypothesized that people who were adults during the years 1950–1970 might still consider all environments with wall-to-wall carpeting to be "commercial" settings and thus *predicted* that these individuals would prefer and be more comfortable in senior housing that used only the similar hard-floor flooring found in most Toronto homes during the last 60 years. As a matter of due course, this student should further verify and validate this prediction by interviewing this group of people.

GIS can be of value to the design researcher through the use of prediction. Consider a hypothesis such as the following:

> Increased urbanization has brought about the need for more diesel trucks to transport goods, while at the same time increasing the number of buildings and diesel particulate matter in the air. Because of the incidence and prevalence of asthma being tied to diesel pollution, it stands to reason that we will see greater numbers of people developing asthma-related conditions as urban densities continue to increase into the future.

A researcher can then go about proving this statement through the use of GIS mapping. First he or she would develop maps that trend or predict the densification of a given urban area. Then, he or she would forecast the incidence and prevalence of asthma within that urban area over the same periods of time. Through these maps the researcher should see (if the hypothesis is indeed true) over time a correlation between increased densification, diesel truck routes, and increased levels of asthma. From this point, the researcher can make projections about the growth of asthma as a growing issue based on the master plan of a city. This projection will include increased projections for development, increased population expectancies, and increased needs for alternate routes for the diesel vehicles.

Like all research methods, a key factor is the degree of creativity in the use of methods. Once a tool such as BIM or GIS has been identified, the job of the researcher is to then outline how he or she will use that tool. The term used in research is "method," but when we look at the synonyms of methods, we can see that this also means process, approach, and way. Hence, the researcher must ask himself or herself, "What is the process or approach that I will take to find things out while using GIS?" Instead of just saying what this process or approach is, researchers need to write down *in detail* their plan of action, so that another researcher can conduct the same research at another time, perhaps in another area.

Summary

In many ways, experiments can be thought of as the backbone of research. When considering evidence-based design, experimentation can provide visual, hands-on opportunities that many students find very beneficial. The key with experimentation is repetition; that is, repeating the experiment to make sure the same results occur consistently and reviewing the data over and over to identify the subtleties and sensitivities of the process. The more comfortable a researcher becomes with the procedures of experimentation, the more successful and confident he or she will be when performing the actual experiments and then presenting those results.

With the experimental method, the researcher manipulates the independent variable in order to determine whether and how much *or* how and to what degree it affects something else (the dependent variable). Ultimately, the scientific experiment allows the researcher to study a subject at an advanced level and allows for reanalysis or for the entire research to be replicated. Experimenting is an excellent way to increase the significance and relevance of design research. Experimental methods that use simulations are well suited for a design studio class because the researcher-designer is already trained to build models and subjecting the models to different conditions—testing. Taking that skill to the next level involves subjecting those models to different *controlled* conditions—experimentation. However, the researcher must take care to record his or her processes and findings.

One way to do this involves video-recording the experiments so that they can be more rigorously analyzed.

Many younger people have grown up with various incarnations and applications of the computer. As a research tool, computer-based applications can add another level of richness to the experimental process. Through hypothetical situations, the researcher can predict the building's future behavior and then create a design that becomes the solution to the situation. BIM is a series of computer modeling applications that allows the design to be developed as a three-dimensional representation that can then be tested to see how the building responds to its surroundings or the way light or outside air enters the building, or to perform material cost/benefit analysis. Another important software tool for the design researcher is GIS. This mapping software has the ability to demonstrate in a plan view the effect a building will have on its surroundings and the identification of significant natural and man-made variables that will affect a building, and can help predict certain conditions, human disorders, or the fluidity of movement throughout a city. A significant factor in the use of computer software in the research process is the variables and data points put into the software applications. One faulty calculation can skew all of the results, thus invalidating the research. Hence, the researcher must be meticulous when identifying his or her data points and make sure that they are accurate.

Glossary

Building information modeling (BIM)—The process of developing, administering, and analyzing three-dimensional computer-generated models featuring real-time dynamics.

Computational fluid dynamics (CFD)—Airflow and temperature predictions through the use of computer and software.

Confounding variables—One or more variables not under the control of the experimenter that affects experimental results.

Control group—A group of test subjects not exposed to some intervention, but compared to a group of subjects who were exposed to the intervention.

Control variable—A variable held constant in order to analyze the relationship between other variables.

Dependent Variable—A variable that is measured.

Double-blind—Neither the participants in a trial nor the investigators are aware of which participant group are given the intervention.

Extraneous variable—An uncontrollable variable that offers an alternative explanation of the results.

Functional magnetic resonance imaging (fMRI)—Diagnostic imaging machinery used to measure brain activity. Commonly used to determine the specific location of the brain where a certain function, such as speech or memory, occurs.

Geographic information systems (GIS)—A computer mapping system designed for storing, manipulating, analyzing, and displaying data in a geographic context.

Independent variable—A variable which is manipulated by the designer.

Placebo-controlled—When an inactive substance (such as a sugar pill) is given to one group of participants.

Quasi experiment—When the experimenter lacks control over the independent variable.

Reliability—The measure of consistency for an assessment instrument

Replicability—The degree to which an experiment can be reproduced in other locations.

Simulations—The imitation of something real.

Single-subject experiment—A single study examined over a period of time.

True experiment—When there are control and experimental variables.

CHAPTER 12 The Final Phase

chapter outline

Introduction

General Guidelines

Resources
- *Time Management*

Formatting

Citations

Embellishments
- *Fold-out Pages*
- *Pocket Materials*
- *Miscellaneous*

Final Assembly

The Title and Cover Page

Front Matter
- *Copyright Page*
- *Signature Page*
- *Dedication Page*
- *Table of Contents Page*
- *List of Tables, Figures, Illustrations, Charts, and Graphs*
- *Nomenclature List*
- *Abstract Page*

Main Text
- *Chapter Headings*
- *Review of the Literature*
- *Methods*
- *Results*
- *Discussion and Design Application*

Back Matter
- *References (APA) or Works Cited (MLA)*
- *Appendices*
- *Glossary of Terms*
- *Curriculum Vitae or Author's Biography*

Electronic Submission

Electronic Thesis or Dissertation
- *Security Concerns*

Summary

> "My task which I am trying to achieve is by power of the written word . . . to make you **see**. That, and no more, and it is everything."
>
> —Joseph Conrad

chapter objectives

By the end of this chapter, students should be able to:

- Develop a schedule for completing his or her thesis or dissertation.
- Understand the formal/traditional layout of a thesis.
- Create a structure and format for presenting his or her ideas with the thesis.
- Compile all of the previously completed sections into a cohesive research document.
- Utilize the feedback from others to refine his or her work with words, graphics, or examples to explain the thesis subject.
- Complete and verify all citations for inclusion to the reference list.
- Prepare all required front and back matter to ready the final document for submission and printing.

Introduction

Unique to the design thesis or dissertation is the application of the research results into a space, building, landscape, or environmental design. Students incorporate the results into computer simulations, physical models, or hand drawings as a means to complete the exploration of the ideas and concepts derived through scientific research. This complex and sophisticated collaboration between art and science takes the research process to a higher level than the theses and dissertations of many other traditional academic disciplines. Thesis candidates should be proud of themselves for arriving at this advanced position within the research document and their academic careers.

The final stage of a thesis or dissertation is the submission of the final document, electronically submitted or printed and bound into a hardcover book. The assembly of a thesis or dissertation requires the researcher to organize all of the individual parts researched (theory, ROL, methods, and so on) and put them into one logically sequenced document. The completion of the document should take readers through the thought process of the researcher, beginning with the issue of concern—all the way to the final design. Each chapter shows how the researcher refined his or her ideas and how the new information influenced the design. The main sections of a thesis or dissertation are the: **front matter**, **main text**, and **back matter**.

This chapter describes the assembling of a traditional thesis document. However, it is up to thesis and dissertation candidates to refine this format to better communicate their message while conforming to the requirements of their college or university. At this stage, students will need to consider the readers of their thesis to be the audience whom they must plead their case to—or *prove* their case. Readers from the design community will want to see justification for the design solution, as they might be thinking the following while reading the thesis:

- So what?
- Why this design?
- Why this location?
- Why not some other design?

However, readers from the scientific community will want empirical data—that is, relevant proof. They will be thinking, "Convince me why I should consider you an expert in this subject." Or "Prove to me that your analysis is accurate." To successfully answer both perspectives of design and science, candidates must lead readers through their explorations, their readings, and their studies to explain the manifestation and evolution of their final design.

General Guidelines

Students should begin writing as soon as possible, starting with a rough draft of ideas and then developing a list of objectives that may be used in the forming of an outline that leads readers down a logical path for clarifying the subject matter and then ending with the design solution. All work that is completed early provides students with a psychological boost and helps them maintain motivation. Therefore, it is suggested that the easiest chapters be written first, thereby leaving the conclusions and introductions for last, when the students have a better understanding of their subjects and can write a comprehensive and concise passage. In order to begin the final assembly of the research document, the vital resources for students must be discussed: computers, people, and reader feedback.

RESOURCES

Most students use computers and word processing software to write their papers. If a student does not have this skill set, he or she should take classes or hire a typist. The software available today has wonderful features to make the lives of researchers much easier:

- Checking for spelling or grammatical errors
- Database managing
- Table of contents formation and indexing
- Footnoting and annotation

However, students should err on the side of caution and protect their files at all times by creating multiple backup copies. Suggestions for backup storage locations: email a copy to yourself, print a hard copy occasionally, save to flash drives frequently, or burn a CD once a week. Warning: do not keep all research (especially the ROL) on one computer—make copies.

One of the best resources a thesis student has is people: friends, family, and thesis advisors. Students should have someone read, examine, and return (with notes and critique) their thesis several times before final printing. It is always a good practice to prepare the reader by identifying some specific questions and concerns with the current draft: Does the information flow? Are there enough citations? This feedback is invaluable to students, who will undoubtedly be spending enormous amounts of time writing their theses alone. Errors are often overlooked when the writer becomes the reader. In fact, *all* authors need a "fresh set of eyes" occasionally; that is, an audience who can read the draft line by line without a preconceived idea of what may or may not have been written.

Feedback should always be accepted gracefully and professionally, as reading a thesis from cover to cover is typically arduous, time-consuming, and not typically considered a "light read." Although a small gift for your readers is not a required formality, it may be appropriate. One last note: some candidates (depending on the discipline) will be encouraged to publish their results once the thesis is completed. Any publishing matters should be discussed with advisors and school administration prior to graduation, as to not delay the publishing process.

Time Management

It is recommended that students develop a timetable or schedule for writing their thesis or dissertation. The timetable should include a listing of dates for when the rough draft of each chapter should be completed and a schedule for when it will be reviewed and then be returned. It is crucial for students to allow adequate "turn around" time at each major junction in their research. It is more likely that students will meet every deadline, when a schedule has been handed to a thesis advisor or mentor, rather than the student having a single *mental* due date for everything. See Activity 12.1.

ACTIVITY 12.1 Develop a Schedule

Develop a schedule for your research document. Final stages include: outlining, researching, rough draft #1, sending out for review, revisions (rough draft #2), graphic additions, and final product. These are only seven possible stages; add any missing steps that can be anticipated with your individual research.

NOTE: Toward the end of the thesis, it is quite likely loose ends or technical difficulties may occur, so expect to complete your manuscript three or four weeks prior to the deadline to minimize stress. Here is an example of a thesis timeline/schedule. (Using boxes to check items off as they are completed makes weary students feel a sense of accomplishment at each stage.)

Done	Month	Chapter	Outline	Research	Draft	Review	Revise	Graphics	Final
☐	September								
☐	October								
☐	November								
☐	December								
☐	January								
☐	February								
☐	March								
☐	April								
☐	May								

Table 12.1 Formatting Reference Guide

Thesis Element	Typeface	Size	Style	Paragraph Spacing	Indent After?	Pagination	Publication Style
Entire Document	Times New Roman	12 point	Normal	Double-spaced	—	Front matter varies	Follow your university's specifications
Title		Less than 20 point	Bold	Single	—	No	
Chapter Title		Less than 20 point	Bold	—	No	Yes: Each chapter starts on a new page.	
Chapter Headings		12 point	Normal	—	No	—	
Chapter Subheading		12 point	Italic	—	Yes	—	
Exceptions							
	Typeface/font	Use same typeface/font throughout					
	Italic	Only for foreign words, titles, and emphasis					
	Bold	Only for special symbols and glossary terms					
	Type Size	Never less than 9 points or greater than 18 points; 9-point type is used only for tables, figures, and the like					

FORMATTING

One of the universal constants in traditional research writing is the formatting of the document. Documents are double-spaced and every page is numbered in a systematic fashion (called **pagination**). The standard typeface is 12-point, Times New Roman, not bold or italic. As a general rule of thumb, all thesis formatting (font, size, and style) should remain consistent throughout the document. Adhering to a coherent and consistent format reduces confusion and frustration for the readers. Table 12.1 offers a quick reference for standard theses formatting.

Some additional guidelines include:

- Avoid typing less than two lines of text or a heading at the bottom of any page.
- Use only graphics and photographs that are clear, sharp, and include a color profile that the printing company can reproduce accurately (i.e., ask for their "printer profile").

Pagination is the systematic ordering of the pages within a formal document. Certain pages receive special numbering to notify the reader of the changes between the reference pages and the body of the text. There are two types of numbers used: Roman numerals and Hindu–Arabic (also known as *algebraic*) numerals. See Box 12.1 for a guide to the typical thesis numbering system.

CITATIONS

Citations are the official recognition of another author's work. It is more than the "credit" that they are due—it is the legal obligation of all authors to point out ideas, quotes, and information that came from someone else.

BOX 12.1 Pagination

Roman Numerals: Used in the beginning of the thesis document, which is called the front matter.

Symbol	Meaning	Thesis Use	Example
I	1 (one)	Signature page: Lower-case	ii
V	5 (five)	Dedication	iii
		Table of contents	iv
		Tables and figures list	v
		Abstract	vi
X	10 (ten)		
L	50 (fifty)	(Not commonly used)	
C	100 (one hundred)		

Hindu-Arabic Numerals: Used in the body of the document (example: 1,2,3,4 . . .).

Page	Type	Location on page
Every page	Hindu-Arabic	Upper right-hand corner, at least 1 inch from top and side edges

(Please refer to Chapter 2 for a detailed discussion of APA and MLA styles.) Depending on the requirements of the individual college or university, systems of citing sources within the text of the document generally fall into these three arrangements:

- Author-date-page
- Number (indicating a reference list either at the end of the chapter or book)
- Footnote or endnote

Thesis writers must double-check their manuscript prior to printing to guarantee that all sources are cited, are included in the References or Works Cited list, and that author and publisher information is accurate. Students are reminded to investigate which publication style is required at their institution and learn more about the rules pertaining to that style.

EMBELLISHMENTS

The thesis for a design degree often becomes an object of art and design, in and of itself. If the college or university allows thesis or dissertation candidates to embellish upon the format, in either construction or presentation, students are compelled to be consistent throughout their manuscript and to consider the long-term ramifications and implications of their design choices.

Fold-out Pages

Many design-related images and drawings are best viewed in a large format; therefore, a fold-out page may become necessary. Oversized material should be thought out and rehearsed long in advance of the printing process. Because these pages can be awkward to handle and subject to damage, the following suggestions should aid students in mitigating such constraints. The image(s) should not be larger than the dimensions of the book while lying open flat. If a book is 8 inches by 8 inches square, the foldout page should be roughly 8 inches by 14 inches. (Please refer to Figure 12.1.) The left side of the page will be bound into the rest of the thesis book, and the vertical fold should be about 1 inch away from the edge. The right side of the fold-out page will be loosely tucked about 1 inch from the center binding. In this way, the page will not be cut while the pages are trimmed at the printers during the binding process.

The same general parameters are involved with large-format images that are centered in the thesis book and stretch across both pages. They are "tricky" at best and oftentimes are visually distracting, as readers attempt to view the image within the book fold. Thus, students who wish to tackle this challenge should confer with the book

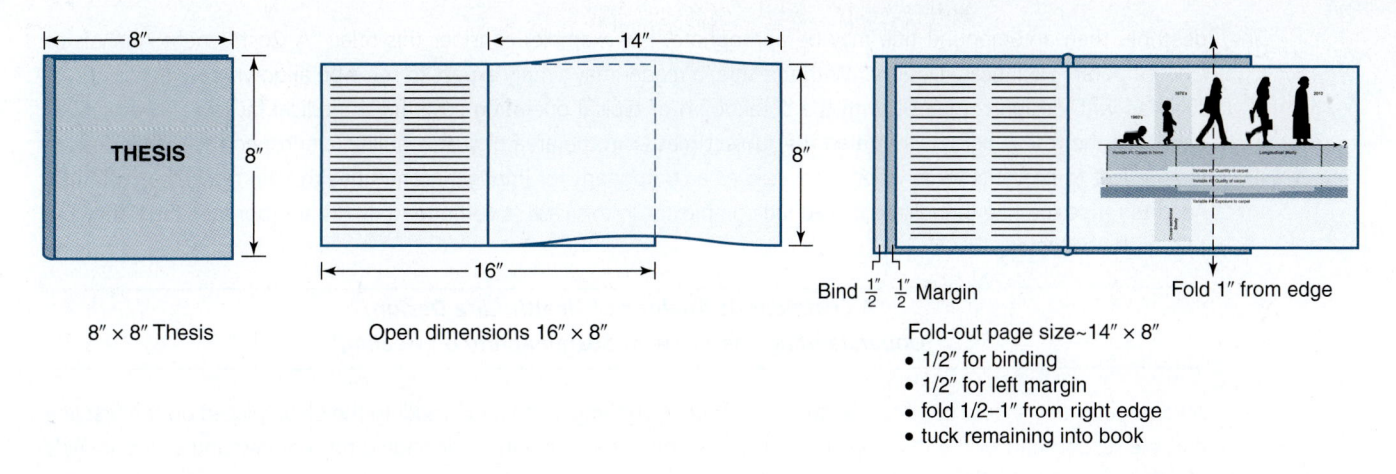

FIGURE 12.1 Example of a Fold-Out. This illustrates one way of including a fold-out page in a thesis or dissertation document. The arrangement and sample dimensions are only examples. Check with the specific printing company to verify requirements.
Source: Sinclair, E. (2009).

publisher as early as possible on how to best accomplish the seamless printing of a large image with the binding running through the center.

Pocket Material

Another way to handle large items is to insert them into a pocket built into the thesis book cover. Pocket materials may include:

- CD or DVDs
- Material or fabric samples
- Tactile objects relevant to the research

Pockets are best attached to the inside back cover of hard-bound books to minimize the chances of the material falling out. A pocket closure with a fastening device can also be incorporated. With regard to the table of contents, the words "in pocket" should be used instead of a page number for location.

Miscellaneous

Cover material, textiles, paper (20 lb. paper is typical), photographs—in fact, any and all components—should be of high quality, and great thought should be put behind the longevity and durability of each article. Students should objectively ask themselves the following questions when considering factors of constructing their final thesis product (their book): What will be the condition of all the components in 5 years after 50 people have paged through my thesis? Will the message—my "material language"—communicate in the same way in the future compared with today?

Final Assembly

First and foremost, the difference between **thesis structure** and **thesis layout** must be established. The structure of a thesis belongs completely to the author. The student-author builds the argument, constructs the arrangement of information, and organizes the flow of facts to the reader. The layout of a thesis is solely predicated by the institutional requirements. Whatever the college or university thesis standards are, students should staunchly adhere to them. To reiterate: thesis structure is up to students and thesis layout is up to the school. The most basic thesis structure and layout is discussed in the next section in order to provide an overview of research writing for all students. Traditional research writings are composed of three main sections: the front matter, the main text, and the back matter.

THE TITLE AND COVER PAGE

The title that a student-researcher selects should be an accurate description of the information contained within the thesis. If the thesis or dissertation contents are an aspect of something greater than what a single title can accurately describe, then a compound title may be appropriate. For example, consider this title: "A Cost/Benefit Analysis of Contemporary Healthcare Design." With this title, a reader may simply expect to see a breakdown between costs associated with design compared with the breakdown of typical operating costs for a medical facility. However, suppose that the researcher concentrated the subject matter in the area of sustainability (a subspecialty within design) in an effort to prove its value when measured as a component for improving one's health. The researcher will then need to refine the title to indicate this added complexity. In this case, a compound title is appropriate. Thus, the new title might become:

"A Cost/Benefit Analysis of Health-Care Design:
Understanding the Value of Sustainability on Healing"

A compound title should be shown as two lines, with everything up to and including the colon placed on the first line and the second part of the title appearing on the second line. The entire title should be centered and approximately five lines (single-spaced) down from the top 1-inch margin.

The next items to appear on the cover are the words, "Thesis Presented to the Faculty of the University XYZ" because the faculty must authenticate and recommend the candidate for graduation. The researcher therefore has an obligation to ensure that the work has been done and represented within the standards set forth by the institution.

It is important to use the proper name of the school. In many instances, a college university may change its name or students may get used to using some abbreviated name for the school. For example, "*The*" is in the title of "The Ohio State University" but the word "the" is not in the title of "University of Massachusetts." A second issue arises when a university alters its name, or if an alternative name of the school is used. For example, many people know of the state school in Long Beach, California, as "Long Beach State." However, the proper name of the university is "California State University, Long Beach." Another common issue is that titles are often exempt from common grammatical errors. For example, "NewSchool of Architecture and Design" merges the two words "*new*" and "*school*" but capitalizes them as if they were two separate words. In addition, rather than using the word "and" the school officially uses the ampersand sign (&) as part of its official name. The last more common issue is the use of acronyms. One might argue that the acronym UCLA has more brand recognition than the actual name of the school, University of California, Los Angeles. However, the latter is the official name of the school. Thus, each school has its own set of rules regarding what is acceptable for a thesis or dissertation cover and each student should consult with his or her thesis advisor for clarification.

The next line is the degree that the candidate is seeking. Within design, there are professional degrees and academic degrees. Make sure that the appropriate degree appears on the title, for example: Master of Architecture (M.Arch) or Master of Science in Architecture (MS). The final line is the author's name as it will appear on his or her diploma. Students who have been married during the course of their education should check with the registrar to confirm that the preferred name on the thesis or dissertation matches the student's transcripts and diploma.

Regarding cover appearances, most theses or dissertations will use a simple monochromatic hard color with gold or silver lettering indicating the title, school, and author of the thesis or dissertation. Some schools may allow some latitude in the cover design; however, most opt for the long tradition of simplicity. Students need to check with their respective school to determine room for cover design. See Figure 12.2.

FRONT MATTER

Once the initial title page is done, the researcher must assemble the front matter. This is the part of the document that provides various logistical information of the research, such as subject background, the advising committee, and the location of all the key components within the document. It also contains the researcher's personal inspiration and an overview of the entire document. Included in this part of the document are the following pages:

- Inside cover
- Copyright
- Signature
- Dedication
- Table of contents

```
                    Title of the Document



                    Thesis Presented to
               the Faculty of the Name of School



          In Partial Fulfillment of the Requirement for
                the Degree of Name of Degree




                    By: Researcher's Name
```

FIGURE 12.2 Title Page
Source: Sinclair, E., (2009)

- Tables, figures, illustrations, charts, graphs
- Nomenclature list
- Abstract

The first page—the inside cover—is merely an exact copy of what is found on the outside cover of the thesis or dissertation.

Copyright Page

The researcher has the choice of whether to copyright his or her thesis or dissertation. The purpose of a copyright is to protect the author from others making copies of the work, distributing copies of that work, making derivative forms of the work, or displaying the work without the researcher's permission. Should a student researcher decide to copyright the work, he or she is guaranteeing that the work is original and that he or she has followed accepted standards for documenting the references and listing citations for all other work used throughout the document. Examples of other works include photographs, charts, graphs, tables, and diagrams. A copyright remains in effect for the lifetime of the author plus 50 years.

Before copyrighting the work, the researcher should consult with his or her advisor. In most cases, all work produced as part of an educational program belongs to the school. This is similar to the standards used in the workplace. When employees generate work as part of their job duties, that work belongs to the company, not the employee. It is therefore best to confer with the advisory committee prior to initiating a copyright.

If the degree-granting institution and committee members allow the researcher to copyright the work, the copyright page should follow the title page in the sequence of the front matter. The page should be formatted with the following information:

Copyright by:
(Full name as it appears on the diploma)
(Year of thesis or dissertation acceptance)

```
                          Copyright By:
                           Jane Johns
                             2010

                               ii
```

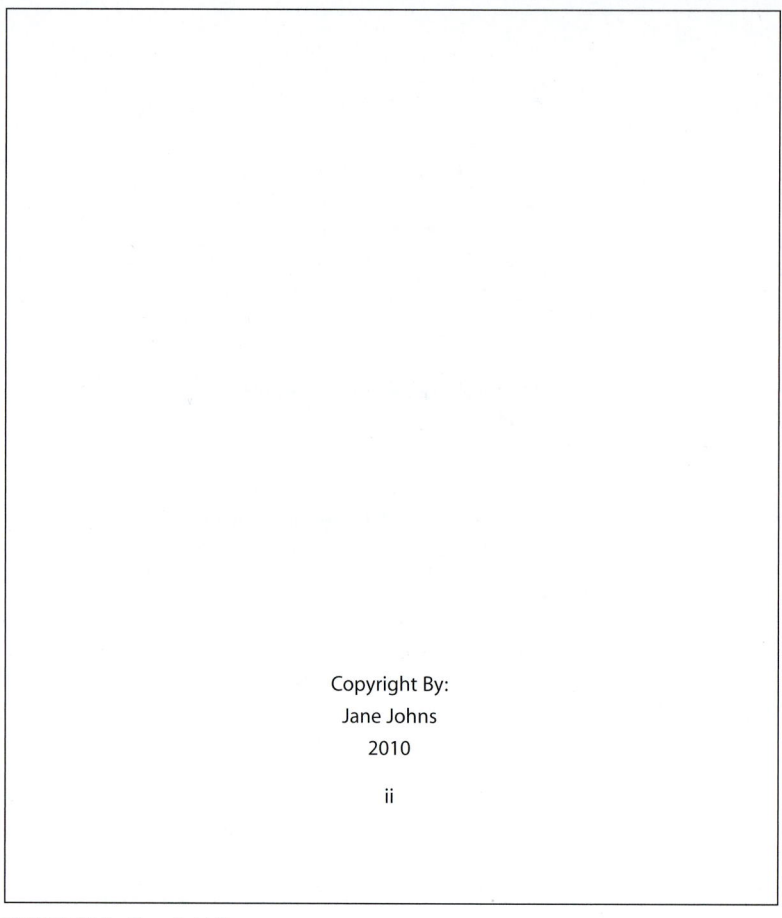

FIGURE 12.3 Copyright Page.
Source: Sinclair, E., (2009)

This information should be located in the center, in the lower third of the page, just above the bottom margin. At the very bottom should appear the Roman numeral "ii" to indicate the second page of the front matter. The title page is the first page of the front matter; although this page is counted, it is not numbered.

Signature Page

The signature page is the page that authenticates the thesis or dissertation. This page should list all committee members, along with their appropriate **appellations** (letters associated with a degree or certification). These people should be listed first by order of title, beginning with the committee chairperson. The next level of committee member to be listed should come directly from the school and be ranked by educational achievement, beginning with research degrees and followed by professional degrees. Please see Box 12.2 for a ranking of appellations. The remaining committee members to be listed on the signature page are outside consultants and peer reviewers. Sometimes these individuals are not formally affiliated with the institution, but instead have agreed to serve on the researcher's committee, pending school approval. Finally, the bottom of the page should contain the Roman numeral "iii" in the center. See Figure 12.4.

BOX 12.2 Appellation Ranking

Doctor of Philosophy (PhD)	Master of Arts (MA)
Doctor of Architecture (D.Arch.)	Master of Architecture (M.Arch)
Doctor of Business Administration (DBA)	Master of Engineering (ME)
Doctor of Education (EdD)	Master of Fine Arts (MFA)
Master of Science (MS)	

```
                    TITLE OF DOCUMENT


            In Partial Fulfillment of the Requirement for
                  the Degree of Name of Degree




     Approved By:
     _____
     Jane Doe, Ph.D., Thesis Advisor

     _____
     John Janes, D. Arch, Studio Advisor

     _____
     Doe Johnson, M. S., Committee Member

     _____
     Maria Gonzales, M. Arch., Committee Member

     _____
     Vu Chen, B.Arch., Peer Reviewer

                             iii
```

FIGURE 12.4 Signature Page.
Source: Sinclair, E., (2009)

Dedication Page

The dedication page should acknowledge significant people in the researcher's life (personal or professional) who have provided support during the research process. Note that it is protocol to list either the researcher's entire committee or none at all. It is inappropriate to acknowledge only one or two committee members; it may indicate that the researcher has difficulty working equally and collaboratively within a team. The dedication should be aligned at the top of the page, double-spaced, with the Roman numeral "iv" located at the bottom center. See Figure 12.5.

Table of Contents Page

The table of contents lists the title, heading number, and page numbers of all the chapters in the book. They can be used to find information quickly and demonstrate how the report has been organized. Each major section of the document should be listed in the table of contents. Additional subheadings may be included in the table of contents to help the reader navigate the document. These subheadings can be beneficial because theses and dissertations often contain long, nondescript sections such as: Review of Literature, Methods, Results, and Application.

Each page of the table of contents should also contain the appropriate Roman numeral page number. Take care to assemble the table of contents in sections: front matter, main text, and back matter. Remember that the front matter is numbered with Roman numerals and the pages of the main text and back matter are numbered with Hindu–Arabic.

Tables, Figures, Illustrations, Charts, and Graphs

Directly following the table of contents is a list of tables, figures, illustrations, charts, and graphs. Each table, figure, illustration, chart, and graph must be labeled with a number and represented in order according to chapter. Please see Box 12.3 for an example.

```
┌─────────────────────────────────────┐
│                                     │
│            Dedication               │
│  This thesis is dedicated to my family for all of the support that they have provided to │
│  me throughout my life. Thank you!  │
│                                     │
│                                     │
│                                     │
│                                     │
│                                     │
│                                     │
│                iv                   │
└─────────────────────────────────────┘
```

FIGURE 12.5 Dedication Page.
Source: Sinclair, E., (2009)

This method has the tables, figures, illustrations, charts, and graphs divided according to chapter. Another way that these items can be divided is according to their heading. This is done by listing all of the tables in the publication, followed by all of the figures, and so forth. In whatever fashion a researcher chooses to depict the tables, figures, illustrations, charts, and graphs, it is important that each category have its own page. Hence, if the researcher opts to list the tables, figures, illustrations, charts, and graphs according to chapter and the thesis consists of five chapters, then the reader would expect to find five pages containing double-spaced information for

BOX 12.3   List of Figures

		Chapter 1
Tables		
	1.1	Comparison of census data for pollution-related deaths according to year
	1.2	Forms of transportation and amount of pollution generated
Figures		
	1.1	Photograph of a diesel truck spewing black smoke from exhaust pipe
		Chapter 2
Tables		
	2.1	Emissions readings from Site No. 1
Figures		
	2.1	Aerial photograph of Site No. 1

```
                    Nomenclature List

        A_g    Gross area of section, defined by the outer dimensions
        A_n    Net area
        C      Compressive force
        D      (1) Diameter
               (2) Deflection
        E      Modulus of elasticity
        I      Moment of inertia
        L      Length (span)
        M      Bending moment
        P      Concentrated load (point load)




                              vi
```

FIGURE 12.6 Nomenclature List.
Source: Sinclair, E., (2009)

all of the tables, figures, illustrations, charts, and graphs, along with their corresponding Roman numeral at the bottom of the page number. The figures should be presented in numeric order according to chapter. Each figure should be accompanied with the citation of where the table, figure, illustration, chart, or graph originated from (called the "Source"). If the table, figure, illustration, chart, or graph was created by the author, then the citation would state "Source: *Author.*"

Nomenclature List

It may be appropriate to provide a list of technical terms, symbols, abbreviations, or acronyms and their corresponding definitions in the front matter if the thesis is highly technical. This will allow readers to peruse the document with confidence and agility. The nomenclature list should also contain the appropriate Roman numeral centered at the bottom of each page. See Figure 12.6.

Abstract Page

The abstract of a thesis or dissertation is a succinct narrative that describes the work, including the purpose, issue, methodology used and the results. Deviating from the standard APA format, the text of the abstract is single-spaced, with an extra line space between the title and text. Paragraphs are indented five spaces and no extra lines are inserted between paragraphs. In addition, the margins are 1 inch on all sides, there are no page breaks, and it is justified to the right margin.

A good abstract is accurate, self-contained, concise, and specific, does not include citations and essentially summarizes the entire research document in less than 500 words. See Figure 12.7. A good guide to writing an abstract is to have several people read it and ask them (at the very least) the following questions:

- Would you read the entire document based on this abstract?
- What is your understanding of the "point" of my research?
- What would you expect to find in the way of "facts" or "proof" within this document?

> **Abstract**
> The purpose of this study was to review existing literature on the development of cognitive functioning and how the brain interprets environmental stimuli. From an extensive review of the literature, exploratory suppositions were developed to inform the design of a prototype model of a nursery for infants and toddlers that could serve as the foundation for future research.
>
> Literature on the cognitive development of both humans and animals was analyzed in order to identify specific developmental capacities of infants and toddlers to perceive environmental stimuli. Among the reviewed literature were publications on children who were deprived of sensory stimulation during their formative years. These findings were then augmented with articles describing the development and process of sensory detection along with evolutionary theories that explain human behaviors that span cultures and socioeconomics. Pertinent factors were extrapolated from the literature to form a prototype model of a nursery that could serve as the basis for further investigations.
>
> The prototype model was developed from evidence-based research with each design attribute purposely selected as a means to enhance the perception and cognition of infants and toddlers. The model was then analyzed and assessed based on existing research to form suppositions related to safety and design feasibility. The intent of this research and prototype model was to provide a foundation for further research to determine if the proposed strategies affect the sensory development of infants and toddlers.
>
> xi

FIGURE 12.7 Abstract Page
Source: Sinclair, E., (2009)

MAIN TEXT

The main text of the thesis is divided into chapters. Each chapter, much like this book, has opening and closing paragraphs or sections, also called the *introduction* and the *conclusion*. These are not to be confused with the actual Introduction and Conclusion chapters. Because the structure of the middle chapters varies amongst theses and students, it will be necessary to devise an organization plan. Box 12.4 shows the sequencing of the main text of a typical design thesis, as well as a few other ways of using the chapters to the advantage of the research subject.

BOX 12.4 Sample Thesis Chapters

Typical design thesis

Chapter 1: Introduction

Chapter 2: Literature Review

Chapter 3: Methodology

Chapter 4: Results

Chapter 5: Discussion and Design Application

Chapter 5: Conclusion

Thesis based on a theory

Chapter 1: Introduction

Chapter 2: Theory

Chapter 3: Methods

Chapter 4: (Title for First Problem)

Chapter 5: (Title for Second Problem)

Chapter 6: (Title for Third Problem)

Chapter 7: New Model

Chapter 8: Conclusion

Thesis based on a process

Chapter 1: Introduction

Chapter 2: Review of Literature

Chapter 3: (Title for technique 1)

Chapter 4: (Title for technique 2)

Chapter 5: (Title for technique 3)

Chapter 6: Process Application

Chapter 7: Conclusion

BOX 12.5   Headings: Position, Numbering, Style, and Indentation

CHAPTER 1: CHAPTER TITLE

(centered, **bold**, and UPPERCASE)

Text starts here, no indentation.

    1.1   **MAIN-LEVEL HEADING** (left-justified, **bold**, and UPPERCASE)
Text starts here, no indentation.

        1.1.1   **Sublevel Heading** (left-justified, **bold**, and Title Case)
Text starts here, no indentation.

            1.1.1.1   *Secondary sublevel heading* (left-justified, *italic*, and Sentence case)
     Text starts here, five-space indentation.

Chapter Headings

Headings are all introductions to a new idea or significant conceptual juncture in the research. They include:

- Chapter titles
- Main-level headings
- Sublevel headings
- Secondary sublevel headings

Headings focus in on or narrow the research to objectives that explain the various stages or points of investigation in a logical order so that readers may track the researcher's thought process and make sense of the information. The basic formatting of the headings is shown in Box 12.5. The numbering system is extended by way of a period (.) and an additional number to indicate the position or level of the information. For example, if a chapter were entitled, "Nutritional Components" (chapter number 1), then a main-level heading might be "Food" (numbered 1.1), and a sublevel heading could be "Vegetables" (numbered 1.1.1), and finally the secondary sublevel heading could be "Minerals" (1.1.1.1). Note how the levels refine the information and research to the specific components that the research will be highlighting.

Review of the Literature

The review of the literature (ROL) is the second chapter following the introduction in a thesis document. Its purpose is to broaden the perspectives and understandings of the thesis topic. It should be the most complete of the first three sections at this final stage of development. However, researchers should revisit, organize, and update (or add if necessary) literary components near completion of their study. In this chapter, thesis students identify and discuss the relevant and similar literary works to show a rational relationship between the past work of others and their own research. Students using this book to navigate the thesis terrain would have written their ROL using the activities in Chapter 5. However, deciding how best the literature they have read can be connected to their thesis and support their claims might be an issue still on the table.

    Students are reminded of the three ways in Chapter 5 for organizing the literature: controversy, method, and position. The *controversy* technique involves grouping authors who support one side of the topic and those who support the opposing view. The *method* technique involves arranging the sections by authors and the empirical method they used to gather their data. The *position* technique clusters all the authors by thesis objective. In this way, other authors and their studies back up each point that the student-researcher wants to make. Once the information has been laid out in such a way as to provide a sturdy and ample foundation for the topic, it can be added to the final thesis document. For specific instructions for assembling a ROL, please refer to Chapter 5.

Methods

The third chapter within a thesis document is called "Methods" or "Methodology"; it is about the acquisition of new knowledge through a systematic and highly structured process in an attempt to gather information which adds reliability and validity to the research. The methods chapter consists not only of the methods used to acquire new knowledge, but also the outcome of that method and how the information was applied to the final design. Each subheading should be between one and two pages in length; for those using qualitative measures such as journaling, photo analysis, and observations, the descriptions will be longer because more detail will be required in order to inform the readers of what happened. Chapter 7 of this book outlines the procedure of writing a "methods" section. The basic arrangement of the methods chapter is as follows:

- A description of the method (*introductory section*)
- How the data was acquired (*implementation section*)
- Discuss and explain the research tool (*discussion section*)
- Traditional design research methods (*site analysis and case study section*)

Results

The "Results" chapter of a thesis or dissertation typically uses four subheadings:

- Implementation
- Description
- Results
- Discussion

Overall, writing up the results chapter should be the easiest part of the whole research project because all of the hard work should have been completed by performing the experiment (or survey, or other method), analyzing the findings, and writing the methods chapter.

The first subheading in the results chapter, entitled "Implementation," explains to the reader what actually happened while executing the research method. (In the methods chapter, the researcher explains what he or she *will do*—this section tells the reader what *actually happened*.) This is done because regardless of how well-prepared a researcher is, when it comes to the actual implementation, factors arise that force the researcher to modify the method. It is the scientific way of saying, "I wanted to do this but I ended up doing this." For example, say one researcher planned to observe activities at three different but randomly selected parks during a given weekday. However, when the researcher went to one of the parks, it was discovered that a local school was given exclusive use of the park during school hours. Hence, the researcher was not able to conduct the observations at that particular park. Therefore, the researcher was forced to modify the method by excluding that park.

Unforeseen situations that occur while implementing a research method have the potential of confounding the data and must be acknowledged by the researcher within the thesis document. One way to address a confounding event is to discuss it and the situation that arose from that event in the implementation section of the results chapter, entitled "**Limitations**." Examples of things that can limit research results range from events such as:

- A typo discovered in a survey
- A participant having a cold
- Events with global significance (war or natural disaster) that disrupted the survey, study, or experiment
- A smaller sample group showed up than desired

One situation that is fairly common when relying upon electronic media for dissemination and delivery is interference of data by email filters, which might stop an email from going through, eliminate the attachment, or eliminate certain attachments such as photographs or illustrations. In the following example, the researcher sent out a survey to an organization as a Microsoft Word document; however, the document arrived without the photographs. The researcher could verify that the survey was indeed complete when it was sent because the original document was carbon-copied (cc'd) to the supervising committee member (instructor) and the instructor's document was received intact. Because of this unforeseen occurrence, the number and diversity of surveys returned was negatively influenced and the researcher was required to address this issue within the results, as described here:

> Participants were sent surveys via email; however, in at least one case the photographs used within the survey were filtered out by the recipient's email system. To address this situation and eliminate the potential for data contamination, the decision was made to omit those surveys from the sample pool. Future attempts to administer surveys through electronic media would need to address this issue in order to avoid the repeat of a similar situation. One solution might include the conversion of the survey document to a PDF prior to dissemination; however, further research would be needed.

In essence, this section should describe in detail how the research was carried out and discuss all of the situations that failed to occur as outlined in the procedures section of the methods section. Researchers must be aware that even the smallest difference between the *planned* implementation and the *actual* implementation must be discussed, because another researcher in the future wanting to duplicate the student's study may end up having different results unless the method is explained thoroughly and accurately.

In the next section in the same chapter, the researcher should discuss any and all procedural factors associated with the research method, including, for example:

- The number of surveys administered versus the actual number returned
- The actual number of photos analyzed
- The actual time each interview lasted

Researchers need to describe in detail what actually happened during the course of carrying out the research method.

The following section is where the researcher should discuss how the data was reviewed and analyzed. Again, this is a procedural step in which the researchers need to explain step by step how the data was analyzed and how he or she decided to display those results. The first half of this section should be an explanation of the strengths and weaknesses of the research tool (method) used, as well as how the data would be demonstrated. Data can be "demonstrated" with charts, graphs, spreadsheets, or diagrams. Because some methods of data demonstration are better than others, researchers must justify their selection. In many instances, surveys and questionnaires will use charts, graphs, and spreadsheets. Journaling, a method for qualitative data gathering, might identify and list key words or phrases that reoccur in the journals, and then examine those words for different meanings associated with the words or phrases.

When detailing the results of a research endeavor, the burden is on the researcher to provide detailed information on how the results were analyzed and depicted. It is imperative that the researcher details the steps used to analyze the data. This detail should be thorough enough that another researcher could duplicate the method and analytic process by basing it entirely on this portion of the document.

The next section of this chapter is the discussion. Here the researcher may wish to restate the thesis statement, along with any other background information. Researchers should also identify early assumptions and how they differ from what was actually discovered via the research. This should be a thoughtful and critical analysis of the results and the meaning of the results. The following is an example of a discussion revolving around the weaknesses of a research process:

> Fifty surveys were disseminated in the three largest cities in the state of California for a total of 150 surveys. Research shows that a sample pool of 150 surveys is too small for any meaningful results (citation). This issue was compounded by the fact that only ten surveys were returned from the smallest of the three cities and only five were returned from the remaining two cities. This is only a 10 percent return rate, which again is too low for any meaningful results (citation). However, the information from those fifteen surveys was analyzed and revealed . . .

Clearly, if this study had actually happened, the researcher would have had to devise a plan for sending out and getting back more surveys to secure a sufficient sample pool. However, the design thesis is a very time-sensitive matter, and as such, researchers are often left with less-than-ideal situations. However, documenting the process and procedures of the method in detail allows a future researcher to replicate the research and (having already being warned of the small sample) to work towards claiming a larger sample pool. The second study could then be compared to the first study to see if the results from a limited sample pool remain valid when compared with the same research done with the larger sample pool. Although it is important that the researcher not attribute more to the results than the data shows, the design researcher can then apply the results to a prototype to assess the design's feasibility. As a point of reference, a good discussion of the results should span two to three pages.

Discussion and Design Application

An added stage to design research is the *application of results*. In this final chapter of the thesis, the researcher uses the studio setting to develop a prototype that has been designed based on the results of the research. Depending on the thesis or dissertation committee requirements, these prototypes can be developed from computer-aided drawings, physical models, or hand-drawn renderings.

In this chapter, it is expected that a student researcher show several different design schematics and evolutions that have been developed and analyzed during the course of the research process. The **design application** chapter records the chronological documentation of how every piece of new information that came to the student caused the design to evolve. Each element and design manifestation should be discussed as to why it was accepted or dismissed.

Using graphic examples with brief captions is a good way to express design decisions. Again, it is very important for the person who reads the thesis or dissertation to be able to follow a researcher's line of thought and understand the rationales and justifications of the final design. Therefore, the discussion of the design elements should include a narrative as to why particular elements were retained and were integrated into the final design and why others were removed. Again, the structure and application of the chapter is entirely up to the student. To illustrate: a thesis measured uncommonly high smog rates on the street of an elementary school, which caused increased asthmatic conditions in the children; every student-researcher, regardless of discipline, would have to prove how his or her design solution would best address the problem. An architectural design student might invent a theoretical wall/filter system to eliminate the smog from entering the building. An urban planning student might propose redevelopment of the area to reduce vehicle smog. An interior design student might recommend an intricate system of wall, floor, window, and furniture finishes and fabrics that will not aggravate the asthmatic children with VOCs and off-gassing. An industrial design student might develop a prototype of lightweight and stylish filtering headgear that children could wear to ward off pollutants. And as a final example, a landscape design student might arrange a mix of perennial and annual plantings along with low garden walls to block and filter smog from coming onto school grounds. This section (called "Design Application") must address with facts from the method findings or literature review every design decision and major stylistic gesture. It is highly suggested that the format of this section be the same as the rest of the thesis and that all graphics be of the highest quality.

BACK MATTER

Once the document has been completed, the author should then assemble the back matter. This section provides clarity, extra information, and terms contained within the body of the document. The first part of the back matter is the references or works cited, which is followed by the appendices, glossary of terms, and sometimes the curriculum vitae or author's biography.

References (APA) or Works Cited (MLA)

It is best to compile the reference list throughout the duration of thesis writing. The reference section allows other researchers to know where a student found the information so that he or she can obtain the same information. The reference section also provides sources to pursue a deeper understanding in a subject area for the readers. Without references, the reader would not be able to tell whether the information presented in the document was based on fact or opinion, which affects the researcher's credibility. (For a detailed explanation of this process, see Chapter 2.) Included in the references or works cited section should be data that the author cited directly within the thesis as a quotation and information that informed the research:

- Author or authors' names
- Title of the document
- Identification information, such as:
  - **Books:** City, state, or country of publication, publisher's name, and year of publication
  - **Journal articles or technical papers:** Journal's name, volume and issue number, date of issue, page numbers
  - **Reports:** Report number, name and location of issuing organization, date of issue
  - **Correspondence:** Name and location of issuing organization, name and location of receiving organization, letter's date
  - **Conversation, conference presentation, or speech:** Name and location of speaker's organization; name, identification, and location of listener; date

Appendices

The **appendix** is a place for information relevant to the subject, but should be kept separate from the main text in order to avoid interrupting the line of logic in a document. Nearly anything can be placed in an appendix as long as it is relevant and there is reference to it in the body of document. One of the items that a researcher should include in the appendices is the method tool that the researcher used to gather information. This tool might be the actual survey or interview questions used to gather information, the matrix that the researcher used to analyze photos, or a long list of criteria that a researcher used when reviewing historical data. The appendix is a good location for the architectural program, as the systematic planning of each space within and around a building can become a lengthy document in and of itself.

Once the researcher has analyzed all of the data, only select pieces will be included in the actual body of the text. The remaining pieces should be placed in an appendix, along with a brief discussion of what that data meant and why it was not included in the main body of the text. This will help the reader to gain greater clarity of the researcher's thought process.

Appendices should be formatted with their own cover page, labeled with a letter (Appendix A, Appendix B, and so on). The relevant information should follow the cover page. Each item included in the appendices should appear in the order in which it was referred to within the document. The first page of each appendix should be numbered separately so that the first page of each appendix begins at 1.

Glossary of Terms

This section is used to provide definitions to important words that a reader may not know. These words include industry jargon or common words used to mean something different than their everyday meaning. An example is the word "skin," which is generally used to describe the biological covering of the human body, but in architectural terms "skin" refers to the outer layer of the building. The glossary is important to an interdisciplinary approach of communication and collaboration between different professions. The glossary should be organized alphabetically with the primary word or term emphasized in bold or italic. Each definition should be at least one sentence in length.

Curriculum Vitae or Author's Biography

Dissertation candidates are generally required to include either a curriculum vitae or biography in their doctoral dissertation back matter. **Curriculum vitae (CV)** is Latin for "the course of life"; it is a complete bulleted listing of all the author's educational credentials, experience, area of specialization, awards, presentations, and past publications. If a CV is required, it must be the last item in the dissertation. There are many resources available online and in libraries on how to write a CV. The basic format is:

- Student's name
- Information and experience in reverse chronological order of: most recent first, then earlier works
- Information in short lists or bulleted style
- The line spacing and font style and size of a CV are not required to match that of the main text.

Electronic Submission

ELECTRONIC THESIS OR DISSERTATION

The electronic submission of a thesis or dissertation is the digitalized version of the research document submitted to an institution to satisfy educational requirements. Though not all schools require that the terminal research document be submitted electronically, those that do most often require the format to be in PDF format (Adobe's Portable Document Format). Many institutions call this an **electronic thesis or dissertation (ETD)**; it contains the exact same contents as the paper (hard copy) version of the thesis or dissertation. Each school has its own requirements for submitting an ETD; therefore, students need to investigate the procedures, costs, and formatting requirements particular to their school long in advance of submitting their document.

An electronic *submission* is different from an electronic *publication*. The **electronic submission** involves furnishing the school with a digital copy of the research document, in lieu of or in addition to a printed and bound copy. An **electronic publication** makes the research document available to others via the Internet. The two ways of electronically publishing theses or dissertations are *traditional* and *open access*. Traditional publishing lists the student's thesis in an online database such as ProQuest. ProQuest is an electronic publisher that archives research documents, newspapers, and journals that can be accessed through online library networks. Generally speaking, with a paid subscription, members can access the complete thesis manuscript, and others can view only the first several pages of the thesis. After the thesis or dissertation committee approves the research, they may grant open-access publishing of the ETD. Open-access publishing means that everyone with access to the Internet database can view and print the entire ETD document.

The benefits of traditional electronic publishing include lower cost and the possibility of the student earning royalties if someone purchases the right to read the entire research manuscript. Open-access publishing offers the thesis or dissertation student more acknowledgment and a wider audience. The hard copy of a student's thesis or dissertation is typically kept in the school's library. All may view and/or print from the work, although only people associated with the school may enter the library and gain access to the academic works. With open-access publishing, nearly all members of every college, research institution, and universities around the world can access the research.

Universities provide instructions on how to convert a thesis or dissertation into a PDF file as well as on specific file size. Generally, it is required that the thesis be made into one file under 50 MB in size. The most common problem seems to be embedding all fonts into the PDF prior to electronically submitting the thesis.

Security Concerns

Some students are concerned about safeguarding their work from intellectual piracy. Copyrighting a thesis or dissertation provides the legal protections needed if the copyright is violated. If a student participates in the open-access publishing of his or her thesis work, a time delay (also called an *embargo*) can be placed on the release of the manuscript into the database. Or the student may opt for a *restricted thesis*, which allows the thesis or dissertation to be withheld from publication for a period of up to two years—a sufficient amount of time to secure a patent or for other commercial reasons.

As far as security protocol goes, most schools mandate that the thesis be printable, and therefore do not allow password-protected documents to be electronically submitted. However, there are certain cases in which security measures should be considered; recently, some thesis students have been seen "blogging" or otherwise sharing their research within the public domain. In these situations, students should protect their work. As PDF is the dominant document format of colleges and universities, students should familiarize themselves with the software necessary for creating and viewing this format as soon as possible. At the time of this printing, Acrobat 9 Professional has these safeguard options available for a document:

- Limited printing of document
- Limited copying text and images within the document
- Excludes changing or merging the document
- Limit the number of times a document can be opened

With all electronically submitted theses and dissertations, the school's guidelines must be followed precisely.

Summary

The thesis is a piece of written communication; therefore, it must have a central message. With the actual research, students conceive of a design; with the actual thesis, students tell the story of the design. Researchers have all of the necessary pieces of the final document and all he or she has to do is put it together in a meaningful order, although the specific layout of a thesis or dissertation varies greatly across institutions.

The front matter includes document formalities and the tradition of proving scholarly discipline. The introduction sets the tone of the paper and outlines the journey of discovery the researcher has taken. The ROL explains the lengths the researcher has taken to gain past information regarding his or her subject matter. The methods set the framework and strategies the researcher has developed to gain new information on his or her topic. All components of the lengthy process have been analyzed and findings are reported in the results. Thoughtful considerations on the research, findings, and design implications have been written and expanded upon within the discussion chapter. The design application chapter explains the rationale and reason for all the design decisions made by the student. The conclusion exemplifies the professional, scholarly, and design dexterity of the student as he or she pulls the immense amount of information into one profound yet straightforward statement that can be translated into a building, a space, or an environment for a purpose far greater than just beauty.

Evidence-based design and the design thesis are complex and sophisticated collaborations between art and science that propel the research process to a higher level than many other disciplines. Students should be proud of their accomplishments; by contributing their theses to design scholarship, they have successfully completed a great feat.

Glossary

Appellations—A name, title, or designation.

Appendix—Supplementary material that is collected and appended at the back of a book

Back matter—The appendix, bibliography, glossary, and index printed at the back of a book.

Citations—A reference to a published or unpublished source.

Curriculum vitae (CV)—A detailed listing of educational achievements, publications, presentations, professional activities, and honors.

Design application—The way that research has been applied to the design process.

Electronic publication—Publications that are available via the Internet.

Electronic submission—The ability to submit a paper or graphic via the Internet for publication.

Electronic thesis or dissertation (ETD)—A thesis or dissertation available as an electronic document as opposed to as a paper-bound product.

Front matter—Written matter preceding the main text of a book that generally consists of a title page, a copyright page, table of contents, and preface.

Limitations—An imperfection or shortcoming that limits the value of the research.

Pagination—The system used to number the pages of a book.

Thesis layout—The prescribed visual representation of a research document by a degree-granting institution.

Thesis structure—The prescribed organization of a research document by a degree-granting institution.

REFERENCES

Allport, G. W. (1937). *Personality: a psychological interpretation*. New York: Holt, Rinehart, & Winston.
Altheide, D. L. (1987). Ethnographic content analysis. *Qualitative Sociology, 10,* 1, 65–77.
Belton, B.K. (n.d.). *A design foundation for information architecture*. Retrieved June 12, 2006, from http://eprints.rclis.org/archive/00000087/02/Design_Foundation_for_Information_Architecture.pdf
Berger, K. S. (2005). *The developing person through child and adolescence*. New York: Worth Publishers.
Cernoch, J. M., & Porter, R. H. (1985). Recognition of maternal axillary odors by infant. *Child Development, 56,* 1593–1598.
Cook, L. (1995). *A guide to good survey design*. Wellington, New Zealand: Statistics New Zealand, Te Tari Tatau.
Creative Research Systems. (2008). *Survey design*. Retrieved October 13, 2008, from http://www.surveysystems.com/online.html
ESRI. (n.d.). *The guide to geographic information systems*. Retrieved February 16, 2010, from http://www.gis.com
Evans, G. W. (1996). Current trends in environmental psychology. *International Association of Applied Psychology, 8,* 2.
Fisher, T. (2004). Architects behaving badly: Ignoring environmental behavior research. *Harvard Design Magazine*. Retrieved January 1, 2009, from http://www.gsd.harvard.edu/research/publications/hdm/back/21_fisher.pdf
Frederick, C. (1976). *Est—Playing the game the new way: The game of life*. New York: Dell.
Ganoe, C. J. (1999). Design as narrative: A theory of inhabiting interior space. *Journal of Interior Design, 25,* 2, 1–15.
Garrison, J., and Lin, J. (2008, June 7). Prop. 8 protesters target Mormon temple in Westwood. *Los Angeles Times*. Retrieved June 7, 2009, from http://www.latimes.com/news/local/la-me-protest7-2008nov07,0,3827549.story
Gifford, R. (2001). *Environmental psychology: Practice and principles* (3rd ed.). Victoria, Canada: Optimal Books.
Guerin, D. A., & Mason, B. C. (1992). An experiential framework for international interior design education. *Journal of Interior Design Education and Research, 18,* 1–2, 51–58.
Hamilton, D., & Watkins, D. (2009). *Evidence-based design for multiple building types*. Hoboken, NJ: John Wiley & Sons, Inc.
Hammersley, M., & Atkinson, P. (1995). *Ethnography: Principles in practice* (2nd ed.). London: Routledge.
Hemingway, E. (1932). *Death in the afternoon*. New York: Scribner's.
Holl, S. (2000). *Parallax*. New York: Princeton Architectural Press.
IDEO (2003). *IDEO method cards: 51 ways to inspire design*. San Francisco: W. Stout Architectural Books.
Isaac Newton. (n.d.). BrainyQuote.com. Retrieved September 13, 2010, from BrainyQuote.com Web site: http://www.brainyquote.com/quotes/authors/i/isaac_newton.html
Isaac, S., and Michael, W. B. (1997). *Handbook in research and evaluation* (3rd ed.). San Diego: Educational and Industrial Testing Services.
Johansson, M. (2003). Social dangers as constraints for pro environmental travel modes: The perception of parents in England and Sweden. *Medio Ambiente y Comportamiento Humano, 4,* 1, 49–69.
Juhasz, J. (1981). The place of social sciences in architectural education. *Journal of Architectural Education, 33,* 3, 2–8.
Loustau, J. (1988). A theoretical base for interior design: A review of four approaches from related fields. *Journal of Interior Design Education and Research, 14,* 1, 308.
Marshall, C., & Rossman, G. B. (1998). *Designing qualitative research*. Newbury Park, CA: Sage Publications, Inc.
Melhuish, C. (2005). Towards a phenomenology of the concrete megastructure. *Journal of Material Culture, 10,* 1, 5–29.
Merriam-Webster Online Dictionary. (n.d.). Definition of "hyphotheses." Retrieved June 29, 2009, from http://www.merriam-webster.com/dictionary
Moffett, M., Fazio, M., & Wodehouse, L. (2004). *A world history of architecture*. Columbus, OH: McGraw-Hill.
Ortiz, J. (2004, March 1). *The human body: A sensing machine*. Retrieved from http://www.macalester.edu/psychology/whathap/diaries/diariess04/josh/diary_entry6.html
Oyster, C. K, Hanten, W. P., & Llorens, L. A. (1987). *Introduction to research: A guide for the health science professional*. Philadelphia: J. B. Lippincott.
Pallasma, J. (2005). *The eyes of the skin*. West Sussex, England: Wiley-Academy.
Park, M. A. (1999). *Biological anthropology* (2nd ed.). Mountain View, CA: Mayfield Publishing Company.

Phenomenology Center. (2005). *What is phenomenology?* Retrieved June 21, 2006, from http://www.phenomenologycenter.org/phenom.htm

Rapoport, A. (2006). In A. M. Salama, Learning from the environment: Evaluation research and experience-based architectural pedagogy. *CEBE Transactions, 3,* 1, 64–83.

Romice, O. (2003). New partnerships for action: Building on the capital of environmental psychology and architecture. *Medio Ambiente y Comportamiento Humano, 4,* 1, 15–32.

Rossano, M. J. (2003). *Evolutionary psychology: The science of human behavior and evolution.* Hoboken, NJ: John Wiley and Sons.

Salama, A. M. (2006). Learning from the environment: Evaluation research and experience based architectural pedagogy. *CEBE Transactions, 3,* 1, 64–83.

Salama, A. (1995). *New trends in architectural education: Designing the design studio.* Raleigh, NC: Tailored Text and Unlimited Potential Publishing.

Sanoff, H. (1992). *Integrating programming, evaluation, and participation in design.* Avebury, England: Ashgate Publishing Limited.

Santayana, G. (1905). *The life of reason: Or the phases of human progress.* New York: Charles Scribner's Sons.

Scarre, C., & Renfrew, C. (1995). *Cognition and material culture: The archaeology of symbolic storage.* Cambridge: McDonald Institute.

Schensul, J. J., & Le Compte, M. D. (Eds.). (1999). *Ethnographer's toolkit.* Walnut Creek, CA: AltaMira Press.

Seibert, T. (2002). *Designing surveys that count.* Keene, NH: Community Research Center at Keene State College & Monadnock United Way.

Sense of Smell Institute. (1996). *Living with your sense of smell.* New York: Sense of Smell Institute, Ltd.

Society for Neuroscience. (n.d.). *About neuroscience.* Retrieved June 2006 from http://www.sfn.org

Stanford University. (2006, March 21). *Geographic information systems (GIS).* Retrieved February 16, 2010, from http://library.stanford.edu/depts/gis/whatgis.html

Sutton, S. (1984). Should behavioral studies be integrated into the design studio. *Architectural Record,* July, 43–48.

Thoreau, H. D. (1854). *Walden, or Life in the woods.* Boston: Houghton Mifflin

Trochim, W. M. K. (2006). *Research methods knowledge base.* Retrieved May 6, 2008, from http://www.socialresearchmethods.net/kb/strucres.php

Von Eckartsberg, R. (1998). Introducing existential-phenomenological psychology. In R. Valle (Ed.), *Phenomenological inquiry in psychology: Existential and transpersonal dimensions*, pp. 227–246. New York: Plenum Press.

Vonnegut, K. (1985). How to write with style. In B. S. Fuess, *How to use the power of the printed word,* 33–38. Garden City, NY: Anchor Press. Retrieved September 12, 2010 <http://www.novelr.com/2008/08/16/vonnegut-how-to-write-with-style>

INDEX

A

Abstract, process beginning
   corner stones, 53
   defined, 53
   evidence-based procedures, 54
   examples, identification
      problem, 53
      product development, 54
      solution, 54
   writing, 53
American Society of Interior Design (ASID), 5
Appellation ranking, 182
Architectural Graphic Standards, 3
Argument dissecting and topic of research. *See also* Research methods
   budget cuts, 57
   efficient grading techniques, 59
   evaluation methods, 59
   intellectual capabilities, 58
   kinesthetic activities, 57
   litigation fears, 57
   logic mapping, 59–60
   low student/teacher ratios, 59
   one-to-one relationship, 58
   predesign programming, 59
   reintroducing vocational style learning environments, 58
   researcher-identified methods, 59
   student evaluation methods, 59
ASID. *See* American Society of Interior Design (ASID)
Assembly. *See also* Final phase documentation in research
   back matter
      curriculum vitae and author's biography, 191
      glossary of terms, 191
      references and works cited, 190
   front matter
      abstract page, 185–186
      copyright page, 181–182
      dedication page, 183
      illustrations, charts and graphs, 183–185
      nomenclature list, 185
      pages, 180–181
      signature page, 182
      table of contents, 183
      tables and figures, 183–185
      title page, 181
   main text, 186
      chapter headings, 187
      discussion and design application, 189–190
      methods, 188
      results, 188–189
      review of literature (ROL), 187
   title and cover page, 179

B

Building information modeling (BIM), 166–169

C

Case study, 110–111
   building typology
      outline, 126
      process design, 125
      sample, 127
      sources of designer, 125
      symbolism, 125
      usage, 126
   defined, 121–122
   overlay format, 122
   research criteria, 122–123
   resources, 125
   technique and process
      cover page format, sample, 124
      ideal project, 123–124
      parameters outlining, 123
Causal–comparative research and experimental research, 13–14, 106
Causal inferences, 10
Chain of logic, 149
Citations
   format examples, 26–28
   plagiarism, form of, 20–21
   purpose, 18–19
   styles, 18
   terminology and fundamental differences, 20
      in-text, 19
      parenthetical reference, 19
      references, 19
      works, 19
Close-ended and open-ended questions, 103
Cohort study, 14
Computer-related methods, 166
Concept mapping
   defined, 49
   "down and dirty" information, 50
   idea mapping, 51–52
Confounding variables, 165
Correlational research, 13–14
Cross-sectional study, 14

D

Data gathering and analysis
   qualitative approach
      representation illustration, 100
      use of, 100
   quantitative approaches
      hypothetical research, 100
      replicable, 99
Deductive process, 10
   reasoning, 37
Dependent variable, 163
Descriptive research, 13–14
Design
   disasters, 80

Design (*continued*)
   education, 2
   professionals, 1
   research, 2
     chain of logic developing, 8
     ex post facto (after fact) reasoning, 11
     illogical argumentation, 39
     issues and opportunities exploration, 4
     issues of logic, 40
     leap of faith, 40
     measurement of indicators, 13
     mystification, 11
     overstating, 41
     overviews, 37
     perspectives, 6
     position developing, 9
     positivism, 8
     postpositivism, 8
     process, 7
     pursuit, 10–13
     question, 32
     reasons for, 8
     reliability and validity, 13
     researcher over-involvement, 11
     stages, 31
     thesis/dissertation completion, 7
     thought process, 8
     variables and attributes, 11
   studies types
     causal-comparative, 13
     correlational, 13
     descriptive, 13
     experimental, 13
     historical, 13
     qualitative, 13
Determinism, 35
Developing questions, 129
   interpretation uniformity, 131
   misinterpreted question, 131
   objectives, 130
   test-piloting, 131
Double-blind, placebo-controlled experiment, 162–163, 166

E

Ecological fallacy, 12
Electronic submission
   thesis or dissertation security concerns
     electronic publication, 191
     security concerns, 192
     security protocol, 192
Ethnography
   acquisition of data, 104
   analytical, 102
   cultural patterns, 102
   modes of information
     direct observation, 103
     participant observation, 103
     scientific objectivity, 104
   primary tools, 103
   self-report journaling, 104
   studies, 102–103
   symbols, 102
   theory development, 104–105
Evidence Based Design, A Process for Research and Writing, 2
Evidenced-based research, 31
Experimental research, 13–14
Experimental variables, 106
Experimentation and computer modeling
   analysis, 165–166, 169–170
   BIM, 165–166
   "cause and effect" relationships, 162
   control and experimental groups, 163
   example, 164
   GIS, 166, 170–173
   reliability and replicability, 161
   software tools, 161
   types
     double-blind, placebo-controlled, 162–163
     quasi, 162–163
     single-subject, 162–163
     true, 162
   variables, 163–165
Exploratory study, 3

F

Farmers Almanac, 3
Final phase documentation in research, 174
   application of, 175
   assembly
     back matter, 190–191
     front matter, 180–186
     main text, 186–190
     title and cover page, 179–180
   electronic submission
     thesis or dissertation, 191–192
   figures list, 184
   guidelines
     citations, 177–178
     embellishments, 178–179
     resources, 175–177
   headings
     position and numbering, 187
     style and indentation, 187
   justification for, 175
   pagination, 178
   schedule development, 176

G

Geographic information systems (GIS)
   analysis, 171
   data and information, 170
   densities, 171
   hypothesis, 172
   mapping system, 170
   quantities, 171
Guidelines for research documentation
   citations arrangements, 177–178
   embellishments
     fold-out pages, 178–179
     miscellaneous, 179
     pocket material, 179
   formatting pagination, 177
   reference guide formation, 177
   resources
     database managing, 175
     footnoting and annotation, 175
     grammatical errors, 175
     indexing and contents formation, 175
   time management, 176

H

Harvard Design Magazine, 5
Heating, ventilation and air conditioning (HVAC) systems, 37
Historical analysis method
   architectural adaptive-reuse techniques, 147
   areas of, 146
   benefits of, 148
   books, 149
   census data, 149–150
   cross-referencing, 148

data analysis, 150
documents
 documentation process, 145
 documents
  media, 148–149
  supposition via comparison, 149
 multiple sources, 151
 post-diction, 149
 post-hoc fallacy, 151
 public records, 146, 150
 remote sensing, 152
 research plan, 147
 sustainability of environment, 147
Historical research, 13–14
HVAC systems. See Heating, ventilation and air conditioning (HVAC) systems
Hypothesis, 32–33

I
Illogical thought process, 39
Independent variable, 163
Inductive and deductive reasoning, 36, 38
Inductive process, 10
Information gathering, 35
Institutional review boards (IRB)
 consent by, 82
 FDA, 81
 purpose of, 82
Interviews, 129–130
 communication types, 136–137
 community forums and focus groups
  advantages and disadvantages, 139
  groupthink, 139
  interview practice, 140
  responsibility, 140
  typical group settings attendance, 140
 electronic media
  advantages and disadvantages, 141
  instant messaging, 141
  video conference Websites, 141
  webcam interactions, 141
 face-to-face method
  body language guide, 139
  nonverbal assessment, 138
  participant responds, 138
 human communication types, 137
 initiating interviews
  community forums and focus groups, 138
  location identification, 138
  participant identification, 138
  query letter sample, 137
 methods, 135–136
 participant's role, 136
 person's level of trust, 136
 questionnaires, 136
In-text sources
 paraphrasing, 22–23
 quotation
  direct quote, 23
  long, 24
  with signal phrase, 23–24
 summarizing, 21–22
Introduction, process beginning
 dissertation statement, 56
 economic theory of supply and demand, 56
 initial drafts, 54
 preliminary
  affordable housing, 54
  housing cost, 54
  new model, 55
  typology, 55

social and architectural solutions, 57
sustainability and ethics, concepts of, 57
thesis statement
 development, 56
 practice, 55
Invariance, 35
IRB. See Institutional review boards (IRB)
Issues in research, 79
 bias
  expectation, 88
  external, 85
  internal, 85
  maturation, 86
  measurement, 86
  problems, 87
  publication, 86
  referral, 86
  results, 87
  selection, 86
  spatial, 86
  statements, 85–86
  timing, 86
  volunteer, 86
  withdrawal, 86
 ethics
  conundrum, 80
  design, 80
  designers, 80
  IRB, 81
  language and guidelines, 81
 postoccupancy evaluation, 81
 responses placed into clusters, 93
 review of literature, 80
 sampling, 88–92
  method, 93
 variables
  behavioral, 82
  conditions, 83
  confounding, 83
  constant, 82
  dependent, 82
  extraneous, 83–84
  independent, 82
  organismic, 82–83
  relationship between, 83
  stimulus, 82

J
Journal excerpts, 104

L
Learning style evaluation, 32
Logical thought process, 39
Logic mapping, argument dissecting
 defined, 59
 format of, 60
 time management, 59–60
Longitudinal study, 14–15

M
Match terms and ideas, 105
Methods-based research, 31
Methods of research, 107
Mixed-methods approach, 34
Motivations, 33

N
Nominal definition, 9

O

Observations, 129–130
  defined, 141
  methods, 141–142
  types, 142
Operational definition, 9
Operationalism, 35
Organizations
  and documentation tools
    citation management, 25
    formatting final lists, 25–26
    references, 26
    works cited, abbreviations, 26, 28
  objectives
    action verbs, 62
    analysis, 62
    assess, 62
    discuss, 62
    explore, 62
    identification, 62
    used for, 61

P

Photo analysis method
  approaches
    formal contextual, 153
    intertextual and contextual, 153–154
  criteria, 154
  data collection table, 157
  environment controlling, 153
  factors, 152
  facts regarding, 155
  levels, 154
  modification, 155, 158
  process, 153
  reasons, 152
  symbolic/metaphorical meanings, 155
Positions, positivism and postpositivism, 33
Positivism, 8
Postpositivism, 8
Probabilistic inferences, 10

Q

Qualitative research, 13–14
Quantitative and qualitative approaches, 33–34
Quasi experiment, 162

R

Recognition objectives
  fictional research project, 60
  preliminary introduction, 60
  statements discussed, 61
Reductionism, 12
Research approaches
  causal–comparative
    dependent, 105–106
    independent, 105
  correlational research, 105
  descriptive, 105
  experimental studies
    controlled group, 106–107
    external validity, 106
    group, 106
    Hawthorne effect, 107
    internal validity, 106
  mixed methods, 107
  placebo effect, 107
Research methods, 96. *See also* Design
  approaches
    causal–comparative, 105
    correlational research, 105
    descriptive, 105
    experimental research studies, 106
    external validity, 106
    mixed, 107
  data gathering and analysis
    framework, 100
    quantitative and qualitative approaches, 99–100
  ethnography
    analytical, 102
    cultural patterns, 102
    modes of information, 103–104
    primary tools, 103
    studies, 102–103
    study, 102
    symbols, 102
  evidence-based design, 97
  formatting
    approach justification, 98
    discussion, 99
    implementation, 98–99
    preliminary method outline, 99
    site analysis, 98
  phenomenology design
    graphic representation, 102
    haptic sensation, 101
    holistic experience, 101
    strength, 101
    study, 101–102
  process, 97
  stages formation, 32
Review of literature (ROL), 187
  assembling
    basic of, 75
    body, 75–76
    introduction, 75
    literature summary example, 76
    organizing, 75
    purpose of, 74
    sample excerpt, 76
    tie-back, 76
  assessing
    academic research degrees, 68
    biases, 69
    credential, 68
    limitations, 68
    peer-reviewed publication, 67
    performance-based funding, 69
    press articles, examples of, 67
    professional degrees, 68
    publication, 69
    scholarly publication and popular press, 67
    Schools and Design, The Autistic Child, 68
    socratic method, 69
    textbooks, 68
    title, 68
  concerns and considerations
    invalid results, 77
    plagiarism, 77
  critical evaluation, 66
  developmental stage
    formative, process and summative, 35–38
    information gathering, 34–36
    outcome, 38–42
    time periods, 35
  evidence-based design researcher's process, 66
  importance, 66
  perspectives, 66
  preparation
    analyze and interpret, 73–74

chart, 69
checklist, 71
connections, 69
controversy, 72–73
databases, 72
define topic, 70
design prototyping, 69
evaluate and assess, 73
features, 70
logical and concise way, 69
method and position, 72
organizing literature, 70
reliable sources, 69
researcher's project, 69
sample outline, 74
search and organize, 70–73
subject areas, 71
purpose of, 66
ROL. See Review of literature (ROL)

S

Sampling
  deterministic statement, 36
  examples, 93
  exercise, 90
  nonprobability
    availability, 91
    purposive, 91
    quota, 91–92
    snowball, 91–92
  probability
    cluster sampling, 90
    simple random, 88
    stratified random, 88–89
    systematic sampling, 89
  sample thesis chapters, 186
  spelling error question, 87
Schools and Design, The Autistic Child, 68
Self-plagiarism, 21
Single-subject experiment, 162–163
Site analysis, 110
  criteria
    climatic surveys, 113–114
    legal aspects, 113–114
    physical characteristics, 113–114
    sociocultural perspectives, 113–114
  defined, 113
  implications and purpose
    academic project, 113–114
    criteria, 113–114
  interpretation
    checklist of sample features, 119
    document, 118
    legal aspects, 118
    "plan," 118
  log, 112–113
  presentation of findings
    asset/liability format, 120
    checklist, 119
    general practice tips, 120–121
    overlay format, 120
    program needs format, 121
  process and procedure
    documentation, 118
    preliminary information, collection, 117
    recording information, 118
  project base map, 112
  subsections, 111
  tools and diagramming
    audio recorder, 115

criteria evaluation, 116
evidence-based design, 117
postsite analysis, 117
presite analysis, 114–115
requirements, 115
site elements in plan view, 116
site visit documentation, 116
usage, 112–113
Specification objectives
  changes track, 61
  defined, 61
  discussion, 61
  documentation, 61
  review, 61
  summary, 61
Surveys, 129–130
  advantages and disadvantages, 132
  defined, 131
  electronic surveys
    emails, 135
    length as universal concern, 135
  question format, 132
  response mechanisms, 131–132
  survey construction
    coercive question, 133
    fatigue, 133
    process, 132–133
    response categories, 133
  survey dissemination
    approaches, 134
    development and delivery, 133
    electronic data via Web, 134
    oral modes, 134
    sample size, 135
    written document, 134
Symbolism and visual metaphors, 156

T

Time-specific evaluations, 35
Topic of research
  argument dissecting, 48
    budget cuts, 57
    efficient grading techniques, 59
    evaluation methods, 59
    intellectual capabilities, 58
    kinesthetic activities, 57
    litigation fears, 57
    logic mapping, 59–60
    low student/teacher ratios, 59
    one-to-one relationship, 58
    predesign programming, 59
    reading comprehension rates, 59
    reintroducing vocational style learning environments, 58
    researcher-identified methods, 59
    student evaluation methods, 59
  formation of, 45
  identification
    area of inquiry, 45
    collage, 48
    design buzzwords, 45
    evidence-based design research, steps of, 45–47
    health-care environment, defined, 46
    narrowing, 45–46
    research method, 46
    students examples, 46–47
    sustainability, 45
  process beginning
    abstract, 53–54
    introduction, 54–57

Topic of research (*continued*)
   question formation
      concept mapping, 49–51
      conceptualization of, 51–52
      deductive reasoning, 53
      development of, 49
      evidence-based design thesis, 53
      inductive reasoning, 53
   selecting research objectives
      defined, 62–63
      organization, 61–62
      recognition, 60–61
      specification, 61
   thesis statement, preparation
      issues discussed, 48
      provable claim, 48
      sustainability issues, 49
True experiment, 162

V

Variables, 165
   conditions, 83
   confounding, 165
   defined by nature
      behavioral, 82
      organismic, 82–83
      stimulus, 82
   defined by use
      dependent, 83
      independent, 83
   host of
      confounding, 83
      covariates, 84
      extraneous, 83
   independent and dependent, 12, 163
   nominal, 11, 263
   ordinal and interval, 11, 163
   ratio, 11
   use in research methods
      constant, 82
      dependent, 82
      independent, 82